Including Families and Communities in Urban Education

A volume in
Issues in the Research, Theory, Policy, and Practice of Urban Education
Denise E. Armstrong and Brenda J. McMahon, *Series Editors*

Issues in the Research, Theory, Policy, and Practice of Urban Education

Denise E. Armstrong and Brenda J. McMahon, *Series Editors*

Including Families and Communities in Urban Education, 2011
   Edited by Catherine M. Hands and Lea Hubbard

Inclusion in Urban Educational Environments: Addressing Issues of Diversity, Equity, and Social Justice, 2006
   Edited by Denise E. Armstrong and Brenda J. McMahon

Including Families and Communities in Urban Education

Edited by

Catherine M. Hands
Family Diversity Education Council

Lea Hubbard
University of San Diego

INFORMATION AGE PUBLISHING, INC.
Charlotte, NC • www.infoagepub.com

Library of Congress Cataloging-in-Publication Data

Including families and communities in urban education / edited by Catherine
M. Hands, Lea Hubbard.
    p. cm. – (Issues in the research, theory, policy, and practice of
urban education)
 Includes bibliographical references.
 ISBN 978-1-61735-399-4 (pbk.) – ISBN 978-1-61735-400-7 (hardcover) –
ISBN 978-1-61735-401-4 (e-book)
1. Education, Urban–United States. 2. Education–Parent
participation–United States. 3. Community and school–United States. 4.
Children of minorities–Education–United States. 5. Educational
equalization–United States. I. Hands, Catherine M. II. Hubbard, Lea, 1946-

 LC5131.I46 2011
 379.2'6–dc22

                                                        2011005761

Printed in the United States of America

CONTENTS

PART I

STRUCTURE

PART II

CULTURE

PART III

AGENCY

PART IV

STRATEGIES FOR INCLUSION AND PROGRAM ASSESSMENT

PART V

CONCLUSION: THEMES FROM INITIATIVES INCLUDING FAMILIES AND COMMUNITY MEMBERS IN EDUCATION

SERIES EDITORS' PREFACE

Denise Armstrong and Brenda McMahon

This series focuses on contemporary issues in the theory, practice, and policy of urban education. Our primary aim is create a substantive body of research and scholarship that (a) examines how urban education is currently conceived, enacted, and transformed in educational contexts; (b) provides critical and/or innovative perspectives on urban education that contribute to our understanding of how it is conceived, enacted, transformed in educational contexts.

Including Families and Communities in Urban Education, edited by Catherine Hands and Lea Hubbard, is the second book in IAP's Issues in the Research, Theory, Policy and Practice of Urban Education Series. This volume underscores the significant role that families play in student achievement, the success of urban students, and the importance of co-constructing authentic and sustainable partnerships at the school, district and community levels. It combines issues from the partnership and reform research in order to highlight the critical role that urban families and their communities play in the success of these reforms. In considering and communicating the complexity of these phenomena, the contributors draw on a wide variety of methodologies to highlight historical patterns and endemic social, economic, and political issues related to the structure and culture of schooling that underlie issues of parental involvement and engagement. The articles illustrate how traditional arrangements related to classism, racism, and sexism restrict individual and collective agency while maintaining and repro-

Including Families and Communities in Urban Education, pages ix–x
Copyright © 2011 by Information Age Publishing

ducing the power and privilege of dominant groups. Together they raise critical questions such as:

- How can school communities be reconstructed to center children and their families at the heart of schooling?
- What are authentic partnerships?
- What are the factors and processes that facilitate and impede school/community partnerships?
- Who benefit and who are disadvantaged by educational policies, practices, partnerships?
- What is the role of school leadership in constructing the cultures and structures which impact family-school relationships?
- How can these traditional barriers be deconstructed and reconstructed to support student success?
- How can schools distribute power and leadership with parents and community groups in order to create meaningful and resilient partnerships?
- What leadership lessons can be learned from the research and practice?

We anticipate that this book will provide K–12 educators, parents, communities, academics, and policy makers with in-depth theoretical insights and practical strategies that can build productive partnerships that are characterized by respect, diversity, inclusion, and ethical action.

ACKNOWLEDGEMENTS

There has truly been community involvement—and in some cases, family involvement—in this collection of writings on diversity and inclusion in education. As such, we would like to thank a number of people whose assistance has been invaluable to us as we put this book together.

First, the authors contributing their work and expertise in the field presented thoughtful and thought-provoking research and commentary. We are grateful for the opportunity to have worked with the team of Elvira Armas, Julie Carter, Janet Chrispeels, Linwood Cousins, Michael Evans, Susan Faircloth, Mary Finn, Margarita González, Erin Horvat, Lauri Johnson, Novella Keith, Magaly Lavadenz, Makeba Jones, Roslyn Mickelson, Bonnie Stelmach, and Susan Yonezawa. Throughout the book's production, the authors' willingness to engage in ongoing dialogue and debate around parent and community engagement and their professionalism regarding our feedback were tremendously appreciated. Collectively, we are consequently able to share decades of experience and thought in the field of family and community engagement with our readers.

To assist us in putting together a volume of outstanding quality, a cadre of individuals willingly shared their expertise on family and community involvement in education by their careful reading and insightful comments as chapter reviewers. The efforts in this capacity of Jo Bennett, Jenifer Crawford, Judy Doktor, Kim Fields, DeMarquis Hayes, Ron Heredia, Ollie Moles, Rema Reynolds, Lee Shumow, and Adriane Williams were and continue to be appreciated through their important contributions in the field of family and community engagement in education.

Including Families and Communities in Urban Education, pages xi–xii
Copyright © 2011 by Information Age Publishing

As well, we would like to thank the series editors, Doctors Denise Armstrong, and Brenda McMahon, whose vision of inclusive urban education had families and communities members taking vital roles in the education of their children. They saw the importance of this topic, they made this book possible, and they gave us the needed support along the way. Similarly, we thank the president of Information Age Publishing, George Johnson, and his team for their support and guidance.

Lastly, we thank the students, families, community members and school personnel who gave their time to the research projects discussed in these chapters. Their voices and experiences give both shape and purpose to our work and move us toward the inclusion of all families and communities in urban educational settings characterized by diversity.

CHAPTER 1

UNDERSTANDING FAMILY AND COMMUNITY INCLUSION AND ENGAGEMENT

Catherine M. Hands and Lea Hubbard

ABSTRACT

In an overview of family and community engagement in education, Catherine Hands and Lea Hubbard discuss the importance of inclusion. In this introductory chapter, they consider the importance of structure, culture and agency when developing initiatives that engage the communities and families in students' education. They operationalize the term, and make the case that assumptions are made by school personnel regarding the way education is and should be organized, the nature of families, and the contributions they should or should not make to their children's education. The introduction illustrates the negative impact on students and their education when these assumptions are not challenged. The authors then provide an overview of the chapters in the book and their contributions to a deeper, more nuanced understanding of parent and community inclusion in educational issues.

Including Families and Communities in Urban Education, pages 1–14
Copyright © 2011 by Information Age Publishing

1

The importance of social support in the form of family and community involvement in education has implications, particularly in terms of student achievement. The gap in student achievement between advantaged and disadvantaged groups is widening (Davies, 2002), and schools are finding it increasingly difficult to create educational programs to address the diverse needs of the students within the geographic community they serve (Merz & Furman, 1997). Moreover, schools cannot close the gaps in academic achievement alone (Davies, 2002). Partnerships between schools, families and communities may serve to provide a support net for each student. Such support is characterized by caring environments that place the students' interests as the focal point for partnership efforts.

With frequent interactions between these partners, it is more likely that common sentiments regarding the importance of school, of exerting academic effort, of assisting others, and of staying in school will be reiterated and subsequently reinforced by a variety of influences on the students (Epstein, 1995). In their urban education study, Shapiro, Ginsberg and Brown (2002) found that a lack of attention and support, an absence of discipline, and not "staying on them" or prodding the students, were considered the most important barriers to success by educators, community mentors and the students. They concluded that caring adults could have an effect on a student's life, and consequently, it is crucial to forge links between schools, families and communities (Shapiro et al., 2002).

Much focus has been placed on the critical role that families play in students' success. Yet, school-family partnerships may not always be realized to their fullest extent. Teachers, overburdened by the demands of high stakes testing, concentrate their efforts in the classroom, not in outreach to the families. Moreover, in a society with high mobility and high levels of occupational specialization, families may find that job obligations, for example, compete with their desire to be involved in their children's schooling (Hands, 2009). More families may have both parents working and in jobs without flexible work hours, making it difficult for them to attend school-related events (Hands, 2009) as they are currently scheduled. In some cases, parents' limited or past negative educational experiences cause them to be less willing to be involved with educators (Hands, 2009). Children consequently may have less family support for their educational needs at a time when the economy is demanding higher levels of education to obtain entry-level occupations (Darling-Hammond & Lieberman, 1993). Hence, in our contemporary society, it may be particularly important to cultivate partnerships with community organizations and citizens in addition to families, in order to address the needs of all students.

Toward that end, various national- and state-level structures have been designed and implemented to encourage partnership development. Legislation such as the No Child Left Behind Act of 2001 and 2009's Race to the Top in the United States of America, and the institution of a Parent Engagement Office within the Ontario Ministry of Education in Canada, for example, both reflect the importance currently being placed on family and community engagement in education (Hiatt-Michael & Hands, 2010). Organizations such as the National Network of Partnership Schools and the Family Involvement Network of Educators, with a priority to cultivate collaborative family–school–community relationships, have been created to provide support to educators, researchers and policymakers who have a similar interest. Moreover, there is some evidence that school–community partnerships may be becoming more prevalent at the district level, particularly among charter schools in the U.S., as increasing numbers of educators view support external to the school as a viable avenue to address financial shortcomings and to meet the academic, social and emotional needs of their diverse student populations (Wohlstetter, Malloy, Hentschke & Smith, 2004).

A promising avenue for family and community members to have a direct influence on education is through the cultivation of partnerships at the school level that provide opportunities for parents and community members to work with school personnel to craft the learning experiences of the students. For example, some scholars have found that opportunities for the co-construction of learning opportunities and school reform initiatives with input from all stakeholders are most likely to contribute to enhancing student achievement, reducing achievement gaps and engaging families (Comer, Haynes, Joyner & Ben Avie, 1996; Jeynes, 2005; Pushor, 2007; Pushor & Ruitenberg, 2005). In the same vein, other scholars call for the creation of authentic partnerships, characterized as "respectful alliances among educators, families, and community groups that value relationship building, dialogue, and power-sharing as part of socially just, democratic schools" (Auerbach, 2010, p. 729; Henderson, Mapp, Johnson & Davies, 2007).

Well-intentioned educators, community members and families have recognized the need for communication, collaboration and partnerships, but all too often these important alliances do not occur, or if they do, they are not sustainable (Darling-Hammond, 1996). Why are such arrangements so difficult? What factors challenge and/or support them, and what lessons can we learn from investigations recently conducted on these issues?

FORCES OF STRUCTURE, CULTURE AND AGENCY ON PARTNERSHIP DEVELOPMENT, ENGAGEMENT AND LONGEVITY

In this book, we meld concepts from both the partnership and school reform literature to examine the contextual issues that are brought to bear on partnership development and sustainability. Currently, parent and community involvement does not draw on school reform and educational change literature, and conversely, school change literature often ignores the crucial role that communities play in educational reform. Yet we know from the work of Gibson, Gandara, and Koyama (2004), Moll, Amanti, Neff, and Gonzales (1992), and others that the connections among families, communities and schools impact educational outcomes.

Parent and community engagement initiatives can and should be viewed as part of the school reform literature. Additional research has alerted us to the helpfulness of a theoretical frame that takes into account issues of structure, culture and agency in understanding educational change. In an investigation of district reform, researchers found that organizational structure, cultural beliefs about teaching and learning, community politics and individual actions, all were found to influence a district wide reform effort (Hubbard, Mehan & Stein, 2006). Although building relationships was essential to the work, district administrators who were motivated by structured inequality—specifically, the need to improve the learning for all students—embarked on a fast paced and comprehensive reform that resulted in deferring relationship-building to the back-channel and ultimately undermining the reform. Consequently, concepts that highlight or explicate the complexities of educational change may be particularly useful when examining the contextual features that facilitate or impede partnership establishment.

We take the position that to understand the complexity of negotiating parent and community partnerships we need to examine the ways they are influenced by the *structure* of schooling and its position within a broader economic system (Bowles & Gintis, 1976; Anyon, 2005). Structure refers to the external forces that impose upon and attempt to define social action, particularly, the institutional arrangements that schools, families and communities have traditionally held in relationship to each other and to the district, state and federal government. Education is tied in the U.S, for example, to a capitalist system of class relations that structures racism, classism and sexism in response to the desire of dominant groups to preserve their privilege and power (Anyon, 1997; Giroux, 2009). Thus, the economic position of low-income, ethnic minority students—the population we find most frequently in urban schools—is merely reproduced. Students and families from these backgrounds often feel alienated and marginalized and therefore do not engage actively with schools that are viewed as representing the interests of the white middle class (Cooper, 2007).

Understanding the success and failures of school, family and community partnerships also demands that we examine the *cultural* factors that are involved. They both influence the presence of partnerships and shape the nature of the collaborative activities. Lareau (2003), Darling-Hammond

(2001), Heath (1982) and others have shown that when the cultural background of students and families do not match that of the school, educational outcomes are affected. "Instead of working together to support the academic and social development of students, teachers and parents find themselves operating in isolation or, in the worst cases, in opposition to one another" (Bryk & Schnieder, 2002, p. 6). Bryk and Schnieder (2002) argue that relationships among schools, families and communities are at the heart of successful reform and that they must involve "trust." When schools and communities establish trust, this trust can act as a dimension of social capital that is able to promote school improvement. Without it, and when problems in parent and teacher relationships are exacerbated by race and class differences, which is often the case in urban schools, communication is challenged (Bryk & Schneider, 2002). By looking at culture, both that of the school and the community, we gain a better understanding of how the ideologies, beliefs and values held by the various constituents give rise to ideological conflicts that may impede collaborations.

Partnerships are driven by the individual *actions* or *agency* of those involved. We learn through previous research on the academic achievement of minority students that students construct their own educational outcomes. We also learn how their actions are tied to structural and cultural factors, including their racial, ethnic, class, linguistic and gendered positions. Research in this area shows the power of individuals to affect change or become part of the reproduction of inequality. Willis's Lads (1977) and MacLeod's Hallway Hangers (1987) were critical of the system and these students believed that the diploma was not necessarily the avenue to economic success. Their resistance resulted in disadvantaging them and limiting their future. More recently, Morris's (2002) study of two predominantly African American elementary schools in the south showed how the schools' strong relations with the community brought about "African American agency in contemporary schooling and society" in ways that led to their success (p. 72). Similarly, the work of Hoover-Dempsey and her colleagues looks at the motivation for parents' engagement in their children's education. Over a number of studies, the researchers found that parents' perceptions of their roles in their children's education, their feelings around how effective they are in participating, as well as school personnel's and students' invitations for parent involvement all play a part in parent engagement (Hoover-Dempsey, Bassler & Brissie, 1992; Walker, Wilkins, Dallaire, Sandler, & Hoover-Dempsey, 2005). In each of these cases, the actions of the individuals, whose dispositions and aspirations—formed by their cultural context—led to specific outcomes.

A constructivist approach to understanding outcomes relies on the belief that actions—like the participation in collaborative activities—occur as the result of the face-to-face interactions among constituents, over time, during everyday practice, and across contexts (Hubbard, et al., 2006). This relational sense of context is important because it calls our attention to the idea that actions are not the result of situatedness or embeddedness in a context that is shaped solely by top down mandates (Pressman & Wildavsky, 1973). Actors are not passive, but rather, outcomes are the result of the interactions among participants, across contexts. Actions shape and are shaped by the participants involved, and are influenced by structural and cultural factors (Datnow, Hubbard & Mehan, 2002).

We take the position that formulating family, community and school partnerships is a co-constructed process that in order to understand fully, we must take structure, culture and agency into account. Following Cole (1996) we see these elements as a "mediational system" in that they construct each other reflexively (Datnow et al., 2002, p. 16). We view structure, culture and agency as an interrelated set of conditions: "a web of conditions where the consequences of actions in one context may become conditions for the next" (Hall & McGinty, 1997, p. 461; see also Datnow et al., 2002).

THE BOOK'S CONTRIBUTION TO FAMILY–SCHOOL–COMMUNITY PARTNERSHIP CONVERSATIONS

As with any educational change and the presence of diverse voices, the work of school, family and community partnerships is complex and messy. This book proposes to plumb the depths of partnerships by attending conceptually to the way structural, cultural and individual actions influence these important relationships with particular attention paid to urban educational settings. To this end, the volume contributes to the ongoing conversations in academia as well as in the profession around effectively engaging all families as well as community members and organizations in their children's education, and building relationships with diverse community members around common educational goals. Specifically, the book does this in several ways.

Nationwide surveys in the United States indicate that school personnel want to establish partnerships; however, they do not always know how to go about developing strong relationships with community members (Sanders, 1999, 2001). Moreover, existing research in urban education indicates that there is inconsistency between the expectations of teachers (who are typically white, female and of middle- or working-class backgrounds) and those of the families and students from different cultural backgrounds and/or social status (Darling-Hammond, 2001; Lareau, 1987; Metz, 1986, 1990). In an urban environment, which is often characterized by diversity, it is likely that educators need to meet the needs of students and families from a wide range of backgrounds. This book illustrates the pitfalls as well as the successes that schools, districts and community-based organizations have had in creating collaborative activities to engage these families and community members. As such, it is hoped that the insights shared by the authors and their study participants are informative for teachers, principals and support staff in their own partnering practices.

Toward the same end, there is an increased push for principal and teacher preparation programs at universities to provide more guidance to pre-service candidates in developing family–school–community partnerships (Dotger & Bennett, 2010; Henderson & Mapp, 2002) as well as gaining a better understanding of how such partnerships can improve or attend to school reform. A number of post-secondary institutions recognize this need, and are offering courses in family and community involvement in education. This book is intended to provide academics teaching in colleges and universities with the background to assist practitioners to develop partnerships in communities characterized by diversity.

Lastly, there is a call for case study investigations that address the processes by which school–community partnerships, in particular, are developed and implemented, in an effort to assist schools experiencing challenges to partnering (Sanders, 2001). We seek to provide a perspective of partnerships that includes the social contexts that come to bear on the types of partnerships needed and subsequently developed, and that are found to facilitate or impede partnership establishment, and we feel that is best done in studies with a qualitative component. We are of the opinion that although generalizability of the findings can be limited in qualitative studies, the presence of rich description enables readers to reflect on the study context and its applicability to their own particular circumstances. As such, it is anticipated that individual academics and practitioners will find the literature reviews and research findings to be of use to their own research, post-secondary teaching, and K–12 practice.

OVERVIEW OF THE CHAPTERS

The chapters featured in this book represent a broad cross-section of current thinking and understanding around family and community engagement in education. Together, the contributing authors provide a picture of family–school–community partnerships that illustrates their complexity while promoting optimism that co-constructed, mutually beneficial partnerships with student achievement and well-being at their core are a real possibility. Because the authors contributing to this volume emphasize the influence of structure, culture or agency, either separately or in combination with one another, we artificially separate the chapters in this book along the lines of these conceptual elements. Each of the first three sections of the book addresses an element. Structural considerations regarding education and its organization, the impact of school-level and family culture on school-family-community partnerships, and the agency of school personnel, family members, community citizens and students are interrelated and reflexive in their impact on social action. The book concludes with a section on the strategies for the development of strong, mutually beneficial relationships and the evaluation of these school-family-community partnerships.

While the chapters are separated out into sections, we invite readers to look at the book holistically, to make connections across the sections rather than to view the chapters as separate entities. After all, the authors' contributions are part of the same conversation around partnership development in urban settings and the need for strong family–school–community relationships that include all persons impacted by education.

Part I: Structure

This section addresses issues of structure, and the external forces and institutional arrangements that serve to shape the actions of educators, families and students around educational issues. The authors make a case for reforming the education system on several levels in order to promote the inclusion of all families in their children's education in more meaningful ways.

In Chapter 2, Bonnie Stelmach begins by outlining a categorization of the family–school–community partnership literature that helps to provide context for the various research traditions in this area of investigation. It also provides a useful backdrop for understanding the differing traditions around partnerships and their goals that are discussed in the chapters that follow. Stelmach opens the discussion on structure by analyzing the language of parents around their relationship with their children's school and the school personnel in her case study. The language parents and teachers use provides a window into their perceptions of the relationship, and the implicit and explicit structures in place that impact parents' engagement with their children's education. The author offers a number of descriptive metaphors that encapsulate their perceptions and enhance our understanding of home-school relations.

While Stelmach examines the perceptions of families and notes the implicit us-them relationship with schools and school personnel, Chapter 3 examines the structures and subsequent relations that impact family–school–community relationships. In their chapter, Lea Hubbard and Catherine Hands provide an overview of the interrelatedness of structure, culture and agency with regard to family–school–community partnerships, and they examine the relationships through the actions of a school leader. In their ethnographic case study of a magnet school, the authors look at the role that structure plays in shaping both the culture of a school and the agency of school leader as well as the families and community members. Noting the important role of school leaders in fostering strong family–school–community ties, the authors show how an individual in a formal leadership position can influence a culture and school-level structures that either facilitate or impede family and community engagement in education.

Chapter 4 presents an explicit depiction of the us-them relationship and the existing hierarchical structures at the board and school levels that impede parent engagement. In their chapter, Lauri Johnson, Julie Carter and Mary Finn examine four parent projects that attempt to give voice to parent concerns and advance the interests of the community and the interests of their children. Educators and administrators who privilege a traditional individualistic parent involvement paradigm—one more typical of middle class, white parents—challenge the actions taken by each of the diverse group of parents in this study. This chapter shows efforts for inclusivity and collaboration are undermined when district expectations of parents come into conflict with parents' beliefs about how they should be treated.

Part II: Culture

This section addresses school- and community-level cultures, and their impact on inclusion. Issues of socio-economic status, race and ethnicity are discussed in relation to school structures and assumptions made by educators and parents as to the current state of family–school–community relations.

Magaly Lavadenz and Elvira Armas use a mixed methods approach to take up the important issue of building effective home-school collaborations by focusing on the English Language Learner (ELL) and Standard English Learner (SEL) population of students in Chapter 5. The authors' examination of one district and its culture of inclusion shows that although schools often formally include parents in some school organizations, in the absence of authentic meaningful participation, minority parents feel a general dissatisfaction with district programs. In response, Lavadenz and Armas present a framework for change to strengthen home-school partnerships.

In Chapter 6, Susan Faircloth also looks at ways to build and enhance home-school partnerships for students from a cultural minority. She weaves traditional native storytelling into her chapter as she presents a literature review of the existing research on Native American families' experiences with mainstream education and the implications of the findings. Her inclusion and use of secondary data is important, for it provides insight into how Native American students in urban schools have accessed and experienced the education system over time. Faircloth looks at ways in which school personnel may foster a more inclusive environment, and she advocates shaping the cultural contexts in schools with the addition of school-level structures such as cultural liaisons to bridge the current divide between school personnel and Native American families.

In Chapter 7, Michael Evans examines how culture and structure are interwoven in the education system and influence opportunities for members of community-based organizations to become involved in education at the district level. The author traces the experiences of one interfaith community-based organization in his ethnographic case study as it attempted to become involved in a school reform initiative that would see the implementation of a conflict resolution program to address violence among youth in the community. In this chapter, Evans exposes the potential challenges to the organization members' involvement in curricular change. He shows that without a culture at the school and district levels that supports community engagement in educational decision-making, and in the absence of structures in place that support it, community involvement of this kind is severely limited.

Chapter 8 switches the focus from schools and districts that experience difficulty engaging groups of parents and community members to an illustration of a school that is meeting with success in this area. In her historical case study examination of a school with a culture of parent engagement over a 30-year period, Erin McNamara Horvat highlights the parent characteristics and agency that thrived in a school culture that both welcomed and supported parent engagement. An important contribution to the literature focuses on parents' collective efforts toward school change. They were involved in their children's education through authentic, collaborative activities that required the participation of all parents for the benefit of the students and the school overall.

Part III: Agency

The section focuses on the action individuals take to construct family–community–school partnerships. Principals, teachers, parents, students and community leaders are key players, but as the chapters in this section show, assumptions, beliefs and expectations about appropriate roles for the various constituents often challenge the actions of individuals to form collaborations in the interest of school reform.

In Chapter 9, Roslyn Mickelson and Linwood Cousins show how the agency of school- and district-level personnel and parents are interrelated, and can impact the success of a program to enhance parents' knowledge of the school system, their access to social and professional networks as well as their advocacy skills. The authors focus on a program designed for a school district by a university-based team to increase the presence of black students in top-level mathematics and science high school courses. Rich descriptions of the Math/Science Equity Project offer opportunities for reflection on the types of programs that could be put in place to promote agency among all actors for the achievement and well-being of all students.

As the family members most intimately affected and intrinsically involved in schooling, students' agency in promoting family and community engagement as well as other school reform initiatives requires investigation. Susan Yonezawa and Makeba Jones discuss the role that students can play when they are provided the opportunity to be involved as researchers investigating issues specifically related to their school communities in Chapter 10. Through a district-university partnership, the authors trained students to conduct research at their schools. Structural issues such as training and the workspace available for it, as well as cultural norms established among the group members, shaped the students' agency with regard to their research practice. Further, school-level structures such as policies and the school culture impacted both the issues chosen for investigation by the students as well as the school personnel's receptivity to the students' findings. Empowered by their research findings, high school students in this study were able to inform adults within their schools about needed changes to improve student achievement. They were challenged, however, by teachers accustomed to long-standing differential power relations.

Part IV: Strategies for Inclusion and Program Assessment

In this final section, the authors take a look at what it takes to develop the relationships that give way to partnership creation that involves all participants and enhances parents' agency in particular. It is proposed that the establishment of trust and an understanding of the social contexts in which parents, community members and educators engage provides fertile ground for co-constructed, mutually beneficial partnerships that involve all constituents.

Novella Keith's Chapter 11 offers an in-depth look at Transformational Social Therapy (TST), a strategy that is designed to foster collaborative action among organizations and communities. Fractured relationships and mistrust in one French community expose a rich context in which to examine how social relationships, torn apart by various expressions of violence, can develop trust when they are provided with supports—or structures—for the emotional understanding of self and other.

Once the foundation of trust and understanding is laid, and partnership programs are in place that encourage parent and community engagement, attention is turned to evaluating the efforts. Chrispeels and González demonstrate a useful assessment strategy in their evaluation of two community-based parent education programs in Chapter 12. The authors demonstrate that although the programs experienced somewhat different outcomes, an in-depth look at their ability to match an espoused theory of parent support with their theory-in-use led to successful outcomes for parents and students. The research shows the benefits of intermediary organizations as cultural brokers able to link Latino families and schools. Through their efforts, parents became empowered by the knowledge they gained from the programs and were better able to support their children's academic needs.

In the final contribution, Catherine Hands and Lea Hubbard provide their culminating thoughts on inclusion for families and community members in urban environments. They draw on their own research and practical experience in the field, and connect the chapters with the broader context of diversity and inclusion in urban education. Taken together, it is hoped that this volume fosters the thought-provoking conversations, research and implementation of insightful partnership programs required to ensure that the needs of all students, their families and members of communities surrounding the schools are represented in education.

REFERENCES

Anyon, J. (1997). *Ghetto schooling: A political economy of urban educational reform.* New York: Teachers College Press.

Anyon, J. (2005). *Radical possibilities: Public policy, urban education, and a new social movement.* New York: Routledge.

Auerbach, S. (2010). Beyond coffee with the principal: Toward leadership for authentic school–family partnerships. *Journal of School Leadership, 20*(6), 728–757.

Bowles, S., & Gintis, H. (1976). *Schooling in capitalist America.* New York: Basic Books.

Bryk, A., & Schneider, B. (2002). *Trust in schools: A core resource for improvement.* New York: Russell Sage.

Cole, M. (1996). *Cultural psychology: A once and future discipline.* Cambridge, MA: Harvard Belknap.

Comer, J., Haynes, N., Joyner, E., & Ben Avie, M. (1996). *Rallying the whole village: The Comer process for reforming education.* New York: Teachers College Press.

Cooper, C. W. (2007). School choice as "motherwork": Valuing African-American women's educational advocacy and resistance. *International Journal of Qualitative Studies in Education, 20*(5), 491–512.

Darling-Hammond, L. (1996). The right to learn and the advancement of teaching: Research, policy and practice for democratic education. *Educational Researcher, 25*(6), 5–17.

Darling-Hammond, L. (2001). *The right to learn: A blueprint for creating schools that work.* San Francisco: Jossey-Bass.

Darling-Hammond, L., & Lieberman, A. (1993, April). *James P. Comer, M.D., on the School Development Program: Making a difference for children.* New York: National Center for Restructuring Education, Schools, and Teaching.

Datnow, A., Hubbard, L., & Mehan, H. (2002). *Extending educational reform: From one school to many.* New York: RoutledgeFalmer.

Davies, D. (2002). The 10th school revisited: Are school/family/community partnerships on the reform agenda now? *Phi Delta Kappan, 83*(5), 388–392.

Dotger, B. H., & Bennett, J. (2010). Educating teachers and school leaders for school-family partnerships. In D. B. Hiatt-Michael (Ed.), *Promising practices to support family involvement in schools* (pp. 129–149). Charlotte, NC: Information Age Publishing.

Epstein, J. L. (1995). School/family/community partnerships: Caring for the children we share. *Phi Delta Kappan, 76*(9), 701–712.

Gibson, M., Gandara, P., & Koyama, J. (2004). *School connections: U.S. Mexican youth, peers, and school achievement.* New York: Teachers College Press.

Giroux, H. (2009). *Youth in a suspect society.* New York: Palgrave Macmillan.

Hall, P., & McGinty, P. (1997). Policy as a transformation of intentions: Producing program from statures. *Sociological Quarterly, 38*(3), 439–467.

Hands, C. (2009, April). *Efforts to enhance parent engagement: What can we learn from an assemblage of district-wide initiatives?* Paper presented at the Annual Meeting of the American Educational Research Association, San Diego, CA.

Heath, S. B. (1982). Questioning at home and at school: A comparative study. In G. Spindler (Ed.), *Doing the ethnography of schooling* (pp. 96–101). New York: Holt, Rinehart and Winston.

Henderson, A. T., & Mapp, K. L. (2002). *A new wave of evidence: The impact of school, family, and community connections on student achievement.* Austin, TX: Southwest Educational Development Laboratory.

Henderson, A. T., Mapp, K. L., Johnson, V. R., & Davies, D. (2007). *Beyond the bake sale: The essential guide to family–school partnerships.* NY: The New Press.

Hiatt-Michael, D. B., & Hands, C. M. (2010). Family involvement policy, research and practice. In D. B. Hiatt-Michael (Ed.), *Promising practices to support family involvement in schools* (pp. 1–8). Charlotte, NC: Information Age Publishing.

Hoover-Dempsey, K. V., Bassler, O. C., & Brissie, J S. (1992). Explorations in Parent-school relations. *Journal of Educational Research, 85,* 287–294.

Hubbard, L., Mehan, H., & Stein, M.K. (2006). *Reform as learning: School reform, organizational culture, and community politics in San Diego.* New York: Routledge.

Jeynes, W. H. (2005). A Meta-Analysis of the Relation of Parental Involvement to Urban Elementary School Student Academic Achievement. *Urban Education, 40*(3), 237–269.

Lareau, A. (1987). Social class differences in family–school relationships: The importance of cultural capital. *Sociology of Education, 60,* 73–85.

Lareau, A. (2003). *Unequal Childhoods: Class, race and family life.* Berkeley: University of California Press.

MacLeod, J. (1987). *Ain't no making it: Aspirations and attainment in a low-income neighborhood.* Boulder, Colo: Westview

Merz, C., & Furman, G. (1997). *Community and schools: Promise and paradox.* New York: Teachers College Press.

Metz, M. H. (1986). *Different by design: The context and character of three magnet schools.* London: Routledge and Kegan Paul Inc.

Metz, M. H. (1990). How social class differences shape teachers' work. In M. W. McLaughlin, J. E. Talbert, & N. Bascia (Eds.), *The contexts of teaching in secondary schools* (pp. 40–107). New York: Teachers College Press.

Moll, L., Amanti, C., Neff, D., & Gonzales, N. (1992). Funds of knowledge: Using a qualitative approach to connect homes and classrooms. *Theory into Practice, 31*(2),132–141.

Morris, J. (2002). A communally bonded school for African American students, families and a community. Retrieved June 25, 2010, from http://www.coe. uga.edu/morris/Kappan%20communally %20bond. Pdf

Pressman, J., & Wildavsky, A. (1973). *Implementation.* Berkeley: University of California Press.

Pushor, D. (2007, January). *Parent engagement: Creating a shared world.* Paper presented at the Ontario Education Research Symposium, Toronto, Ontario, Canada.

Pushor, D., Ruitenberg, C., with co-researchers from Princess Alexandra Community School. (2005, November). *Parent engagement and leadership* (Research report, project #134). Saskatoon, SK: Dr. Stirling McDowell Foundation for Research into Teaching.

Sanders, M. G. (1999). Schools' program and progress in the National Network of Partnership Schools. *The Journal of Educational Research, 92*(4), 220–232.

Sanders, M. G. (2001). The role of "community" in comprehensive school, family, and community programs. *The Elementary School Journal, 102*(1), 19–34.

Shapiro, J. P., Ginsberg, A. E., & Brown, S. P. (2002, October). *Family and community participation in urban schools: The ethic of care.* Paper presented at the 7th annual Values and Leadership in Education conference, Toronto, Ontario, Canada.

Walker, J. M. T., Wilkins, A. S., Dallaire, J. R., Sandler, H. M., & Hoover-Dempsey, K. V. (2005). Parental involvement: Model revision through scale development. *Elementary School Journal, 106*(2), 85–104.

Wohlstetter, P., Malloy, C.L., Smith, J., & Hentschke, G. (2003). *Cross-sectorial alliances in education: A new approach to enhancing school capacity.* (Working paper). Los Angeles: University of Southern California, Rossier School of Education, Center on Educational Governance.

Willis, P. (1977). *Learning to labor: How working class kids get working class jobs.* Westmead, England: Saxon House.

PART I

STRUCTURE

CHAPTER 2

METAPHOR AS INSIGHT INTO PARENTS' CONCEPTUALIZATIONS OF THEIR ROLE IN SCHOOL IMPROVEMENT

Bonnie L. Stelmach

ABSTRACT

While educational policy strongly endorses the idea of parent-teacher unity in principle, it tends not to be founded on deep understanding of parents' and teachers' views about schooling and education. Drawing on three case studies of schools in Alberta and Saskatchewan, Canada, Bonnie Stelmach demonstrates that despite claims that parents are partners, parents continue to conceptualize themselves in ways that push them to the educational peripheries, and make questionable their ability to be natural collaborators with teachers. In keeping with their argument that metaphors mirror conceptual understanding, Lakoff and Johnson's orientational and structural metaphors are applied as an interpretive lens. Data interpretations are presented as motifs that show a persistent dissonance between parents' understanding of their place among educators and the educational rhetoric of meaningful parent involvement.

Including Families and Communities in Urban Education, pages 17–40
Copyright © 2011 by Information Age Publishing
17

In *The Sociology of Teaching* (1932), Willard Waller surmised:

> From the ideal point of view, parents and teachers share much in common in that both, supposedly, wish things to occur for the best interests of the child; but in fact... parents and teachers are natural enemies, predestined each for the discomfiture of the other. (p. 68)

Waller's assessment of the relationship between teachers and parents might seem overly glum for contemporary times because the notion of "partnership" has been popularized as the new optimistic prophesy for parent-teacher relations. Through this apparent volte-face, parents and teachers have been recast as "natural collaborators." To this effect, educational policies such as the United States of America's much discussed *No Child Left Behind Act* (2001) include as a parameter the participation of parents in curriculum-related planning. This expectation is echoed across other continents (see Boylan, 2005; Department for Education and Skills, 2005; Dom & Verhoeven, 2006; Ho, 2006; Hong Kong Education Department, 2000; New Zealand Ministry of Education, 2005). In Canada, all provinces and territories have mandated parent involvement through school councils as recently as 2005 (Saskatchewan Learning,[1] 2005; Young & Levin, 2002).

Though recorded nearly seventy years ago, Waller's (1932) statement continues to resonate because while educational policy strongly endorses the idea of parent-teacher unity in principle, it tends not to be founded on deep understanding of what Lawrence-Lightfoot (2003) describes as the "complex and tender geography [of the] borderlands between families and schools" (p. xi). Thus, while it is assumed that parents and teachers are bonded by the common interest of improving schooling for children, both groups have potentially different views about schooling. Lawrence-Lightfoot (2003) has investigated these apparently opposing views and found that "every time parents and teachers encounter one another in the classroom, their conversations are shaped by their own autobiographical stories and by the broader cultural and historical narratives that inform their identities, their values, and their sense of place in the world" (p. 3).

In this paper, I extend Lawrence-Lightfoot's sentiment to explore from parents' perspectives their metaphorical constructions regarding their role in education relationships with their children's teachers. Drawing on data collected in Alberta (Stelmach, 2005, 2006) and Saskatchewan, Canada (Stelmach & Preston, 2008), I argue that parents and teachers are aligned rhetorically as partners, but parents continue to conceptualize themselves in ways that push them to the educational periphery or make questionable their ability to be natural collaborators. I echo Lawrence-Lightfoot's urging to "see the necessary and crucial claims of each other's position" (p. 243); however, I depart from her methodologically. While Lawrence-Lightfoot employs a combination of portraiture and narrative, or what she calls "parables of wisdom" (p. xxx) to understand in an archaeological and historical sense the behavior of teachers and parents, I was interested in how the expressions and descriptions parents used in interviews could be understood as metaphors reflecting their conceptualizations of parental roles. I believe my searching beneath and beyond what is reported as self-evident about parents' places in schools may contribute to Lawrence-Lightfoot's project of explicating viewpoints from both sides of the desk.

OVERVIEW OF LITERATURE ON PARENT INVOLVEMENT

Theoretical positioning of parent involvement literature can be thought of in three broad ways corresponding to Guba and Lincoln's (2005) epistemological and ontological paradigms. Post-positivist orientations render parent involvement to a science that can be objectively understood. These studies embrace a cause–effect formula in which parent involvement is claimed to have a direct, positive impact on students' learning. Joyce Epstein's (2001) work has been influential in this regard. Her categorization of six types of parent involvement has come to be the most frequently cited and applied framework for involving parents in supporting better student achievement (e.g., Baker & Soden, 1998; Canadian School Boards Association, 1995; Dietz, 1997; Hara & Burke, 1998; Lyons, Robbins, & Smith, 1984; Mapp, 2003; Norris, 1999; Simich-Dudgeon, 1993). Other parent involvement models, such as the Comer Process (Comer, Haynes, & Joyner, 1996) have been built on similar assumptions, structures, and practices.

Quasi-experimental studies, though rigorous in their statistical analysis and scope, have been most useful for understanding parent involvement in elementary schools. In contrast to studies conducted in elementary school contexts, where parents are assumed to be a key, unidirectional factor in students' achievement, secondary school studies factor students into the equation and suggest a bidirectional relationship in which students' response to parent involvement is actively negotiated (Deslandes, Royer, Turcotte, & Bertrand, 1997; Hoover-Dempsey & Sandler, 1995). Parent involvement, then, is not an unquestioned "good" beyond elementary school.

A second position, borne out of the critical paradigm, troubles ethnicity, class, and gender for their effects on parents' ability or inability to participate within schools according to current discourses of parent involvement (David, 2002, 2004; de Carvalho, 2001; Fine, 1993; Lareau, 1996; Vincent, 1996, 2000). Rooted in Marxist theory, critical theorists focus on macro-level socioeconomic sources of power among parents, locating the challenge for parent involvement in broad social and economic realities (Caines, 2005; Crozier, 2000; de Carvalho, 2001; Fine, 1993; Lareau, 1996; Vincent,

1996, 2000). The feminist poststructuralist account departs from critical theory on this matter, and instead examines from a micro-perspective how some parents choose and others do not choose to participate in schools in traditional ways. Like critical theorists, feminist poststructuralists acknowledge power differentials among parents and between parents and teachers, but feminist poststructuralists argue that all parents have agency, and that *not* participating in school-constructed opportunities is a demonstration of this. Both views encourage questioning of schoolcentric (Lawson, 2003) discourses through the examination of ethnic heritage, race, socioeconomic class, and/or gender, and the way these factors contribute to the banking (or bankruptcy) of parents' cultural capital (Bourdieu & Passeron, 1990) in relation to schools.

A third position in the literature is interpretivist/constructivist. This position suggests both congruities and incongruities with the way parents and educators experience programs and strategies involving parents (Pushor & Murphy 2004). This lens suggests educators have a particular expectation of parents to be involved in ways that correspond to or mimic school practices such as discipline, homework completion, attendance, teaching (Lawson, 2003). Rarely stated by teachers, although implicit, are educators' assumptions of a division between professionals and parents in terms of roles and what counts as knowledge (Allen, Thompson, Hoadley, Engelking & Drapeaux, 1997; López & Vázquez, 2005). The parent experience often suggests an acceptance of this dichotomy, particularly at the secondary level (Westergård & Galloway, 2004). With few exceptions in the literature (Ruitenberg & Pushor, 2005), parents' voices are eclipsed by educators' positions on parent involvement. For this reason, I sought a more in-depth and nuanced understanding of parents' views.

METHODOLOGY AND CONCEPTUAL ORIENTATION

Scholarship on parent involvement tends to report on elementary schools in urban centers characterized by low socio-economic conditions and minority ethnic families (e.g., Lareau, 1987, 2002; Lawson, 2003), assuming that low socio-economic status and the impersonal environment of larger schools dissuade parents from participating in their children's schools. My professional and research experiences in rural contexts compelled me to question these assumptions. I was curious how a close-knit community in a smaller urban center might differently impact upon parent-teacher relationships and influence how parents thought about their role in education. Further, I wondered whether children's grade levels might create different challenges for parent involvement.

The Study's Parent Participants and Community Contexts

I purposefully (Mertens, 2005) selected a sample composed primarily of parents of secondary students (grades 7–12); twenty out of the 24 parents interviewed represented the secondary level. The parents selected can be described as middle- to high-income earners. Most of parents were of European descent, but the sample also included Aboriginal[2] parents and Elders, immigrant parents, and foster parents of First Nations children.

All parents were from two school divisions[3] in the Western Canadian provinces of Alberta and Saskatchewan. These provinces were particularly suitable for my research because they were engaged in policies and/or programs that made specific recommendations to involve parents. In Alberta, the *Alberta Initiative for School Improvement* (AISI) (Alberta Learning,[4] 1999), a school improvement project implemented in 2000, expected schools to directly involve parents in the development of school improvement plans aimed at enhancing students' academic achievement. School councils had also been in place since 1995 (Alberta Education, 1995). In 2005, Saskatchewan revised its *Education Act* to legislate School Community Councils (SCC). The SCC mandate was similar to AISI in Alberta in that Saskatchewan parents were to contribute to the development of schools' learning improvement plans. These characteristics suggested to me that Alberta and Saskatchewan were committed to parent involvement.

The communities in which I conducted the research were described by the participants as "bedroom communities" and "hubs." One research site had a population under 7000, and because it was located two hours from a major urban center, it served as a hub for an extensive geographic region. The other research site was a community of less than 1000, but was called a bedroom community because it was within commuting distance to an urban center. The community was characterized by a substantial population of families with professional and social lives concentrated in the city.

Data Collection

Over the course of three instrumental case studies (Stake, 2005) investigating parents' perspectives on contributing to school improvement (Stelmach, 2005, 2006; Stelmach & Preston, 2008), I interviewed parents individually using Fontana and Frey's (2005) semi-structured process. Proforma questions were used to elicit emic information about the participants, and open-ended questions encouraged interview participants to express their understanding of "parent involvement" as Patton (1990) would say "in their own terms" (p. 290). The semi-structured approach enabled me to adapt to unexpected responses and pursue salient aspects as they were introduced (Maykut & Morehouse, 1994). My aim in interviews was to gain insight into their conceptualizations of their role in school improvement generally, and within specific school improvement initiatives relevant to the provincial contexts.

Interviews were the primary data source and were supplemented with document analysis and school observations. I used these approaches to access multiple meaning with the hope of establishing methodological rigor in my studies. The research was premised on the belief that knowledge is constructed through interaction with a social world, and that meaning is filtered through interpretations by actors in situ (Schwandt, 1994). Guba and Lincoln (2005) referred to this epistemological stance as "transactional/subjectivist" (p. 195) in which knowledge is construed as a "community *negotiation*" (p. 204, emphasis in original). Importantly, they earlier suggested that interpretation is the conduit to understanding how constructions are brought out and refined through researcher-respondent interactions (Guba & Lincoln, 1998). Given this, I acknowledge that a penumbra of my own beliefs, values, and expectations as a former high school teacher and current researcher was cast upon these data. I addressed this to the extent a researcher can by checking my interpretations orally and in written form with these parents. By virtue of the case study method, I was able to investigate to some depth parents' perspectives on their educational roles, recognizing that data collected in case studies are bound by time, place, and space.

Metaphor as a Conceptual Framework

Traditionally, metaphor analysis has been reserved for the domains of literature, linguistics, and cognitive science. Morgan's (1986, 2006) use of metaphors in organizational theory introduced a connection between metaphor and educational organization and management, and more recently metaphor has become a medium for understanding educational policy (Baker, 2002; Yanow, 2000). In their classic work, *Metaphors We Live By*, Lakoff and Johnson (1980) suggest that metaphors mirror conceptual understanding; the way people think and what they experience is understood through principles that are metaphoric in nature. They argued, "metaphorical expressions in everyday language can give us insight into the metaphorical nature of the concepts that structure our everyday activities" (p. 7). Yanow (2000) defines metaphor as the "juxtaposition of two superficially unlike elements...in a single context" (p. 42). She contends metaphor can be a useful tool for deciphering policy meaning, and, citing Lakoff and Johnson (1980), shows her thesis is an extension of their refutation that metaphor is merely decorative:

Metaphor is not a harmless thing. It is one of the principal means by which we understand our experience and reason on the basis of that understanding. To the extent that we act on our reasoning, metaphor plays a role in the creation of reality. (p. 42)

Metaphor, then, is an access point to the descriptive content and prescriptive forces that shape perceptions and policy. Applied to my research, the way parents talk about their role in their children's school performance mirror their conceptualizations of parent involvement, and, in Lakoff and Johnson's terms, structure their behavior as a result.

To interpret the data, I applied Lakoff and Johnson's definitions of orientational and structural metaphors. Orientational metaphors "[organize] a whole system of concepts with respect to one another" (p. 14). Most orientational metaphors are spatial orientations such as up/down or central/peripheral. Structural metaphors refer to concepts that are metaphorically structured in terms of other concepts (e.g., argument as war). Parents' understanding of their role in their children's schooling was interpreted through metaphoric descriptions, as derived through inductive content analysis (Krippendorff, 2004).

Inductive Content Analysis

Inductive content analysis involves a systematic reading of text (Krippendorff, 2004) for the purpose of recognizing meaning and intention as well as consequences associated with them (Downe-Wamboldt, 1992). Because I was interested in how language may impact upon parents' conceptualizations of their role vis-à-vis teachers, and how this may ultimately play into parent-teacher collaboration, content analysis was an appropriate method. Using orientational and structural metaphors as a premise for analysis, I mined interview transcripts for language that reflected parents' positioning and orientation with respect to teachers. Words and phrases that expressed orientation or structure, such as "stand *behind* your school" and "dodged a bullet", were the unit of analysis (Krippendorff, 2004). In this first stage of open coding (Warren & Karner, 2005), I noted in the margins of transcripts the most compelling, novel, surprising and recurrent ideas.

In keeping with inductive content analysis, the next phase of the analysis involved thematic unitizing (Krippendorff, 2004). General impressions created from the first phase of analysis were further coded into what I called motifs where my interpretations were supported by key themes. Parents' understanding of their role in their children's schooling was interpreted through metaphoric descriptions.

Metaphors and Motifs

According to Lakoff and Johnson (1980), our daily actions are manifestations of a conceptual system that is metaphorical in nature. Metaphors figure prominently in an unconscious logic that can be deciphered through the examination of language. Language is like a key that gives access to conceptual systems.

Orientational Metaphors

In examining the words these parents used to describe their role in their children's learning, I noted that they employed various orientational metaphors that were spatial in nature (Lakoff & Johnson, 1980). These spatial metaphors were expressed through words and phrases that predominantly distanced or inferiorly positioned them with respect to professional educators and schools: "overstepped," "above," "welcome you *in*," "stand *behind* your school," and "this came from . . . somewhere *higher up*" were suggestive examples. These parents' descriptions of their supportive or indirect role may be clarified through such orientational metaphors.

Motif of Support

Parents described their role as being one of support with respect to teachers and schools, educational policy, and their children. I discuss these in turn below.

In support of teachers and schools. A number of parents reinforced an educational script whereby curriculum and school improvement design were policy makers' and educators' domains:

> I think most parents see themselves more as a support. . . . They're asking what they're doing, they're assisting with projects. . . . They're supporting the school, but it's not direct. (Lewis[5])

> Personally, I think parents should be behind the scenes and be supportive. [Teachers] have to provide good programs for the kids to undertake and for parents to be supportive. (Surin)

These comments correspond to other research documenting a separation between teacher and parent roles (de Carvalho, 2001; Waggoner & Griffith, 1998). These parents clearly held an expectation that curriculum matters belonged to the educators:

...overall the educators should know what is to be taught, I think it's fine educational-wise to leave it in their hands. (Melanie)

I kind of see them (teachers and principals) as having the guiding hand as far as programs and curriculum. (Clarence)

Admissions such as Jill's, "When I went to high school it's nothing like what these children are doing now," implied high school material might have been too unfamiliar for some parents, including those who held university degrees. Being intimidated by curriculum content partially explained why most of these parents described their role in terms of monitoring students' performance, meeting with teachers during parent-teacher interviews, participating in parent workshops, encouraging their children to seek extra help, and attending awards ceremonies when their children were honored. Supportive roles such as these suggest that these parents understood themselves as somewhat external, yet necessary, to their children's schooling. In earlier work, I called this position "off-center stage" (Stelmach, 2006, p. 184).

I most noted a tone of respectful distance when these parents spoke about their role vis-à-vis teachers and educational administrators. Some parents expressed a democratic interest in participating in educational decisions but were aware that their position as parents allowed them to only weigh in on them lightly. Rita, who had participated on a school improvement planning team at her children's school reported, "If there were things you wanted to get done, I mean if everyone voted, 'Okay, let's do this' it wouldn't get done. If the administration didn't buy into it, it didn't really matter what you said." (Stelmach, 2005, p. 179) While Rita was resigned to her lack of authority, other parents readily accepted this arrangement:

I've always been behind the teachers... I've always dealt with the school as if it's in the school power to go ahead and do what they want to do, go ahead. (Guy)

In fact, power was non-negotiable in educators' courts for Fritz:

I hate to see the parents in control. I think the school should stay in control... because it will automatically become more of a political ball... Some parents will get on their high horse.

Hierarchy was evidently preferable for Fritz. Very telling was his sardonic use of the term "high horse" to indicate that parents should be positioned lower than teachers. His reference to parents' politicization speaks to Lightfoot's (1978) binary of parents' particularistic interests in their children versus educators' universalistic interests for all students. Betty, on the other hand, saw hierarchy contingently:

> It's like a ladder where you put the parents—well, it depends on what you're referring to or looking at. The parents would be high on one aspect, but the teachers would be high in another aspect. Parents should be there for support, although the teacher should be there for support, too, but probably in different areas.

Even parents who argued for opportunities to voice their opinions revealed through their language that ultimately they all "[saw] teachers as an authority in some way" (Victoria). In their suggestions that parents should "stand *behind* [the] school" (Ada), or that they felt "[teachers] totally welcome you *in*" resonate with the idea that parents have an understanding of themselves as peripheral. Lakoff and Johnson (1980) argue that we talk about the world in the way we conceive of it, and our everyday activities are structured accordingly. If this is the case, then it helps to clarify why neither the Alberta nor the Saskatchewan parents believed strongly in their role in school improvement, despite both provinces having mandated such a role for them. It also explains why the transition from parents as social organizers for schools to improvement planners has been negligible (Stelmach & Preston, 2008).

In support of educational policy. The AISI and SCC policies in Alberta and Saskatchewan, respectively, emphasized parent involvement as a central strategy to improving schools. I was, therefore, interested in parents' views on their interactions with policy design and implementation. Similar to their descriptions of engaging with teachers, these parents invoked a metaphor of spatial distancing when it came to their relationship to educational policy.

Sometimes against their judgment or wishes, parents supported school policy as a matter of duty. Victoria provided two examples regarding school programming and fees:

> Their (school's) policy is all students will attend Religion.... Parents may or may not be happy with those things, but I think parents should generally support the school in implementing those policies.

> It was really hard for me to sit there in those meetings and vote for a fee increase, which I knew the school needed... I was thinking that means whatever less for me, you know? But I always voted for the fee increase because that was what the school needed; it was the best for the school even though it had a negative impact on me personally.

Ann recollected her experience in the AISI project as follows:

> I was asked to sit on this board. I didn't really know exactly what board I was sitting on, what I was doing, what my involvement was supposed to be. So that

was cloudy. So when this...model came in, it was kind of like, 'Oh, okay, I guess if this is what they want...' (Stelmach, 2005)

These examples convey an oppositional stance of "we/me versus they/them." Parents seemed to regard themselves at the bottom of a hierarchy, as highlighted in the following:

This came from [school] division office or somewhere *higher up*....There's a policy *coming down* from division office. (Gina)

...the [school] board *above* us....so many *levels* to go through. (Ada)

The upshot of this stratification was parents classified themselves as "just parents" (Ada) or "just listeners" (Dee) meant to passively receive policy decisions made by those who "run the show" (Gina). As evidence that parents' commentary on policy carried no force, Dee shared the experience of organizing the SCC's participation on a school division policy. After asking parents to collect input from others about a proposed policy, Dee recounted how a school administrator took over and changed the process, "They (parents) were overstepped quickly and brutally," according to her. She conjectured that this incident was a "power trip." From a critical theory point of view, one might argue that historical relations of hierarchy are entrenched such that parents are essentially disenfranchised from educational processes. However, Dee demonstrated a more poststructuralist response. Instead of succumbing to what she perceived as a power struggle, Dee reported that she was going to avoid "going through the school" on another project she was working on. Notably, however, her use of the word "through" indicates recognition of potential confrontation, a metaphor I take up in a later section.

In support of their children. The reference to parents as their children's first teachers (Canadian School Boards Association, 1995; Gestwicki, 2004; Hargreaves & Fullan, 1998) prefaces many arguments for parents to be continuously at the center of their children's educational lives. Neither with regard to the school, nor to their children did these parents, however, orient themselves in this way. But departing from literature which describes parent involvement as simply declining as children progress through the grades (Epstein, 2001), these parents described themselves as "coach[es] in the background" (Fritz), indicating a shifting of their positioning as their children matured. Some parents explained their expectation for their children to become independent learners:

I tell my kids this (school) is their job. This is your job, and I want you to treat it as such. You need to be on time, you need to do a good job or you're going to get fired. (Angela)

Their education is their responsibility. (Martine)

One parent suggested that after grade seven or eight, parents should not have to hold children "by the hand" (Betty). Thus, support was something that came from a distance. Some parents felt it was particularly important to avoid "meddling." I cite Martine to illustrate:

> At that age they don't want to see you around, so it's sometimes a detriment. It's kind of like playing the field of the child. Is it important that I'm there? If [son] tells me I know—because I know him—then it's important for me to be there. He doesn't have to say, "Mom, I'd really like you to be there."

The position in the literature has been that the parental role is a negotiation between parents and teachers (Beck & Murphy, 1999; Keyes, 2002; Lawson, 2003; Pushor & Murphy, 2004; Ruitenberg & Pushor, 2005; Skau, 1996; Waggoner & Griffith, 1998). Martine's comment suggests that parents may face boundaries with their children as well, a point that Hoover-Dempsey and Sandler (1995, 1997) articulate in their model of parental involvement. The way these parents spoke about mediating against being a "nag" (Jill) or "push[ing] too much" (Melanie) indicates that for the sake of youth's privacy and autonomy, negotiation occurs more between parents and children. Crozier (2000) found students draw a fine line between support and control. This emphasizes the conciliatory nature of parent involvement at the secondary school level. Education policy seems to deny this outright because it rarely includes students in policy design.

These parents' insights confront the parent-teacher relationship as the pinnacle of parent involvement. Parents are context-bound by their parent status. One might assume that the virtue of parenthood is the ability to lead, influence, and orchestrate children's learning, yet these parents' orientation metaphors indicate their role is more likely to be one of followers of teachers, and at the secondary level, their teenage children.

Structural Metaphors

Lakoff and Johnson (1980) claim that:

> Structural metaphors allow us to do much more than just orient concepts, refer to them, quantify them . . . they allow us, in addition, to use one highly structured and clearly delineated concept to structure another. (p. 61)

Thus, structural metaphors imply other concepts. They define reality through what Lakoff and Johnson call "entailments" (1980, p. 147). In other words, a structural metaphor such as likening life to climbing a mountain generates a network of entailments such as the fact that there are difficult ascents and occasional plateaus and descents; that there is a peak to be reached through physical, psychological, and spiritual investment; and that every mountain climbed leaves one with a sense of conquest or reward. In this section I explicate two structural metaphors that offer valuable insight into how these parents conceptualized their educational role and relationships. With regard to their children, I interpreted parents as safety nets. With respect to their relationship with teachers, the metaphor of battle seemed appropriate.

The Motif of the Safety Net

Though these parents' use of spatial metaphors would suggest that they are indirectly involved in or sometimes removed from their children's learning, they occupied a significant crucial space. In trying to understand what parents meant when they defined their role as "just being there" (Angela), I noted references to a role that I interpreted as a safety net.

The need for a safety net implies imminent danger or potential injury. Indeed, these parents saw schooling as sometimes embodying risk, threat, failure, and disappointment. Rather than swoop in and prevent their children from these experiences, what their language revealed was that the safety net was there to catch their fall. It was not statically positioned, but rather, it shifted. The safety net oscillated between being near and far, depending on the circumstances, and depending on the parenting style.

Martine and Yves took an approach that to educators might seem radical: "It's not my problem if you choose to have low marks . . . We encourage, but . . . I already did grade 9, and it's your responsibility to do it." Melanie shared this opinion: "They learn by their mistakes; I can't do it all for them at this stage." Other parents were more prepared to move in, setting up meetings with teachers, for instance, but only in the event of persistent problems. Some educators might accuse these parents of being apathetic when they appear to be standing back, but clearly these parents trusted their children and, for better or worse, felt they had to allow them "to grow up" (Hans). This is not, however, how policy constructs the parent role, especially for those parents whose children do not exhibit the ability to manage their learning according to educator expectations. A *White Paper* in the United Kingdom (Department for Education and Skills, 2005), for example, puts the onus on parents to discipline their children in accordance with school rules. This is especially problematic for some parents. Pushor and Murphy (2004) explain that non-mainstream parents tend to be judged as negligent because their families' domestic routines diverge from the white, middle class structures upon which schools are based (Lareau, 1996).

Further, teachers tend to want parents to immediately jump in when things go wrong (Stelmach, 2006), but this was not how these parents perceived their responsibilities. These parents of secondary students emphasized the need for their children to mature and develop their independence; thus, parents were less inclined to intervene at the first sign of trouble. They reported that their children had to learn responsibility through mistakes and challenges. Whereas teachers focused on grade achievement and homework completion, and expected parents to prioritize these as they did, parents spoke more holistically about their children's development. Parents' decisions to remain in the background even when their children were struggling academically was sometimes viewed by teachers as apathy. I interpreted an unarticulated dissonance in perspective, which perhaps created some frustration for both teachers and parents.

The assumption around safety nets is they are a last resort to impending disaster. In this regard, they took an unobtrusive stance. Some parents saw school itself as creating pressure for their children:

> I find these kids have a lot on their plates, and higher expectations. I think a lot of them are stressed out, and I think you see more depression with these kids, and more emotional and psychological issues than in our days . . . I will try to support them in that way to try to encourage them so that they're doing something positive.

Thus, the safety net may have been positioned away from school-related activities, something of which teachers might not be aware. The idea that their children had to sometimes suffer to learn was expressed by many parents. They said:

> We've all had good and bad teachers. Deal with it. I mean, that's life. (Karla)

> Sometimes they need to fall in order to pick themselves up again, unfortunately. (Melanie)

Relating negative experiences to "real life" was one way Ada justified not rushing in to the school in response to her children's complaints:

> I will let them complain and I will listen to them. Then I will say, "In the real world you will probably have a boss like that, or you might have a co-worker like that." They say, "Well, that's not fair." Well, I'm sorry . . . You have to deal with it and move on.

Issues of justice seemed to be one instance that motivated parents' deployment of the safety net. Some of these parents confronted teachers on such issues as perceived unfair disciplinary action and grades. Parents seemed to recognize, however, that this type of behavior resulted in them being labeled, as Victoria euphemistically put it, "difficult," and not what educators wanted from "involved" parents (Casanova, 1996; Ogawa, 1996). The metaphor of the safety net, in Victoria's case, was enacted quite differently. Instead of waiting to soften a blow for her child, she engaged the teachers as a form of safety net. For instance, she insisted on participating with her child in the development of his special needs program. In this way, she encouraged her child's teachers to legitimate her knowledge (Pushor, 2008) about her child and his needs in the process of addressing his learning requirements. Thus, the metaphor of the safety net is not necessarily straightforward, always implying that parents act alone in this regard. But the co-constructed safety net seemed to be used only when parents could forecast with certainty that their children were in some sort of danger.

The Motif of Battle

In my field notes I recorded one administrator at a staff meeting as having claimed to have "dodged a bullet" when describing an incident with a parent. Another time this administrator characterized parent involvement as a "double-edged sword." I was intrigued that these parents, too, invoked such language. Either directly or indirectly in their metaphors, these parents invoked battle terminology, suggesting a combative relationship that involved winners and losers. An examination of these parents' language made a compelling case that Waller's (1932) sobriquet of parents and teachers as "natural enemies" still holds sway.

The metaphor of battle may be interpreted as parents demarcating where/when they belong, and in what instances they may advance or must retreat. Curriculum decisions appeared to be an area in which these parents understood they were out of bounds. In describing what she perceived was a limitation of the SCC, Margaret stated that parents cannot "step way across the line." She added that her school principal would be receptive to the SCC's ideas only if it "[didn't] maker her feel like they [were] treading too much in her (the principal's) territory." One father commented that the "educational community is closed" (Oskar). These descriptors speak to the protective structures erected and political boundaries adhered to during battle.

Even the SCC which was intended to provide Saskatchewan parents with direct opportunities to contribute to a school learning improvement plan faced barriers, in Dee's experience. She reported that the SCC had limited power because legislation required that all decisions be approved by the School Board. The Board was like a "wall" that worked against parents having a place in school improvement planning.

It seemed that parents who had concerns that the school was not addressing critical issues, such as drug abuse in the community, were prepared to
battle with teachers. After failing to reach community members about this
particular issue, Oskar said he "attacked it from the other end at parent-
teacher interviews." No doubt these parents did not purposely choose these
words to describe their relations with the school, but it is precisely this unconscious use of metaphorical language that Lakoff and Johnson (1980)
argue is a window to conceptualization.

Some parents were overwhelmingly supportive of their children's schools
and felt they were engaged in an equal partnership with their children's
teachers. Surin described her child's school as having "opened its doors." On
the surface, this expression creates a welcoming impression of the school.
However, the metaphor of a door suggests it can be closed (slammed shut?)
for the purpose of privacy. Elsewhere I have argued that the schoolhouse
door is often only rhetorically open because parents are decoupled from
the school's technical core of teaching (Stelmach, 2004), and the organizational structures of school do not really allow for non-educator presence.
Thus, even Ada's comment that she felt the school "welcomed her in" indicates a boundary to be negotiated.

Those parents who questioned or challenged educators' decisions un-
equivocally aligned with the metaphor of battle. Oskar expressed this sentiment when he shared a debate he had with teachers over the school's improvement project: "I got yelled at . . . I was cut off." In this scenario, Oskar
was painted as the aggressor to be confronted, surrounded, and silenced.
Oskar believed there were definite "boundaries" between the school and
home. Somewhat jokingly he said, "When there's an issue it's, 'Oh my God,
he's coming,' you know?" He believed teachers saw him as a "threat." In
other words, Oskar, and parents like him who disagreed with teachers, was
an enemy.

Parents were aware of their limits with teachers, and had a sense of how
much pressure they could exert. Melanie, for example, had tried to deal
with what she felt was unjust disciplinary action against her child: "I've also
seen where my son has been wrongfully punished, but I'm not going to go
fight a war over it either." She, like other parents, knew how to "pick her
battles" (Ada), and understood that surrender was sometimes inevitable. In
some cases, lack of specialized information stifled parents' positions. Consider Dee's comment about curriculum:

> I don't have any background . . . I can't go in and attack them (teachers) . . . be-
> cause I don't have the background.

In a sense, parents lacked ammunition to advance their position. They
also readily admitted to defeat, another element of battle. When a school

administration team was facing a forced transfer to another community, Trisha explained that parents "fought tooth and nail...and lost" in the battle to keep them. Though both the Alberta and Saskatchewan ministries of education had granted parents legal power, neither parents' conceptualizations nor the teachers' led to a development of equitable relations.

The establishment of formal structures such as school councils does not itself disrupt entrenched assumptions about parents' roles vis-à-vis teachers' for a number of reasons. Nakagawa (2000) has argued that the discourse around parents re-entrenches a hierarchy of power, and controls which parents are encouraged and discouraged to participate and in what ways. Along the same vein, Dehli (2004) has argued that parent involvement policies advance a neoliberal agenda, which essentially organizes exclusion as well as inclusion of parents. Through "politics of recognition" (p. 62), parents are invited to participate on the school's terms. The spaces parents are given for involvement entail closures and exclusions, and establish boundaries and practices of surveillance based on moral injunctions on what good parents ought and ought not to do. Additionally, parents who are encouraged to participate on committees or school councils often lack the training and confidence to move beyond a "compliance orientation" to a "capacity-building orientation" (Boylan, 2005, p. 51); thus, they serve a representation function rather than a contributory one. The shift from a traditional perspective of parents' roles is also a matter of pre-service teachers' education and socialization. As Graue and Brown (2003) found, teacher education re-entrenches the notion that parents should be held at a distance.

Of importance, notions of lines, territories and fortresses are prominent features of battle where aggressors and defenders attempt to advance over and protect, respectively. Research on teachers' perspectives on parent involvement has made clear that impermeable boundaries persist in the collective voice of the profession. Isolationism, protectionism, and exclusion are clear and common themes (Allen et al., 1997; Casanova, 1996; Crozier, 2000; Davies, 1993; de Carvalho, 2001; Henry, 1996; Lawrence-Lightfoot, 2003; McKenna & Willms, 1998; Moles, 1993; Ogawa, 1996; Ravn, 1998; Sanders & Epstein, 1998; Sarason, 1995; Vincent, 1996; Walsh, 1995).

What conditions are necessary, then, for barriers to be broken down or arms retired?

CONCLUSION

Some scholars have attempted to explain parent involvement from a behaviorist standpoint (e.g., Hoover-Dempsey & Sandler, 1995). In these analyses, parents are thought to be motivated or demotivated by environmental or interpersonal cues. Thus, from a behaviorist perspective, parents can be encouraged or conditioned to respond differently to schools and teachers. Ruitenberg and Pushor (2005) advance this viewpoint. They argue for schools to demonstrate genuine hospitality rather than offer perfunctory invitations to parents. These sorts of ideas typically form the foundations of parent involvement models (e.g., Epstein, 2001). The behaviorist position is useful yet somewhat dissatisfying because of its tendency to oversimplify parent-teacher interactions. Lakoff and Johnson's (1980) thesis ultimately has behaviorist elements as well, and their idea of metaphor as the conceptual content rests on foundational assumptions that language itself holds a truth. These concerns aside, however, I contend that linking behavior and language supplements current thinking about parents because it lends explanation for how parents' conceptualizations influence their actions. This is valuable insight. This connection may dispel the reliance on technocratic approaches to engaging parents and inspire more sophisticated dialogue based on belief systems, values and how these are intricately layered within action. Rather than focus on ways to stimulate parents into action, language provides clues to the complexity of behavior, and forces new approaches.

Alberta's and Saskatchewan's educational policies purport to be premised on "grassroots initiative[s]" (Alberta Learning, 1999), and principles of partnership and shared responsibility (Saskatchewan Learning, 2005). These policies presuppose that parents are reneging on their duties to schools. Though these duties are couched in democratic language, ultimately policy assumptions are derivative of binaries, which portray parents as involved/uninvolved, responsible/irresponsible, or good/bad (Nakagawa, 2000). This deficit mentality is a result of research that currently drives schools to increase parent involvement, and the assumption that educators know best how this can happen. This mindset prevails among parents, too, as I have demonstrated here.

Thus, space must be created for both groups to disclose their assumptions and understandings. It is typically the case today that discussion and debate occur separately, and so while parents and educators may understand their peers and colleagues better, they do not necessarily gain insights into each other's positions. Staff meetings are usually closed to parents; professional development for teachers and parents occurs separately. Similarly, policy makers must consider how processes of consultation may reinforce dominant voices. Different modes of inquiry—beyond committees or school councils—may be required because a parent representative is not necessarily a representative parent.

Moreover, while listening is often advocated as central to communication, what one listens for is imperative. Specifically, analyzing what language is used to articulate a point is a necessary part of summarizing and synthesizing viewpoints taken in consultation. Language is not benign, but rather, is a carrier of deeply engrained conceptualizations. Paying heed to this may begin a process of dislodging the seemingly inclusive vocabulary that currently pervades educational discourse and misleads policy-relevant groups into believing change is occurring. This implies more research employing approaches such as discourse analysis or semiotics to examine sub-text and symbolism may be helpful.

Following from the above, if conceptual systems influence behavior, as Lakoff and Johnson (1980) posit, then can these conceptual systems altered? And how? Lakoff and Johnson contend that new metaphors can change our realities, and in fact cultural change arises from the introduction of new metaphorical concepts. This offers optimism. But, how do Lakoff and Johnson account for rhetorical language? Partnership, for example, has become an educational slogan that parents and educators alike easily recite. What do they mean by partnership? Do they mean partnership at all? Further exploration around these questions would be helpful. One potential implication is educator and parent conversations must move below exchange of factual information about student progress so that deeper, more philosophical ideas are engaged. In other words, parents and teachers must explore what Lawrence-Lightfoot (2003) calls the tender borderlands.

NOTES

1. On November 7, 2007, Saskatchewan Learning was renamed the Saskatchewan Ministry of Education.
2. I used the word *Aboriginal* in this work when referring to Canadian First Nations, Métis, and Inuit Peoples because the participants in my study invoked this term. I acknowledge that all indigenous communities view and describe their ethnicity uniquely.
3. In Alberta and Saskatchewan, as in most Canadian provinces and territories, the term school division is interchangeable with school board or school district.
4. On November 24, 2004 Alberta Learning was renamed Alberta Education.
5. In the interest of anonymity participants were invited to select a pseudonym.

REFERENCES

Alberta Education. (1995). *School councils handbook: Meaningful involvement for the school community.* Edmonton, AB: Alberta Education.

Alberta Learning. (1999, December). *Framework for the Alberta Initiative for School Improvement.* Edmonton, AB: Author.

Allen, S. M., Thompson, R., Hoadley, M., Engelking, J., & Drapeaux, J. (1997, March). *What teachers want from parents and what parents want from teachers: Simi-*

larities and differences. Paper presented at the Annual Meeting of the American Educational Research Association, Chicago, IL.

Baker, E. L. (2002). *The struggle to reform education: Exploring the limits of policy metaphors.* (Report No. CSE-TR-576). Los Angeles, CA: National Center for Research on Evaluation, Standards, and Student Testing. (ERIC Document Reproduction Service No. ED 476865)

Baker, A., & Soden, L. (1998). *The challenges of parent involvement research.* ERIC Clearinghouse on Urban Education, New York. (ERIC Document Reproduction Service No. ED419030).

Beck, L., & Murphy, J. (1999). Parental involvement in site-based management: Lessons from one site. *International Journal of Leadership in Education, 2*(2), 81–102.

Bourdieu, P., & Passeron, J. (1990). *Reproduction in education, society and culture* (2nd ed.). London: Sage.

Boylan, C. R. (2005). Training needs of rural school council members. *The Australian Educational Researcher, 32*(2), 49–64.

Caines, P. (2005). Rethinking parental participation in educational governance: Quality matters. *Principals Online, 1*(1), 22–25. Retrieved from http://www.principalsonline.com/

Canadian School Boards Association. (1995). *Parent involvement and school boards: A partnership.* Ottawa, ON: Author.

Casanova, U. (1996). Parent involvement: A call for prudence. *Educational Researcher, 25*(8), 30–32 + 46.

Comer, J. P., Haynes, N. M., & Joyner, E. T. (1996). The school development program. In J. P. Comer, N. M. Haynes, E. T. Joyner, & M. Ben-Avie (Eds.), *Rallying the whole village: The Comer process for reforming education* (pp. 1–26). New York: Teachers College Record.

Crozier, G. (2000). *Parents and schools: Partners or protagonists?* Trent, UK: Trentham Books.

David, M. (2004). Partnerships and parents: Issues of sex and gender in policy and practice. In B. Franklin, M. Block, & T. Popkewitz (Eds.), *Educational partnerships and the state: The paradoxes of governing schools, children, and families* (pp. 213–236). New York: Palgrave Macmillan.

David, M. (2002). Gender equity issues and public policy discourses. In C. Reynolds & A. Griffith (Eds.), *Equity & globalization in education* (pp. 183–210). Calgary, AB: Detselig Enterprises.

Davies, D. (1993). Benefits and barriers to parent involvement: From Portugal to Boston to Liverpool. In N. Chavkin (Ed.), *Families and schools in a pluralistic society* (pp. 205–226). Albany, NY: SUNY Press.

de Carvalho, M. E. P. (2001). *Rethinking family–school relations: A critique of parental involvement in schooling.* Mahwah, NJ: Lawrence Erlbaum Associates.

Dehli, K. (2004). Parent involvement and neo-liberal government: Critical analyses of contemporary education reforms. *Canadian and International Education, 33*(1).

Department for Education and Skills. (2005, October). *Higher standards, better schools for all.* Retrieved from http://www.dfes.gov.uk/publications/schoolswhitepaper/

Deslandes, R., Royer, E., Turcotte, D., & Bertrand, R. (1997). School achievement at the secondary level: Influence of parenting style and parent involvement in schooling. *McGill Journal of Education, 32,* 191–207.

Dietz, M. (Ed.). (1997). *School, family, and community: Techniques and models for successful collaboration.* Gaithersburg, MD: Aspen Publishers.

Dom, L., & Verhoeven, J.C. (2006). Partnership and conflict between parents and schools: How are schools reacting to the new participation law in Flanders (Belgium)? *Journal of Educational Policy, 21*(5), 567–597.

Downe-Wamboldt, B. (1992). Content analysis: Method, applications and issues. *Health Care for Women International, 13*(3), 313–321.

Epstein, J. L. (2001). *School, family, and community partnerships: Preparing educators and improving schools.* Boulder, CO: Westview Press.

Fine, M. (1993). [Ap]parent involvement: Reflections on parents, power, and urban public schools. *Teachers College Record, 94*(4), 682–709.

Fontana, A., & Frey, J. H. (2005). The interview: From neutral stance to political involvement. In N.K. Denzin & Y.S. Lincoln (Eds.), *The Sage handbook of qualitative research* (3rd ed.) (pp. 695–727). Thousand Oaks, CA: Sage.

Gestwicki, C. (2004). *Home, school, and community relations: A guide to working with families* (5th ed.). Clifton Park, NY: Delmar Learning.

Guba, E., & Lincoln, Y. (1998). Competing paradigms in qualitative research. In N.K. Denzin, & Y. Lincoln (Eds.), *The landscape of qualitative research: Theories and issues.* Thousand Oaks, CA: Sage.

Guba, E., & Lincoln, Y. (2005). Paradigmatic controversies, contradictions, and emerging confluences. In N.K. Denzin & Y.S. Lincoln (Eds.), *The Sage handbook of qualitative research* (3rd ed.) (pp. 191–215). Thousand Oaks, CA: Sage.

Graue, E., & Brown, C. P. (2003). Preservice teachers' notions of families and schooling. *Teaching and Teacher Education, 19,* 719–735.

Hara, S., & Burke, D. (1998). Parent involvement: The key to improved student achievement. *School Community Journal, 8*(2), 9–19.

Hargreaves, A., & Fullan, M. (1998). *What's worth fighting for out there?* New York: Teachers College Press.

Henry, M. (1996). Parent-school collaboration: *Feminist organizational structures and school leadership.* Albany, NY: SUNY. Retrieved from http://www.netlibrary. com/Reader/Tools/EbookDetailos.aspx

Ho, S. E. (2006). Educational decentralization in three Asian societies: Japan, Korea and Hong Kong. *Journal of Educational Administration, 44*(6), 590–603.

Hong Kong Education Department. (2000). *Transforming schools into dynamic and accountable professional learning communities: School based management consultation document.* Retrieved from http://www.info.gov.hk/archive/consult/2000/ SBMconsult_e.pdf

Hoover-Dempsey, K., & Sandler, H. (1995). Parental involvement in children's education: Why does it make a difference? *Teachers College Record, 97*(2), 310–331.

Hoover-Dempsey, K. V., & Sandler, H. M. (1997). Why do parents become involved in their children's education? *Review of Educational Research, 67,* 3–42.

Keyes, C. (2002). A way of thinking about parent/teacher partnerships for teachers. *International Journal of Early Years Education, 10*(3), 177–191.

Krippendorff, K. (2004). *Content analysis: An introduction to its methodology* (2nd ed.). Thousand Oaks, CA: Sage.

Lakoff, G., & Johnson, M. (1980). *Metaphors we live by.* Chicago, IL: University of Chicago Press.

Lareau, A. (1987). Social class differences in family–school relationships: The importance of cultural capital. *Sociology of Education, 60,* 73–85.

Lareau, A. (1996). Assessing parent involvement in schooling: A critical analysis. In A. Booth & J. Dunn (Eds.), *Family–school links: How do they affect educational outcomes?* (pp. 57–64). Mahwah, NJ: Lawrence Erlbaum Associates.

Lareau, A. (2002). Invisible inequality: Social class and childrearing in black families and white families. *American Sociological Review, 67*(5), 747–776.

Lawrence-Lightfoot, S. (2003). *The essential conversation: What parents and teachers can learn from each other.* New York: Random House.

Lawson, M. (2003). School-family relations in context: Parent and teacher perceptions of parent involvement. *Urban Education, 38*(1), 77–133.

Lightfoot, S.L. (1978). *Worlds apart: Relationships between families and schools.* New York: Basic Books.

López, G. R., & Vázquez, V. A. (2005, April). *Parental involvement in Latina/o- impacted schools in the Midwest: Effective school leadership for a changing context.* Paper presented at the annual meeting of the American Educational Research Association, Montréal, QC.

Lyons, P., Robbins, A., & Smith, A. (1984). *Involving parents: A handbook for participation in schools.* Ypsilanti, MI: The High/Scope Press.

Mapp, K. (2003). Having their say: Parents describe why and how they are engaged in their children. *School Community Journal, 13*(1), 35–64.

Maykut, P. S., & Morehouse, R. (1994). *Beginning qualitative research: A philosophic and practical guide.* Washington, DC: Falmer Press.

McKenna, M., & Willms, D. (1998). The challenge facing parent councils in Canada. *Childhood Education, 74*(6), 378–382. Retrieved November 23, 2004, from Wilson Education Abstracts.

Mertens, D. (2005). *Research and evaluation in education and psychology: Integrating diversity with quantitative, qualitative, and mixed methods* (2nd ed.). Thousand Oaks, CA: Sage.

Moles, O. (1993). Collaboration between schools and disadvantaged parents: Obstacles and openings. In N. Chavkin (Ed.), *Families and schools in a pluralistic society* (pp. 22–49). Albany, NY: SUNY Press.

Morgan, G. (1986). *Images of organizations.* Beverly Hills, CA: Sage.

Morgan, G. (2006). *Images of organizations.* Thousand Oaks, CA: Sage.

Nakagawa, K. (2000). Unthreading the ties that bind: Questioning the discourse of parent involvement. *Educational Policy, 14*(4), 443–472.

New Zealand Ministry of Education. (2005). *Parent mentoring initiative evaluation.* Retrieved from http://www.minedu.govt.nz/web/downloadable/dl10718_v1/parent-mentoring-initiative-evaluation.pdf

Norris, C. (1999). Parents and schools: The involvement, participation, and expectation of parents in the education of their children. *Education Quarterly Review, 5*(4), 61–80.

Ogawa, R. T. (1996). Bridging and buffering relations between parents and schools. UCEA *Review, 37*(2), 2–3, 12–13.

Patton, M. Q. (1990). *Qualitative evaluation and research methods* (2nd ed.). Newbury Park, CA: Sage.

Pushor, D. (2008). *Parent knowledge, acKNOWLEDGing parents.* Paper presented at the Annual Meeting of the American Educational Research Association, New York, NY.

Pushor, D., & Murphy, B. (2004). Parent marginalization; marginalized parents: Creating a place for parents on the school landscape. *Alberta Journal of Educational Research, 50*(3), 221–235.

Ravn, B. (1998). Formal and informal parental involvement in school decision-making in Denmark. *Childhood Education, 74*(6), 375–377. Retrieved from Wilson Education Abstracts.

Ruitenberg, C., & Pushor, D. (2005). Hospitality and invitation in parent engagement. *Principals Online, 1*(1), 32–25. Retrieved from http://www.principalsonline.com/

Sanders, M., & Epstein, J. L. (1998). International perspectives on school-family-community partnerships. *Childhood Education, 74*(6), 340–341.

Sarason, S. (1995). *Parental involvement and the political principle: Why the existing governance structure of schools should be abolished.* San Francisco: Jossey-Bass.

Saskatchewan Learning. (2005, November). *Towards SchoolPlus. Policy directions for school community councils: Provincial response to the local accountability and partnerships panel final report.* Retrieved from http://www.sasked.gov.sk.ca/branches/comm/minister/speeches/PolicyDirections_ Nov05.pdf

Schwandt, T. (1994). Constructivist, interpretivist approaches to human inquiry. In N. Denzin & Y. Lincoln (Eds.), *Handbook of qualitative research.* Thousand Oaks, CA: Sage.

Simich-Dudgeon, C. (1993). Increasing student achievement through teacher knowledge about parent involvement. In N. Chavkin (Ed.), *Families and schools in a pluralistic society,* (pp. 189–203). Albany, NY: SUNY.

Skau, K.G. (1996). Parental involvement: Issues and concerns. *Alberta Journal of Educational Research, 42*(1), 34–48.

Stake, R. (2005). Qualitative case studies. In N. Denzin & Y. Lincoln (Eds.), *The Sage handbook of qualitative research* (3rd ed.) (pp. 443–466). Thousand Oaks, CA: Sage.

Stelmach, B. (2004). Unlocking the schoolhouse doors: Institutional constraints on parent and community involvement in a school improvement initiative. *Canadian Journal of Educational Administration and Policy, 31.* Retrieved from http://www.umanitoba.ca/publications/cjeap/issuesOnline.html

Stelmach, B.L. (2005). A case study of three mothers' experiences in the Alberta Initiative for School Improvement: Having a voice versus getting a hearing. *International Journal of Leadership in Education, 8*(2), 167–185.

Stelmach, B. (2006). *The role of parents in school improvement: Secondary school parent and student perspectives.* Unpublished doctoral dissertation, University of Alberta.

Stelmach, B. L., & Preston, J. P. (2008). Cake or curriculum? Principal and parent views on transforming the parental role in Saskatchewan schools. *International Studies in Educational Administration, 19*(2), 1–18.

U.S. Department of Education. (2001). *No Child Left Behind.* Retrieved from http://www.ed.gov/nclb/landing.jhtml

Vincent, C. (1996). *Parents and teachers: Power and participation.* London: The Falmer Press.

Vincent, C. (2000). *Including parents? Education, citizenship, and parental agency.* Buckingham: Open University Press.

Waller, W. (1932). *The sociology of teaching.* New York: Wiley.

Walsh, M. (1995). Parental involvement in educational decision making. Unpublished doctoral dissertation, University of Western Ontario, London, Ontario, Canada.

Waggoner, K., & Griffith, A. (1998). Parent involvement in education: Ideology and experience. *Journal for a Just and Caring Education, 4*(1), 65–77.

Warren, C. A. B., & Karner, T. X. (2005). *Discovering qualitative methods: Field research, interviews, and analysis.* Los Angeles, CA: Roxbury Publishing Company.

Westergård, E., & Galloway, D. (2004). Parental disillusionment with school: Prevalence and relationship with demographic variables, and phase, size and location of school. *Scandinavian Journal of Educational Research, 48*(2), 189–204.

Yanow, D. (2000). *Conducting interpretive policy analysis.* Thousand Oaks, CA: Sage.

Young, J., & Levin, B. (2002). *Understanding Canadian schools: An introduction to educational administration* (2nd ed.). Scarborough, ON: Nelson.

CHAPTER 3

THE ROLE OF LEADERSHIP IN FORGING FAMILY– SCHOOL–COMMUNITY RELATIONSHIPS

Lea Hubbard and Catherine M. Hands

ABSTRACT

Well-intentioned educators, community members and families have recognized the need to construct family–school–community partnerships that would support improved educational outcomes for urban students. In this chapter, Lea Hubbard and Catherine Hands examine issues of structure, culture and agency that enhance or impede family–school–community partnership development. This ethnographic account, which is focused on the history of one U.S. public school's conversion to charter status, deepens our understanding of the role these issues play. Findings from this study, which were based on interviews, observations, and document analyses of the historical events related to the conversion, indicate that despite overwhelming challenges imposed by the local school district, this predominately Latino and African American urban community became pro-active in improving the educational lives of their children. School–community collaboration was compromised due to the actions of school leaders, cultural beliefs that supported deficit perspectives of students and community, and the institution

Including Families and Communities in Urban Education, pages 41–68
Copyright © 2011 by Information Age Publishing
All rights of reproduction in any form reserved.

of organizational arrangements that were insufficient for or detrimental to supporting and sustaining effective partnerships. With the recent increase in the number of conversion charter schools and strong evidence to suggest that family–school–community partnerships can benefit urban education, the authors make the case that it is imperative to look more closely at the factors that facilitate and challenge this work.

In our economically and culturally diverse society, schools are finding it increasingly difficult to create educational programs to address the various needs of the students (Merz & Furman, 1997) with the finances and the resources available to them. This realization has influenced some school- and district-level educators to collaborate with families and communities (Hands, 2005a; Sanders, 2001) in order to establish "connections between schools and community individuals, organizations, and businesses that are forged to promote students' social, emotional, physical, and intellectual development" (Sanders, 2001, p. 20). Although family–school–community partnerships have been considered important for students' academic success, creating an effective relationship among the entities has proven difficult.

Explanations for the problem have typically focused on structural *or* cultural *or* agentive reasons. According to some research, since authority over issues of education has arguably been contested territory, school personnel structure a private domain (Boyd & Crowson, 1993; Keith, 1996; Mawhinney, 1994). They institute formal policies and practices unfamiliar to many low-income and minority families (Delpit, 2002; Lareau, 1989; Valenzuela, 1999), creating physical, intellectual or psychological barriers that dissuade families and communities from interacting with school educators. Other research points out that schools and communities have historically constituted two disparate cultures, and the resulting discontinuity has led to unreliable and uneasy relationships (Curtis, 1988; Epstein, 2001; Tyack, 1974).

Studies to date relying solely on structural, cultural or agentive explanations for school and community relationships have under-theorized and oversimplified the complexity of these factors and have inadequately attended to their interrelatedness. We learn from research on educational reform that principals are often at the "heart" of school change (Hubbard, Mehan & Stein, 2006; Fullan, 2008). Yet, research has largely ignored the role of school leadership in constructing the structures and impacting the culture, and the actions and reactions that influence school–community relationships. This gap in our understanding demands a more careful examination of school–family–community interactions.

In 2007, we began an ethnographic study of middle school that had recently converted to charter status to address this gap. Conversion charter schools are particularly interesting sites in which to examine the complexity of school/community relationships because they are restructured specifically to meet the needs of the local community. Families and school educators, attempting to rally from what may have been years of academic failure often position themselves to work together to improve the academic lives of students.

We used a socio-cultural analysis because it allowed us to understand how meaning was constructed in interactions between individuals. We paid attention to the actions and dispositions of school leadership, teachers and support staff toward the community, and the political and social tensions that facilitated and challenged interactions. Through a sustained examination of the school personnel's and community members' relationship *before, during and after* the conversion process, we investigated the structural, cultural and agentive reasons for the school's relational stance to its community and the community's response to the school. In the sections that follow, we provide an overview of what we mean by family and community involvement, as well as the concepts of structure, culture and agency and how they relate to each other. We then discuss their impact on the family and community involvement at the school in our study.

FAMILY AND COMMUNITY ENGAGEMENT IN EDUCATION

The importance of social support in the form of family and community involvement in education has implications, particularly in terms of student achievement. Schools, together with families and community citizens, need to work together to close achievement gaps, for schools operating alone are not able to address academic achievement disparity across advantaged and disadvantaged students (Davies, 2002; Lareau, 2003). Families and community members can support the messages students are receiving from school personnel regarding the importance of education and sustaining academic effort throughout their schooling, and actively participate in collaborative activities in the school as well as outside of it (Epstein, 1995), provided there is a welcoming school culture and organizations such as action teams in place to promote and foster partnerships (Sanders, 1999; Sanders & Harvey, 2002). More than this, though, families in particular shape the educational experiences their children have outside of the classroom, and the quality and quantity of these experiences have an impact on achievement (Lareau, 2003). For instance, the extracurricular activities in which children are engaged such as social clubs, camps, sports and arts activities, and visits to cultural venues such as museums, art galleries, theaters and libraries, all have the potential to affect students' academic achievement. The disparity in families' abilities to access these services and extracurricular activities notwithstanding, family–school–community partnerships hold possibilities for pooling resources for the benefit of the students both in schools and outside of their walls.

Families and community members are able to provide human resources in the form of time, knowledge and skills to share with school personnel and students (Hands, 2005a). As well, some individuals have material resources such as supplies, equipment and financial assistance, for example, that schools may not otherwise be able to access for their programs and students (Hands, 2005a). Partnerships among schools, families and communities that focus on the students' needs can provide academic, social, physical, and emotional support needed by each student (Epstein, 1995, 2001; Hands, 2005a).

Structure, Culture and Agency, and Their Interconnectedness in Family–School–Community Relations

A number of school districts and individual schools and community organizations are coming to the same conclusion that partnerships are an invaluable support for educational programming and students' needs.[1] As we outlined in the introductory chapter of this book, we suggest that in order to create and sustain authentic partnerships, issues of structure, culture and agency need to be addressed. Moreover, we need to understand their relationship to one another and their collective impact on family–school–community partnerships. In the sections that follow, we elaborate on the structure-culture-agency framework as it relates to parent–school–community relations.

Structure as an Influence on Culture and Agency

Structure plays a key role in shaping the nature of home–school–community relationships and the possibility of collaboration. Structure may result from an intangible entity such as policy, or take a more direct and tangible form as organizations or committees, for instance. Regardless of its nature, structure serves to influence social action (Datnow, Hubbard & Mehan, 2002).

The institutional relationships that schools, families and communities have traditionally held, as well as the relationships these entities currently have with the district, as well as with state and federal governments, are influenced by structural issues of politics and policy (Giroux, 2009; Wilson, 1997). The historical relations among schools, families and communities and the accompanying structures yield insight into the structures of today that are shaping relationships. For instance, families and community members had control of the schools' curricula, schedules and hiring practices during the early 19th century in the United States of America and Canada (Curtis, 1988; Epstein, 2001). A central public education office was created by the late 19th century, and the control that parents and local school supporters enjoyed in the early 19th century was transferred from the communities to public officials instructed by the central office (Tyack, 1974).

A hierarchical, bureaucratic model for schools was established (Merz & Furman, 1997) that allowed upper- and middle-class citizens more opportunities to influence education (Merz & Furman, 1997; Murphy, 1997); however, most citizens' participation in public education was severely limited as a result of the politics and policies (Curtis, 1988) that saw these structures put into place. District policies that prohibited families' and community members' involvement in schools or even setting foot on the premises (Curtis, 1988), combined with increasingly differentiated roles and responsibilities of families, community citizens and school personnel, served to effectively separate schools from their communities (Hands, 2010). Since the mid-20th century, there have been closer connections among home, school and community. Yet the fact that partnerships are not more widespread may reflect past relationships. Indeed, the hierarchical, bureaucratic model established for the education system more than a century ago remains as its structural underpinning. This maintains the potential for inequities in the relative levels of power and influence over educational issues among families, community members, and district and school personnel.

At the state, district and school levels, community-based organizations serve as structures that promote the agency of families and communities in education.[2] Some exist to provide families and community members with the skills and knowledge necessary to advocate on behalf of the students, while some focus on promoting the students' own agency and ability to advocate for themselves. Examples of these types of organizations are most notably illustrated elsewhere in this book.

More narrowly focused, the presence (or absence) of organizational structures at the school level enhances (or discourages) parent and community engagement. The establishment of multiple opportunities in schools for family and community members to be involved in their children's education is advocated by a number of scholars (see for example Epstein, 1995, 2001; Harvard Family Research Project, 2002). The presence of school-based organizations such as action teams (Epstein, 1995, 2001; Sanders, 1999), steering committees, PTAs or school councils (Hands, 2010) are intended to facilitate this. Through the agency, or social action of the organizations' members, collaborative activities are developed that meet the students', families' and communities' needs while promoting their agency. Whether these structures are present and/or functional is largely an issue of school culture and the people charged with establishing them, which is addressed in the sections that follow.

School Culture, and Its Impact on Family and Community Engagement

Understanding the successes and failures of school, family and community partnerships also demands that we examine the *cultural* factors that are involved. Here, we are concerned with both the school environment's ethos, as well as issues of race and ethnicity, class and gender. As indicated in a comprehensive study of educational reform, "culture involves power and is the site of social differences and struggles... [it] is of equal importance and profoundly impacts both structure and agency" (Datnow et al., 2002, p. 16).

Some scholars have shown that a mismatch of cultural and socio-economic backgrounds between families and the school personnel can negatively impact student achievement (Heath, 1982; Lareau, 2003; Metz, 1986). In response, Dei and his colleagues, for instance, discuss the importance of having faculty members of ethnicities that match those of their students in order to provide role models and to promote student engagement (Dei, James, Karumanchery, James-Wilson & Zine, 2000).

Moreover, disparities in the lived social contexts between families and the school personnel can adversely affect family engagement. In their research on Latino parent participation, Quiocho and Daoud (2005) found that parents wanted to be more involved in their children's education but felt excluded. They also noted that some teachers had misconceptions about the parents' roles and ability to support their children's education (Quiocho & Daoud, 2005). These findings illustrate the importance of challenging thinking and a school culture that may limit parent engagement, a point that is taken up elsewhere in this book.

Implied here is the need for a school culture of receptivity and openness to others. A welcoming environment and two-way communication are two keys to establishing a foundation upon which partnership programs can be developed (Hands, 2009a; Sanders & Harvey, 2002). Over a number of years, Hoover-Dempsey and her colleagues have demonstrated that parents' motivation to be involved is in part due to invitations from school personnel to participate in their children's education (Hoover-Dempsey, Bassler & Brissie, 1992; Hoover-Dempsey & Sandler, 1997; Walker, Wilkins, Dallaire, Sandler & Hoover-Dempsey, 2005). Focused specifically on urban education, research on a multicultural group of parents in an urban district similarly found a strong relationship between teachers' invitations to parents to become involved in their children's education and the parents' actual participation (Anderson & Minke, 2007).

While school personnel have the responsibility to initiate family and community engagement, communication is a key feature of a school culture that supports partnerships among school personnel, parents and community members (Epstein, 1995, 2001; Hiatt-Michael, 2010; Sanders & Harvey, 2002). This begins with actively seeking out and listening to views of parents (Cooper, 2007) and community members. For example, a district in Ontario, Canada held a speakers' series tailored to the educational needs of the students and families in three aboriginal communities within the district. The proportion of aboriginal students in the district was on the rise. At the same time, the mistrust of school personnel and negative perceptions of the public education system harbored by families of aboriginal heritage resulting from their historically poor relations with the education system ensured low family engagement (Hands, 2009a). To encourage family and community involvement, school personnel and families participated in cultural traditions such as communal feasts during the sessions. The research findings indicated that communication, trust and parent engagement in education were promoted among families that were typically disengaged from the school and its functions (Hands, 2009a). Here we see structures, such as feasts and speakers' sessions, created as a vehicle for establishing communication and a culture conducive for family and community agency through their engagement in education.

Other structural elements can assist in creating a school culture for engagement. For families whose members are English language learners, having a liaison person to connect families with the school (Quiocho & Daoud, 2005) or at the district (Hands, 2005a), having staff members who speak the languages represented in the school community, and translating materials being sent home into the commonly spoken languages (Hands, 2009a; Quiocho & Daoud, 2005) are some recommended strategies. Holding school–family–community meetings in the community can also assist in promoting two-way communication (Hands, 2009a). The presence of these structures or accommodations may serve as a sign that families' and community members' engagement in their children's education is welcomed by school personnel. With respect to the potential misunderstandings and assumptions made by school personnel based on cultural and socio-economic differences, these structures may provide opportunities to learn about the community and gain a deeper understanding of the lived social contexts of the students and their families (Hands, 2010). Similarly, it provides families and community members with opportunities to get to know school personnel on personal as well as professional levels (Hands, 2009a).

As we demonstrate, school culture plays an important role in family–school–community partnerships. More than this though, the school and community cultures—and the structures that shape them—have a direct influence on families' and community members' agency, or ability to participate in education issues (Hands, 2005a). By looking at both school and community culture, then, we gain a better understanding of how the ideologies, beliefs and values held by the various constituents give rise to ideological conflicts that may impede collaboration, or present common ground for partnership development.

School Personnel and Families' Agency is Influenced by Issues of Structure and Culture

The initiation of partnerships and the participation of school, family and community members in them are driven by the individual actions or agency of those involved. We learn through previous research on the academic achievement of minority students that they construct their own educational outcomes (MacLeod, 1987; Ogbu, 2003; Willis, 1977). Outcomes, however, are also mediated by structural and cultural factors (Mehan, Villanueva, Hubbard & Lintz, 1996). Institutional arrangements within schools, as well as those within the larger political context in which the schools are embedded, interact with the racial, class and gendered identities of students and parents, and shape actions, including those taken to create family–school–community partnerships.

As previously mentioned, the hierarchical structure of the education system has consequences for agency. Those with formal authority as determined by central office personnel are the ones responsible for reaching out to families and initiating partnerships (Davies, 2002; Epstein, 1995, 2001). Sanders (1999) identifies guidance and leadership as key elements in the development of successful partnership programs. Indeed, school leaders play an important role in fostering a culture that is welcoming (Auerbach, 2009), and often function as facilitators of school–community relationships at their inception (Hands, 2009b), as well as gatekeepers, determining who comes into the school and under what circumstances (Hands, 2009b; Sanders & Harvey, 2002). School personnel—teachers, in particular—are the ones who usually initiate partnerships, based on their perceptions of what their programs and students need (Hands, 2005a). With the existence of structures such as action teams or school councils at some schools, this activity may be shared across school personnel and family members (Hands, 2009a; Sanders, 1999). Here, agency is influenced by the school- and community-level contexts; the characteristics, needs and resources available in the school and community shape the school programs' and students' needs (Hands, 2005a), as do the individuals' personal social contexts.

In other cases, families and community members take the initiative to become involved in education. Some organizations work with schools as part of their mission. Public Health, for instance, has a mandate to work with youth, and the most direct way to do this is by presenting co-constructed wellness programs through the schools (Hands, 2005a). Some organizations get involved with education as a way to address a pressing social issue in their communities or the education available to their children, as discussed in detail within other chapters in this book. Similarly in other research, African American mothers sought power through advocacy and the school choice available to them within their community, in order to combat inequitable access to resources and to make sure educational opportunities were available for their children (Cooper, 2007). Here, agency is rooted in, and driven by individuals' racial, cultural (both professional and personal), socio-economic, and gendered positions. In other words, the actions of the individuals, whose dispositions and aspirations are influenced by their cultural context and mediated by the structures around them, shape partnership goals, activities and outcomes.

In this chapter, we attempt to illustrate how political structures shape school personnel's agency—the school leader's in particular—which in turn, influences the school structures that serve to shape the school's culture. We aim to show how the structures and culture impact the agency of the families and community members, and influence possibilities for home-school collaboration. Here, we highlight the role of structure as a lynchpin, subsequently shaping the cultures and influencing the agency of others.

METHODOLOGY

Noting the need for a deeper understanding of participants' experiences of the phenomenon (i.e., school changes related to the charter school conversion), the research team chose a qualitative case study research design. Case study methodology was chosen to allow the examination of the process and consequences of school conversion in the real-life context in which it is occurring (Yin, 2008). With this goal in mind, case study methodology is the best strategy available for exploring situations in which the intervention being evaluated (i.e., school conversion) has no single set of outcomes (Yin, 2008). It allowed the research team to examine and to present the perspectives of those involved with and impacted by the school's conversion from a traditional public school to a charter school.

In conducting the case study, data were collected over numerous site visits during the 2007–2008 school year. Additional data was collected on events before, during and immediately after the conversion of the charter school from 2004 until 2008. Interviews were conducted with students, six community members, board members, some of whom are also community members, and the executive director. The semi-structured interviews were approximately one hour in length. Observations were conducted during the researchers' attendance at community and board meetings, as well as at school events, and field notes were taken. Finally, a document analysis of the historical events related to the conversion of the charter was conducted, using archival materials such as newspaper articles and PBS program transcriptions on charter schools including the subject of this research. Multiple sources of data were sought to establish construct validity through the triangulation of the data (Merriam, 1998; Rothe, 2000; Yin, 2008).

All of the interviews were audiotaped and transcribed verbatim. The constant comparative method was utilized in which the data obtained from each participant and event were continuously examined and incidents were compared across the data (Bogdan & Biklen, 1982; Merriam, 1998). In this way, new categories and themes were developed and existing ones were evaluated and modified. The data and interpretations thus far represent an examination of the school's reculturation and the roles played by the parents and community citizens outside the school. They are part of an ongoing effort to understand the school's efforts at reform.

FINDINGS

In the sections that follow, we outline the relations among school leadership, families and community members from their beginning days of collaboration in converting Barbara Jordan Middle School to charter status, to their troubled relational status at the time our study ended in 2008. We explicate these findings in light of the school leader's influence on the structural factors that served to shape the cultural and agentive elements that together impacted school–family–community relationships. We begin with a brief historical background on the school and its community.

Barbara Jordan Middle School: A Phoenix Rising?

School administrators most frequently sited the troubled academic history of Barbara Jordan Middle School[3] (BJMS) as evidence of the need to convert the public school to charter status. After being part of California's Immediate Intervention for Underperforming Schools Program (II/USP) and failing to meet its performance targets under the No Child Left Behind Act, the school was placed in Program Improvement. In the spring of 2000, only a third of the school's nearly 700 students tested at or above 50% on the state's Standardized Testing And Reporting assessment of mathematics and reading. Although student achievement began to improve in 2001 under the leadership of a newly appointed principal and former teacher at BJMS,[4] it remained in Program Improvement status through the 2004–2005 school year, when a new Executive Director[5] was appointed.

Perceptions of the school's immediate surrounding community were pointed to as evidence of low performance and dysfunctionality. From the early days of Executive Director Laura Pendleton's tenure until today, the school's website has described the surrounding community as: "undeniably gang-ridden and struggling economically to survive." This predominately Latino and African American community was frequently viewed as the cause of students' low academic achievement. Before conversion to charter status, one principal after another left the school, and it was difficult to keep qualified teachers. For these educators, the determination of the community as the locus of the problem may have precipitated their departure from the school. As Metz (1986) notes, teachers' pride is intimately connected with their students' achievement. Teachers in schools where students have poor academic performance "suffer public opprobrium along with their students" (Metz, 1986, p. 223). White enrollment in the district hovered around 26% since 2001–2002, but it then dropped sharply, reaching a low of 2.6% in 2006–2007. The "white flight" reflected by these numbers is also likely linked to the poor reputation of the neighborhood and school.

Differing Opinions Regarding the Students' Low Achievement

Parents viewed the cause of student failure somewhat differently than school administrators and teachers. While they recognized gang problems and economic hardships in their community, they believed it was the education system that had failed them and their children, and they were ready to lead the effort to reform the school.

Standing in front of an applauding audience of African American and Latino community members, an African American parent addressed the predominantly white district school board on January 7, 2005, the board that would ultimately decide whether or not the public school could become charter. He enthusiastically claimed, "You cannot kill our momentum. You cannot stop or kill our spirit. And you will not stop our determination." His words, highlighted in a PBS feature (Merrow, 2007), were followed by the equally impassioned words of another African American parent: "We will clean the house you refuse to clean." And another parent explained that she was willing to take the risk of converting to a charter school because she felt that district leaders had failed her school: "They haven't been paying attention to us 'til now. We need to do something to turn around our children's achievement." These parents embodied the anger, frustration, and empowerment that provided the impetus for the charter conversion. "The frustrated parents, teachers, and principals . . . saw the radical restructuring options of No Child Left Behind as a golden opportunity" to help their kids, according to one journalist (Merrow, 2007). Parents advocated for a school that would challenge and support their children and spur progress in the community. They perceived that the community of which they were a part had suffered from society's neglect.

Here, the causes of low student achievement were identified as being beyond the immediate community but were also the result of inadequacies in the broader society and their blatant disregard for the community in which the school was located. BJMS families exemplified the parents' democratic participation in education through their advocacy for school reform and improved school performance (Harvard Family Research Project, 2002; Robinson, 2007). Consistent with the Harvard Family Research Project (2002) model of family–school–community relations, parents' advocacy fostered both confrontation and collaboration, and this was a path toward mutually beneficial partnerships with a focus on school reform.

Community Members and Educators Work Together

Although school administrators and community members viewed the cause of poor achievement and the source of the community's troubles differently, they were unanimous in their agreement that reforming the school and converting it to charter status would help to address their problems. The community members and educators worked together toward educational change. Executive Director Pendleton explained how the process started: "We gathered together what we called a workgroup, and we started talking about a dream school. What are the qualities of a dream school?" During these conversations, momentum gathered around the notion of converting to a charter school. Parents, community members, students, and staff began going door-to-door with petitions to present to the school board. Determined to achieve charter status by the start of the new school year, parents and teachers worked through the December holidays and into the evenings in January to prepare a charter. One Latino parent explained:

> So what we did was we gathered up all the signatures that we hadn't received and we went door to door. It took us two weeks, two to three days a week. Where we would drive around and go to people's homes. We would say, "We're coming from Barbara Jordan Middle" and then explain what we were doing. We told them it was a good opportunity to now have a voice in the school. For years the school was there but we didn't have a voice in what the school would do, what kind of curriculum the school would offer. We just told them the parents would have more control over what they were gonna have, what the child would be offered.

BJMS's website reports that this resistance from the district only fueled greater efforts by community members: "When faced with obstacles created by local school board members who feared losing one of 'their' schools to the charter movement, parents, staff, and students banded together to fight for control of their school's staffing, budget, and curriculum." Despite overwhelming challenges imposed by the local school district stemming primarily from their reluctance to relinquish control and funding for yet another charter school in their district, the intense involvement by this group of concerned parents secured the requisite number of signatures needed to convert the middle school to charter status and to free themselves from what they perceived to be a district that had not supported their children. Pendleton testified along with some community members in front of over one hundred supportive community members and the local school board.

These efforts were rewarded on February 28, 2005, when the trustees of the city's schools voted unanimously to approve the school's five-year charter, along with those of a local elementary school and another middle school also attempting to convert. One school district trustee said he "couldn't defy community wishes and California law to reject charter petitions when the schools have met all the requirements." Hundreds of parents who had gathered at the meeting celebrated the board's decision.

In successfully petitioning for BJMS to become a charter school, the families and community citizens demonstrated the knowledge, resources, skills and the influence needed to engage in problem-solving strategies around education issues, consistent with the literature (Epstein, 2001; Goldring, 1993; Harvard Family Research Project, 2002). They had come together around a common vision—improving the academic achievement of their underserved children. Their collaboration had opened the door for additional opportunities for further collaboration between school personnel, families and community members (see Keith, 1999).

Structural Changes Have the Potential to Enhance Family and Community Engagement

Families and community members used the existing political structures and those of the education system to exercise their democratic rights for educational change. For their part, the school personnel wanted structures in place for a charter school that would see greater autonomy and subsequent agency granted to the school's leadership team, and they needed the support—and agency—of the community. In the months that followed conversion, aided by private grant funding, including a $100,000 grant from a local city foundation, charter status paved the way for further structures to be created by the Executive Director that would impact the culture of the school and the agency of others. These structural and cultural changes set into place conditions that eventually led to a formidable rift between school and community.

By design, charter schools are meant to combine greater academic autonomy than is normally associated with traditional public schools; however, they must function under an authorizing agent, typically a district, and be held accountable for producing positive educational outcomes (Hubbard & Kulkarni, 2009; Wells, 2002; see also Wohlstetter, Wenning & Briggs, 1995). This structure drives the demand for certain governance structures and, although not strictly proscribed, the need for partnerships.

The first structural change instituted by BJMS leadership was the establishment of a school board to oversee the school and help the leadership interact with their new "authorizing agent," the local school district. Representatives from the parent community, business community and a local university sat with a teacher representative and the Executive Director to ensure support for the school's fiscal viability and long-term sustainability.

Following the university's support of the school during the conversion, another structural change was made. The Executive Director created a partnership with the university to help them face an array of challenges. Although neither side had clearly articulated their expectations when the partnership was created, over the course of several years, the school personnel facilitated university faculty research projects, and the university professors provided staff development, arranged university campus tours for students, provided scholarships, sat on the board, gave counseling support and provided university tutors for the middle school students. In addition, a partnership action committee of school and university faculty, parent representatives, a member of the leadership team and a student representative was formed to establish and maintain partnerships and collaborative activities with the families and the broader community (Epstein, 1995, 2001; Sanders, 1999).

When BJMS became a charter school, a position was created specifically for parent and community outreach. Without a parent council or PTA at the school, the parent involvement director in charge of parent support became vital to the success of communicating with the approximately 50% Hispanic families that BJMS served. Rosa was from the community, of Mexican heritage, familiar and often friends with the parents, and fluent in Spanish. An actively involved parent volunteer observed, "parents [approached Rosa] for advice and support." As research indicates, a culture conducive to family and community engagement includes effective communication strategies such as the capacity for translating materials and information into the commonly spoken languages, having accessible translation services, and a community liaison person (Hands, 2005a, 2009a; Quiocho & Daoud, 2005).

While these structures had the potential to facilitate school reform, and families' and community members' engagement in learning, teaching and decision-making, they were not used in this capacity. We demonstrate in the sections that follow that the school's leadership team created further structures that impacted the school's culture in keeping with their vision for Barbara Jordan Middle School.

Leadership Drives Cultural Changes Based on Perceptions of Student and Family Needs

Understandably the Executive Director and her administrative staff that took on the leadership of BJMS (and the parents that had been part of the group envisioning their "dream school") believed that the school needed a culture change. Research suggests that the success or failure of any educational reform often hinges on the extent to which attention has been given to changing the culture of schooling (Hargreaves, 1994; Fullan, 2001). The vision and plan that was set for the school was, however, constructed by the school leadership team with minimal input from the community, and ultimately it was crafted in a way that demonstrated a deficit perspective of both the students and community whom the school would serve.

The overwhelmingly positive support and activism on the part of the community never translated in the minds of BJMS's leadership team into anything other than the idea that the students and the community needed repair. Executive Director Pendleton's comments about her first day on the campus reflect the attitudes that set the stage for her reform:

> My first day here, I thought, 'Oh, my goodness, what am I in for?' At any point in time, I would see 20 to 100 students just roaming the campus, many stories of setting fire in the bathrooms, destroying property, a campus of chaos.

In essence, both students and the community surrounding the school were seen as in chaos and out of control. Pendleton admits that her husband tried to convince her not to take the job, but after spending a year on campus as a principal intern, she knew she wanted to help the students and their community. She saw the school's conversion as her opportunity to transform the children by "produc[ing] leaders to revitalize the community," a community that she felt desperately needed her knowledge, expertise and missionary spirit.

Leadership Develops Strategies to Transform Culture Through Structure and Structures

About half of the school's teachers left the school upon its conversion, causing Pendleton, along with parents and the remaining staff, to interview and hire new teachers who fit the school's mission. The group also worked hard to recruit the requisite number of students to ensure adequate daily attendance figures. The students were drawn mostly from the local neighborhood. School leadership and staff improved the school grounds and focused on ensuring that the environment was a safe place for their students. They instituted a block schedule to protect instructional time, prepared a detailed discipline plan and a character education program, with students required to wear uniforms, conform strictly to school rules, and learn a back to basics curriculum with an academic tracking arrangement.

In striking contrast to pre-conversion descriptions of chaos, aimlessness, and deterioration, post-conversion descriptions emphasized orderliness. Visitors noted how quietly students lined up before class, and how engaged and respectful students were in class. Suspension rates were down—enough to publicly post on a board outside the office. "Within weeks, the former 'culture of chaos' was converted to a 'culture of learning,'" according to a 2008 feature article about Jordan's transformation. The school seemed to be on its way toward improved student achievement.

To move the school from "chaos," low achievement, and an unqualified teaching staff to a successful charter school required a sea of change, and from her perspective, that meant one of Pendleton's first steps was to clean house. Out from under the rules of a union contract, which gave principals limited choice as to which teachers they could hire, Pendleton fired teachers she viewed as ineffective and used incentive pay to keep promising teachers. The union president argued that the best, most experienced teachers would transfer to a district school to regain union protection. Some did, but others were let go. The school's teacher demographics shifted as a result. In 1998–1999 before the conversion, the school's teaching staff was more diverse than that of the entire district.[6] The most substantial changes in teacher demographics took place after the charter conversion. The percentage of white teachers at the school rose in 2004–2005 after the conversion to 60%, even as the population of white students dropped during those years. Most of the teachers who were hired were young, recently credentialed, white teachers, with some teaching out of their field. As noted in existing research, discrepancies in demographics such as these have the potential for the disengagement of students who do not see themselves or their lived social context reflected in the faculty (Dei et al., 2000), and the potential for misunderstandings on the faculty's part regarding the students' and their families' contexts (Metz, 1986, 1990). The culture that was fostered further contributed to such a likelihood.

As Deal and Peterson (1999) have emphasized, culture plays a central role in creating successful schools. For Pendleton, creating a new culture at BJMS meant constructing a heroic break from the previous culture—a transformation. One of Pendleton's early efforts was to form a "ladies lunch group" for students. She formed this group the year before she became Executive Director when she served as a principal intern. Surprised by the "un-lady-like behaviors of the girls" at BJMS, she felt that part of her mission was to teach etiquette and behaviors that were more typical of the girls she had worked with in the overwhelmingly white and middle class communities where she previously taught.

For further inspiration, she visited a charter school on the east coast and returned enthusiastically advocating for many of the policies and procedures that were in place in this college prep school for low-income, black students. Primarily it was a call for a strict code of discipline. Students were always required to line up as they entered and left the school in an orderly fashion. Five hundred students, all dressed in uniform, entered through the newly named "Gates of Wisdom," each shaking hands with Laura Pendleton every morning. These "Gates," while clearly signaling that students were entering a place of learning, also suggested a symbolic representation of the dividing line where wisdom began—the entrance to the school—and wisdom ended—the broader community.

Since students were struggling academically, as indicated by standardized test scores, academic strategies were put in place. Students were assigned to specific homeroom classes that would offer academic support called college prep classes. The back to basics curriculum focused on studying vocabulary words. While all students received this instruction, one group of more proficient students was able to take an accelerated, rigorous mathematics and science course. Other tracking arrangements were institutionalized when advanced math classes were added. Unlike their less fortunate peers, the students placed in the college prep class received an academically enriched class, but according to school administrators there just were not sufficient funds for everyone to get the same opportunity (Hubbard & Spencer, 2009). In their work on detracking, Oakes, Wells, Jones and Datnow (1997) caution that conceptions of intelligence, ability and giftedness are socially constructed by school personnel, parents and students. In turn, these "conceptions of and responses to intelligence are grounded in ideologies that maintain race and class privilege through the structure as well as the content of schooling" (Oakes et al., 1997, p. 484).

The Effects of the School Culture's Newly Instituted Policies and Practices on Engagement

The families' and citizens' roles in education were peripheral and not reflective of the level of school-family-collaboration that could have developed following the conversion. Their "influence was less a parental prerogative and more one of conflicting social and political coalitions who lobby the central office on various issues" (Metz, 1990, p. 93). They had been involved in capacities supported by BJMS in order to serve the purposes of the school, as defined by the educators in the school, so the school could then further its agenda (see Pushor, 2007). As Metz (1986) noted in her study of three magnet schools, the influences from outside the school interact with internal processes to affect the context of the school. In this case, the school personnel's and families' perceptions of the causes for the students' low achievement were external ones; however, they were not aligned. School personnel saw the community as the locus of the problem, while the community viewed the district and broader education system as failing to address their needs and those of the students.

This misalignment in perspectives did not affect either side's understanding that change was necessary; however, it may have influenced the strategies used by the Executive Director to change the culture and the nature of the policies and practices that were put into place. Instead of engaging BJMS parents in the co-construction of the education as advocated by some scholars (Pushor & Ruitenberg, 2005), reculturing efforts, particularly the emphasis on discipline, were grounded in perceptions of what the administration felt students and families needed. It may have also contributed to the community's belief that that they were being systematically marginalized and alienated from the school. Although the school leadership team would tell the story repeatedly for the next several years that school and community had worked together, the community's right to weigh-in on student learning was minimal, as was their inclusion in decision-making.

Research describes the structures needed for comprehensive partnership programs, such as funding, time to develop relationships, guidance, leadership and an action team or steering committee to support and coordinate the collaborative activities (Sanders, 1999). Efforts to operationalize a partnership steering committee were met with obstacles in a culture that was not supportive of family and community engagement. The Executive Director distanced herself from the work of the steering committee and the needs and goals identified by the committee. The proposed partnerships were not supported by Pendleton, and there were no effective avenues for communicating the committee's work to the school community. With no PTA, school council, or other structures to enable engagement, there was no place for the previously involved families and community members. The deficit perspective that framed the work of school administrators seemed to impede the possibilities for collaboration (Keith, 1999). In essence, structures to reculture the school were put into place without an understanding of the community context and the lived social contexts of the families, and this served to minimize the agency of others.

Agentive Factors Create a Silo of Control

The key to home-school understandings is communication and the active participation and collaboration of parents with school personnel (Epstein, 2001; Jeynes, 2005; Pushor & Ruitenberg, 2005; Sanders & Harvey, 2002). Learning environments that do not acknowledge—or worse, devalue— the everyday life experiences of students run the risk of marginalizing and alienating students (Lee, 2007). In her efforts to reculture BJMS, Executive Director Laura Pendleton and her staff made assumptions about students' lives, which shaped actions and conveyed very specific messages to students and parents. Instead of interacting with students and parents in ways that would expose the complexity of issues impacting the ways students engaged with school, they acted on their assumptions.

Several instances typified the relations among the school personnel and the families. One staff person explained an encounter between the Executive Director and parent:

> The Executive Director was quick to suspend the student without trying to understand the family circumstances that prompted the behavior. The mother spoke to me right after the meeting and explained that her husband, the boy's father had just left them and she felt the boy was acting out because of that.

Instead of attempting to investigate the cause of the behavior, this Jordan employee felt the Executive Director had made assumptions about the student and "took the easy way out" by suspending him. She explained that this is a common occurrence, where administrators and teachers do not attempt to really know the student or their family, which leads to students and parents feeling like "they don't belong" at the school. Moreover, a partnership with a counseling team designed to provide support to and understanding of the students and families was dissolved after two years due to a lack of support from the leadership team. To overcome deficit assumptions about communities and the students themselves, "it means de-constructing colonizing mentalities and ethnocentric assumptions" that create what Edmund Gordon has called "communicentric bias," which limits understanding of areas of study as well as of those who are taught (Lee, 2007, p. xx). At BJMS, there were limited structures in place and opportunities made for the reflection necessary to deconstruct communicentric bias.

Leadership Crafts Policies and Practices That Limit Family and Community Engagement

The following incident occurred during a Fall Awards ceremony and illustrates that the leadership team felt that not only the children needed to be controlled, but the parents did as well. As the Executive Director announced student GPAs, a parent sitting next to our student researcher in the audience leaned over to him and said with a grin, "I never got above a 2.0—in anything." The researcher remarked: "Yeah, these kids are pretty impressive." There was a large amount of audience conversation and much fanfare with the announcement of names. Families shrieked with pride for some students. A balloon that read "Congratulations" intermittently played "Celebration" by Kool and the Gang. The student researcher stated that after a while, the Executive Director announced, "We are here in praise of academics and citizenship. No hooting and hollering! Clapping is okay." The researcher reported that

> honestly, it was kind of off-putting. The crowd was kind of silent for a brief period after this announcement. I kind of changed my posture and really felt kind of uncomfortable. The staff behind the Director, after she made this command, was expressionless.

According to one BJMS staff person, events at this awards ceremony were typical of the way that parents were treated. She had felt it herself as a Latina parent and had been told repeatedly by Latino parents, particularly those who were not fluent English speakers that the administrators "run the show" and they felt "less than others."

The dismissal of the parent involvement director served to further dismantle the relations among the school personnel and families. Despite the support that Rosa had provided to the parent community, the Executive Director fired her in the spring of 2008 and did not fill the role. The actions of the Executive Director limited opportunities for school personnel and families to communicate and collaborate, particularly for those parents who were English language learners, and she sent a clear message that the school was not amenable to parent and community engagement. This caused parents to become increasingly detached from the school, a finding that is supported in the existing literature on the positive impact of a welcoming culture and invitations from school personnel for parents to become involved (Deslandes & Bertrand, 2005; Hoover-Dempsey et al., 1992; Hoover-Dempsey & Sandler, 1997; Quiocho & Daoud, 2005, Walker et al., 2005).

With avenues for communication and parent and community influence cut off, it was not surprising that we heard such phrases from teachers as: "Parents don't care; they don't come to back-to-school night, and they can't help with homework." School personnel evaluated the parents' level of concern for their children's education based on their assumptions regarding how they felt parents should be involved in the school (see Lareau, 1987; Metz, 1986, 1990).

Although it is likely that parents felt pushed out, this concept was never discussed to our knowledge among the teachers and administrators. It was not evident that the school leadership took any action to get to know the parents and community, or to understand their needs and expectations for their children's education. Apart from the initial working group that was struck to convert the school, there were no subsequent meetings to discuss the students', school's, families' and community's needs, of the kind called for by a number of scholars (Epstein, 2001; Hands, 2005b; Harvard Family Research Project, 2002). Used successfully in some instances as a strategy to connect middle class teachers with families from minority groups, face-to-face, one-to-one meetings have the potential to reduce the social distance that may promote unanswered concerns and negative perceptions (Hiatt-Michael, 2010). To our knowledge, there were no structures to support teacher-home, or community visits that would assist school personnel to understand the lived contexts of their students and families.

The Effects of Structural and Cultural Factors on Agency

Actions and inactions caused relationships to be strained. With the passage of time, the school leadership and some BJMS faculty members came to view the university as self-serving, failing to provide the level of monetary and tutoring support that was expected and that the school needed. For their part, the university representatives came to feel that no matter how much support they provided, it was never considered enough by their charter partners. Research indicates liaisons that meet the needs of the partners have clearly articulated goals based on those needs (Epstein, 1995, 2001; Hands, 2005b), involve negotiation to determine mutually beneficial collaborative activities and include some assessment of the activities' abilities to meet the goals of the partnerships, followed by any necessary adjustments to the activities to ensure all partners' needs are met (Hands, 2005b). In this case, there were none of the requisite communication structures in place to create a favorable situation for all parties. For instance, it was not known until the final year of the partnership that tutoring to be provided by the university was a primary goal for BJMS faculty and administration. There were no arranged opportunities for assessments, nor were channels to provide feedback created by either side until the partnership had already suffered from the absence of these important institutional arrangements and was deemed to be at its conclusion. Ultimately, the university partnership was dissolved, which ended several years of financial and human capital support.

The principal's leadership is an essential component in strong partnership programs (Epstein, 2001) in part because school leaders establish priorities for their schools, allot resources, and impact school culture (Knapp, 1997; Newmann, King & Youngs, 2000). They have the task of accommodating and incorporating the genuine needs of individuals, groups, organizations, communities and cultures within the school (Begley, 2001). Board-school and university-school relationships had called for the Executive Director to mediate relationships, but this charter school leader was unprepared formally and experientially for the task. She privileged autonomy and top-down decision-making, and the existing hierarchical school structures accommodated these leadership preferences. The Executive Director came to view the school board as top-heavy with university support and the school board was angered by the Executive Director's dismissal of key personnel. More importantly, there were protests from the community members that their voices were not adequately represented on the board or in the school.

While important structures had been put in place initially to help support the work of the charter school, none of the constituents had foreseen the importance of establishing communication structures to ensure its ongoing success. What began as a concerted and coordinated effort on the part of school personnel, families and community members to effect school change to support the students ended with a division between the school and the community.

CONCLUSIONS: THE INTERRELATEDNESS OF STRUCTURAL, CULTURAL AND AGENTIVE FACTORS

Schools are challenged to build strong, lasting school–community relationships. We make the case in this chapter that it is necessary to attend to issues of structure, culture and agency. Each has an important role to play in the partnering process, and not attending to one or more of these issues has consequences for the creation and longevity of mutually beneficial partnerships. Conversion charter schools are ideally situated to include the community in their reform efforts. For this reason, they are apt subjects for investigation. In this research, BJMS would not have become a charter without the support of the community. Together they recognized the need to improve the academic lives of the students who had been underserved for decades. The school leadership and the community worked side by side to effect change and in doing so set the stage for a supportive relationship.

That said, leaders of conversion charter schools typically face uncharted waters, and this Executive Director's experiences were not the exception. Their interactions with key constituents require skills that are not often taught in principal leadership programs. The structural arrangement of the conversion charter necessitated the need for leadership to interact with a board and with school partners on an ongoing basis. This posed substantial challenges for BJMS leadership. The only common goal was to convert the school to a charter school. The families' and school personnel's cultural contexts and goals for the students (apart from overall improvement), and each of their roles in the process, remained unexamined by the parties concerned. Cultural discord grew out of the actions of the school leadership. Pendleton set into policy practices that fostered a school culture based on deficit perspectives in which many families did not feel welcome. Instead of cultivating relationships with the families and community, Pendleton and her staff acted on assumptions about the community and their perceived needs. Community members began to think that their voices were not represented or valued, and that the board, the university partner and the Executive Director did not represent their interests. Parents felt marginalized and withdrew support. Unfortunately, as the leadership team worked to restructure and reculture the school, the school–community relationship deteriorated.

By examining the school leader's role in family–school–community partnering, we have been able to understand the structural, cultural and agentive factors, as well as their interrelatedness and their individual importance in partnering. While this research is presented as a cautionary tale, it serves to illustrate the importance of creating structures and spaces for school personnel, families and community members to come together to discuss their goals and needs for their children (Harvard Family Research Project, 2002), as well as what each party brings with it to a potential partnership (Hands, 2005b). Further, it highlights the value of a welcoming environment and culture conducive to collaboration (Sanders & Harvey, 2002).

Hopeful Signs

During the summer of 2008, Laura Pendleton resigned her position under some pressure from the board, raising opportunities for the school personnel to forge a new collaborative culture with families and the community in an effort to meet the needs of the students. The newly reinstated parent involvement director recently wrote in an online letter, "[Barbara Jordan Middle School] will stand to protect, improve, and impact the entire Community with the time and effort that we will give to our children today." Her words reflect the sense among parents that a strong community school is essential to the health of the neighborhood.

As we concluded our research, the interim leadership team, with the assistance of the parent involvement director, was doing what previous research has helped us to understand best supports school–family–community partnerships. They were actively recognizing the important role that the family and community can play in supporting educational outcomes, devising ways to equip parents with the tools to assist their children at home and to contribute to school-level decision-making, as well as to access community resources to meet the needs of the students and their families (see Epstein, 2001; Harvard Family Research Project, 2002).

The hopeful signs that have emerged since the departure of the former Executive Director come with caution. The leadership team would do well to develop a culture that recognizes the strengths of students, families and communities. Further, leadership needs to be able to work collaboratively with the school board and the other organizational factions that are necessary for the support of the school, and adequately include the community in governance decisions. Even with a leadership team that is supportive of partnering, school personnel may lack the capacity to develop partnership programs. Scholars note the need for pre-service and in-service teacher and principal courses and programs that address the research base behind the value of partnering as well as the strategies for cultivating these relationships (Dotger & Bennett, 2010; Henderson & Mapp, 2002). Without the creation of policies and structures designed to promote collaboration among all constituents, any actions aimed at constructing improved academic outcomes and school–family–community relationships will be limited at best.

NOTES

1. As of 2005, the National Network of Partnership Schools, for example, reported working with over 1000 schools, 100 school districts and 17 departments of education to establish and strengthen their partnership programs (Epstein, 2005), nationally and internationally.
2. The Harvard Family Research Project's (2002) model of families' involvement in school reform identifies community-based organizations as a key to providing the negotiating skills and knowledge necessary for families to engage effectively with school and district personnel in an educational arena to advocate for school change. For a discussion of the types of organizations and their roles in family engagement, please see Hands (2010).
3. All names have been changed for anonymity.
4. The students' scores on the Academic Performance Index (API) climbed from 546 in 2001 to 629 in 2004.
5. The title of Executive Director was given to the appointed principal of Barbara Jordan Middle School.
6. While 73.8% of the district's teachers were white, only 45.2% of Jordan teachers were white. Although this number was still disproportionate to the school's student population, the percentage of African American and Latino teach-

ers—32.3% and 16.1%, respectively—was closer than the district to mirroring its student body (41.1% African American and 35.7% Latino) at the time.

REFERENCES

Anderson, K. J., & Minke, K. M. (2007). Parent involvement in education: Toward an understanding of parents' decision making. *The Journal of Educational Research, 100*(5), 311–323.

Auerbach, S. (2009). Walking the walk: Portraits in leadership for family engagement in urban schools. *School Community Journal, 19*(1), 9–32.

Begley, P. T. (2001). In pursuit of authentic school leadership practices. *International Journal of Leadership in Education, 4*(4), 353–365.

Bogdan, R. C., & Biklen, S. K. (1982). *Qualitative research for education: An introduction to theory and methods.* Boston: Allyn & Bacon.

Boyd, W. L., & Crowson, R. L. (1993). Coordinated services for children: Designing arks for storms and seas unknown. *American Journal of Education, 101*, 140–179.

Cooper, C. W. (2007). School choice as "motherwork": Valuing African-American women's educational advocacy and resistance. *International Journal of Qualitative Studies in Education, 20*(5), 491–512.

Curtis, B. (1988). Patterns of resistance to public education: England, Ireland, and Canada West, 1830–1890. *Comparative Education Review, 32*(3), 318–333.

Datnow, A., Hubbard, L., & Mehan, H. (2002). *Extending educational reform: From one school to many.* New York: RoutledgeFalmer.

Davies, D. (2002). The 10th school revisited: Are school/family/community partnerships on the reform agenda now? *Phi Delta Kappan, 83*(5), 388–392.

Deal, T., & Peterson, K. (1999). *Shaping school culture: The heart of leadership.* San Francisco, CA: Jossey-Bass Publications.

Dei, G. J. S., James, I. M., Karumanchery, L. L., James-Wilson, S., & Zine, J. (2000). *Removing the margins: The challenges and possibilities of inclusive schooling.* Toronto, Ontario: Canadian Scholars' Press.

Delpit, L. (2002). *The skin that we speak: Thoughts on language and culture in the classroom.* New York: The New Press.

Deslandes, R., & Bertrand, R. (2005). Motivation of parent involvement in secondary-level schooling. *Journal of Educational Research, 98*(3), 164–175.

Dotger, B. H., & Bennett, J. (2010). Educating teachers and school leaders for school-family partnerships. In D. B. Hiatt-Michael (Ed.), *Promising practices to support family involvement in schools* (pp. 129–149). Charlotte, NC: Information Age Publishing.

Epstein, J. L. (1995). School/family/community partnerships: Caring for the children we share. *Phi Delta Kappan, 76*(9), 701–712.

Epstein, J. L. (2001). *School, family, and community partnerships: Preparing educators and improving schools.* Boulder, CO: Westview Press.

Epstein, J. L. (2005, September). Developing and sustaining research-based programs of school, family, and community partnerships: Summary of Five Years of NNPS Research. Research report. Baltimore, MD: National Network of

Partnership Schools, Center on School, Family, and Community Partnerships, Johns Hopkins University.

Fullan, M. G. (2001). *Leading in a culture of change.* San Francisco, CA: John Wiley & Sons.

Fullan, M. G. (2008). *The six secrets of change.* San Francisco, CA: John Wiley & Sons.

Giroux, H. (2009). *Youth in a suspect society.* New York: Palgrave Macmillan.

Goldring, E. B. (1993). Principals, parents, and administrative superiors. *Educational Administration Quarterly, 29*(1), 93–117.

Hands, C. (2005a). Patterns of interdependency: The development of partnerships between schools and communities. Unpublished doctoral dissertation. University of Toronto, Ontario, Canada.

Hands, C. (2005b). It's who you know and what you know: The process of creating partnerships between schools and communities. *The School Community Journal, 15*(2), 63–84.

Hands, C. M. (2009a, April). Efforts to enhance parent engagement: What can we learn from an assemblage of district-wide initiatives? Paper presented at the annual meeting of the American Educational Research Association, San Diego, CA.

Hands, C. M. (2009b). Architect, advocate, coach and conciliator: The multiple roles of school leaders in the establishment of school–community partnerships and the impact of social context. In K. Anderson (Ed.), *The leadership compendium: Emerging scholars in Canadian educational leadership* (pp. 193–213). Fredericton, NB: Atlantic Centre for Educational Administration and Leadership.

Hands, C. M. (2010). Parent engagement in school decision-making and governance. In D. B. Hiatt-Michael (Ed.), *Promising practices to support family involvement in schools* (pp. 97–127). Charlotte, NC: Information Age Publishing.

Hargreaves, A. (1994). *Changing teachers, changing times.* New York: Teachers College Press.

Harvard Family Research Project. (2002). Concepts and models of family involvement. Retrieved March 11, 2004, from http://www.gse.harvard.edu/hfrp/projects/fine/resources/case_study/intro.html#top.

Heath, S. B. (1982). Questioning at home and at school: A comparative study. In G. Spindler (Ed.), *Doing the ethnography of schooling* (pp. 96–101). New York: Holt, Rinehart and Winston.

Henderson, A. T., & Mapp, K. L. (2002). *A new wave of evidence: The impact of school, family and community connections on student achievement.* Austin, TX: Southwest Educational Development Laboratory.

Hiatt-Michael, D. B. (2010). Communication practices that bridge home with school. In D. B. Hiatt-Michael (Ed.), *Promising practices to support family involvement in schools* (pp. 22–55). Charlotte, NC: Information Age.

Hoover-Dempsey, K. V., Bassler, O. C., & Brissie, J S. (1992). Explorations in Parent-school relations. *Journal of Educational Research, 85,* 287–294.

Hoover-Dempsey, K. V., & Sandler, H. M. (1997). Why do parents become involved in their children's education? *Review of Educational Research, 67*(1), 3–42.

Hubbard, L. Mehan, H. & Stein, M.K. (2006). *Reform as learning: School reform, organizational culture, and community politics in San Diego.* New York: Routledge.

Hubbard, L. & Kulkarni, R. (2009). Charter schools: Learning from the past, planning for the future. *Journal of Educational Change, 10,* 173–189.

Hubbard, L. & Spencer, J. (2009). Achieving Equity: More than tinkering at school structure. *Perspectives in Education, Special Issue.*

Jeynes, W. H. (2005). A meta-analysis of the relation of parental involvement to urban elementary school student academic achievement. *Urban Education, 40*(3), 237–269.

Keith, N. Z. (1996). Can urban school reform and community development be joined? The potential of community schools. *Education and Urban Society, 28*(2), 237–259.

Keith, N. Z. (1999). Whose community schools? New discourses, old patterns. *Theory Into Practice, 38*(4), 225–234.

Knapp, M. S. (1997). Between systemic reforms and the mathematics and science classroom: The dynamics of innovation, implementation, and professional learning. *Review of Educational Research, 67,* 227–266.

Lareau, A. (1987). Social class differences in family–school relationships: The importance of cultural capital. *Sociology of Education, 60,* 73–85.

Lareau, A. (1989). *Home advantage: Social class and parental intervention in elementary education.* London: Falmer Press.

Lareau, A. (2003). *Unequal childhoods: Class, race and family life.* Berkeley, CA: University of California Press.

Lee, C. (2007). *Cultural literacy, and learning: Taking bloom in the midst of the whirlwind.* New York: Teachers College

MacLeod, J. (1987). *Ain't no making it: Leveled aspirations in a low-income neighborhood.* Boulder, CO: Westview Press.

Mawhinney, H. B. (1994). *The policy and practice of community enrichment of schools.* Paper presented at the Education and Community conference, Toronto, Ontario, Canada.

Mehan, H., Villanueva, I., Hubbard, L., & Lintz, A. (1996). *Constructing school success: The consequences of untracking low achieving students.* Cambridge and New York: Cambridge University Press.

Merriam, S. B. (1998). *Qualitative research and case study applications in education.* San Francisco: Jossey-Bass.

Merrow, J. (2007). Failing San Diego schools work to meet standards. *The News Hour with Jim Lehrer.* MacNeil/Lehrer Productions. Retrieved May 5, 2008 from http://www.pbs.org/newshour/bb/education/july-dec07/nclb_08-15.html

Merz, C., & Furman, G. (1997). *Community and schools: Promise and paradox.* New York: Teachers College Press.

Metz, M. H. (1986). *Different by design: The context and character of three magnet schools.* London: Routledge and Kegan Paul.

Metz, M. H. (1990). How social class differences shape teachers' work. In M. W. McLaughlin, J. E. Talbert, & N. Bascia (Eds.), *The contexts of teaching in secondary schools* (pp. 40–107). New York: Teachers College Press.

Murphy, M. F. (1997). Unmaking and remaking the "one best system": London, Ontario, 1852–1860. *History of Education Quarterly, 37*(3), 291–310.

Newmann, F. M., King, M. B., & Youngs, P. (2000). Professional development that addresses school capacity: Lessons from urban elementary schools. *American Journal of Education, 108*, 259–299.

Oakes, J., Wells, A. S., Jones, M., & Datnow, A. (1997). Detracking: The social construction of ability, cultural politics, and resistance to reform. *Teachers College Record, 98*(3), 482–510.

Ogbu, J. (2003). *Black American students in an affluent suburb: A study of academic disengagement.* Mahwah, N.J.: Lawrence Erlbaum Associates.

Pushor, D. (2007, January). Parent engagement: Creating a shared world. Paper presented at the Ontario Education Research Symposium, Toronto, Ontario, Canada.

Pushor, D., Ruitenberg, C., with co-researchers from Princess Alexandra Community School. (2005, November). Parent engagement and leadership. Research report, project #134, Saskatoon, SK: Dr. Stirling McDowell Foundation for Research into Teaching.

Quiocho, A. M. L., & Daoud, A. M. (2005). Dispelling myths about Latino parent participation in schools. *The Educational Forum, 70*, 255–267.

Robinson, D. V. (2007, November). Grasping the ideal of parent engagement in schools: No Child Left Behind, Title 1 and opportunities for participatory democracy. Paper presented at the annual meeting of the University Council on Educational Administration, Washington, DC.

Rothe, J. P. (2000). *Undertaking qualitative research.* Edmonton, Canada: The University of Alberta Press.

Sanders, M. G. (1999). Schools' program and progress in the National Network of Partnership Schools. *The Journal of Educational Research, 92*(4), 220–232.

Sanders, M. G. (2001). The role of "community" in comprehensive school, family, and community programs. *The Elementary School Journal, 102*(1), 19–34.

Sanders, M. G., & Harvey, A. (2002). Beyond the school walls: A case study of principal leadership for school–community collaboration. *Teachers College Record, 104*(7), 1345–1368.

Tyack, D. B. (1974). *The one best system: A history of American urban education.* Cambridge, MA: Harvard University Press.

Valenzuela, A. (1999). *Subtractive schooling: U.S. Mexican youth and the politics of caring.* New York: SUNY Press.

Walker, J. M. T., Wilkins, A. S., Dallaire, J. R., Sandler, H. M., & Hoover-Dempsey, K. V. (2005). Parental involvement: Model revision through scale development. *Elementary School Journal, 106*(2), 85–104.

Wells, A. (2002). *Where charter school policy fails: The problem of accountability and equity.* New York: Teachers College Press.

Willis, P. (1977). *Learning to labor: How working class kids get working class jobs.* Westmead, UK: Saxon House.

Wilson, W. J. (1997). *When work disappears: The world of the new urban poor.* New York: Vintage

Wohlstetter, P., Wenning, R., & Briggs, K.L. (1995). Charter schools in the United States: The question of autonomy. *Educational Policy, 9*(4), 331–358.

Yin, R. K. (2008). *Case study research: Design and methods.* Thousand Oaks, CA: Sage.

CHAPTER 4

PARENT EMPOWERMENT THROUGH ORGANIZING FOR COLLECTIVE ACTION

Lauri Johnson, Julie Carter, and Mary Finn

ABSTRACT

In this chapter, Lauri Johnson, Julie Carter and Mary Finn chronicle four grassroots initiatives for parent empowerment instituted by parent and community activists and their university allies over several years in an urban district in the Northeast. Efforts included the development of a parent advocacy organization, creation of a public education forum, parent literacy workshops, and a parent-driven small schools initiative. Findings focus on the resistance that arose from administrators and school district officials, different expectations of parent involvement between parents and educators, and the "bonding" social capital that developed amongst parent activists. Implications for developing "bridging" social capital that supports collective action by diverse groups as well as the university's role in community organizing efforts are considered by the authors.

Just from growing up in the same area and stuff, you think nobody really has these concerns, and then you walk in here and its like, wow, *there are other people out there*. It might help if we get together and maybe make some

Including Families and Communities in Urban Education, pages 69–95

69

changes for our children. (Jan, Lakeview School parent) (Finn, Johnson, & Finn, 2005, p. 193)

Advocates for parent involvement in education are often divided between those who see the goal as greater effort on the part of individual parents to improve their child's education outcomes, and those who campaign through collective action in the community organizing tradition of Saul Alinsky (1946, 1971) for system changes that can benefit all students. While all parent involvement advocates understand the importance of education and want to help children do well in school, those who approach the topic from a social justice perspective take a broader view of school reform. They seek to redress inequities long acknowledged to be deeply rooted in the education system (Apple, 1996; Giroux & Shannon, 1997), such as the racial and social class achievement gaps that reflect the larger social and economic structure (Anyon, 1997, 2005; Ayers, Hunt & Quinn, 1998; P. Finn, 2009; Noguera, 2005; Rothstein, 2004).

As Oakes and Rogers (2006) discovered in their organizing efforts, school reforms that threaten the social status quo will not be firmly enacted without contestation and changes in the balance of decision-making power. Anyon (2005) has gone so far as to call for a new civil rights movement to bring a measure of equity to education in this country. Social justice educators who seek ways to further democracy through public education see parent participation in school change through collective action as more efficacious than parents advocating individually for their own children (Gold, Simon & Brown, 2002; Mediratta, Fruchter, & Lewis, 2002; Mediratta, Shah, & McAlister, 2008; Shirley, 1997; Warren, 2001).

Parent Activism Research

Much of the parent involvement research has focused on the role of the individual parent advocate in contrast to the collective role of parents involved in community organizing for school reform. Schools are more familiar and more comfortable with the types of parent involvement where the focus is on what individual parents do or do not do to increase individual student's achievement. In an extensive review of parent involvement research, Pomerantz, Moorman, and Litwack (2007) distinguish between two types of individual parent involvement and conclude that the type that produces the most increase in student achievement is when parents are involved on the "school front," such as attending general school meetings and parent-teacher conferences, and volunteering in classrooms. The type of individual parent involvement that is most common, however, is on the "home front", such as helping with homework.

Auerbach (2009) found many of the thirty-five administrators she interviewed for a previous study (Auerbach, 2007) were adept at "talking the talk" of parent involvement; however, they focused primarily on parents who attended school events, as they considered these parents to be the ones supporting their children's school work. Such views may be especially true of educators' perceptions of African American mothers, whose "lack of school site presence and school activity participation" leads many to question whether the parents promote learning at home, and whether or not they are concerned about their children's school achievement (Cooper, 2007, p. 492). Lack of home/school communication can contribute to misunderstanding of how parents view their role in their children's education, and what they need from the school to fulfill that role. Quiocho and Daoud (2006) sought to dispel negative myths held by teachers that result from lack of knowledge about Latino parents. Public meetings were held and parents were encouraged to share their views. The large turnout and parents' articulate explanations impressed the teachers, but their outspoken criticism also offended some and resulted in steps taken to constrain the parents' participation in the meetings.

In the conventional type of parent involvement, whether on the school or home front, schools expect students' parents to match their involvement to the school's practices and thus to reinforce the school paradigm of success through individual achievement (Schutz, 2006). Such involvement has been labeled the "transmission school practices model," where parents emulate school learning at home to ensure that they and the school are acting in accordance with one another (McCaleb, 1997). Fine (1993) concludes that efforts such as these often result in "(ap)parent involvement," where programs designed for parents by others fail to authentically include the voices of parents or to challenge existing power relations at the individual school site and the district level.

Critics of the transmission model cite the hidden assumptions of many such programs, noting they often are structured as if there is something wrong or lacking in the family environment (De Carvalho, 2001). When parents do not appear to know the school's practices and/or reinforce them with their own children it is too often assumed that they cannot conform to school expectations because of some deficit in their parenting ability. Deficit-oriented views of students and their families are particularly common in high-poverty urban schools. In two studies by Warren, 70% of the teachers in one school "held negative beliefs about... [students in urban schools] and their families" (Thompson, Warren, & Carter, 2004, p. 6) and 64% of the teachers surveyed in another underperforming urban high school agreed with the statement: "I believe that parents or guardians are largely to blame for students' low achievement" (p. 8).

But there is another substantial problem with the transmission model beyond the deficit assumptions associated with it; that is, it ignores the systemic problems with the way schools, especially urban schools, are structured and operate (Anyon, 2005; Oakes & Rogers, 2006). Parents and students experience fiscal and student achievement inequities, lack of respect for diversity, and violence on a daily basis; these are systemic problems where solutions other than fixing each individual child are needed. Community organizing for educational justice is a version of parent involvement in education that seeks to address such structural problems.

Henderson and Mapp (2002) reviewed studies that examined the impact of parent-community organizing on improving schools: "Strategies of community organizing are different from traditional parent involvement and are openly focused on building low-income families' power and political skills to hold schools accountable for results" (p. 7). As they note, "There is a strong inside-outside tension in this work.... Because it is based outside schools, is focused on accountability, and is demanding of improved performance, school administrators and teachers may see organizing as threatening and hard to control" (Henderson & Mapp, 2002, pp. 59–60). According to Lopez (2003): "When parents and community members press schools on sensitive issues and demand accountability, conflict often erupts. The stakes are extremely high when school leaders are publicly exposed and can lose office. Thus, community organizing is perceived to be threatening to many educators" (p. 4).

Parent engagement through community organizing around structural power imbalances and inequities can be seen as a form of resistance to the transmission model. Community organizing enhances parent agency through collective action (M. Finn, 2009; Gold, Simon & Brown, 2002; Shirley, 1997; Warren, 2001), as opposed to the anger-based resistance of individual parents who react to the cultural deficit assumptions of the transmission model (Zaretsky, 2004; Quiocho & Daoud, 2006; Cooper, 2007).

Parent engagement through organizing, however, can quickly escalate to political and power struggles. As Zaretsky's (2004) study of parents of special education students indicates, "parent advocates gradually become more politicized as they engage in the struggle to achieve what they believe to be their own children's rights... but they quickly learn that connecting with other parents of disabled children is a vital way of gaining collective strength to achieve their goals..." (p. 272). Outside organizations, such as those that support parents of special education students, can be crucial partners at this stage of parent activist development as parents "transform their parenthood into political parenthood and begin to engage in political activism in schools" (Zaretsky, 2004). Since not all educators accept Freire's (1973) notion that all education is political (it either reinforces the social status quo or contributes to changing it), the political transformation of parent activists can set the stage for greater conflict and controversy.

Shirley (2002) uses social capital concepts to contrast the benefits of a "'parent engagement' approach that develops parents' leadership capacities to attack social injustices in a school or community" with the traditional "'parent involvement' strategy in a school that uses parents for cafeteria duty or photocopying" (p. xvi). For social capital theorists, parent involvement strategies can strengthen social networks within an institution such as a school when parents share the school's expectations and conform to their assigned role, but parent engagement or empowerment strategies must have a broader base. As Shirley (2007) explains, "organizers must move beyond *bonding* social capital—which refers to strong social ties among individuals similar to them in terms of categories such as race, gender, religion, or profession—to develop *bridging* social capital" (p. 82).

Building bridging social capital, or "strong lateral ties between individuals across organizational boundaries," (Shirley, 2002, p. xv) is exceptionally difficult. It is easier to organize individuals who share a group identity than it is to organize across diverse group lines because racial and economic diversity keep opportunities for mixed-group encounters where social relationships can develop to a minimum.

In the parent engagement projects described in this chapter, interview and observational data indicate that parent activists learned how community organizing could provide new avenues to achieve their goal of shared power in school decision-making, which in turn created resistance from school district officials. With the offer of partnership from local state university educators, in a city well known for its racial segregation, they reached across racial boundaries to establish parity among racially and ethnically diverse parents. Only the social class divide blocked their attempts to create authentic power sharing. Social capital theory helps to explain this outcome.

DATA SOURCES AND METHODOLOGY

The study used interpretive methods to examine how parents moved from involvement to empowerment through collective action, and the resistance they encountered from urban principals and district level administrators along the way.

- Interviews were conducted with four parent leaders in an effort to document their transition from parent to parent-activist and their views on school reform and parent empowerment.

- Parent perspectives were recorded and analyzed during a series of community dialogues through videotaping, audiotaping, and field notes.
- Interviews were conducted with 13 parents who participated in a series of parent literacy workshops that arose out of these community dialogues.
- Newspaper articles were retrieved and analyzed retrospectively to help provide a historical context for the key events described in the parent narratives.

Participant observations were also conducted by two of the three co-authors within the parent organization that is the subject of this analysis. These data were analyzed using Denzin's (2002) notion of "triadic interactional" process, in which data is first coded through the teller's linguistic lens and then through the interpretive framework of the researchers. Major conceptual themes were identified in the data through a constant comparative approach (Glaser & Strauss, 2006) and discussed and verified with one of the parent activists who is profiled in this chapter.

The authors' participant/observer roles varied along a researcher/organizer continuum. The first author (Lauri Johnson) served as a collaborator-organizer, the second author (Julie Carter) as a consultant-educator, and the third author (Mary Finn) as an initiator-organizer, although these roles themselves blurred at times. Stoecker (1999) explores the challenges of academic researchers who also play the role of community organizers collaborating for social change. In a meta-analysis of participatory research studies, he concludes that the roles that must be simultaneously fulfilled when engaged in research and community organizing include "animator, organizer, educator and researcher," each with its own skill set and rarely embodied in any one academic researcher (p. 847). The challenges of sustaining the community's role in the work after the researchers have moved on is explored in the concluding sections of this chapter.

FINDINGS

This chapter looks at four interrelated projects (the development of a parent advocacy organization, creation of a public education forum, parent literacy workshops, and a parent-driven school reform initiative). The projects aimed to promote structural reforms within an urban school system in the Northeastern United States through a focus on parent empowerment by organizing for collective action. Different expectations for parent involvement, the networking that develops among diverse groups of parents and their allies, and the resistance that arises from administrators and school district officials when parents voice their concerns and organize collectively to advance their interests and the interests of their children are explored. Instances of attempts to build bridging social capital and to develop shared value relationships among diverse groups of parents, community activists, and university researcher/activists are also described.

The District Context

The mid-sized urban school district under study (Steeltown) is often described as a post-industrial "rust belt" city. The city's current population of about 270,000 (down from a high of almost 600,000 in the 1960s) represents the flight of younger residents to other parts of the U.S. and a gradual population shift to the surrounding suburbs with a resulting loss of jobs and the property tax base to support the public schools (Institute for Local Governance and Regional Growth, 2006). The public school population has declined to an all-time low of just under 33,000 students, as both middle class and working class parents have placed their children in one of the 14 new charter schools that have opened up in the area in the last ten years. The current student population is composed predominately of students of color (i.e., 57% African American, 15% Hispanic/Latino, 1% Native American and 3% Asian American and other). Only just under a quarter of the district's students (24%) are white, and 82% of the students qualify for free or reduced school lunches (NySTART, 2009).

Previous school reform efforts in Steeltown took place in the mid 1970s, when several magnet schools and early childhood centers were created as part of a court-ordered desegregation plan. In the 1990s the court order was rescinded and the school district removed race and gender as selection criteria for placement in the magnet school programs. Twelve years ago school reform efforts resurfaced in the district, largely as the result of a group of parent activists and their university allies who continually pressed for greater parental and community input in school and district decision-making processes. This chapter illustrates a series of "flash points" in the district's relationship with parent and community activism over a period of several years from the vantage point of the parents themselves and three of their university allies who are the co-authors of this chapter.

The Growth of Parent Activism in Steeltown

Increased parent participation was mandated for all school districts in the state in the early 1990s through the initiation of Site Based Management Teams (SBMTs). Each school team was to be composed of teachers, administrators, parents, and community members who were to have input in the school's decision-making. A much stronger version of this decentralization concept had already begun in Chicago in 1988, where legislation gave parents a majority of the seats on each Local School Council (LSC), which was empowered to hire and fire the school's principal. Dissatisfaction with the weaker Steeltown SBMTs, which were universally controlled by principals, led to a public forum initiated by the chair of the City Council's Education Committee (who had children in the Steeltown school system) and the third co-author who was a community member of a SBMT in the district.

Two leaders of the Chicago Local School Council movement were invited to talk to Steeltown parents, teachers, and university faculty about their experience with LSCs in November 1997.[1] A new parent organization was formed as an outcome of this meeting. Three of the four parents featured below became prominent leaders in the new organization. Two of these parents also attended a training session in Chicago in January 1998 where they learned more about the Cross-City Campaign for the Urban School Reform model of organizing parents for powerful participation in school decision-making. At the same time, a new community/grassroots organizing campaign was forming in Steeltown and several local education activists, including two leaders of the new parent organization, took the week-long training based on Alinsky's (1946, 1971) organizing model.[2]

Getting Involved: Conversations at a Bus Stop

Four parent leaders in Steeltown—one black, one white, one Puerto Rican, and one Native American—all describe how their first efforts at parent activism arose through concerns with their child's school. Audra Wood,[3] an African American woman who was a diversity coordinator at a local community college at the time, characterized her initiation into parent activism as "conversations at the bus stop." She and her neighbor Mary Watson, a white, middle class stay-at-home mom, would talk about school politics daily while waiting with their children at the school bus stop on their block. Mary was the president of the Parent Teacher Organization at their magnet school, and during the course of their daily conversations she urged Audra to help her "bust up the all white PTA" at the school.

Mary Watson traces her first involvement to the birth of her daughter who was born with Down's syndrome shortly after she moved to the district. Similar to the experience of parents of special needs children studied by Zaretsky (2004), in the process of advocating for pre-school services for her daughter, Mary started a Parent Network for other parents of children with disabilities in the district. When her two younger children entered the school system, Mary got involved in the PTA at their magnet school as well.

Painfully aware that the PTA was not "inclusive of other parents, particularly parents of color," she enlisted Audra's help to integrate the group. Together they encouraged more black and Hispanic parents to join an advocacy group that they formed at the school to help negotiate conflicts between parents and the school administration.

Sonia Rodriguez, the third parent interviewed, started by volunteering every morning in her son's school, which was a large high school with lots of immigrant parents. She notes that the Vietnamese and Russian parents in the school "didn't know how this system worked and they were afraid." For parents in the school from Latin American countries, on the other hand, "the teachers and school policy (were seen as) the best thing and respected by the parents." So in Sonia's view, parent involvement at the school was "*so* slow."

Sonia began sitting on her son's school SBMT as a parent representative. In her interview she described the meeting where the SBMT was to decide how to allocate $4,000 in special funds. A couple of teachers wanted to order a few books, which were quickly approved, and the principal's request for two new photocopiers was also quickly approved, which took up the rest of the funds. Sonia and the other parent present were taken aback, as they had a request to make but had not been asked to present it. When they objected that the parents had been spending their own money to make goods for the bake sales along with other fund raising projects, they were allotted $200. In Sonia's mind this incident typified the SBMT culture in Steeltown—parents were to be seen but not heard.

When her son's school became identified for review under No Child Left Behind because of low state test scores, Sonia became involved in the committee that was charged with developing a comprehensive plan to address changes in the school that would lead to improved student achievement. Because she disagreed with aspects of the plan and felt that parent input had been disregarded, she refused to sign the final plan sent to the State Education Department. Sonia's relationship with the school's principal was severed as a result. In her words,

> The principal insulted me in the meeting and he raised his voice. I thought he was gonna even hit me. And I said, you know, "too bad." . . . If he makes a parent meeting in the school, it's so controlled. . . . so the parent movement (at the high school) died there.

In Sonia's view, parent involvement includes

> . . . a community who's conscious. I don't believe that "parent" per se is somebody who has a child in the school. To me, "parent" is anybody in the community who is conscious of the responsibility of the community to educate a child.

Wanda Hare, a fourth parent leader in the district, describes the year she spent "sitting on the bench outside the principal's office" at her younger child's elementary school. A magnet school with a Native American cultural infusion program, Wanda visited the school hoping to volunteer. In her words, "I spent one year sitting on the bench because the principal at that time didn't really believe in parent involvement. And even though I came in almost every day to school, there was really nothing for me to do besides sit on the bench."

She spent her days talking with "kids who join(ed) me (on the bench) because they were bad in class." Because of her constant presence, some of the teachers began to invite her into their classroom to, in her words, do "work that they didn't have time to do." The following year Wanda "took over the reins" of the defunct PTA and became the President. She went on to become the chairperson of the Native American Cultural Infusion program at the school and got more involved at the district level when she noticed, "there was no Native American representation in anything."

Getting Fed Up: The Parent Walk-Out

In an effort to meet the statewide mandate, the superintendent formed a District Stakeholders' Committee (DSC) that produced the first district SBMT plan in 1994. The expanded committee of 32 formed in 1997 to revise the plan as mandated bi-annually included parents who were active on their school's site-based planning team (SMBT), principals, teachers, and union officials. Wanda, Audra, and Mary were tapped by the new superintendent to become members of this committee.

Audra describes how parents quickly became frustrated with the review process because district officials, building level administrators, and union representatives held a different perception of what constituted "authentic" parent involvement. Participation in personnel decisions was not included in that perception. In her words,

> They wanted to define parental involvement for us. For instance, although it is the superintendent's (decision) to put whomever he likes on the negotiating committee with the unions, the unions kept telling us it was against the contract, which we knew it was not. They didn't want us involved in those big decisions. . . . Hiring, budgets, all those decisions that made an impact, parents were not to be involved in.

The conflict came to a head at the April 27, 1998 District Stakeholders Committee meeting when the principals on the committee left the meeting abruptly without reaching a decision on the parents' proposed changes. When asked about a date for a meeting to continue the process, the president of the administrators' union answered "October." On June 10, 1998 eleven of thirteen parents resigned en masse at the Board of Education's business meeting in order to protest the district's failure to include parents' suggestions for improving the SBMT plan and involving parents in district decision-making in a meaningful way. In her narrative, Mary Watson concluded after attending several meetings that the district "had no intention of implementing site-based decision-making...they liked the way things operated. The union president ran the district, and the superintendent kowtowed to him."

The parent walkout made the front page of the local newspaper. In their report of the meeting, the newspaper noted that district administrators described the committee the parents resigned from as "dysfunctional." In an interview the following day the president of the administrators' union suggested that parents on the District Stakeholders' Committee were "headstrong and unreasonable" (Heaney, 1998). This newspaper article also quoted the parents' perspective: "We were disrespected."

Several of the parents who resigned joined Audra, Mary, and Wanda in the new parent organization that had formed the previous November which intentionally maintained its independence from the district and focused on parent organizing, a type of parent involvement that addresses power imbalances (NCEA, 1999). With increased membership, the group decided to become a more formal organization by establishing by-laws, electing officers, obtaining 501c status, and affiliating with a national parent organization that advocated and provided support for independent, community-based parent organizations (Parents for Public Schools, 1998). Wanda Hare and her co-chair described their first objective for the new PPS committee: "(to) convince parents to change their perception of what schools are...the schools are something they have ownership of" (Campagna, 1999).

PPS drafted a parent involvement policy for the district that would establish a city-wide Parent Council, assist families with parenting skills, improve communications between parents and schools, boost parent volunteerism, increase student learning at home, and encourage parent involvement in school decision-making and governance, which largely followed the Epstein (2001) model. Under this policy, however, PPS parents expected to participate in union contract negotiations and be represented on staff hiring teams, powers similar to those the parents in Chicago's LSCs enjoyed through their role in selecting principals. In the newspaper article that announced the proposed policy, one of Steeltown's school board members commented: "It just seems to me we're talking about some dramatic fundamental changes. We set up structures that continue to invite conflict and confrontation" (Simon, 1999). While this parent involvement policy was eventually adopted by the Board of Education, it has remained largely symbolic and was never implemented in the way the parent activists who drafted it intended.

PPS was a multi-racial, multi-ethnic group composed of well-connected, well-educated, middle class parents whose children were most often admitted to the city's top rated schools. Their social network was strong and they often acted in concert when bringing their grievances to the school or district's attention, as Horvat, Weininger, and Lareau (2003) noted is typical of middle-class parents. They were largely responsible for the mayor's decision to fund parent literacy workshops such as the ones described below (Finn, Johnson, & Finn, 2005). Two of their members eventually ran for and were elected to seats on the district Board of Education. Their proposals regarding input into decision making regarding hiring, firing, and promotion decisions, however, were soundly rejected. PPS had developed bonding social capital but failed to build sufficient bridging social capital to mount the sort of political campaign necessary to realize their goals (Shirley, 2002).

Building Alliances: The Community Dialogues

A key arena for networking between parent activists and other school reform advocates in Steeltown proved to be a series of community dialogues initiated by the new Urban Education Institute at the local state university. The first dialogue in April 1999 brought together 70 participants who met in stakeholder groups as parents, teachers, administrators, university faculty, or community members. Issues that emerged from this meeting included the increased involvement of parents and community members in school and district decision-making, greater responsiveness to cultural and racial diversity in the district, teacher empowerment, effective teacher preparation for urban schools, and improved access to the city schools for university faculty, parents, and community members. A key concern that emerged at the end of this dialogue was the need for more information about the views and concerns of parents in the district.

Following this dialogue, a core group of parents (including PPS members), teachers, and university faculty formed the Coalition for Urban Education which collaborated with three other community groups to conduct a door-to-door survey of 250 Steeltown parents in October 1999 to discover parents' perceptions of their child's schooling and their views on parent involvement (Johnson, 2005). The second community dialogue (May 2000) asked stakeholder groups to respond to the results of the parent survey; a listening panel identified the lack of communication and cooperation between the area's various teacher preparation programs as a key concern. As a result, the third dialogue (December 2000) invited the deans and chairs of local teacher education programs to form a listening panel to hear each stakeholder group's ideas about how to improve the preparation of urban teachers and administrators. Commitment to the idea of collaboration seemed sincere but the culture of cooperation among local institutions was weak and this venture fell by the wayside before it could engage such important topics as how to prepare their students to enhance school/community partnerships (Epstein & Sanders, 2006).

The Council of Great City Schools had conducted a site visit to Steeltown district schools in 1999 and recommended 243 changes that needed to be made in the district bureaucracy if student achievement was to be improved. During the fourth community dialogue (March 2001), small breakout groups deliberated on the five areas of school reform identified in the Great City Schools Report: student achievement, decentralization, professional development, school choice, and accountability. Recommendations that came out of these breakout groups included the need for culturally relevant instruction, fair discipline practices, and the importance of schools as caring communities.

At the conclusion of this day-long dialogue, parent and community members presented their issues to a listening panel composed of the superintendent and several members of the Board of Education. They urged the district to include teachers, parents, and community members in the five district task teams charged with planning the reforms. One of the organizers of the dialogue from the local state university's Urban Education Committee confronted a school board member directly, insistently questioning, "Why aren't parents included on these task teams? Why doesn't the community know what's happening?"

Sonia Rodriguez's narrative expressed the skepticism of many of the parent activists about the school board's willingness to seriously consider community input in the reform process: "They (the board of education) already had their report...they have all the resources. It's not going to happen (school reform) because they're not willing to give. They are not willing to open themselves up." Mary Watson characterized the parents in the meeting as co-opted by the district administration: "The reality is the superintendent took control of the morning and it looked like her event. She took credit for it (being open to the community). Everybody's so busy trying to please (the superintendent and the board) that they're not holding them accountable." After this dialogue, the local state university severed its connection to the Coalition for Urban Education as a result of complaints from the superintendent for being publicly confronted about the exclusion of parents from reform planning.

While the local state university had ostensibly made a commitment to urban education by forming a new Institute and a faculty committee to provide oversight, too few faculty, particularly junior faculty, felt they could devote time from their research and publication agenda to be actively involved in local school concerns. Even fewer saw their professional role as involving endeavors that had political implications. To quote Shirley (2002), "...work on school reform and community development falls outside the boundaries of most of the dominant rhetoric of 'professional development' and indicates just how removed our concepts of professionalism have become from the emphasis on active citizenry that has been the foundation of American concepts of liberty..." (p. 94).

Finding Our Voices: Is Anybody Listening?

As an outgrowth of the community dialogues, the Coalition for Urban Education obtained a grant from the mayor's office to conduct a series of "Powerful Parent Literacy" workshops at Lakeview Elementary School, located in a poor and working class neighborhood near downtown. The workshop participants, none of whom were members of PPS, reflected the student population at Lakeview that was approximately one third white, one third African American, and one third Latino. For a two-year period (2000–2002) Mary Finn and Patrick Finn, who had participated in the Alinsky training cited above, served as co-facilitators of the workshops. Lauri Johnson participated as a parent and participant observer who collected qualitative data about parents' responses to the workshops (Finn, Johnson, & Finn, 2005).

There were three strands of workshop activities: building community (Vopat, 1994), parent involvement in their children's literacy learning (P. Finn, 2009), and parent empowerment through organizing (Gamaliel Foundation, 2010; Swarts, 2008). Parent empowerment was defined as acquiring and using language to influence people and events in the public sphere and to negotiate to advance the group's collective self-interest—or in this case the children's interests—in two ways: 1) through activities that taught the use of explicit language and negotiating techniques, and 2) through experiences in negotiating with those in authority.

For instance, in an organizing exercise called "Cutting an Issue" the facilitator described a good issue as one that is easy to understand, affects a lot of people, and has a reasonable chance of achieving positive results quickly (Cortes, 1993; Cross-City Campaign, n.d.). When asked what issue they would be willing to organize around, parents identified two issues involving the lunchroom. Some of the meals were nearly universally detested. Macaroni and cheese was one such meal. It wasn't that the children and teachers didn't like macaroni and cheese, they didn't like *that* macaroni and cheese. Secondly, children who qualified for free lunch (most of the children in the school) were required to pay for chocolate milk most days, and parents were aware that at some other schools chocolate milk was free every day.

Although these were not the most pressing problems facing the school, experienced organizers know that the first issues parents organize around tend to be less profound than you might expect, but that's good from an organizing point of view (Cortes, 1993; Cross-City Campaign, n.d.). When the issue is low test scores, for example, parents are intimidated by their lack of knowledge and specialized vocabulary, but parents feel entitled to their opinions about macaroni and cheese and free chocolate milk. Organizing around the lunch issues allowed them to enter their first negotiations on familiar turf, and success here gave parents the experience and confidence to address more significant issues.

With very little advice from the facilitators, the parents formed a committee and made an appointment with the lunch room manager. The first meeting was a big success. The lunchroom manager said if they didn't want macaroni and cheese, she would not order it any more. Parents also learned that a previous principal believed chocolate milk was not good for children and had decided it would be included with free lunches only one day a week. The next day it was announced that chocolate milk could be included with the free lunch every day and there would be no more macaroni and cheese. The parents who met with the lunchroom manager were elated. They then requested a meeting with the food supervisor for the district, got a list of all the meals available, and conducted a survey among upper-grade children and teachers regarding their likes and dislikes. They took the results to the lunchroom manager so she could consider this information in menu planning.

During the course of the project, as organizers would expect, parents began to address more pressing issues: children had only ten minutes to eat the free breakfast at school, and they had no recess. A committee of three parents and one of the workshop facilitators met to draw up a list of demands and arranged a meeting with the school principal to discuss their issues. When they arrived at her office, the principal had called in the Assistant Principal as well as the District Parent Liaison. The parents left the meeting feeling angry and outgunned. Loretta, one of the parents who organized the meeting, describes how she felt:

> I felt very peed-off. I felt like she was so condescending. She tried to overtalk us and then invite other people into the room that weren't supposed to be there for the meeting—like facilitators of hers—and it just kind of threw off what we were there for. She never let the smile off of her face, but just the way she did things was so...we really didn't get our questions answered like we wanted to...I mean we all did this on our lunch break, me and a few other parents.

Loretta notes that the three parents "all kind of drifted after that. Because I think we all got discouraged after that meeting."

The workshop facilitators had hoped to continue to build on parent empowerment strategies so that parents would take on bigger issues like the school curriculum, teaching methods, the school budget, discipline, and parents' role in school governance, but this was not to be. The school board announced that several schools in the district would have to be closed because of shrinking student numbers and budget considerations. Lakeview Elementary School was one of the schools that was closed, but not before a small number of parents from the workshops organized themselves, got 1,000 names on a petition and turned out 200 parents for a meeting with the superintendent and several school board members. The decision, many felt, had been irrevocable before it was announced. Lakeview Elementary School was closed, its students and teachers scattered across the city in the new "choice" program adopted by the district.

The isolation of the working-class parents who participated in the literacy workshops, as expressed by "Jan" in this chapter's opening quote, as well as other parents we interviewed, underscores research by Horvat, Weininger, and Lareau (2003) regarding "the variation in the architecture of social networks" and the "class differences in the mobilization or activation of network ties by parents in school settings" (p. 344). The social capital that poor and working-class families can call on when addressing school issues is significantly different from that of middle-class families. Working-class families' social networks are based in kinship, in contrast to middle-class families that develop social networks with other parents they meet through their children's mutual school or after-school activities and often include other professionals.

The value of the working-class kinship network is inestimable in terms of the support and assistance it provides families, especially with childcare, but kinship networks typically do not become involved in school-based problems. Here working-class parents "tend to undertake individual responses and do not receive much concrete support through their networks in doing so," in contrast to middle-class parents who may act individually while holding "the possibility of collective involvement in reserve" (Horvat et al., 2003, p. 344). While the Powerful Parent Literacy Workshops made great strides in building bonding capital among the working-class participants, it neglected to build alliances with other more affluent and powerful groups that could have built bridging social capital (Shirley, 2002), and form the basis of a political alliance that might have been able to reverse the closure decision.

Direct Parent Engagement: The Small Schools' Initiative

The fifth and final community dialogue in the fall of 2001 focused on "small schools" as a way to counter the growing popularity and fiscal calamity resulting from the growth of charter schools in the district. A leader of the Pilot School movement in Boston (Khanna, 2008; Meier, 2002) facilitated the dialogue in which many PPS parents participated. The parents quickly recognized the benefits of small schools as a component of the district's choice program, and they began to inform parents and others of the possibilities. Important to PPS was the fact that small schools are often independent of district mandates while still maintaining their status as public schools. An additional benefit is that parents play substantial roles in the leadership and decision-making of small schools (Ayers, Klonsky & Lyon, 2000; Meier, 1995).

PPS took the lead in promoting their message about small schools with support from the Urban Education Institute (UEI) at the local state university. As a multiracial parent group, PPS used their awareness of racial politics to gain access to decision-makers. They leveraged the privilege and connections of white middle-class parents in the group like Mary Watson to gain access to meetings and spaces into which most parents of color were not welcome, and subsequently to position themselves to deliver their message through a collective voice (Carter, 2007). Through collaboration with the Urban Education Institute, PPS was able to create networks of interested constituents from the community, the school board, the district superintendent's office, the local state university, and the district's university-based educational consulting group. These players were vital in assuring consideration of small schools at the highest levels of decision-making in the district.

At this point, Mary Finn retired as Director of UEI and was not replaced, which significantly reduced the state university's public commitment to urban education. Julie Carter, then a graduate student, became the lead educator and consultant to the project. The university agreed to convene several community meetings to gauge parent and district interest in small schools. While PPS saw the work they had done to accumulate and disseminate knowledge about small schools in the community as key to their leadership role, from the local state university's perspective school administrators were the most vital participants in these encounters. Its earlier withdrawal from the Coalition for Urban Education and the appointment of a part-time graduate student left the parent initiative with little institutional support.

For individual student problems, PPS had developed a direct parent "involvement" model in which parents helped other parents co-create individual action plans using culturally sensitive intervention strategies to enlist teacher or school support for solving individual student problems. In their work on the small schools initiative they wrote grants, arranged meetings with the superintendent, school board and university players, and provided information about the research on small schools as a viable option. These efforts culminated in a community meeting attended by 100 people where a panel of educators talked about successful small school projects in other districts. As PPS parents worked together to create interest among key players, they soon encountered the now familiar resistance to the idea of parent "engagement." Both the university and district administrators expressed discomfort with PPS's direct parent engagement approach and the "reputation" the group was said to have developed in the community as a result of their campaign for authentic power sharing.

After ten months of effort, the university moved forward alone, using the resources the parent group had garnered even though PPS parents were poised to do the outreach work. These resources included help from a national small schools incubator that had been invited to town through the efforts and financial support of PPS. When it came time to re-invite parents into the "conversation" about small schools, the district turned instead to its in-house Parent Liaison Coordinators, individuals hired by the district to represent parents. PPS parents were left with few resources to re-insert themselves into the small schools reform initiative, which never materialized beyond one or two ineffectual efforts made by the district. Julie Carter's position as a graduate assistant on the project was eliminated, and the connection between PPS and the university was lost.

DISCUSSION: LESSONS LEARNED FROM PARENT ACTIVISM

Each of the four initiatives to increase parents' engagement in their children's education that are discussed here—Parents for Public Schools (PPS), Community Dialogues, Powerful Parent Literacy Workshops, and the Small Schools Initiative—aimed to empower parents through organizing for collective action. As we have noted, however, collective action by parents was threatening to the administration of this urban school district. The district maintained that appropriate parent involvement was individual parents helping individual students increase their academic achievement, a model of parent involvement that flows naturally from schools' traditional individualistic paradigm. While this paradigm may work well in middle-class and suburban schools, it is less successful in poor and working-class neighborhoods where it contributes to the schools' failure to close the racial and class-based achievement gap.

PPS, a racially and ethnically diverse group of educated, middle-class parents, knew the survival of public schools in Steeltown meant helping the district develop an educational system that reduced the achievement gap, a gap they attributed to the systemic problems in the district. They believed that addressing this problem required organizing for collective action, which meant building an economically as well as a racially and ethnically integrated parent political power base. Outreach to less affluent parents such as those in the Powerful Parent Literacy Workshops was essential to establishing the necessary power base.

Attempts made by PPS to bridge the social class divide between themselves and other potential parent activists included writing and obtaining a grant to develop parent workshops facilitated by PPS members using the model of school-based Powerful Parent Literacy Workshops that brought parents and teachers together. While the Powerful Parent Literacy Workshops had been successful for a time in a school-based setting (perhaps because local university faculty had clout with the district and experience working in schools), the proposed PPS workshops never got off the ground. PPS parents did not have the same expertise and professional connections that their university allies did and so were never able to connect with a school willing to collaborate with them.

The real problem, however, was that PPS had ignored its own imperative to remain community-based and independent of the district as mandated by the national organization of Parents for Public Schools to which the local group belonged (Parents for Public Schools, 1998). Independence would have meant organizing workshops for progressive change that linked urban neighborhoods, schools, and stakeholder groups that were not dependent on, or in any way linked to, the district. Indeed, the Powerful Parent Literacy Workshops would have been stronger and might even have weathered the closing of Lakeview School if the participants had also built a strong, independent political base on which to establish a more collaborative relationship with the district.

Professional organizers may have helped build more workable school/ community relations. Auerbach (2009) describes four administrators she selected for an in-depth study of their success in establishing parent engagement programs in their schools. Two of the principals brought in professional organizers (from MALDEF, a Hispanic organization, and One LA, an Alinsky model group) to prepare parents with new roles in shared decision-making (pp. 19–20). These initiatives eliminated the need for parents to seek such training themselves and also prepared the schools for new relationships with parents. Auerbach (2009) found these principals had a greater awareness of social justice issues, which resulted in a stronger community focus and less fear of what one principal called "professional parents," the "power players who knew the right people" and used their power to manipulate others (p. 16).

The idea of organizing around school reform has been gaining ground nationally. Having a U.S. President with a background in organizing has expanded the public's knowledge of the term if not the process involved. In the case of the small schools initiative, a professional organizer could have helped build independent support for the parent group so that when the university pulled back, there would have been community support to replace it. The parents' dependence on the university proved a weak point and suggests an area where future research is needed to better understand the symbiotic relationship between a university education program and the local school district. While we have ample research on school-university partnerships and their challenges, there are no studies we know that explore the political expediency of universities maintaining positive relationships with school systems, for example research on the competition universities face in locating and maintaining practicum placements, securing district partners for federal grants, and even attracting local administrators to their programs. These might be considerations when a university decides to distance itself from a parent group that the local district considers too "radical."

CONCLUSIONS

Our work with parent activists and advocacy groups over the last several years has led us to conclude that the following three endeavors are worthy of further investigation:

1. Development of on-going community dialogues;
2. Preparation of teachers and school leaders to work with community organizers;
3. University support for community engagement and parent empowerment.

Creating a Level Playing Field: Community Dialogues

For the two years they were enacted (1999–2001), the community dialogues among parents, community members, teachers, and university faculty in this community verged on becoming the kind of small democratic community advocated by Fields and Feinberg (2001), which reflects a coming together of citizens from different backgrounds, races, and classes who deliberate about the prospects of improving the responsiveness of public education to community concerns. Analysis of the transcripts from the small group breakout sessions indicates that this dialogical approach created "free spaces" (Evans & Boyte, 1986) where parents could honestly share their concerns about the district's school reform agenda on an equal basis with other stakeholders.

A level playing field has not been the norm in school–community relations in this urban district. The district's traditional expectation of deference from parents, and their desire to be treated as fellow professionals by university faculty, made it difficult for teachers and administrators to listen to and take advice from other stakeholders. We believe that this type of critical inquiry approach is worth refining in order to create school–community relations that both promote democracy as well as identify oppression by linking knowledge with action to further more just, equitable, and trusting relations between stakeholder groups in urban communities (Oakes & Rogers, 2006).

Perhaps the most beneficial use of community dialogues is to serve as a place where the social class divide between middle-class and working-class parent activists might be bridged. As Shirley (2007) notes, "For networks in civil society to promote social learning, individuals need public spaces in which they can articulate their beliefs, hear others' points of view, and negotiate their differences…" (p. 142). Building this bridge means ensuring that such dialogues are not held in university or school district buildings, but in locations that are familiar enough places to attract parents from public housing projects and other areas of the city that house low-income families. Encouraging poor and working-class parents to participate in such dialogues must also consider their child care and transportation expenses. In addition, low-income parents should have an opportunity in their own neighborhood settings to practice dialogue behaviors, where they are expected to see themselves as the equal of teachers, administrators, university faculty, and other middle-class parents who are more experienced in vocalizing their views in such settings.

Building political power by bridging parents' economic, education, and experience gaps will also need to be an explicitly stated goal of community dialogues. Collective action implies an organization capable of bringing out large numbers of individuals to press for the changes parents identify as desirable. Building such a membership organization requires purposeful training and development of strategies to insure that organization-building is a priority. Institutions of higher education can play a crucial role in supporting the growth and stability of independent parent and community organizations through community dialogues by using their prestige to assure that equity, the key component of dialogue, is maintained.

Dealing with Resistance: Rethinking Urban Teacher and School Leadership Preparation

Our interviews with activist parents are filled with stories of teachers and school leaders who proved resistant, insulting, or at best patronizing to poor parents and parents of color who raised concerns about their individual school, or collectively advocated for policy changes in the district. Parent activists cannot sustain their efforts if they feel they are being treated like pawns and not respected as change agents (Fine, 1993). School personnel are not given adequate preparation in understanding or collaborating with collective action to reform urban education, even though potentially they have much to gain, especially in terms of community support for campaigns for equitable funding in urban school districts (Rebell, 2005).

Shirley (2002) concludes, "part of the preparation of teachers and administrators must entail learning about the social networks that characterize any given community, and then working carefully and strategically to ensure that the children and parents who make up those networks have opportunities to engage with and enjoy the fruits of the process of schools..." (p. 98). The preparation of too many administrators, however, is primarily in public relations. While most school leadership textbooks acknowledge the need for schools to be "responsive and accountable," their central focus is on "tools that administrators can use to lead their schools' 'publics' in the directions the administrators themselves desire" (Schutz, 2006, p. 707).

Restructuring urban school leadership and teacher preparation programs may be our best hope for helping future public school educators learn how to work with parent activists and community organizers. Epstein and Sanders (2006) surveyed 161 teacher preparation programs to determine what courses and content are currently offered to prepare "graduates to conduct family and community involvement activities." They found that "deans and department chairs recognize the importance of partnerships," however they "need to become change agents and team builders at their institutions ... to actively influence faculty attitudes" and increase their graduates' preparation for community work (p. 113). There is a special need for teacher education students to participate in field-based experiences that directly deal with families and communities: "There is only so much telling and talking. After a time, some type of practicum is called for" (p. 105).

Auerbach (2009) heard a similar recommendation regarding the preparation of school leaders. For "leadership programs to produce leaders who not only espouse a belief in family engagement but actively walk the walk to promote it in urban schools... [they] need more field experience working with parents and exposure to community-oriented leaders (p. 28). Teacher education faculty themselves could benefit from more hands-on community experience, which could have prevented the naive plan to immerse students in central city neighborhoods that Lauricella (2005) describes. Home visits are another way to assure opportunities to better understand families (Rose, 2009).

Teachers and school leaders must learn how to support independent parent organizations that use collective action for social and educational justice in urban communities even when they ruffle the feathers of the powers that be. Teacher education curricula can include courses on grass-roots organizing. Warren, Director of the Harvard Family Research Project, teaches such a course (Warren, 2003), as does Schutz (2006) at the University of Wisconsin, Milwaukee. Mary Finn and Patrick Finn developed a grassroots organizing course at Antioch University, Los Angeles (M. Finn, 2009) to help educators learn from and engage with parents and other community members. "Because nearly all levels of education focus on the empowerment of relatively isolated individuals," according to Schutz, "this is a radical challenge for schools" (p. 727–728), but one that schools of education in urban institutions of higher education have a responsibility to help meet.

University Support for Community Engagement

Parent activists need material resources, technical expertise, and allies who have access to broader networks that can help build "bridging" social capital (Lopez, 2003). Universities could be an excellent source for these types of resources, yet community organizing is often risky business for university faculty. There has not been a longstanding history or culture of public engagement in urban education among the faculty of most colleges and universities. Public service is encouraged but not rewarded when it comes to tenure and promotion. More often than not, public service by faculty that rankles power centers is undermined or even punished. In addition, research conducted by faculty members in urban schools has often not filtered down to the practitioner. The local state university in the current study is no exception. While the mission statement of their college of education expresses social justice concerns, the best way to put that concern into practice has not been articulated. While the university president pays lip service to "civic engagement," the faculty reward system remains unchanged.

As university faculty who have worked with parent activists and community organizers, we advocate for the development of a "scholarship of civic engagement" that would include rethinking the tenure and promotion process and faculty reward system to give credit and recognition to emerging scholars for the application and dissemination of knowledge through collaboration with grassroots parent and community organizations (Johnson, 2003). Universities that provide leadership in this area will make significant contributions to improving urban schooling outcomes and increasing confidence in, and support for, public education. We believe that they will also contribute substantially to educating citizens in their collective self-interest, a democratic imperative.

NOTES

1. Presentations were made by representatives of the Cross-City Campaign for Urban School Reform which was organized in 1993 by school reform leaders in Chicago, Denver, New York, Philadelphia, and Seattle to support policy and practices that move authority, resources, and accountability to the local school level. This organization disbanded in 2007.
2. The Gamaliel Foundation assists local community leaders to create, maintain, and expand independent, grassroots, and powerful faith-based community organizations so that ordinary people can impact the political, social, economic, and environmental decisions that affect their lives. It also provides these organizations with leadership training programs, consultation, research and analysis on social justice issues. It is also a network for mutual learning environments and working coalitions. (See http://www.gamaliel.org/default,htm; Swarts, 2008.)
3. All parent activist and place names are pseudonyms.

REFERENCES

Alinsky, S. (1946). *Reveille for radicals.* Chicago: University of Chicago Press.

Alinsky, S. (1971). *Rules for radicals: A pragmatic primer for realistic radicals.* New York: Vintage.

Anyon, J. (1997). *Ghetto schooling: A political economy of urban educational reform.* New York: Teachers College Press.

Anyon, J. (2005). *Radical possibilities: Public policy, urban education, and a new social movement.* New York: Routledge.

Apple, M. (1996). *Cultural politics and education.* New York: Teachers College Press.

Auerbach, S. (2007). Visioning parent engagement in urban schools: Role constructions of Los Angeles administrators. *Journal of School Leadership, 17*(6), 699–735.

Auerbach, S. (2009). Walking the walk: Portraits in leadership for family engagement in urban schools. *The School Community Journal, 19*(1), 9–31.

Ayers, W., Hunt, J. A., & Quinn, T. (Eds.). (1998). *Teaching for social justice: A democracy and education reader.* New York: The New Press.

Ayers, W., Klonsky, M., & Lyon, G. H. (Eds.). (2000). *A simple justice: The challenge of small schools.* New York: Teachers College Press.

Campagna, D. (1999, September 6). Parent activism rekindled in new advocacy group. *Steeltown News.*

Carter, J. (2007). The challenge of parent engagement in urban small schools reform. In P. Chen (Ed.), *American Educational Research Association 2007 E-yearbook of urban learning, teaching, and research* (pp. 46 – 55). Retrieved from http://www.aera-ultr.org/Publications/Archive.html.

Cooper, C. M. (2007). School choice as 'motherwork': Valuing African-American women's educational advocacy and resistance. *International Journal of Qualitative Studies in Education, 20*(5), 491–512.

Cortes, E. (1993). Reweaving the fabric: The iron rule and the IAF strategy for power and politics. In H. Cisneros (Ed.), *Interwoven destinies: Cities and the nation* (pp. 294–319). New York: Norton.

Cross City Campaign for Urban School Reform. (n.d.). *Resources on schools and communities for urban school leaders.* Chicago: Author.

De Carvalho, M. E. P. (2001). *Rethinking family–school relations: A critique of parental involvement in schooling.* Mahwah, NJ: Lawrence Erlbaum.

Denzin, N .K. (2002). The interpretive process. In A. M. Huberman & M. B. Miles (Eds.), *The qualitative researcher's companion* (pp. 349–366.) Thousand Oaks, CA: Sage Publications.

Epstein, J. L. (2001). *School, family, and community partnership: Preparing educators and improving schools.* Oxford, UK: Westview Press.

Epstein, J, & Sanders, M. (2006). Prospects for change: Preparing educators for school, family, and community partnerships. *Peabody Journal of Education, 81*(2), 81–120.

Evans, S. M. & Boyte, H. C. (1986). *Free spaces: The sources of democratic change in America.* New York: Harper & Row.

Fields, A. B. & Feinberg, W. (2001). *Education and democratic theory: Finding a place for community participation in public school reform.* Albany: State University of New York Press.

Fine, M. (1993). (Ap)parent involvement: Reflections on parents, power, and urban public schools. *Teachers College Press, 94*, 682–710.

Finn, M. (2009). Grassroots organizing and teacher education. In R. Linne, L. Benin, & A. Sosin (Eds.), *Organizing the curriculum* (pp. 250–265). Rotterdam: Sense Publications.

Finn, P. (2009). *Literacy with an attitude: Educating children in their own self-interest.* (2nd ed.). Albany: SUNY Press.

Finn, P., Johnson, L., & Finn, M. (2005). Workshops with an attitude. In L. Johnson, M. Finn, & R. Lewis (Eds.), *Urban education with an attitude* (pp. 193–217). Albany: State University of New York Press.

Freire, P. (1973). *Education for critical consciousness.* New York: Seabury.

Gamaliel Foundation. (2010). Retrieved from http://www.gamaliel.org/default.htm

Giroux, H. & Shannon, P. (1997). *Education and cultural studies: Toward a performative practice.* New York: Routledge.

Glaser, B. G. & Strauss, A. L. (2006). *The discovery of grounded theory: Strategies for qualitative research.* New Brunswick, NJ: Aldine Transaction.

Gold, E., Simon, E., & Brown, C. (2002*). Strong neighborhoods, strong schools: The indicators project on education organizing.* Chicago: Cross City Campaign for Urban School Reform.

Heaney, J. (1998, June 11). Parent activists resign in protest. *Steeltown News.*

Henderson, A. T. & Mapp, B. (2002). *A new wave of evidence–The impact of school, family, and community connections on student achievement.* Austin, TX: National Center of Family & Community Connections with Schools: Southwest Educational Development Laboratory.

Horvat, E., Weininger, E. B., & Lareau, A. (2003). From social ties to social capital: Class differences in the relations between schools and parent networks. *American Educational Research Journal, 40*(2), 319–351.

Institute for Local Governance and Regional Growth (2006). *The young and the restless.* Steeltown: Author.

Johnson, L. (2003). Multicultural policy as social activism: Redefining who "counts" in multicultural education. *Race, Ethnicity, and Education, 6,* 107–121.

Johnson, L. (2005). Giving voice to urban parents: A collaborative community-based survey about parent involvement. In L. Johnson, M. Finn, & R. Lewis, *Urban education with an attitude* (pp. 157–172). Albany: State University of New York Press.

Khanna, M. (2008). Families and schools partner for student success. *Middle Matters, 16*(4), 1–3.

Lauricella, A. M. (2005). Community Walk-about: Finding hope in hopelessness. In L. Johnson, M. Finn & R. Lewis, *Urban education with attitude* (pp. 121–134). Albany: SUNY Press.

Lopez, M. E. (2003). *Transforming schools through community organizing: A research review.* Cambridge, MA: Harvard Family Research Project. Retrieved from www.gse.harvard.edu/hfrp/projects/fine/resources/research/lopez.html.

McCaleb, S. P. (1997). *Building communities of learners: A collaboration among teachers, students, families, and community.* Mahwah, NJ: Lawrence Erlbaum.

Mediratta, K., Fruchter, N., & Lewis, A. (2002). *Organizing for school reform: How communities are finding their voice and reclaiming their public schools.* New York: Institute for Education and Social Policy.

Mediratta, K., Shah, S., McAlister, S., with Fruchter, N., Mokhtar, C. & Lockwood, D. (2008). *Organized communities; stronger schools: A preview of research findings.* Providence: Annenberg Institute for School Reform.

Meier, D. (1995). *The power of their ideas: Lessons for America from a small school in Harlem.* Boston: Beacon Press.

Meier, D. (2002). *Creating communities of learning in an era of testing and standardization.* Boston: Beacon Press.

NCEA (National Coalition of Education Activists). (1999). *Newsletter: Action for Better Schools, 6*(3).

Noguera, P. (2005). The racial achievement gap: How can we assure an equity of outcomes? In L. Johnson, M. Finn & R. Lewis, *Urban education with attitude* (pp. 11–20). Albany: SUNY Press.

NySTART. (2009). New York State School District Report Cards for School Year 2008–2009. Retrieved from https://www.nystart.gov/publicweb/Home.do?year=2009

Oakes, J. & Rogers, J. (2006). *Learning power: Organizing for education and justice.* New York: Teachers College Press.

Parents for Public Schools. (1998). Decisionmakers, policymakers, advisors: Parent-owners participate in school governance. *Parent Press.*

Pomerantz, E. M., Moorman, E. A., & Litwack, S. D. (2007). The how, whom, and why of parents' involvement in children's schooling: More is not necessarily better. *Review of Educational Research, 77,* 373–410.

Quiocho, A. & Daoud, A. (2006). Dispelling myths about Latino parent participation in schools. *The Educational Forum, 70,* 255–267.

Rebell, M. (2005). Court-ordered reform of New York State school aid. In L. Johnson, M. Finn & R. Lewis, *Urban education with attitude* (pp. 33–40). Albany: SUNY Press.

Rose, C. (2009). The Parent teacher home visit project. *Family Involvement Network of Educators (FINE) Newsletter, 1*(1). Retrieved from http://www.hfrp.org/family-involvement/publications-resources/effective-home-school-communication.

Rothstein, R. (2004). *Class and schools: Using social, economic and educational reform to close the black- white achievement gap.* New York: Teachers College Press.

Schutz, A. (2006). Home is a prison in the global city: The tragic failure of school-based community engagement strategies. *Review of Educational Research, 76*(4), 691–743.

Shirley, D. (1997). *Community organizing for urban school reform.* Austin: University of Texas.

Shirley, D. (2002). *Valley Interfaith and school reform: Organizing for power in south Texas.* Austin: University of Texas Press.

Shirley, D. (2007). Teacher education and community organizing. In P. Finn & M. Finn, *Teacher education with an attitude: Preparing teachers to educate working-class students in their collective self-interest.* Albany: SUNY Press.

Simon, P. (1999, March 18). Parental role sought in school contracts, hiring. *Steeltown News.*

Stoecker, R. (1999). Are academics irrelevant? Roles for scholars in participatory research. *American Behavioral Scientist, 42*(5), 840–854.

Swarts, H. (2008). *Organizing urban America: Secular and faith-based progressive movements.* Minneapolis: University of Minnesota Press.

Thompson, G. L., Warren, S., & Carter, L. (2004). It's not my fault: Predicting high school teachers who blame parents and students for students' low achievement. *High School Journal, 87*(3), 5–15.

Vopat, J. (1994). *The parent project: A workshop approach to parent involvement.* York, Maine: Stenhouse.

Warren, M. R. (2001). *Dry bones rattling: Community building to revitalize American democracy.* Princeton: Princeton University Press.

Warren, M. R. (Fall, 2003) Education organizing: Course description. Retrieved from http://www.hfrp.org/family-involvement/publications-resources/education-organizing

Zaretsky, L. (2004) Advocacy and administration: From conflict to collaboration. *Journal of Educational Administration, 42*(2), 270–286.

PART II

CULTURE

CHAPTER 5

LISTENING TO PARENT VOICES

Home–School Collaboration for Diverse Communities

Magaly Lavadenz and Elvira G. Armas

ABSTRACT

This chapter is based on a study that was conducted as part of a district-wide effort to improve home-school partnerships with Latino and African American parents in a large, diverse urban school district. Magaly Lavadenz and Elvira Armas used a mixed methods approach to collect survey data through a purposeful sampling of 16 parent leadership groups. A total of 513 surveys, $n = 366$ (Spanish) and 147(English), were collected. Results indicate a general dissatisfaction with the district's programs for English Learners and Standard English Learners and with the overall district's support for parent programming. The authors present a framework for change to strengthen home school partnerships through a three-pronged approach including (1) parental involvement programs that are culturally relevant and linguistically appropriate; (2)support for teacher and administrators' preparation that draws from community funds of knowledge; and (3) improvement of advocacy-oriented bi-directional communication.

Including Families and Communities in Urban Education, pages 99–118

99

English Language Learners (ELLs) are among the largest group of underserved students in the nation. Currently there are over five million ELLs in the United States, representing an increase of 57% over the past ten years (Ballantyne, Sanderman, & Levy, 2008). The requirement for strong home-school partnerships to address the needs of ELLs has never been more acutely important. Study after study reveals great academic achievement gaps according to race, language, and socioeconomic differences. Simultaneously, parents of ELLs face significant barriers in attempting to become informed and involved in their child's school experience. Common barriers have been identified as: (1) school-based barriers; (2) lack of English language proficiency; (3) parental educational level; (4) disjunctures between school culture and home culture; and (5) logistical issues (Arias & Morillo-Campbell, 2008).

Another group of students and parents experiencing similar challenges is identified in this study as Standard English Learners (SELs). This group includes students who speak a nonstandard English dialect and are of African American, Mexican American, Hawaiian, and Native American descent (Le Moine, 2002). California was the first state in the U.S. to focus on the needs of nonstandard English speaking children. The State Board of Education and State Department of Education acknowledge this group of students, include accommodations for them in state frameworks, and expect districts to address their needs. Furthermore, they recommend that instructional strategies targeting nonstandard English speakers' needs and informing the public and parents of focused support be developed and implemented. Districts in California, Texas, and Florida have been at the forefront of establishing programs for non-standard English Speakers (SELs). However, little or no research has been documented in the area of parental involvement in these programs (Taylor, 1987/1990).

This study was conducted in a large, urban school district (District A) by an interdisciplinary team of bilingual researchers from Loyola Marymount University's Center for Equity for English Learners (CEEL). Our focus was on the parents of both ELLs and SELs, who represent a significant and growing population of students. We developed the *Achieving Parent Survey* and administered it to parent leaders from both of these groups, focusing on the central question: "What do parents of English Language Learners and Standard English Learners say about the education of their children and about parent education and involvement in District A?" The impetus for this research was a dedicated effort on behalf of District A to attend to the growing needs of the two student groups. District A initially recognized that home-school partnerships are at the core of district-wide reform and that gathering parent voices around issues concerning the education of their children is a necessary, responsive approach to building partnerships for more effective home-school collaboration.

FRAMING PARENTAL INVOLVEMENT FOR CULTURALLY AND LINGUISTICALLY DIVERSE COMMUNITIES: THEORETICAL AND EMPIRICAL PERSPECTIVES

Parental involvement is one of the most critical components in the educational outcomes of our children. Despite this emphasis on home-school partnerships, teachers, principals, and parents involved in implementing such programs are often frustrated by the lack of success in establishing programs that foster meaningful and lasting connections with families, particularly with culturally and linguistically diverse communities (Mapp, 2003). For minority parents, who represent the majority of parents and students in District A's city and district (U.S. Census, 2000), scholars point to the importance of interpersonal ties and connections that cross institutional, ethnic, family and cultures (Stanton-Salazar & Spina, 2000; Horvat, Weininger & Lareau, 2003).

In this study, we frame the educational context as a system of dynamic interrelationships among institutional, situational, and societal levels, all of which influence each other. This definition is influenced by sociocultural theories that characterize learning in ways that promote relevancy in the relationship between participants to promote change in home-school collaboration. Because social constructivism concerns itself with the construction of knowledge and meaning through the social involvement of agents within a social context, we contend that it is necessary to gather multiple parental perspectives to answer the question posed in this study. These interrelationships determine the ways we approach the types of parental involvement within District A's various organizational levels—district, school, and community. Accordingly, our orientation towards data collection and analysis therefore includes multiple constructions of meaning, based on diverse viewpoints of those engaged in the interaction (Berger & Luckmann, 1966; Crotty, 1998). Especially because we engaged with a district in which the majority of the population is comprised of culturally and linguistically diverse communities, we sought to expand on traditional/mainstream orientations to parental involvement. The empirical parental involvement literature often excludes or ignores the unique characteristics, values and norms within these communities.

Perhaps the most influential and often-cited work on parental involvement is that of Joyce Epstein (2001), who identifies six types of parental involvement as a framework for building partnerships: developing parenting skills, building two-way communication, volunteerism, learning at home, decision making, and collaborating with the community. However, the perspectives of minority parent groups in culturally and linguistically relevant ways are only minimally referenced. Carren, Drake and Barton (2005) argue that parental involvement moves beyond merely being present at the school site. It must also provide for roles and contributions that can be constructed in more personal, informal spaces, often created by parents themselves. Parental engagement in formal spaces such as the PTA is one traditional example of a social network of support. Minority parents often rely on informal processes or resources both within the school and outside of the school for active participation to take place in a more supportive and relevant context, as opposed to the formal agendas and structures of school organizations such as PTA. Embedded in these less formal processes are opportunities to make connections using shared language and cultural similarities (Arriaza, 2003).

In a similar vein, Jasis and Ordoñes-Jasis (2004/2005) address the development of social networks as parental *convivenicia,* or an avenue for the empowerment of parents to exercise their rights through collective action. A series of questions can be posed around these notions. *How are empowering social networks created within a large, urban school district? What information is provided for parents, and how is that reflective of responsive home-school collaboration? How do parents perceive their role in this process? How do large, urban school districts honor and capitalize on parental funds of knowledge to promote home-school partnerships?* These questions guided our investigation as we sought to expand on existing parental involvement models through elucidating parent voices for the purpose of promoting a culturally and linguistically responsive home-school collaboration framework.

Epstein and Sheldon (2006) assert that advancement in this area does not come from a simple identification of methodology, but rather must include empirical research that will answer critical research questions to support equity in programs for all learners. A review of the literature reveals that while empirical research in this area is limited, there have been some attempts at collecting parent voices for the examination and refinement of parental involvement programs with diverse learners. Carreen, Drake, and Barton (2005) report on narratives of working-class immigrant parents in an effort to bring forth parent voice on issues faced as they work to participate in their children's schooling. They contend that because most of the literature on parental involvement refers to parents in a homogeneous manner, there is limited attention paid to the perspectives offered by this group of parents. Mapp (2003) gathered parents' *own* descriptions of their participation in their child's education to determine how their responses fall within existing definitions. Findings from her study indicate that the most important factor in creating effective home-school programs was to establish caring and trusting relationships with parents.

Some researchers purport that student achievement is negatively affected when school personnel do not acknowledge the differences between the dominant school culture and the culture at home (Reyes & Capper, 1991). Pena (1998) contends that understanding the dynamic interrelationships among the institutional, situational, and societal levels is essential for diverse communities. In this study parental groups and district leadership espoused differing ideologies that impacted decisions made regarding purposes, procedures, and program definition for diverse learners. Accordingly, this research afforded researchers the opportunity to collect parental perspectives on how institutional decisions affected the implementation of school-wide bilingual, dual language or other instructional programs that meet the linguistic and academic needs of ELLs and SELs. Interview and focus group data collected in this study found that parents believed their needs were not being met by the school, resulting in their mistrust about the district's long-term efforts to improve academic achievement and ability to respond in culturally receptive ways. Findings such as these underscore the need for researchers to examine what different individuals say, believe, and do in educational contexts, particularly when working with diverse learners.

The parent leadership groups that participated in our study exemplified some of the structures and processes that can lead to active participation in a school system such as District A. These groups were selected on the criteria of having strong histories of involvement in district training and because they had been elected by school-level parents to represent and advocate for the needs of the larger school community at the district level. Yet, research has found that when minority parent groups become informed, they are often met with resistance when it comes to making meaningful changes (Christie & Cooper, 2005). As such, the methods employed for this study were reflective not only of a sociocultural framework, but also provided structures for parent leaders to voice concerns and opinions about the relationship between the institution, the community, and the parents as change agents within home-school collaborations. Noguera (2008) states that real reform occurs when schools are "more responsive to the parents and families they serve through systems of mutual accountability" (p. 182). We concur with Noguera's notion of "mutual accountability" as manifested in the actions that should follow traditional mechanisms for gathering "parent voices" such as meetings and school site councils. This study presents findings from diverse parent leaders who have been involved in reform processes, have evaluated the district's efforts for reform and express their views on what is needed to actually create change in this large metropolitan district allowing us to examine this notion of "mutual accountability" in home-school partnerships.

METHODS

District A has had a long history of providing parent education programs through traditional structures such as PTA, School Site Council, and DELAC/ELAC. Nonetheless, district leadership recognized the need to augment and refine practices for home-school collaboration with linguistically and culturally diverse students based on feedback parent groups had provided at many of these meetings. Subsequently, the central office sought out support from university partners to conduct research to gather data on parent perspectives. To that end, this study used mixed-methods to report findings from a survey instrument developed specifically to examine the perspectives of African American and Latino parents regarding District A's programs for English Language Learners and Standard English Learners and parent education and involvement opportunities. We report on both the quantitative (descriptive) results from the Likert-scale questions and on qualitative results, using a grounded theoretical approach from the two open-ended questions.

Grounded theory served as the way to identify constructs from the parent's responses via the constant-comparative method (Hutchinson, 2001). Schwandt (2001) defines this methodology in the following way:

> Grounded theory requires a concept-indicator model of analysis, which in turn employs the method of constant comparison. Empirical indicators from the data (actions and events observed, recorded, or described in documents in the words of interviewees and respondents) are compared, searching for similarities and differences. (2001, p. 110)

Theoretical sampling guided the selection of our participants and also allowed us to code our data to identify key themes from the data (Draucker, Martsolf, Ratchneewan & Rusk, 2007).

Participants and Setting

Through a selective sampling process, we identified 16 parent leadership groups within the large urban school district. The district has 995 schools with a student population that is 3.7% Asian, 11.2% black/African American, 2.2% Filipino, 73.3% Hispanic, .3%, Pacific Islander, and 8.95% white. We sought to engage with a variety of parental involvement spaces in the greater Los Angeles area—to include both traditional, school-based parent groups as well as the socially-networked parental groups that exist outside of formal school and district jurisdiction. Formal, district and school-based groups included parent groups that are organized around Title I, District English Learner Advisory Committees (DELAC and ELAC), and Special Education Multicultural Advisory Committees (SEMAC). These parent leadership groups consisted of elected parent representatives from within the district.

Community-based recruitment as part of our selective sampling process led to the selection of several parent leadership groups consisting of families living within district boundaries and which functioned independently from the district. These parent groups included cross-region groups such as Parent Organizational Network (PON) and Padres Unidos, as well as local groups (San Fernando Community Partnerships). These grass-roots parent organizations focused on empowering parents within each of their respective communities by providing parent development courses and leadership training. In addition, these organizations served as informational centers and advisory groups responding to the social and academic needs faced by families in the community. They were organized as clearing-houses for parent advocacy on a variety of educational and social services for low-income and diverse communities within the larger metropolitan area within District A.

Survey Instrument

The survey was developed collaboratively by the bilingual research team at our university with multiple phases of feedback with our district partner. The research team also convened an expert panel to review the survey. The survey consists of 19 items for the English version and 17 for the Spanish version.[1] We report only on the seven survey questions directly related to the District's support of parents, and on the education of English Learners or Standard English Learners in the district. Two open-ended questions designed to provide adequate opportunities for parents to elaborate on these issues and to provide feedback for District A are included in this paper. The survey is included in the Appendix.

Data Collection

Data collection took place between October and December 2007. One of four lead members of the research team, accompanied by a research assistant, attended one or more meetings of the parent meetings for each of the 16 school and community-based groups. Participants volunteered to complete the surveys at each of the meetings.

Data Analysis

Analysis of the survey began immediately after the surveys were completed. We used Survey Pro® for both creating the instrument and for inputting and analyzing the quantitative data. We also verified the data input process for accuracy by having a second person cross-check each entry. The descriptive statistics were generated by the program. For reporting purposes, we converted the 5-point Likert-scale with rating levels ranging from unacceptable to very well to a grading scale ranging from F to A. Table 5.1 reports on the descriptive findings for the two research questions.

We used Hutchinson's (2001) constant comparative method to analyze the two open-ended questions in the survey. The constant comparative method allows for the development of categories through theoretical sampling, and is a key feature of grounded theory (Strauss & Corbin, 1990). Theoretical sampling from a sociocultural framework was used to select the central themes. The researchers validated the coding of the data by examining the degree to which the theoretically relevant features of the parents' answers were represented (Hak & Bernts, 1996).

Data from the open-ended survey responses were triangulated with anecdotal notes, and there were opportunities for stakeholders to comment on themes and to discuss results as compared to previous research on parental involvement in District A. After coding the survey responses and studying them across the two parental groups, specific concepts and themes started to emerge and reemerge. A team of bilingual researchers identified these concepts and themes and began classifying responses that corroborated the frequency of themes. We established inter-coder reliability by going through the data several times to 1) check the consistency of coding system by independent coders, and 2) compare the identified categories by the two separate coders (Hak & Bernts, 1996).

Parental responses were coded and then sorted by theme. A tally of responses was conducted to establish which themes reoccurred more frequently within the qualitative data set. This examination led to the refinement of themes, changes in classification, and abandonment of others (Hak & Bernts, 1996). The themes were used to further categorize responses, ensuring that they complemented each other and that they told the story of

TABLE 5.1 Parents' Ratings of Districts' Support for SELs/ELLs and Their Parents

	Parents' Overall Rating of District Support			District's Support of Parents of ELLs or SELs			Parents' Rating on Districts' Education of ELLs			Parents' Rating on the Education of SELs		
	Mean	%	Grade	Mean	%	Grade	Mean	%	Grade	Mean	%	Grade
Spanish	3.05	61	C	2.61	52	D	2.57	51	D			
English	2.88	58	D	2.92	58	D	2.87	57	D	2.72	54	D

Note: Using a 5-point scale, 1 = Unacceptable; 5 = Excellent

the district-parent-community interactions, as opposed to simply describing parental feelings or events.

FINDINGS

The results are reported in two sections: quantitative findings and qualitative findings. We collected 513 surveys of the 785 surveys distributed (65% response rate) from the participating 16 parent leadership groups.

Descriptive Results

The great majority ($n = 384$, 75%) of respondents have two or more children enrolled in LAUSD schools (Spanish $n = 236$, 62%; English $n = 80$; 58%). Table 5.1 is a composite of four of the survey items that asked parents to "rate" District A's efforts and outcomes in the education of Standard English Learners and English Language Learners, as well as those items that address parent education and parental support. Table 5.1 represents responses from all 513 surveys, differentiated by parents of SELs, and parents of English Learners.

Overall, all parent leadership groups have relatively low ratings for District A's parent education efforts, along with their efforts to provide educational programs for their children. The analyses of the open-ended survey responses provide examples and elaborations on these key issues.

Qualitative Results

A total of 280 parents responded to two open-ended questions:

1) What do you believe District A needs to do to educate the Standard English Learners of English Language Learners in the District?

¿Que debería hacer el distrito para major educar a los estudiantes desarrollando el inglés?

2) What type of information regarding the education of English language Learners or Standard English Learners would you like to have?

¿Qué información le gustaría recibir acerca de la educación de los estudiantes desarrollando el inglés?

Both groups of parents identified similar themes; however, there was a variation in the number of times a specific topic/recommendation was mentioned for each theme as well as in the emphasis provided by each group of parents, as evidenced by the delineation of their respective, "representative comments." These comments are included to elucidate parent voices since all parent leadership groups surveyed emphatically expressed the desire to have a collective representation of parent voices heard throughout the district. Five recurring themes emerged from the analyses of both parent groups' open-ended responses: 1) respectful and responsive home-school collaboration, 2) professional development in parental involvement for school staff, 3) rigorous and relevant curriculum & instruction, 4) responsible accountability process, and 5) extended learning opportunities.

Themes are reported holistically in Table 5.2 according to language of response (Spanish or English). We used language of response as a proxy for parent group membership (Spanish for designating parent of English Language Learners, English for parent of Standard English Learner). Additionally, there were three Korean, one Chinese, one Vietnamese, and one German for a total of six responses given in English; these were also considered part of the ELL parent group.

TABLE 5.2 Theme Identification and Representative Comments for Parents of ELLs and SELs

Theme 1: Respectful and Responsive School and Home Collaboration

Parents of English Language Learners:	Parents of Standard English Learners:
• *Hay que crear conciencia en que se les eduque en la casa y la escuela es para aprender* [There is a need to create awareness that moral/values education is provided at home and school is a place for learning] • *Información a los padres sobre servicios y programas* [Information for parents about services and programs] • *Involucrar más a los padres y no solo con información, también aceptando ideas y opciones* [Involve parents, not only with information, but also accepting their ideas and opinions]	• Genuine parent involvement and customer service that serves the actual population. Only through the Academic English Mastery Program is there any support for Standard English Learners; they need to feel a part of the district • Strategic collaborations building between parents and teachers, staff & parents, staff to staff. • Need more town hall meetings with the teachers and the principals together with the parents, and need to feel less intimidated so they can really speak to the issues

Theme 2: Improved Professional Development in Parental Involvement for School Staff

Parents of English Language Learners:	Parents of Standard English Learners:
• *Mejor profesores, consejeros y programas que verdaderamente ayuden a los estudiantes* [Better teachers, counselors and programs that truly help students] • *Educar primero al distrito escolar, a los directores en la oficina, y a los maestros que entiendan el idioma y la cultura* [Educate the district first, principals in the office, and teachers so they understand the language and the culture]	• Need more teachers who are culturally aware of their students (learn about the community's culture) and to teach accordingly • Parents mentioned **curriculum and instruction** both in general terms and specific to curricular areas including Reading/Language arts, instruction of English, class size, and other subject areas

TABLE 5.2 (continued)   Theme Identification and Representative Comments for Parents of ELLs and SELs

Theme 3: Rigorous and Relevant Curriculum and Instruction

Parents of English Language Learners:

- *Darles clases de inglés adicionales no solo la instrucción en inglés porque al no entender el idioma el estudaiante se frustra* [Give students additional English classes, not merely provide instruction in English because a student can become frustrated if he doesn't understand the language]
- *Más apoyo en el idioma que habla como primer idioma y permitir en todas las escuelas la educación bilingüe para valuar el lenguaje que ya tienen* [More primary language support and allow bilingual education in every school to value the language they come with]

Parents of Standard English Learners:

- I think each Standard English Learner needs support. SEL students are being left behind. Students need dual languages and culturally relevant curriculum. It's hard for them to compete for jobs. Dual languages will help in our community
- Continue support for the Academic English Mastery Program for SEL students[a]
- Need more money and support to fund the AEMP program so that other schools may benefit from the program

Theme 4: Responsible Accountability

Parents of English Language Learners:

- *Monitoriar los directores sobre los planes de educación que se está llevando en las escuelas* [Monitor principals in regards to educational plans that are being implemented in schools]
- *Que el Plan Master se implemente en las escuelas* [That the Master Plan is implemented in the schools]

Parents of Standard English Learners:

- I believe that schools should be held accountable (principals), make sure teachers are being effective and that children are learning on a daily basis.
- Establish a monitoring system that measures the progress of Standard English Learners. The system should be district wide and AEMP should be instrumental in monitoring the Standard English progress

Theme 5: Extended Learning Opportunities

Parents of English Language Learners:

- *Sería excelente que se les diera la oportunidad de tener más apoyo, ejemplo tutor o mentor uno a uno por estudiante 2 horas por semana dentro de la escuela* [It would be excellent to provide opportunities for additional support, for example tutors or mentors one-on-one for students, 2 hours per week during school]
- *Más programas en las vacaciones para los niños y después de escuela* [More programs during students' vacation and after school]

Parents of Standard English Learners:

- Additional educators (teachers and tutors) and one-on-one tutoring is needed.
- Supply us with all the valuable resources to assist us to achieve and more books, resources and a variety of educational tools

---

[a] The Academic English Mastery Program in District A has been in place for over a decade with the intent of providing professional development and guidance to educators of Standard English Learners (SELs) in support of language and literacy development for this group of students. SELs are predominantly African-American, but can include other native English speakers who speak other varieties of English, including Chicano English. The professional development provided by AEMP targets narrowing the achievement gap for these students.

DISCUSSION

The descriptive reporting of the Likert-scale allowed us to capture minority parents' ratings of this large district's *performance* in the two main areas addressed by this study: 1) the education of Latino and African American students, and 2) the quality of parent education and involvement opportunities. The open-ended responses resulted in empirical indicators that allowed us to identify the themes and describe the level of interactions between parents and schools in District A. We contend that District A exhibited a climate where minority parents felt marginalized, regardless of the type of parent leadership constituency they represent (Arias & Morillo-Campbell, 2008). Formal spaces for parental involvement exist; nonetheless these structures include groups such as PTA, School-site Council and DELAC (District English Learner Advisory Council) that provide only physical places and prescribed agendas when parents come together. As such, these findings indicate that district personnel hear, but are not truly listening to their voices, opinions and recommendations. The excerpts selected address parents' ability to pinpoint areas of curriculum, instruction, leadership and collaboration that need restructuring.

Researchers presented results of this survey at District A's Summit for ELLs and SELs. Additionally several follow up meetings, including a presentation to District A's board, were held; yet to date, parent leaders and district leadership report that few of these recommendations have been acted upon by the district. Responsible accountability, which we define as actual movement towards implementing recommendations for authentic home-school collaboration for diverse communities, is a central aspect of our findings. Parent leaders from these communities do not just want to be heard, they want their recommendations advanced to a level of concrete action.

In order to promote more positive interactions, responsible accountability processes, knowledge of school policies and procedures must be made available to all types of parents in a clear and concise manner and in parents' primary language. Parents in this study clearly communicated this desire, as reflected by representative comments in Theme 1: Respectful and Responsive School and Home Collaboration. Additionally, all district personnel should have a clearly defined role in the accountability process with multiple opportunities to report on progress to community stakeholders, most especially to parents.

Educational and Policy Recommendations for Parent Involvement and Leadership

There is no question of the centrality of parents in their children's progress in school and of the corresponding mandate to schools to provide access and opportunities for parent involvement (Epstein, 2001). This mandate is underscored and must be differentiated for culturally and linguistically diverse districts such as the one in our study. The parent opinions and voices collected through the *Achieving Success Parent Survey* provide a critical avenue for change with regards to the education of English Learners and Standard English Learners within the district. Three central recommendations emerged from our study.

Expand Culturally Responsive Home–School Collaborations

Theme 1 describes the ways in which Latino and African American parents define *respectful* outreach to parents from diverse communities. They desire that schools: 1) move beyond traditional uni-directional approaches, 2) consider the talent and skills parents bring to the conversations, 3) listen to them with sincere consideration, and 4) follow up with measureable actions to implement changes. School and district teams should establish on-going ways to "listen to parent voices"—to survey parents and community members on their funds of knowledge to be used as a foundation for home-school collaboration (Moll, Amanti, Neff, & Gonzalez, 1992). Special attention should be given to linguistic and cultural assets that exist within communities (Arias & Morillo-Campbell, 2008). This type of responsive approach to capitalizing on parents' assets must be part of district and school plans.

Focus Professional Development on Curriculum and Instructional Needs of Bilingual Learners

This includes language acquisition programs, culturally responsive instruction, and during and after school learning models. Jasis and Ordoñes-Jasis (2004/2005) and Epstein (2001) recommend that existing parent social networks should be included as providers of this type of professional development to create effective instructional programs for linguistically diverse students. This would reduce the uni-directionality that is typical of most parent involvement and professional development efforts at school sites. Parents can and should be active participants and leaders in professional development efforts along with other experts. As Theme 2: Improved Professional Development on Parental Involvement for all School Staff illustrates, parent leaders expressed that all school staff members, from the secretary to the administration, need more preparation about who their students are in order to serve them better. By knowing their students better, school staff members understand the entire communities' needs in deeper and more meaningful ways. Parents surveyed indicated that responsive and deepened professional development would have greater impact during the school day and in after school experiences for their children (Theme 5: Extended Learning Opportunities).

Greater Accountability for Local and District Level Personnel in the
Implementation of Programs for ELLs and SELs

Care and trust in the relationships between home and schools require reciprocal efforts (Mapp, 2003). Parents expressed a strong desire to ensure that all of the adults in their children's schools are held responsible for ensuring positive change in the education of their children (Theme 4: Responsible Accountability). As active participants in the development of local plans, parents want to participate in the monitoring of the school site and other action plans on a more consistent basis with a focus on improvement. These models of mutual accountability traditionally do not exist in diverse communities (Noguera, 2008; Noguera & Wing, 2006). School systems must work together with parent leadership groups and/or school site councils to create them. While there is no formula for this, tools and procedures can be created collaboratively to monitor leadership, instructional practices and program effectiveness for ELLs and SELs, resulting in a system of checks and balances for all stakeholders.

Implications for Culturally and Linguistically Relevant Parent Involvement and Research

If we are to significantly affect positive change in the education of language minority children and youth, we must continue to raise questions around issues of school, family, and community partnerships. Schools and school systems must challenge themselves to critically examine family involvement practices, especially as it pertains to those who are typically underrepresented. This study allowed us to highlight parent voices around key issues related to home-school partnerships. An analysis of the findings provides a framework for change whereby a district can refine efforts for building home-school partnerships through a three-pronged approach: 1) implementation of parental involvement programs that are culturally relevant and linguistically appropriate, 2) support for teacher and administrators' preparation that draws from community funds of knowledge for curricular development, and 3) improvement of advocacy-oriented bi-directional communication between home and school that creates change in school policy.

Further research is needed to expand theoretical and explanatory models of minority parent involvement. The emerging body of research addressing parent involvement for these populations (Noguera, 2008; Noguera & Wing, 2006; Mapp, 2003) has just begun to problematize this issue. We also need empirical studies of minority parent involvement to support our increasingly diverse student population. The collaborative professional development called for in this study does not currently exist. Subsequently, the examination of the knowledge and skills for culturally responsive practices needs to be documented through research efforts about the development and outcomes of these programs. A final implication for research is the identification of measures and data for the study of new approaches to mutual accountability.

NOTES

1. We eliminated the two questions that addressed the needs of Standard English Learners from the Spanish version.

REFERENCES

Arias, M.B., & Morillo-Campbell, M. (January 2008). Promoting ELL parental involvement: Challenges in contested times. Arizona State University: *Great Lakes Center for Education Research & Practice.*

Arriaza, G. (2003). Schools, social capital and children of color. *Race Ethnicity and Education,* 6(1), 71–94.

Ballantyne, K.G., Sanderman, A.R., & Levy, J. (2008). *Educating English language learners: Building teacher capacity.* Washington, DC: National Clearinghouse for English Language Acquisition. Available at http:// www.ncela.gwu.edu/practice/ mainstream _ teachers.htm.

Berger, P. & Luckmann, T. (1966). *The Social construction of reality: A treatise in the sociology of knowledge.* London: Penguin.

Carreen, P., Drake, C., & Barton, A.C. (2005). The importance of presence: Immigrant parents' school engagement experiences. *American Educational Research Journal,* 42(3), 465–98.

Christie, C.A., & Wilson Cooper, C. (October 2005). Evaluating parent empowerment: A look at the potential of social justice evaluation in education. *Teachers College Record,* 107(10), 2248–2274.

Crotty, M. (1998). *The foundations of social research: Meanings and perspectives in the research process.* St Leonards: Allen & Unwin.

Draucker, C.B., Martsolf, D. B., Ratchneewan, R., & Rusk, T. B. (2007). Theoretical sampling and category development in grounded theory. *Qualitative Health Research,* 17(8), 1137–1148.

Epstein, J. L. (2001). *School, family, and community partnerships: Preparing educators and improving schools.* Boulder, CO: Westview Press.

Epstein, J. L. & Sheldon, S. B. (2006). Moving Forward: Ideas for Research on School, Family, and Community Partnerships. In C.F. Conrad & R. Serlin (Eds.), *SAGE handbook for research in education: Engaging ideas and enriching inquiry* (pp. 117–138). Thousand Oaks, CA: Sage Publications.

Hak, T., & Bernts, T. (1996). Coder training: Theoretical training or practical socialization? *Qualitative Sociology,* 19(2), 235–257.

Horvat, E., Weininger, E. B., & Lareau, A. (Summer 2003). From social ties to social capital: Class differences in the collaboration between schools and parent networks. *American Educational Research Journal, 40*(2), 319–351.

Hutchinson, S. 2001. Education and grounded theory. In R. Sherman, & R. B. Webb (Eds.), *Qualitative research in education: Focus and methods* (p. 135). London: RoutledgeFalmer.

Jasis, P., & Ordoñes Jasis, R. (Dec 2004/Jan 2005). Convivencia to empowerment: Latino parent organizing at La Familia. *The High School Journal, 88*(2), 32–42.

Le Moine, N. (2002). Academic English mastery program for Standard English Learners: Empowering students through communication. LAUSD: Los Angeles, CA.

Mapp, K. L. (2003). Having their say: Parents describe why and how they are engaged in their children's learning. *School Community Journal, 13*(1), 35–64.

Moll, L. C., Amanti, C., Neff, D., & Gonzalez, N. (1992). Funds of knowledge for teaching: Using a qualitative approach to connect home and classrooms. *Theory into Practice, 31*, 131–141.

Noguera, P. A. (2008). *The trouble with Black boys and other reflections on race, equity and the future of public education.* San Francisco, CA: Wiley, John & Sons.

Noguera, P., & Wing, J. Y. (2006). Closing the achievement gap at Berkley High School. In P. Noguera & J. Y. Wing (Eds.), *Unfinished business: Closing the racial achievement gap in our schools* (pp. 3–27). San Francisco, CA: Jossey-Bass.

Pena, R. (1998). A case study of parental involvement in a conversion from transitional to dual language instruction. *Bilingual Research Journal, 22*(2), 3 & 4, Spring, Summer & Fall, 103–125.

Reyes, P., & Capper, C. (1991). Urban principals: A critical perspective on the context of minority student dropout. *Educational Administrative Quarterly, 27*(4), 530–547.

Schwandt, T. A. (2001). *Dictionary of qualitative inquiry* (2nd Ed.). Thousand Oaks, CA: Sage.

Stanton-Salazar, R. D., & Urso Spina, S. (2000). The network orientations of highly resilient urban minority youth: A network-analytic account of minority socialization and its educational implications. *The Urban Review, 32*(2), 227–261.

Strauss, A., & Corbin, J. (1990). *Basics of qualitative research: Grounded theory procedures and techniques.* Newbury Park, CA: Sage.

Taylor, O. (1990). *Cross cultural communication: An essential dimension of effective education.* Chevy Chase, MD: The Mid-Atlantic Equity Center, 21–25. (Original work published 1987)

U.S. Census Bureau. (2000). *State and country quickfacts.* Retrieved from http://quickfacts.census.gov/qfd/states/06/0644000.html.

APPENDIX A
English Learner Summit
(District A) Unified School District
Parent Survey

Please take a few moments to respond to the following questions. The results of this survey will be used to provide information to (District A) regarding parent involvement, parent education, and needs for parents of English Language Learners and Standard English Learners in the district. All individual survey responses will remain confidential and results will be reported collectively. This information will be instrumental in supporting parents of English Learners and Standard English Learners in the district.

Background Information

1. How many children do you have that attend (District A) schools?
   ☐ 0 ☐ 1 ☐ 2 ☐ 3 ☐ 4 ☐ more than 5

2. What level school (s) do your children attend? (mark all that apply)
   ☐ elementary ☐ high school ☐ adult school
   ☐ middle school ☐ continuation school ☐ Other: _____

3. How many years has your oldest child attended (District A) schools?
   ☐ less than 3 ☐ between 3 and 5 ☐ more than 6 ☐ Other: _____

4. How many years have your children attended schools in the U.S.?
   ☐ less than 3 ☐ between 3 and 5 ☐ more than 6 ☐ Other: _____

5. Do your children participate in programs for Standard English Learners?
   ☐ Yes ☐ No ☐ I don't know

6. Do your children participate in programs for English Language Learners?
   ☐ Yes ☐ No ☐ I don't know

7. What language (s) are spoken in your home?
   ☐ English ☐ English and Spanish ☐ Spanish
   ☐ Another language (please specify)
   ☐ Other: _____

(District A) Parent Support

8. Overall, how well do you believe that (District A) helps parents in the district?
   ☐ Very Well ☐ Well ☐ Average ☐ Poor ☐ Unacceptable

9. How many times during 2006–2007 did the district provide you with information regarding your child's progress in his/her English Learner and Standard English Learner instructional program?
☐ never ☐ 1 time ☐ more than 3 times ☐ more than 5 times
☐ Other: _____

10. How well do you believe (District A) supports/informs parents of Standard English Learners or parents of English Learners?
☐ Very Well ☐ Well ☐ Average ☐ Poor ☐ Unacceptable

Involvement with Children at Home

11. How much time do you spend helping your children with homework?
☐ 1–15 minutes daily ☐ 16–30 minutes daily ☐ 30–60 minutes daily
☐ 60–90 minutes daily ☐ Other: _____

12. How much time do you spend daily reading to or with your children?
☐ 1–15 minutes daily ☐ 16–30 minutes daily ☐ 30–60 minutes daily
☐ 60–90 minutes daily ☐ Other: _____

Parent Education and Involvement

13. How many (District A) parent education workshops have you attended in the past 2 years? _____

14. How many parent education workshops on Standard English Learners in the district have you attended in the past 2 years? _____

15. How many parent education workshops on English Learners in the district have you attended in the past 2 years? _____

Educating English Learners in (District A)

16. Please rate how well you believe the district has educated Standard English Learners
☐ Very Well ☐ Well ☐ Average ☐ Poor ☐ Unacceptable

17. Please rate how well you believe the district has educated English Learners
☐ Very Well ☐ Well ☐ Average ☐ Poor ☐ Unacceptable

18. What do you believe (District A) needs to do to educate the Standard English Learners or English Language Learners in the District?

19. What type of information regarding the education of English Language Learners or Standard English Learners would you like to have?

Thank you very much!

English Learner Summit (Spanish translation)
Distrito Unificado (A)
Encuesta para padres

Favor de tomar unos momentos para responder a las siguientes preguntas. Los resultados de este estudio se utilizarán para proporcionar información al Distrito Unificado de (A) en relación a la participación, educación y necesidades de los padres de alumnos quienes son aprendices del inglés en el distrito. Todas las respuestas tendrán carácter confidencial y los resultados se comunicarán colectivamente. Esta información será fundamental en el apoyo de los padres de niños aprendices del inglés en el distrito.

Antecedentes

1. ¿Cuántos hijos tiene matriculados ahora en escuelas en el Distrito?
   ☐ 0   ☐ 1   ☐ 2   ☐ 3   ☐ 4   ☐ más de 5

2. ¿En qué nivel (es) están sus hijos? (favor de indicar todas las que aplican)
   ☐ pre-escolar   ☐ preparatoria   ☐ primaria   ☐ educación especial
   ☐ secundaria   ☐ otro, favor de indicar _____

3. ¿Por cuántos años ha asistido su hijo/a mayor a las escuelas del (Distrito A)?
   ☐ menos de 3   ☐ entre 3 y 5   ☐ más de 6
   ☐ otro, favor de indicar _____

4. ¿ Han asistido a las escuelas de los EE.UU.?
   ☐ Sí   ☐ No

5. ¿Participan sus hijos en programas para aprender inglés?
   ☐ Sí   ☐ No   ☐ No se

6. ¿Cuál(es) idioma(s) habla(n) en su hogar?
   ☐ inglés   ☐ español   ☐ inglés y español
   ☐ Otro idioma (por favor especifique) _____

Apoyo a los Padres del Distrito Unificado (A)

7. ¿Qué tan bien cree usted que el (Distrito A) ayuda a los padres en el distrito?
   ☐ Excelente   ☐ Muy bien   ☐ Adecuado   ☐ Pobre   ☐ Inaceptable

8. ¿Cuántas veces durante 2006–2007 le proporcionó el distrito información con respeto al progreso de su niño/a en su aprendizaje de instrucción en inglés?
   ☐ nunca   ☐ 1 vez   ☐ más de 3 veces   ☐ más de 5 veces
   Comentario _____

9. ¿Qué tan bien cree usted que el (Distrito A) apoya/informa a los padres de alumnos desarrollando del inglés?
☐ Excelente   ☐ Muy bien   ☐ Adecuado   ☐ Pobre   ☐ Inaceptable

La participación con los niños en el hogar

10. ¿Cuánto tiempo ayuda a su hijo (a) con la tarea?
☐ 1–15 minutos al día   ☐ 30–60 minutos al día
☐ 16–30 minutos al día   ☐ 60–90 minutos al día   ☐ otra _____

11. ¿Cuánto tiempo pasa diariamente leyendo con su hijo (a)?
☐ 1–15 minutos al día   ☐ 30–60 minutos al día
☐ 16–30 minutos al día   ☐ 60–90 minutos al día   ☐ otra _____

Educación de los padres y participación familiar

12. ¿Cuántos talleres para la educación de padre ha asistido en el distrito en el último año? _____

13. ¿Cuántos talleres ha asistido con respeto a estudiantes de aprendizaje de inglés en el último año? _____

Educando a Aprendices del inglés en el (Distrito A)

14. Por favor califique que tan bien cree que el distrito ha educado a estudiantes de aprendizaje del inglés
☐ Excelente   ☐ Muy bien   ☐ Adecuado   ☐ Pobre   ☐ Inaceptable

15. ¿Qué debería hacer el distrito para mejor educar a los estudiantes desarrollando el inglés?

16. ¿Qué información le gustaría recibir de la educación de los estudiantes desarrollando el inglés?

¡Muchas Gracias!

CHAPTER 6

FOSTERING INCLUSIVE EDUCATIONAL ENVIRONMENTS FOR AMERICAN INDIAN PARENTS AND FAMILIES IN URBAN SCHOOLS AND COMMUNITIES

Susan C. Faircloth

ABSTRACT

Susan Faircloth addresses ways in which parent and family involvement may be facilitated among American Indians residing in urban areas in this chapter. Although American Indians comprise less than two percent of the total U.S. population, they reflect an extraordinary array of cultural and linguistic diversity, seldom adequately acknowledged by the educational system. Failure to acknowledge, respect and incorporate such diversity has resulted in a system of education through which American Indians have been acculturated, assimilated and disenfranchised. This is evidenced by chronically low academic achievement, high dropout rates and low levels of parental and

Including Families and Communities in Urban Education, pages 119–138
Copyright © 2011 by Information Age Publishing
All rights of reproduction in any form reserved.

family involvement. Rather than acknowledge the role of schools in failing to facilitate meaningful parent and family involvement, blame has often been placed on parents and families themselves. To reverse these trends, schools must increase efforts to include American Indian parents and families into their educational programs and services.

When asked to write this chapter, I began to reflect upon my own personal experiences as an American Indian[1] woman growing up in the southeastern United States. I was particularly concerned with the events and people who helped to shape my educational development and subsequent academic trajectory. The challenge for me was figuring out how to relate my experiences as a rural southerner to those of Native[2] children and youth in urban schools and communities. After much reflection, I realized that the connection for me was one rooted and grounded in the stories I heard as a child; stories of aunts, uncles and cousins who no longer lived in the South, having moved to the North, during the 1940s and 1950s, in search of educational opportunities and jobs and away from the rampant racism and prejudices of the South. What my relatives did not fully comprehend was they would continue to encounter oppression in the North.

Traveling back to the South during holidays and summer vacations, they brought with them gifts of clothing and other "hand me downs." When they returned home to the North, they took with them food, stories, and memories, each of which helped to keep them connected to their American Indian roots in the South. Although their physical home was in the North, their emotional, mental and spiritual home remained in the South in our small, rural communities colloquially referred to as "down below," "cross the creek," and "Shiloh." The heart of these communities was and still is the church, a place where families gather to celebrate births, weddings, deaths and homecomings, and a place that was the site of their first formal education for many of our relatives.

Why do I begin this chapter with this story? I do so because it helps to illustrate the tensions that exist between many Native peoples whose forced or coerced movement away from their communities of origin to unfamiliar terrain causes them to constantly struggle to maintain their identities as Native peoples, and to place them at odds with the larger western world.[3]

For the purposes of this chapter, I focus on American Indians in the United States; however, it is important to note that the Native peoples of Canada, New Zealand, Australia, and other locales across the globe share similar stories of forced or coerced relocation, in addition to other means of acculturation and assimilation (e.g., Janovicek, 2003; Armitage, 1995). For many Native peoples in the U.S., urban migration was a direct result of federal policies aimed at depopulating Indian reservations and other tribal communities through the Relocation Act of 1956. This was coupled with the enforcement of terminationist policies with the goal to sever relationships between the federal government and tribes (e.g., Stuart, 1977). Although these policies were enacted in the 1950s and 1960s, removal of American Indians from their homelands has been a recurrent theme in U.S. history. For example, many of the treaties between the U.S. government and Indian tribes involved the exchange of land. In return, the federal government promised to provide for the tribes' general welfare, including education—a promise that more often than not resulted in the loss of Native languages, cultures and lives (e.g., McCoy, 2000).

Although Native children in the U.S. attend both urban and rural schools today, the bulk of educational research has focused on students residing in predominantly rural areas and attending schools operated or funded by the Bureau of Indian Education.[4] As a result of this focus on rural schools, little is known about the educational conditions and subsequent academic outcomes of Native children in urban schools. What we do know anecdotally is that for many Native children and their families, regardless of location, schools are often viewed as unwelcoming. In response, this chapter aims to provide some contextual background on Native families' experiences, and to address ways in which schools may work to create and sustain more inclusive learning environments for Native children and their families residing in urban areas.

DEMOGRAPHIC OVERVIEW OF AMERICAN INDIANS IN THE UNITED STATES

The following sections provide a brief introduction to the social and economic conditions of American Indians in the United States. These data are important in that they help to shape the ways in which Native families and children access and experience the educational system. Moreover, it provides valuable contextual information on American Indian experiences that can inform opportunities for family–school–community collaboration and inclusion.

According to the U.S. Census Bureau (2007), there are four million American Indians in the United States. The majority[5] (61%) reside outside of reservations and tribal communities, with a large number residing in urban and urban fringe areas (National Urban Indian Family Coalition [NUIFC], 2009). American Indians are most likely to reside in California (14%), Oklahoma (10%), and Arizona (8%). Overall, the largest proportion of American Indians live in Alaska, where they represent 19% of the state's population (U.S. Census Bureau, 2007). Metropolitan areas with the highest numbers of American Indians include Phoenix, where they account for 2.8% of the population; Los Angeles, where they account for 1.6%; and Chicago, where they account for less than 1% (U.S. Census, Bureau, 2007).[6]

According to the Census, the American Indian population is relatively young, with 30% under the age of 18 compared to 22% of non-Hispanic whites, and a median age of 31.9 compared to 40.1 for non-Hispanic whites (U.S. Census Bureau, 2007). Approximately 51% of American Indian families with children are led by married couples, while 38% are led by single females and 11% are led by single males (DeVoe & Darling-Churchill, 2008). Approximately 7% of those over the age of 30 are grandparents residing in the same house as their grandchildren under the age of 18, compared to 2% of non-Hispanic whites. Further, nearly 58% of American Indian grandparents who live with their grandchildren assume the role of primary caregiver, compared to 45% of non-Hispanic whites (U.S. Census Bureau, 2007).

Although a majority of American Indians have graduated from high school, approximately 25% live below the poverty level, compared to 9% of non-Hispanic whites. Poverty is most heavily concentrated among Native children, with 31% living in poverty, compared to 11% of non-Hispanic whites (U.S. Census Bureau, 2007). Among this population, the median income is $31,600 compared to $48,000 for non-Native peoples.

Across the nation, American Indians experience a number of socioeconomic and health-related disparities[7] including poverty, disability, low educational attainment, high unemployment rates, large numbers of single-parent families, as well as high rates of accidental deaths, diabetes, liver disease and other alcohol-related deaths. Many expectant mothers also tend to have limited access to prenatal care and experience higher rates of infant mortality. Further, many Native communities are reported to experience higher rates of child abuse and neglect than non-Native communities (NUIFC, 2009). In spite of these disparities, the Native population in the U.S. remains resilient, and the number of young American Indians continues to grow.

American Indian Student Demographics

Today, there are approximately 644,000 American Indian students in kindergarten through twelfth grade. While the majority (91%) attend public schools, nine percent attend schools operated or funded by the Bureau of Indian Education and tribes. Although American Indian students account for only one percent of the total public school enrollment, they reflect a wide range of cultural and linguistic diversity, representing more than 560 federally recognized tribes, more than 60 state recognized tribes and approximately 200 different tribal languages[8] (DeVoe & Darling-Churchill, 2008).

Approximately 46% of American Indian students attend schools in urban areas[9] (DeVoe & Darling-Churchill, 2008). Cities with large populations of Native children include New York (27,031), Los Angeles (15,853),

Phoenix (12,697), Anchorage (10,564), and Oklahoma City (9,690) (Snipp, 2002).[10] The large number of American Indian students residing in urban areas is due in large part to the urban relocation programs of the 1950s and 1960s.

Urban Relocation

Following World War II, the U.S. government adopted the policies of tribal termination and urban relocation (see for example, Szasz, 1998). Termination resulted in the abrogation of treaties between tribes and the federal government and a movement to depopulate American Indian reservations. As a result, between 1951 and 1973, more than 100,000 Native peoples relocated to urban areas (NUIFC, 2009). To facilitate this process of relocation, the federal government established the Adult Vocational Training program, also known as the American Indian Voluntary Relocation program, which provided one way tickets to cities, including St. Louis, Dallas, Denver, Los Angeles, San Francisco, Oakland, San Jose, Cleveland, New York, and Waukegan, Wisconsin, where they were to begin new jobs or engage in job training programs (Ward, 1997).

Relocation was viewed by some as a means of "exterminating" the Indian problem by moving them away from their tribal communities to urban areas where they would be forced to swim or sink. In the cities, they encountered racism, low wages, poor housing conditions and culture shock (Fixico, 2000). Fixico characterizes the early urban Indian experience as one of survival and "a clash of cultures" (2000, p. 7). While some chose to return to their reservations or other tribal communities (Fixico, 2000), relocation resulted in many Native people never returning home "... and their sense of specific tribal identity [being] significantly diminished" (NUIFC, 2009, p. 12).

Urban Indians Today

Today, American Indians living in urban areas account for approximately half of the Native population in the United States (NUIFC, 2009). The Harvard Project on American Indian Economic Development (2004) describes urban Indians as "... the forgotten majority..." (p. 53). According to the National Urban Indian Family Coalition (2009), there are four categories of Native peoples residing in urban areas. These include: long-term residents, forced residents, permanent residents, and medium and short-term visitors, described as those who do not intend to remain in an urban area permanently. A fifth category includes those who live and work in the city, but who return home for ceremonies and other events (Lucero, 2007;

Lobo, 2002). As these categories suggest, there is a wide range of individual and group characteristics among American Indians living and working in urban areas.

According to the Substance Abuse and Mental Health Services Administration (SAMHSA) (2009), many urban Indians "...form a sense of community through social interaction and activities, but are often 'invisible,' geographically disbursed, and multi-racial" (p. 2). Lobo (2003) describes these communities as 1) multicultural and multitribal, 2) lacking a centralized area of residence within the city, 3) comprised of networks of individuals and groups, 4) having a variety of socioeconomic levels and conditions, 5) spanning several generations, and 6) demonstrating both flexibility and fluidity in their ability to move between city life and life in their communities of origin.

Today's urban Indian communities tend to differ, in some ways, from those found among the original waves of American Indians who relocated to the cities. For example, in the early days, many of those relocating to the cities often found themselves living in centralized areas sometimes referred to as "Indian ghettos" (e.g., Fixico, 2000). Urban areas such as Oakland, Los Angeles and New York were part of the original relocation movement. As a result, these cities tended to attract large numbers of American Indians from across the country, resulting in a more heterogeneous Native population than in urban areas closer to tribal communities and reservations (Lobo, 2003).

It is important to note that some researchers (e.g., Lobo, 2003) find the use of terms such as "ghetto" to describe the residential patterns of American Indians in urban areas problematic. Lobo argues that such terms erroneously characterize urban Indians as residing in geographically clustered areas or communities rather than being dispersed throughout the city. This makes it particularly difficult to accurately identify, describe and respond to the socioeconomic and other conditions of this particular population.

Those who have moved to urban areas in recent years have tended to be more geographically dispersed. As a result, many urban Indian communities are not defined by typical geographical boundaries. The lack of a centralized area in which urban Indians are located makes it more difficult for some Native peoples to establish a sense of community or connectedness (Lobo, 2002). The existence or lack of a sense of community is important because it has implications for the ways in which individuals are able to respond to social, economic and cultural pressures. In many cases, one's cultural community has the potential to help mediate or mitigate the effects of external pressures on community members.

THE STATUS OF NATIVE STUDENTS' ACADEMIC ACHIEVEMENT AND WELLBEING AND THE IMPACT OF CONTEXT

As the previous sections of this chapter demonstrate, a substantial proportion of American Indian children live in urban areas where they are in the minority and apt to be overlooked by the educational system. For many American Indians, failure to acknowledge and incorporate their cultural and linguistic diversity into the educational arena is a characteristic failure of Native education in the US. Historically, American Indian students have not fared well in the educational system (Meriam, 1928; U.S. Senate, 1969; U.S. Department of Education, 1991). Today, approximately 14% of American Indian students receive special education services—more than any other racial or ethnic group. Sixty-six percent of 8th graders report being absent from school one or more times during the previous school month, compared to 55% of whites and blacks, 57% of Hispanics, and 36% of Asian/Pacific Islanders. American Indian students also drop out or are pushed out of school at rates higher than their non-Native peers, resulting in graduation rates lower than their peers (DeVoe & Darling-Churchill, 2008).

Parent and family involvement is critical to ensuring children's academic success (see for example, Weiss, Bouffard, Bridglall & Gordon, 2009). Without a culturally-based support net, sometimes missing in large urban areas where there is a not a well-defined, centralized or easily accessible American Indian community, families play an especially important role in promoting student achievement and well-being among Native students. In a recent study of parent involvement among American Indians, Mackety and Linder-VanBerschot (2008)[11] conducted focus groups with parents in seven states within the central region of the United States. When asked to define parent involvement, participants identified two categories of involvement as follows: (1) *school-oriented involvement,* [which entails] "communicating about children, attending student-centered events, volunteering, [and] advocating for...children" (p. iv); and (2) *home-oriented involvement,* which entails "showing interest in children's educational life; helping with school work; encouraging and rewarding children to do their best; reading with children; meeting children's needs; and involving the extended family and community" (p. iv). Although condensed into two categories, these levels of parent involvement are similar to the 6-part model developed by Epstein (1995), which include parenting, communicating, volunteering, learning at home, decision-making, and collaborating with the community.

In the Mackety and Linder-VanBerschot study, participants also identified a number of reasons for getting involved in their children's education, These explanations are supported by existing literature on family involvement (see for example, Epstein, 2001; Walker, Wilkins, Dallaire, Sandler &

Hoover-Dempsey, 2005). Parents wanted to monitor their children's progress and help their children succeed and build confidence; they wished to stay connected with the school or to address a problem; and they wanted to respond to the school's invitation or welcoming environment (Mackety & Linder-VanBerschot, 2008).

Barriers to parent involvement were categorized as both home- and school-related. Home-related barriers included scheduling conflicts, a lack of transportation, a lack of childcare, and economic difficulties (Mackety & Linder-VanBerschot, 2008), which are consistent with challenges to involvement found in other research studies (see for example, Hands, 2009). School-related barriers included an unwelcoming school climate, past experiences in school, perception of cultural insensitivity within the school, and differences in communication styles. These school-level challenges reflect the structures that are in place to shape the educational experiences of Native students and their families. Perhaps to an even greater extent, they highlight the impact of the cultures within the educational organizations that serve to influence families' involvement or lack of involvement in their children's education.

The extent to which many American Indian parents and families are involved in schools and school-related activities is shaped in large part by historical interactions with governmental organizations and agencies that have infringed upon the rights of Native peoples to determine not only the educational path of their children, but the ways in which these children have been reared. Historically, much of the education of American Indians has been planned and implemented with little or no input from Native peoples, tribes or communities (see for example, Fuchs & Havinghurst, 1972). Education has run the gamut from religious-based schools to off-reservation boarding schools to tribal schools funded in part by the U.S. Department of Interior, and public schools receiving limited amounts of funding from the federal government to supplement existing educational services for Native children. The use of education as a tool to acculturate and assimilate has resulted in a lingering distrust of the educational system for many Native peoples (see for example, Szasz, 1998).

DEVELOPING INCLUSIVE EDUCATIONAL CULTURES: RECOMMENDATIONS FOR PRACTICE

Historically, American Indians have been marginalized by the educational system. Their cultures, languages and religious beliefs have been viewed as detriments rather than strengths. As a result, education has been structured and delivered in ways that do little to foster active and meaningful involvement of parents and families. Unfortunately, this is not unique to American Indian children and families residing in urban areas. Nonetheless the potential exists for such exclusionary practices to be magnified in schools and communities where American Indians are among the least visible of all racial and ethnic minority groups. If schools are to reverse this trend, they must move away from the use of deficit approaches to education (Hands, 2006) and begin to view Native students and their parents and families as partners, rather than mere recipients of their services. Some ways in which this reversal can be facilitated are outlined in the following section.

Next Steps: Facilitating More Inclusive Educational Environments for American Indian Parents and Families

If parents are to become more involved in their children's schools, the challenge for educators is to make these schools places in which parents and families feel welcome. Mackety and Linder-VanBerschot's (2008) study on parent involvement found that "... parents' culturally related perceptions of public education and the tenor of the school's efforts to engage them in supporting their children's achievement were at the heart of their motivation—or resistance—to become involved in their children's education" (p.1). This finding underscores the need for educators to work in concert with Native peoples and communities to foster more inclusive learning environments in which schools are viewed not only as places and spaces in which to learn academic subjects, but also to honor and strengthen Native languages, cultures and ways of knowing. This is particularly difficult in urban areas where Native peoples are often viewed as the "invisible minority" (see for example, Carr, 1996).

If schools are to facilitate more active involvement among American Indian parents and families, they are encouraged to:[12]

1. *Acknowledge and respect different conceptions of familial structure found among American Indian peoples and communities.* This requires a recognition and acceptance of the fact that family structures vary. For example, in American Indian communities, families often include extended family members as well as non-relatives who are considered part of the family and play an important role in rearing children (Lucero, 2007).

2. *Acknowledge the role of American Indian women in urban communities.* Native women play an important role in these communities. Their homes serve as gathering spots, offering lodging, food, health and healing, advice, space for ceremonies, emotional and spiritual support, entertainment, transportation, and a sense of community, as

well as a connection to individuals' communities of origin. Lobo (2003) refers to these women as "Urban Clan Mothers".

3. *Recognize and respect Native children's cultural and linguistic diversity* (Lucero, 2007; Mackety & Linder-VanBerschot, 2008). This is particularly important, given the large number of American Indian tribes (more than 600 total) and languages (approximately 200) in the U.S. Avoiding assimilationist teaching practices[13] aimed at forcing Native students to fit into the larger, dominant culture is one way to respect their diversity. This process can be facilitated by selecting curricula and textbooks that include images and stories of American Indians in historically accurate ways, as well as discussing the current status and conditions of the American Indian population today.[14] Such practices help to remind us that American Indians are as much a part of the present as they are of the past.

4. *Facilitate systems of support.* According to the National Urban Indian Family Coalition (2009), many Native children residing in urban areas lack the "safety net" (p. 4) often found in reservation or tribal areas. One way to buffer potentially dangerous conditions is to draw upon the services and supports available through Urban Indian Centers,[15] churches and other religious organizations, which have historically played an important role in the lives of urban Indians. For many Native peoples, Urban Indian Centers served and continue to serve as a source of support and connectedness. For example, the American India Center of Chicago was established in 1953, followed by the Intertribal Friendship House (Oakland, California) in 1954 (NUIFC, 2009). Urban Indian Centers are also found in Minneapolis (Minneapolis Indian Center), Denver (Denver Indian Family Resource Center) and Seattle (United Indians of All Tribes Foundation). According to Laukaitis (1972), in the early years of urban relocation, these centers "... became imperative for survival and cultural preservation" (p. 139). One example of these centers' continued role in the lives of today's urban Indians is found in the work being conducted in conjunction with the American Indian Center of Chicago, which focuses on health and wellness, education and the arts.

5. *Encourage student and family voice and agency.* It is important to listen to their concerns as well as their suggestions (Lucero, 2007). Ask parents and families to define, describe and operationalize their conceptions and understanding of what it means to be actively involved in schools. Be patient. Understand that relationships take time to develop (see for example, Mackety & Linder-VanBerschot, 2008).

6. *When appropriate, work with federally-funded Indian Education Programs.*[16] States with significant numbers of American Indian students are eligible to apply for funding through the Title VII, Indian Educa-

tion Program, administered by the Office of Indian Education, U.S. Department of Education. The Indian Education Program provides funds directly to local public schools, to meet the educational, social, and cultural needs of American Indian students enrolled in public schools. A required component of these programs is the Parent Education Committee.

Similar recommendations are found in Pushor and Murphy's (2004) work with Aboriginal parents in Canada. In response to the lack of "place and voice" experienced by many Aboriginal parents as they seek to participate in their children's education, Pushor and Murphy call for the development of a new model of parent involvement in which parents are viewed as integral to their children's education rather than as obstacles or barriers. This model requires asking parents what their goals are for their children, seeking their input regarding the design and delivery of educational programs and services, and identifying ways in which the relationship between parents and schools can be made more beneficial to both parties. In doing so, educators must first begin to identify and understand the factors that have contributed to parents' lack of involvement in their children's education. Such knowledge is key to building and sustaining meaningful parent-school relations.

As these recommendations suggest, it is important for educators to reach out to American Indian parents and families if they are to become more involved in the education of their children—a conclusion reached by a number of scholars writing more broadly about parent and community engagement in education (see for example, Epstein, 2001; Henderson, Mapp, Johnson & Davies, 2007). Without such outreach, many parents and families may continue to view schools as unwelcoming.

Building a Foundation of Trust for Collaborative Relationships

In working with parents and families, educators are encouraged to acknowledge that the ways in which many Native peoples interact with the educational system are shaped in large part by their past experiences (SAMHSA, 2009). Failure to acknowledge these experiences may further strengthen the divide between parents, families and schools.

Identifying and implementing ways in which educational programs and services may be delivered outside of the physical boundaries of the school building is one strategy for building collaborative relationships. The goal here is to meet parents and families where they are, in an attempt to break down perceived barriers and make services appear more user-friendly

(SAMSHA, 2009). This is particularly important for individuals who have historically been excluded from the educational system.

Implicit is the role of two-way communication in the development of educational partnerships (Sanders & Harvey, 2002; Zaretsky, 2004). This often requires the use of multiple strategies (Hiatt-Michael, 2010; Mackety & Linder-VanBerschot, 2008). For example, promoting family involvement by establishing an open-door policy and talking to parents about their children (Mackety & Linder-VanBerschot, 2008) can be considered preliminary steps to developing positive relationships. The use of cultural liaisons or cultural brokers who are familiar with the school as well as the American Indian community is another way in which to begin breaking down barriers between parents, families and schools. Liaisons can be extremely valuable in helping educators to establish trust among members of the Native community (SAMHSA, 2009).

Although cultural liaisons can help to facilitate relationships between educators and parents and families, much of the success of relationship building is dependent upon one's own ability and willingness to recognize his or her individual biases, beliefs and stereotypes (SAMHSA, 2009). This is a critical first step in becoming what Lindsey, Robins and Terrell (2003) describe as a culturally competent and proficient educator. Although potentially different from one's own, it is important for educators to acknowledge parents' and families' values and beliefs (Mackety & Linder-VanBerschot, 2008). A core value of many Native peoples is one of respect. Respect for elders is particularly important (SAMHSA, 2009). It is important to note, however, that an elder is not necessarily someone who is older, but may also be someone who has earned the respect of others within the community as a result of his or her role within the community.

When meeting in person with parents and families, it is important for school personnel to consider ways in which to make the physical setting more welcoming. One way to do this is to incorporate food into meetings (SAMHSA, 2009). This may be as simple as preparing a plate of vegetables and fruit, cookies, cakes, juices or water or providing more traditional foods such as fry bread, Indian tacos, chili, beef or other meats. In such cases, it is important to identify, when possible, any food allergies or other restrictions family members may have. The provision of food is a symbolic way of demonstrating a sense of sharing and caring, as well as helping to create a safe and welcoming environment (Holkup, Salois, Tripp-Reimer & Weinert, 2007). Although there is a lack of published research specific to the use of food in the educational environment, the incorporation of food in many American Indian gatherings is a commonly known practice.

Similarly, when convening a meeting, school personnel are urged to respect the spiritual or religious points of view and practices of parents and families. For example, some tribal members may ask or expect to begin meetings with a prayer or blessing (SAMHSA, 2009). According to Stubben (2001), others may feel uncomfortable discussing their spiritually or religious beliefs and practices with non-Natives; therefore, it is important to approach such discussions tactfully and with respect, and when possible, to bring in other Native people (e.g., the cultural liaison) with whom the family or community may feel more comfortable discussing such practices or beliefs.

What does this mean for educators? It means that in order for us to work effectively with Native children and families in both urban and rural settings, we must be open to learning from and with these communities rather than imposing western models of education and involvement on them without their input or consent. It is also important to acknowledge the numerous strengths American Indian parents and families bring to the education of their children (e.g., involvement of extended families, Indigenous knowledge and wisdom, as well as resiliency) (SAMHSA, 2009). Acknowledgement of these strengths is a critical first step in moving away from deficit approaches to working with culturally and linguistically diverse parents and families.[17] This means leaving the comfort of our classrooms and venturing out into the communities and homes from which our students come and asking members of these communities what it is that they want for their children and youth. Sometimes, what they want is more than academic learning. What they may want is an opportunity to participate in the education of their children in ways that help to affirm their cultures and languages, rather than using education as a continued tool of assimilation and acculturation.

IMPLICATIONS FOR FUTURE RESEARCH AND THE CREATION OF MORE INCLUSIVE LEARNING ENVIRONMENTS

As demonstrated in this chapter, there is an ongoing need for research into the current status and conditions of urban Indian students (e.g., NUIFC, 2009). According to Blackhawk (1995), the few accounts that do exist often serve to "perpetuate existing homogenous portrayals of American Indians" (p. 19). Such portrayals ignore the cultural and linguistic diversity of the urban Indian population—characteristics that are at the core of their continued survival in settings far removed from their communities of origin. It is important to remember that "although American Indians faced difficult, lonely, and often very tragic struggles within urban environments, to suggest that the challenges confronting American Indians in cities were insurmountable ignores the dynamic and resilient processes of American Indian cultural change and adaptation" (Blackhawk, 1995, p. 20). Such resilience is critical to their continued survival.

In addition to familial-level variables, there is a need for ongoing research to explore differences and similarities between schools with low and high concentrations of Native students. For example, a recent study by DeVoe and Darling-Churchill (2008) found a number of differences in school climate among schools characterized as having high and low numbers of Native students.[18] This study found that the integration of Native language and culture into the curriculum was less likely in schools with less than 25% Native student enrollment. Students in grades four and eight attending schools with smaller Native student populations also reported fewer instances in which representatives from the Native community visited or presented programs related to Native traditions and cultures during the school year (DeVoe & Darling-Churchill, 2008). These are potentially important findings, which should be explored to determine the extent to which the school's willingness to engage in cultural programming and outreach to members of the American Indian community impact the level of active parent involvement within the school. Additional research is also needed to more fully understand the extent to which the incorporation of Native cultures and languages into schools in urban areas may result in improved school climate and an increased sense of inclusivity for American Indian students and their families within these schools.

CONCLUDING REMARKS

I end this chapter as I began, with a story. Several years ago, I attended a conference where I met a fellow attendee who was interested in American Indians. Learning that I was an American Indian, she began to engage me in a conversation about Indian education. She was particularly interested in the Carlisle Indian Industrial School,[19] one of the first boarding schools for American Indians, located in Carlisle, Pennsylvania. During this conversation, she stated how impressed she was by the work of Carlisle and its attempts to educate Native children. I sat and listened until I could listen no more. My response to her was, "How would you feel if someone came to your home and demanded that you allow him to take your young child thousands of miles away to school, where you would rarely be allowed to see or visit with your child—to a place where your child could not speak English or practice his or her religion? Would you think this was an honorable thing to do?" She looked at me with shock. And, as one can imagine the conversation abruptly ended.

This story highlights one example of the ways in which the educational system has served to alienate American Indian parents and families from their children and their education. Throughout history, the places, spaces, and characters have changed, but the basic processes have not. Moreover, the impact of these educational structures on Indigenous peoples may still not be fully understood by scholars, school personnel and—more broadly—citizens alike. The challenge for us as educators is to learn from stories such as this and strive to create learning environments that view parents and families as partners and collaborators.

When I started writing this chapter, I approached it from the perspective of an American Indian student, educator and scholar. Little did I know that during the course of revising this chapter, I would become the mother of a beautiful baby girl named Journey. Her arrival provided an opportunity for an added layer of reflection from the perspective of a parent. I realized that I, as many other American Indian parents, want my daughter to be educated in an environment that values and respects her culture, but that also challenges her to excel academically. This requires collaboration, partnership and trust on the part of parents, families and educators. Each of these is a critical element of an inclusive learning environment—an environment in which each person is valued, regardless of his or her ability and where children and their families are nurtured physically, emotionally, and mentally.

Although much has been written about parent and family involvement, little has been written specific to parents and families of American Indian students in urban schools and communities. Much of what I and other Native scholars know about working with urban Indian schools and communities comes not from formalized research studies, but from lived experiences working in and with Native communities. If we are to create schools that are truly inclusive learning environments for Native children and families, we must open our minds to what Battiste (2005) describes as Indigenous knowledge and ways of knowing, a type of knowledge that is rarely written down in textbooks or peer reviewed journals, but is passed down from generation to generation through stories and personal interactions. According to Battiste (2005),

> ... Indigenous knowledge benchmarks the limitations of Eurocentric theory— its methodology, evidence, and conclusions—reconceptualizes the resilience and self-reliance of Indigenous peoples, and underscores the importance of their own philosophies, heritages, and educational processes. Indigenous knowledge fills the ethical and knowledge gaps in Eurocentric education, research, and scholarship. By animating the voices and experiences of the cognitive "other" and integrating them into the educational process, it creates a new, balanced centre and a fresh vantage point from which to analyze Eurocentric education and its pedagogies (n.p.)

Battiste reminds us that the most important guidance on how best to create and sustain inclusive learning environments for American Indian parents and families comes directly from the voices of these individuals.

NOTES

1. The term American Indian refers to the Indigenous peoples of the United States. Each American Indian tribe has the right to determine membership in the individual tribe.
2. The term Native is used to refer to American Indians in the United States.
3. Although beyond the scope of this chapter, it is important to point out the distinction between state and federally recognized tribes, as these distinctions often determine the extent to which programs and services sponsored by the federal government directly impact their day-to-day life conditions. A prime example of this is demonstrated in the story of the members of my tribe, the Coharie People, who migrated to urban areas. As members of a tribe that was not formally recognized by the state until the 1970s, their migration was not forced at the hands of the federal government, but for some, was a conscious decision to improve their economic and social standing.
4. The Office of Indian Education Programs, within the U.S. Department of the Interior, was recently restructured and renamed as the Bureau of Indian Education. For additional information, see http://www.bia.gov/WhatWeDo/ServiceOverview/IndianEducation/index.htm
5. This represents an increase from 38% in 1970 (NUIFC, 2009).
6. Percentages based on those individuals identifying as American Indian/Alaska Native alone or in combination with another racial or ethnic group.
7. Approximately 20% of Native peoples in urban areas live in poverty compared to approximately 13% of Native peoples nationally. Native peoples are also less likely to graduate high school than their non-native peers. This contributes to an unemployment rate nearly twice that of non-Indians. Native peoples are also three times more likely than non-Natives to be homeless (NUIFC, 2008).
8. More than 25% of American Indian students in grades four and eight report speaking their Native language with family members at least 50% of the time (DeVoe & Darling-Churchill, 2008).
9. Urbanized areas include those with at least 50,000 people. Urban clusters include areas with densely clustered populations ranging in size from 2,500 to 49,999. In addition to urbanized areas and urban clusters, urban includes those areas classified as fringe rural and distant rural as defined by their size and overall proximity to rural or urban areas. See DeVoe and Darling-Churchill (2008) for additional clarification of these definitions.
10. These numbers include students identified as American Indian alone or in combination with one or more other racial or ethnic groups.
11. It is important to the note that this study was limited to parents served by the Central Region. Of 200 parents recruited for this study, only 47 elected to participate. As such, the findings may not be generalizable to this particular population or more broadly to American Indian populations at-large.
12. For a more in-depth look at parent involvement research, see the work of Epstein and her colleagues at the National Network of Partnership Schools (http://www.csos.jhu.edu/P2000/index.htm); Heather Weiss and colleagues at the Harvard Family Research Project, (http://www.hfrp.org/); Anne Hen-

derson at the Annenberg Institute for School Reform (http://www.annenber-ginstitute.org/); and Karen Mapp and staff at SEDL (http://www.sedl.org/)

13. See Deyhle and Swisher (1997) for an in-depth review of education research, including a discussion of assimilation and acculturation as they relate to the education of American Indian students.

14. See the work of Debbie Reese, University of Illinois, Urbana-Champagne for recommendations regarding the selection of culturally appropriate literature (http://americanindiansinchildrensliterature.blogspot.com/)

15. For a listing of Urban Indian Centers, see http://www.nuifc.net/members

16. For additional information, see http://www.ed.gov/policy/elsec/leg/esea02/pg100.html#sec7121

17. See Castagno and Brayboy (2008) for an in-depth review of "culturally responsive schooling" specific to American Indian and Alaska Native students. Although this article focuses on students, its implications are far-reaching and may be applied to the restructuring of educational practices aimed at facilitating more inclusive educational environments for American Indian parents and families.

18. High-density schools are those identified as having an American Indian or Alaska Native student population of 25% or more. Low-density schools are identified as having an American Indian or Alaska Native student population less than 25% (DeVoe & Darling-Churchill, 2008).

19. For more information on Carlisle Indian Industrial School, see http://home.epix.net/~landis/histry.html

REFERENCES

Armitage, A. (1995). *Comparing the policy of Aboriginal assimilation: Australia, Canada and New Zealand.* Vancouver, British Columbia: University of British Columbia Press.

Battiste, M. (2005). Indigenous knowledge: Foundations for First Nations. *WINHEC Journal.*

Blackhawk, N. (1995). I can carry on from here: The relocation of American Indians to Los Angeles. *Wicazo Sa Review, 11*(2), 16–30.

Carr, G. (1996, March/April). Urban Indians: The invisible minority. *Poverty & Race.* Retrieved February 3, 2010, from http://www.prrac.org/full_text.php?text_id=365&item_id=3563&newsletter_id=25&header=Race+%2F+Racism

Castagno, A. E., & Brayboy, B. M. J. (2008). Culturally responsive schooling for indigenous youth: A review of the literature. *Review of Educational Research, 78*(4), 941–993.

DeVoe, J. F., & Darling-Churchill, K. E. (2008). Status and trends in the education of American Indians and Alaska Natives: 2008 (NCES 2008-084). Washington, DC: National Center for Education Statistics, Institute of Education Sciences, U.S. Department of Education.

Deyhle, D., & Swisher, K. (1997). Research in American Indian and Alaska Native education: From assimilation to self-determination. In M. W. Apple (Ed.), *Re-*

view of research in education (Vol. 22) (pp. 113–194). Washington, DC: American Educational Research Association.

Epstein, J. L. (1995). School/family/community partnerships: Caring for the children we share. *Phi Delta Kappan, 76,* 701–712.

Epstein, J. L. (2001). *School, family, and community partnerships: Preparing educators and improving schools.* Boulder, CO: Westview Press.

Fixico, D. L. (2000). *The urban Indian experience in America.* Albuquerque, NM: University of New Mexico Press.

Fuchs, E., & Havinghurst, R. (1972). *To live on this earth; American Indian education* (1st ed.). Garden City, New York: Doubleday.

Hands, C. M. (2006). Seeing the glass as half full: Meeting the needs of underprivileged students through school–community partnerships. In D. E. Armstrong & B. J. McMahon (Eds.), *Inclusion in urban educational environments: Addressing issues of diversity, equity, and social justice* (pp. 71–90). Greenwich, CT: Information Age Publishing.

Hands, C. (2009, April). Efforts to enhance parent engagement: What can we learn from an assemblage of district-wide initiatives? Paper presented at the annual meeting of the American Educational Research Association, San Diego, CA.

Harvard Project on American Indian Economic Development. (2004). The context and meaning of family strengthening in Indian America. A report to the Annie E. Casey Foundation. Cambridge, MA: Author. Retrieved October 3, 2009, from http://www.aecf.org

Henderson, A. T., Mapp, K.L., Johnson, V.R., & Davies, D. (2007). *Beyond the bake sale: The essential guide to family–school partnerships.* New York: The New Press.

Hiatt-Michael, D. B. (2010). Communication practices that bridge home with school. In D. B. Hiatt-Michael (Ed.), *Promising practices to support family involvement in schools* (pp. 25–55). Charlotte, NC: Information Age Publishing.

Holkup, P. A., Salois, E. M., Tripp-Reimer, & Winert, C. (2007). Drawing on wisdom from the past: An elder abuse intervention with tribal communities. *Gerontologist, 47*(2), 248–54.

Janovicek, N. (2003, Fall & Summer). "Assisting our own": Urban migration, self governance, and native women's organizing in Thunder Bay, Ontario, 1972–1989. *American Indian Quarterly, 27*(3/4), 548–65.

Laukaitis, J. J. (1972). Relocation and urbanization: An educational history of the American Indian experience in Chicago, 1952–1972. *American Educational History Journal,* 139–44.

Lindsey, R. B., Robins, K. N., & Terrell, R. D. (2003). *Cultural proficiency: A manual for school leaders* (2nd ed.). Thousand Oaks, CA: Corwin Press.

Lobo, S. (2002, May/June). Census-taking and the invisibility of urban American Indians. *Population Today.* Retrieved February 2, 2010, from http://www.prb.org/Articles/2002/CensusTakingandtheInvisibilityofUrbanAmericanIndians.aspx

Lobo, S. (2003). Urban clan mothers: Key households. *American Indian Quarterly, 27*(3/4), 505–522.

Lucero, N. M. (2007, May). Working with urban American Indian families with child protection and substance abuse challenges. Denver Urban Indian Family Resource Center and the Rocky Mountain Quality Improvement Center Project.

Retrieved October 2, 2009, from www.Americanhumane.org/assets/docs/protectingchildren/PC.rmqic.dif-guide.pdf

Mackety, D. M., & Linder-VanBerschot, J. A. (2008). Examining American Indian perspectives in the Central Region on parent involvement in children's education (Issues & Answers Report, REL 2008–No. 059). Washington, DC: U.S. Department of Education, Institute of Education Sciences, National Center for Education Evaluation and Regional Assistance, Regional Educational Laboratory Central. Retrieved September 27, 2009, from http://ies.ed.gov/ncee/edlabs

McCoy, M. L. (2000). Tribalizing Indian education: Federal Indian law and policy affecting American Indian and Alaska Native Education. Indian Education Legal Support Project. Boulder, CO: Native American Rights Funds. Retrieved February 7, 2010, from www.narg.org

Meriam, L. (1928). *The problem of Indian administration.* Baltimore, MD: The Johns Hopkins Press.

National Urban Indian Family Coalition. (2009). Urban Indian American: The status of American Indian and Alaska Native children and families today. A report to the Annie E. Casey Foundation. Seattle, WA: Author. Retrieved September 30, 2009, from http://www.nuifc.org/index.html

Pushor, D., & Murphy, B. (2004). Parent marginalization, marginalized parents: Creating a place for parents. *Alberta Journal of Educational Research, 50*(3), 221–235.

Sanders, M. G., & Harvey, A. (2002). Beyond the school walls: A case study of principal leadership for school–community collaboration. *Teachers College Record, 104*(7), 1345–1368.

Snipp, C. M. (2002). American Indian and Alaska Native children in the 2000 Census. Baltimore, MD: The Annie E. Casey Foundation and the Population Reference Bureau.

Stuart, P. (1977, September). United States Indian policy: From the Dawes Act to the American Indian Policy Review Commission. Social Service Review, 450–63.

Stubben, J. D. (2001). Working in and conducting research among American Indian families. *American Behavioral Scientist, 44*(9), 1466–81.

Substance Abuse and Mental Health Services Administration (SAMHSA). (2009, January). Culture card: A guide to build cultural awareness, American Indian and Alaska Native. Retrieved October 2, 2009 from www.SAMHSA.gov/shin

Szasz, M. C. (1998). Education and the American Indian: The road to self determination since 1928. Albuquerque: University of New Mexico Press.

U.S. Department of Education. (1991). Indian nations at risk: An educational strategy for action, final report (Report No. ED/OPBE–91–34). Washington, DC: U.S. Government Printing Office.

U.S. Census Bureau. (2007). The American community—American Indians and Alaska Natives: 2004. Community Survey Reports. Washington, DC: Author.

U.S. Senate. (1969). Indian education: A national tragedy, a national challenge (Report No. 91–501). Washington, DC: U.S. Government Printing Office. Retrieved July 16, 2010, from http://www.tedna.org/pubs/Kennedy/toc.htm

Walker, J. M. T., Wilkins, A. S., Dallaire, J. R., Sandler, H. M., & Hoover-Dempsey, K. V. (2005). Parent involvement: Model revision through scale development. *Elementary School Journal, 106*(2), 85–104.

Ward, W. (1997). Outing, relocation, and employment assistance: The impact of federal Indian population dispersal programs in the Bay area. *Wicazo Sa Review, 12*(1), 29–46.

Weiss, H. B., Bouffard, S. M., Bridglall, B. L., & Gordon, E. W. (2009, December). Reframing involvement in education: Supporting families to support educational equity. Equity Matters: Research Review No. 5. Retrieved February 7, 2010, from http://www.hfrp.org/family-involvement/publications-resources/reframing-family-involvement-in-education-supporting-families-to-support-educational-equity

Zaretsky, L. (2004). Responding ethically to complex school-based issues in special education. *International Studies in Educational Administration, 32*(2), 63–77.

CHAPTER 7

LEARNING TO ORGANIZE FOR EDUCATIONAL CHANGE

One CBO's Efforts to Influence Educational Policy

Michael P. Evans

ABSTRACT

Community based organizations (CBOs) across the nation are using "people power" to address education issues ranging from school safety to the achievement gap. Many of these efforts have had a positive impact on the field of education. The Annenberg Institute recently completed a six-year, longitudinal study in which the researchers found that "successful organizing strategies contributed to increased student attendance, improved standardized test score performance, higher graduation rates and college-going aspirations" (Mediratta, Shah & McAlister, 2008, p. vi). While the successes and possibilities of education organizing are well chronicled (Mediratta, Shah & McAlister, 2009; Oakes & Rogers, 2006; Shirley, 1997), there is limited information regarding the obstacles that CBOs may encounter when learning to work for educational change. Drawing on research collected from an ethnographic case study, Michael Evans explores the challenges that emerged for one inter-

Including Families and Communities in Urban Education, pages 139–160

faith CBO when they engaged with education politics for the first time. This chapter focuses on the challenges that arise when CBOs enter into the field of education and has implications for communities seeking to utilize organizing strategies by exploring the knowledge that is required for effective participation in educational change.

Education organizing is the utilization of organizing strategies for the purpose of achieving educational change. The Cross City Campaign defines organizing as "building power for people who are powerless and those whose lives are negatively impacted by the decisions of others" (Gold, Simon & Brown, 2002, p. 5). The process enables otherwise marginalized individuals to work for change through relationship building. Education organizing is grounded in the traditions of community organizing but is also strongly influenced by the history of labor unions, the US settlement house movement, and the Civil Rights, farm worker, and Women's Rights movements of the 1960s (Oakes & Rogers, 2006). Organizing provides an intriguing alternative (or supplementary opportunity) to traditional forms of family involvement by allowing families to become *engaged* and not just involved with education issues. Shirley (1997) describes the critical distinction between involvement and engagement as follows:

> Parental involvement—as practiced in most schools and reflected in the research literature—avoids issues of power and assigns parents a passive role in the maintenance of school culture. Parental engagement designates parents as citizens in the fullest sense—change agents who can transform urban schools and neighborhoods. (Shirley, 1997, p. 73)

Family empowerment through organizing stems from the creation of opportunities independent of schools and school systems, though many CBOs work to develop partnerships with schools and teachers (Schutz, 2006). Moreover, community organizing extends opportunities to be involved in educational reform beyond the family to community citizens. It is an appealing model for individuals who feel excluded or limited by traditional opportunities for involvement (Evans, 2009) and it is an approach that continues to grow in popularity (Mediratta, Shah & McAlister, 2009).

ENCOUNTERING RESISTANCE IN EDUCATION ORGANIZING: A REVIEW OF THE LITERATURE

Existing research literature provides some limited examples of resistance faced by CBOs engaging with education issues. The types of resistance generally fall into one of three categories: professional, bureaucratic, or cultural.

Resistance Rooted in Educators' Profession

Professional resistance is exhibited by teachers and/or administrators who are reluctant to collaborate or who refuse to negotiate because of their desire to maintain their professional autonomy (Rooney, 1994; Shirley, 2002; Zachary & olatoye, 2001). There are several factors that may contribute to professional resistance. First, educators have worked over the past fifty years to build the prestige of the teaching profession. Increased educational requirements have established teaching as a middle-class, white collar career, but in many ways, it remains a "shadowed profession," esteemed for its contributions to society, yet diminished as easy work or a "stepping stone" job (Lortie, 1975). Teachers who are sensitive to these perceptions place great importance on their professional autonomy and expertise, and may be reluctant to share power (Hargreaves, 2001a; 2001b). Second, parent/teacher relationships have a history of tension rooted in what teachers see as a fundamental difference in priorities. The common perception is families are concerned about the needs of their individual children, whereas educators must take into the account the needs of all students (Lawrence-Lightfoot, 2003; Waller, 1932). Third, despite recognition of the impact that teachers have on student outcomes and the value of their contributions to successful school reform efforts (Gitlin & Margonis, 1995; Hubbard, Mehan & Stein, 2006), teacher input is often relegated to small-scale concerns like the selection of classroom materials (Winfield & Hawkins, 1993). Such actions cause teacher resistance and in some cases, reform failure. Shirley (2002) describes one example of professional resistance to organizing he observed among teachers at the Alamo Middle School in Texas:

> Oppositional teachers at Alamo resented Valley Interfaith for agitating the teachers to engage the community when teachers felt that their efforts were better spent on specifically instructional matters. For the teachers, social capitalization between the school and the community represented a distraction from their specifically academic mission and represented what might be termed a "hidden cost" of social capital. (Shirley, 2002, p. 95)

Finally, some professional resistance exists because teachers are burned out, resigned to going through the motions, or mired in a culture that rejects any innovation (Huberman, 1989; Lima, 2000; Payne, 2008).

Policy-Making and Its Influence on Resistance

In addition to professional resistance, reform efforts often face resistance created by school policies or government bureaucracies. The Texas Industrial Areas Foundation (IAF) had successfully organized with numerous schools and built strong relationships with educators across the state (Shirley & Evans, 2007). With an increase in high stakes testing and the implementation of accountability systems, though, teachers and principals felt compelled to focus on test preparation. Collaborative efforts outside of the school were gradually eliminated as teachers were more narrowly focused on adhering to state-mandated curricula. For these educators, No Child Left Behind (NCLB) created an atmosphere that limited both time and capacity for work that was not focused on test preparation (Shirley & Evans, 2007). Fear of government reprisals also hindered organizing efforts by the Southeast Task Force in Baltimore. Howell Baum, a University of Maryland researcher and task force member observed, "Principals had little room for slippage. Parent organizing was risky... the paranoid strand in the system culture made many principals highly anxious about organizing and parents unable to see common interests" (Baum, 2003, p. 153). Threats regarding the loss of employment, state takeovers, or school reconstitution are serious disincentives to educators considering collaboration with CBOs.

Ironically, NCLB features parental involvement as a key component of effective school reform. Yet, family participation is not framed in a manner that readily supports collaboration. John Rogers (2006) has identified three distinct narratives that manage parent power in the legislation: accountability, choice, and involvement. These narratives emphasize the distribution of data about student progress and school performance, the creation of "exit strategies" for students attending persistently low-performing schools, and the use of parents as monitors of school effectiveness. Each of these narratives is based on a free market rationale that assumes educators will be motivated to improve practice by the fear of losing students and funding. Unfortunately these strategies feed into traditional adversarial depictions of parent/teacher relationships by "pitting poor parents against unmotivated educators and a recalcitrant education system" (Rogers, 2006, p. 617). This is hardly a basis for effective collaboration, although some CBOs have embraced elements of NCLB as a tool to force cooperation in districts that are unwilling to work for change (Shirley & Evans, 2007).

The Influence of Cultural Differences Among Organizations

Finally, cultural resistance can cause communication breakdowns between community activists and educators. Cultural differences among key constituents stemming from racial, ethnic, social class, or even professional norms, may pose substantial problems for CBOs attempting to improve or affect change. In his analysis of Chicago school reform efforts, Charles

Payne observed conflict between school board members and community activists over basic issues like time:

> Board people tended to think of the workday as having well-defined limits. If they put in a couple of extra hours, it felt like a significant sacrifice. Community activists, who live in a world where meetings may *start* at 9 or 10 p.m., could not abide this attitude. They had a more visceral sense of schools as being in a state of crisis, and one doesn't respond to crisis by making a big deal over working a couple of extra hours now and then. (Payne, 2008, p. 127)

Other examples of cultural resistance exhibited by schools can be caused by educators' unfamiliarity or discomfort with CBOs and organizing strategies. For example, in collaborations with faith-based CBOs, some educators express concern with overtly religious language and practices like communal prayer. These individuals worry that any collaboration might be a violation of the separation between church and state (Shirley, 1997). Other education leaders are uncomfortable with strategies that emphasize relationship-building over clearly defined objectives, or approaches such as public demonstrations or rallies that may openly promote conflict with district or school personnel (Rooney, 1994).

Encountering resistance while working for change is a familiar experience for CBOs. In fact, CBOs often thrive on the identification of a clear adversary, which provides a tangible focus for organizing activities and personalizes the action (Alinsky, 1969; 1971). Regardless, it is important for CBOs to understand the source of resistance and identify the challenges that have the potential to impede opportunities for collaborative work. As CBOs continue to engage with schools it is important that they learn about the culture of education policymaking (Sarason, 1990; Tyack & Cuban, 1995). This includes the identification of key stakeholders and recognition of the complex sociopolitical contexts that influence their interactions.

LEARNING TO WORK FOR EDUCATIONAL CHANGE

To better understand the resistance that CBOs may encounter when engaging in reform efforts and the organizational learning that must occur for successful reform participation, this chapter frames the experiences of one CBO within the broader literature of educational change. Three perspectives on educational change have dominated the field over the past several decades: technological, political, and cultural (House, 1981; House & McQuillan, 1998). Each perspective is based on a set of assumptions that shape which school reforms are pursued, how other reform efforts are interpreted, and which procedural elements are emphasized (House & McQuillan, 1998). Many reformers adhere to a single perspective and doggedly pursue narrow strategies, yet research indicates that reforms that take a more holistic approach and consider all three elements are more likely to succeed (Fullan, 2001a; Hargreaves, 2003; House & McQuillan, 1998; Oakes, 1992).

The technological perspective on educational reform focuses primarily on the production and outcomes of schools and argues that school improvement requires a technical fix (Oakes, 1992). Here, the central idea is that school improvement is achieved through the research, development, and diffusion of best practices. House (1981) traces this perspective back to education's technical response to the Soviet launching of Sputnik and the resulting National Defense Education Act of 1958. Technological perspectives continue to influence policy debates today, as schools are asked to implement generalized curricula grounded in "scientifically based research." A technological perspective understands school improvement as a matter of finding, perfecting, and implementing the right technique.

The political perspective on educational change shifts away from the emphasis on specific strategies and instead looks toward negotiation and conflict among social groups as the basis for change. It takes into consideration that the interactions between multiple stakeholders are central to the shaping and implementation of education policy. Issues related to power and the balancing of competing interests become central to the creation of effective reforms. Here, learning to navigate the formal and informal change processes are an essential part of creating an effective and sustainable reform.

Finally, the cultural perspective on educational change emphasizes the social norms of different communities of practice and how they influence various stakeholders' reactions to reform. Implied is the recognition that schools reformers must consider the impact and reception of new policies by various communities. House (1981) uses an example of a curricular modification created in academia to demonstrate this phenomenon. He writes,

> ... an innovation may be developed by a group of university scholars, and the innovation will reflect the norms and values of that culture. As it is disseminated to teachers, it enters a new culture with significantly different norms and values. It will be interpreted differently when used in the new culture. (House, 1981, p. 24)

In order for a reform to be successful, there must be consideration given to the culture in which it is to be used. Reforms that fail to take into account the needs of their target communities are less likely to be adopted and implemented (Fullan, 2001b; Sergiovanni, 2000).

The implication for education organizers is the need for an awareness of these three perspectives to create or influence change. There must be an understanding of the assumptions that inform other stakeholders' positions before effective communication can be achieved, and organizers must be prepared to address these perspectives when participating in the creation of new strategies or reforms. Education policymaking is a complex process, and narrow solutions suggest an incomplete understanding of the problems that a school or district may face. As a conceptual framework, these perspectives serve as a useful guide for examining the work of education organizing and the various forms of resistance organizers may encounter. This chapter explores the experiences of one CBO entering the field of education policy for the first time and seeks to understand the organizational learning that must occur for a stakeholder to effectively collaborate with school and district personnel for educational change.

RESEARCH METHODS

From 2006 to 2008, I used an ethnographic multiple-case study approach to examine the internal workings of three Massachusetts CBOs engaged in education issues. The case studies were selected based on their representation of various organizing models: faith-based, neighborhood-based, and issue-based. This paper draws on the research from one of the case studies, United Interfaith Action (UIA). UIA is an interfaith coalition of twenty religious communities across the cities of New Bedford and Fall River. Separated by roughly ten miles, the cities share a number of the same social concerns that plague post-industrial cities in the United States such as unemployment, urban blight, and high levels of violent crime. UIA is a broad-based organization dedicated to the empowerment of its participants for the purpose of addressing these issues. They work on a wide variety of issues, but only recently have their actions brought them within direct contact of the New Bedford Public Schools (NBPS).

Contextualizing the Work of United Interfaith Action: The City of New Bedford and the New Bedford Public Schools

New Bedford is located in southeast Massachusetts on Buzzards Bay and is home to just under 100,000 residents. It is a working-class community with a median household income of $27,569, which is substantially lower than the state average of $50,502 (South Coast Facts Brief, 2007). The city is ethnically diverse, with over a third of the population claiming Portuguese descent (City of New Bedford, 2000). In January 2007, the Greater New Bedford area had the highest unemployment rate in Massachusetts (despite an increase of 1,200 total jobs) at 9.4% (Fraga, 2007).

Geographically, New Bedford covers twenty square miles and is divided into the North, West and South sides of the city. Longtime residents describe the community as being extremely territorial, and conflict over turf is the impetus for much of the violent crime in the area. There are eleven gangs operating in the city. Five of the eleven are associated with national groups, and the other six are organized at the neighborhood level. Two of these neighborhood gangs, the United Front Projects (UFP) and Monte Park, are recognized by residents as being responsible for the majority of the violence in the city. While gangs have a substantial impact on community life, New Bedford Police estimate that there are only an estimated 272 active gang members in the city, a relatively small portion of the city's youth (Shannon CSI, 2008). Facing a number of social issues, many of the residents are committed to the betterment of the community.

The New Bedford public schools (NBPS) currently serve 13,000 students in 27 schools (Massachusetts Department of Education, 2008). They face some serious challenges. The four-year graduation rate is 56.1% and the official dropout rate is 26.8%, which is significantly higher than the state average of 3.4% (Massachusetts Department of Education, 2008). Of those students who do graduate, the majority (57%) go on to attend four- or two-year public colleges. Only 15 % of graduates plan to attend private institutions of higher education, compared with the state average of 33% (Massachusetts Department of Education, 2008). Results from the 10th grade Massachusetts Comprehensive Assessment System (MCAS) for 2007–2008—which students need to pass in order to graduate—revealed that 50% of students on the English Language Arts (ELA) and 54% of the students in math either needed improvement or were failing. The figures went up to 61% and 68% respectively when examining the performance of low-income youth in the community.

The circumstances and challenges in the schools and in the broader community drew the attention of UIA.

Data Collection

Data for the case study included interviews, observation of various organizing activities, and the collection and analysis of documentation (Miles & Huberman, 1994). Formal, open-ended interviews were conducted with the lead organizer and nine core UIA leaders. The interview protocol was based on a combination of questions generated from a review of the existing literature (Merriam, 1998) on education organizing, community organizing more broadly defined, and organizational change. In addition, informal interviews were conducted with UIA members at UIA events. The UIA lead organizer played an important role in providing access to the organization's

activities and helped to set up individual interviews. The participants themselves were also helpful resources, contributing suggestions for people to
interview, and creating a snowball sample of organization members (Stake,
2002). Twelve formal observations were conducted, including attendance
at two rallies, four meetings with school or civic officials, and six planning
or organizational meetings. Finally, documents related to UIA were also an
important source of data. Meeting agendas, training manuals, working outlines of upcoming events, testimonial scripts, websites, brochures, newspaper clippings and other organizational literature were all collected, coded
and analyzed.

Data Analysis

Data analysis was an iterative process that began during data collection
and continued through the completion of this study. Merriam describes
this process as, "making sense out of data ... consolidating, reducing, and
interpreting what people have said and what the researcher has seen and
read—it is the process of making meaning" (Merriam, 1998, p. 178). Ideas
about possible categories and themes were identified and included in field
notes and memos (Rossman & Rallis, 2003). Based on these ideas, additional literature was reviewed, shaping both future data collection and analysis.
The data sources were triangulated and coded to identify dominant themes
and construct a "holistic understanding" of the case (Mathison, 1988).

UNITED INTERFAITH ACTION ENTERS THE FIELD
OF EDUCATION ORGANIZING

In May of 2006, a beloved member of the New Bedford community was
murdered. Bernadette "Bunny" DePina was a lector at the tight-knit Our
Lady of the Assumption parish, and her death came as a shock to the entire
community. Just days earlier, DePina's son had been charged with the murder of Justin Barry. County Sheriff Thomas Hodgson was quoted in a *Boston
Globe* article stating, "There's nothing in my mind to suggest that it would
be anything other than a form of retaliation. I had told some of my staff that
the expectation would be there's going to be retaliation, not ever thinking
that it would be the mother. This raises it to a whole new level" (Smalley &
Ellement, 2006). While UIA was already working to reduce violence in the
community, this tragedy spurred a redoubling of efforts.

UIA's efforts resulted in an October 2006 action at Our Lady of Guada-
lupe parish, which was attended by over 600 people. The action featured
the testimony of local community members and the presence of local of-

ficials including Mayor Scott Lang, Chief of Police Ron Teachman, and Deputy Superintendent Ronald Souza, who was representing Superintendent Michael Longo. UIA demanded an increase in summer jobs for teens, more transparency by the local police, a commitment to community policing, and the integration of a comprehensive conflict resolution education (CRE) curriculum in the public schools. The group was convinced that the best way to combat violence in the community was to reach the children at an early age before they were caught up in street life. With regard to this last issue, Mayor Lang and Dr. Souza each promised $50,000 from their respective budgets to fund a CRE curriculum. The meeting was considered a success, and UIA began operating under the assumption that the promised funds would be made available for the following academic year. UIA began to research CRE programs in the region, which included a trip to Providence to observe an existing program with New Bedford school officials.

At the beginning of the next school year (2007–2008), UIA began to reach out to NBPS, but they found that it was extremely difficult to connect with Superintendent Longo. Over the summer Superintendent Longo had announced his intention to retire at the end of the following year, and a search for a new superintendent had begun. Throughout the fall of 2007, UIA members repeatedly attempted to meet with him, but each time meetings were pushed back or cancelled. By the time UIA leaders met with Mayor Lang in early January, fifteen months had passed since the initial promise of funding, and the Superintendent had cancelled meetings on six different occasions. Mayor Lang, who worked hard to foster positive relationships with the community, was visibly surprised to learn about the numerous canceled meetings. Eventually, Deputy Superintendent Souza became the point person for NBPS regarding the CRE issue.

At the January meeting, Mayor Lang repeated his promise for funding and said that UIA should allow him to find the money in the school budget, since it is "almost a sure thing." Three weeks later, the money had still not been set aside, but UIA and the NBPS had started moving forward on the creation of a panel to oversee the implementation of a more comprehensive CRE curriculum. In February 2008, the two sides met and determined a course of action that would include a comprehensive analysis of the effectiveness of the programs that are already in place and initial plans for the piloting of CRE in three local schools. Despite setbacks that delayed action for almost two years, UIA members remained hopeful their diligent pressure would lead to the implementation of a pilot program by the 2008–2009 academic year, and that the hiring of a new superintendent would create a more responsive school administration.

As UIA pursued the adoption of a CRE curriculum, they began to learn more about the state of public education in New Bedford. Through a series of one-on-ones in the local community, it was determined that there might be interest in broader actions for improving education in New Bedford. UIA leaders were concurrently working on an action to support the continued funding of the Shannon CSI grants, which provided summer work opportunities for students and teen outreach programs. They decided that they would hold an accountability meeting with local legislators to "pin" their commitment to the funding, and simultaneously use the event to gauge interest in education issues. In addition, UIA actively recruited the participation of the youth of New Bedford for the first time, reasoning that they could offer new insights on education issues and show their commitment to the community.

Through the recruitment of students from a local alternative education program (which required participation among its students), the youth presence outnumbered UIA members by almost two to one. UIA members and the youth swapped stories about overcrowded classrooms and being discouraged to apply to college by guidance counselors who felt that they "didn't have what it takes." UIA members were energized by the inroads they were making with the youth of the community. Many of the struggling youth were quick to shoulder the blame and take responsibility for their own academic failings, but at the same time, they were also able to illuminate a number of substantial issues that were negatively impacting their educational experiences. The youth expressed frustration with the behavior of their peers in the classroom and lamented their teachers' lack of classroom management skills. Others talked about how difficult it was to hold a book discussion in a crowded English classroom. To this end, the kick-off meeting was a success, as UIA was exposed to some of the critical issues that the youth of New Bedford faced, and a starting point was created for further conversations about how to improve NBPS. In the weekly UIA meetings that followed the action, a number of youth attended and became active participants.

The influx of youth generated more enthusiasm and creativity for the next UIA event and a focus on the theme of "Hope in Youth." Recruitment efforts were redoubled following the unsatisfactory turnout of adult participants at the kick-off meeting and this time, UIA recruiters were quick to remind potential attendees of the message that their absence would send to the youth of New Bedford. One leader commented, "It was really important to us to get a good turn out, and I think people responded because we were better organized and had a better idea of what we were asking for." Building on the successful testimony of youth at the prior meeting, more young voices were included in the program, and the evening even featured a dramatic interpretation of the New Bedford dropout rate. Ten students stood in a row at the front of the stage and one by one, five of the students stepped back as a peer read off various drop-out statistics from the city. Mayor Lang had previously commented that New Bedford's dropout rate was not dissimilar from comparable urban districts, but the boos from the crowd made it clear that the community was not satisfied with these results.

As UIA members increased interactions with NBPS staff, they learned that some school officials were wary of collaboration and interpreted questions or challenges as personal criticisms. There was cause to be critical of NBPS because of its dismal achievement record, but UIA members also understood that officials were frustrated by low levels of parental involvement in the city and an apparent lack of support. In planning for the "Hope in Youth" event, UIA leaders determined that in addition to holding community leaders accountable, they needed to demonstrate their own commitment to the children of New Bedford. They came up with a "Community Education Compact" that they would ask the mayor and school committee members to sign as symbol of their commitment to working toward improving New Bedford schools. The compact included the following goals:

- Bring the graduation rate up 18 percent and increase college attendance by graduates by 25 percent in five years.
- Improve parent-school relationships.
- Develop a strategy for paying for the improvements.
- Create a plan of accountability.

In return, UIA called on its own membership to renew their commitment to the youth of New Bedford. Representatives from Big Sister/Big Brother and other youth-oriented organizations were present and set up tables where UIA members could sign up to volunteer. The UIA community was making it clear that they were willing to do their part, and they expected a similar commitment from their public officials. The night was a success.

Framing the Challenges of Learning to Work for School Reform in New Bedford

When this study was conducted, members of UIA had over ten years of organizing experience in the city of New Bedford. They had established cordial relationships with the majority of the local politicians and with various social service agencies. They had achieved several political victories and earned the respect of key political players in the area. Yet, UIA had never worked directly with a school system, and its work was often complicated by deficiencies in technological, political, and cultural knowledge as they related to NBPS. Opponents were able to use their expertise in these areas to block UIA's efforts, or at least complicate the change process. Using the previously outlined theoretical framework, I now turn to an examination of the types of resistance that UIA encountered and an analysis of the organizational learning that took place or was needed to support reform efforts.

Technological Challenges to Collaboration

UIA's first attempt to engage with the New Bedford school system involved the implementation of the CRE curriculum. UIA members were impressed by what they had witnessed in Rhode Island, and this became the curriculum that they identified with during their actions. Admittedly, there was limited research on the efficacy of the CRE curriculum, but the specific curriculum adopted by New Bedford was of little consequence to UIA members. It was more important that the schools take action and help reduce violence in the community.

Unfortunately, as UIA continued to pursue this initiative, a lack of knowledge about the CRE curriculum occasionally hindered their efforts to garner support within the school system. Administrators became caught up with the details of the program and opponents used "eduspeak" to intimidate UIA members. During one meeting, a New Bedford administrator remarked, "Why haven't you considered a curriculum that is based in socio-emotional learning theory?" The UIA members were not prepared to effectively engage in a conversation about the technical merits of various violence prevention curricula, and this delegitimized their efforts in the eyes of some administrators. Implementation is not a major focus for most CBOs, but it is critical element of school reform (Baum, 2003; Payne, 2008). Despite UIA's repeated insistence that their primary concern was simply that *something* be done, school administrators struggled to take action and became bogged down in the details. For UIA, insufficient knowledge regarding the "technological" solution they were proposing became a major obstacle in their communication with NBPS officials. Research also suggests that a lack of training in community relationship development and worries about losing control of the curriculum were likely contributing factors to the resistance exhibited by some administrators (Crowson & Boyd, 2001).

Policies and Unfamiliar Bureaucratic Structures

The school system also raised a number of new challenges in terms of its political structure. In November of 2006, UIA obtained a commitment for funding the CRE curriculum from the mayor and deputy superintendent. These were key leaders in the city, and this format was used by UIA to accomplish many of its previous goals. However, over time it became apparent to UIA that they were largely unaware of the political process for curriculum selection and implementation. As UIA members continued to push for CRE, they learned more about the immense pressures that school leaders and teachers were under as a result of the demands of high-stakes testing and NCLB. Teachers in New Bedford were already feeling overwhelmed, and any additions to the curriculum, especially additions that were being imposed from the district level, were sure to be met with opposition. With few ties to the local schools, UIA struggled to understand these delays and were frustrated by the layers of bureaucracy that they encountered. It was only through conversations with principals and teachers that they became aware of these other issues.

UIA's understanding of the process for curricular change was convoluted by exchanges with various city and district officials. UIA was assured that the mayor could easily acquire funding for CRE, but they never became directly involved in the school board's budget meetings or learned how the school system's resources were being allocated. They assumed that the mayor had the final say over the school budget, but in the end, the curriculum went unfunded for almost two years. School funding is a complicated political issue that involves multiple stakeholders (the superintendent, the school committee, etc.), and the mayor is not capable of making unilateral budgetary decisions.

Furthermore, even if the mayor was capable of making a unilateral decision, there was no guarantee that this would ensure the implementation of CRE. Successful curriculum implementation generally requires the buy-in of both school administrators and teachers (Gitlin & Margonis, 1995). In Binder's study of the campaigns for Afrocentrism and creationism (2002), she found that education outsiders met with more success when they were able to establish "insider resonance." That is, if the agenda of the challengers meshed with the perspectives of the insiders, then they were more likely to receive support for their actions.

Binder's (2002) study also revealed there is an important distinction between political and institutional insiders in an education system. The supporters of both Afrocentrism and creationism were able to build relationships with *political insiders*, or place people into positions of political power with relative ease. One might assume that these political forces would have substantial transformative power in an education system, yet Binder found that it was more important to generate support from the *institutional insiders* (educators or administrators) if one wanted to achieve sustainable change. Institutional insiders had more direct control over reform implementation and were less susceptible to the types of pressure that outsiders were capable of generating.

These findings have important implications for education organizers and illuminate some of the struggles that were encountered by UIA, who acquired the support of political insiders like Mayor Lang, the chief-of-police, and members of the school board, but did not initially secure support from institutional insiders like building principals and teachers. Achieving their goal would ultimately depend on the buy-in of institutional insiders.

School personnel were also learning about UIA, and it was apparent that some were uncomfortable with tactics that were mildly confrontational. Actions like the accountability meetings forced politicians and city workers to take a stand. This approach stems from the belief that in order to effectively negotiate, it is necessary to have a power base (financial, numerical, etc.), and the power of a CBO is primarily derived from the possibility of creating consequences for public officials (Alinsky, 1971; Horwitt, 1989). It is the possibility that these consequences could happen that made Alinsky's groups so powerful. As Stinchcombe notes:

> It appears as if most exercises of power by mobilized collectivities do not consist of actually changing the rewards and punishments of a public official, but instead of giving them the notion that their rewards and punishments might change if they do not behave. Demonstrations, popular organizations, riots, and even revolutionary crowds rarely actually hurt anybody, or collect enough money to run an automobile factory for a day, or deliver a given number of votes on election day, etc. Instead, they give the office holder the notion that perhaps this might happen unless some action is taken. Since this can have the desired effect (either give in or repress the movement), the exercise of popular power turns out to be a matter of "virtual movements," or "potential power." (Stinchcombe, 1989, p. 127)

This conflict-based approach is effective with political officials, but less so with entrenched school bureaucracies where personnel are not publically elected and job security is perceived as being linked to the successful implementation of district or federal policies (Shirley & Evans, 2007). Confrontation can still be an effective and necessary tool for CBOs in situations where they are being ignored or systematically marginalized, but the impact of the use of certain tactics must be considered in light of school culture and the resistance that might emerge if teachers feel that they are under attack.

Cultural Influences on Assumptions, the Educational System, and Communication

The culture of the community can play a significant role in the success of a school reform. Established social norms among various stakeholders and their traditional relationships with one another must be taken into consideration. The challenges UIA faced in their reform efforts were complicated by a legacy of disengagement between the schools and New Bedford families. While there are almost certainly economic and cultural factors that influenced the creation of this situation, UIA members admitted that many families did not engage in traditional forms of involvement and they expressed their own frustrations over the lack of engagement that they observed in the community (Hoover-Dempsey & Sandler, 1997; Lareau, 2000). One UIA member recalled her efforts in the mid 1990s to form a PTO at her son's elementary school:

> Parents in the community aren't verbal enough. We actually tried to get a PTO going there (at her son's elementary school), but it just didn't work out. I was so disgusted. It was hard to get them, it was always the same four or five people who would show up, even though we would send flyers home and make phone calls. It was so discouraging and finally it just fell apart, you can't have a PTO with just four or five parents.

Based on this legacy, UIA members were concerned about the stereotyping of community members by the school personnel and worried that their children or families were being "labeled." As one mother noted, low expectations can be a two-way street:

> It doesn't matter who you are, parent, teacher, or administrator, once you start making generalizations, that opens up the door for a lot of mistrust. Are there parents who are not holding up their end of the bargain in raising children? Yes! But, does that mean that it is always the parents' fault? No. Are there some teachers that are overwhelmed or maybe undertrained, that need something? Yes. Does this mean that they are all bad teachers? No.

Research indicates that teachers' assumptions regarding parents that are based on social class (Lareau, 2000) or culture (Olivos, 2006) are often inaccurate while at the same time, some parents unfairly project negative personal experiences from their own childhoods onto their children's teachers (Lawrence-Lightfoot, 2003). Because of these cultural barriers, part of UIA's work was the need to build trust with the school system (Bottery, 2003; Hands, 2005).

While on the surface, NBPS was receptive to the idea of working with UIA, the district personnel's actions occasionally sent a different message (Hargreaves, 2001a). Perhaps most glaring is Superintendent Longo's dismissal of UIA's early efforts by failing to attend the community action in 2006 and his subsequent cancellation of scheduled meetings. In other interactions, city leaders appeared very defensive. When a meeting was finally scheduled with the mayor, deputy superintendent, and police chief, one of the UIA members gave testimony regarding a large-scale disciplinary action that had occurred the previous day to illustrate the need for CRE. A group of four students were going from room to room in the high school searching for another student who they believed was involved in the murder of a local teen. A large group of twenty-five to thirty students followed as they searched the classrooms. Police were called to the scene, four students were arrested, and a number of others received detentions or suspensions. Upon hearing this description at the meeting, the public officials refuted a number of the fine details from UIA's testimony, and attempted to downplay the severity of the incident, warning that the community needs to be careful about perpetuating rumors. Essentially, the interaction quickly turned into an "us" versus "them" dynamic, yet the concerns of UIA were representative of the community-at-large. An article in the *Standard-Times* that very day noted that "Mr. Longo said that his own home telephone, which is listed in the directory, has been ringing steadily and that he was up late Thursday addressing parents' concerns" (Urbon, 2008). While there were some inaccuracies in the testimony of the UIA member, the point remained that New Bedford could benefit from increased attention to conflict resolution. It became clear that both sides needed to create a space for more open and authentic dialogue (Sergiovanni, 2000).

Even when progress was made and UIA began to work collaboratively with NBPS, there remained a disconnect with the terminology used by each and their modes of practice. For example, in an effort to expedite the launching of the pilot CRE program Deputy Superintendent Souza sent UIA's proposal to all of the principals in New Bedford. Ironically, although members of the NBPS continually warned UIA that school personnel would be resistant to any top-down reforms, they themselves used a top-down approach to disseminate information about the proposal. Three schools responded, which was excellent news, but as an organization based on relationships, UIA was frustrated that they were not able to make more individual connections and spend time talking with principals about their needs and what they are looking for in a program. UIA members were confident that they could have garnered even more support if they could have presented the proposal to the school personnel in person. This difference in approaches speaks to the difficulties inherent in partnership work and the cultural disconnect between UIA and district officials. This type of miscommunication is not uncommon between schools and communities, and it can hinder reform efforts (Bryk & Schneider, 2002). Communities need to feel that their concerns are being taken seriously or they will become completely disengaged (Chrispeels & Rivero, 2001; Mawhinney, 2004). Successful reform will require more effective communication from both sides to avoid exacerbating pre-existing tensions and to more efficiently work for change (Bottery, 2003).

From the perspective of UIA members, they were simply trying to improve the schools and community, but they had grown frustrated with the many obstacles that they had encountered: "Why is it that we can't make them see that if they get a program in there that works...and you can't know if it works until you initiate it, it will make everybody's job easier," one member said. "The teachers, the students, everybody. We can't understand why it is such a struggle." UIA members realized that they did not fully understand the day-to-day operations of the school system, but they wanted a chance to build a mutually beneficial relationship and increase trust. Trust is an essential component of school improvement, but it can only be achieved if there is a sense of efficacy among all stakeholders (Bryk & Schneider, 2002). Traditional forms of family involvement have limited authentic community participation (Hoover-Dempsey & Sandler, 1997; Schutz, 2006), and alternative models require a commitment to the critical examination of dominant education structures (Crowson & Boyd, 2001). Education organizing can empower participants to become more engaged (Evans, 2009; Shirley, 1997) and can provide a foundation for collaboration (Mediratta, Shah & McAlister, 2009), but additional work is necessary to build mutual trust.

CONCLUSION

In New Bedford, violence brought education to the forefront of UIA's organizing agenda. Through recognition of the interrelatedness of social issues in the community, UIA's attempts to address violence evolved from an emphasis on direct solutions like community policing to more indirect approaches like implementing CRE. As UIA became involved with the schools and listened to the challenges that were being raised by members with children, the multifaceted problems facing students in the NBPS became clearer. UIA remains committed to community policing and the implementation of a CRE curriculum, but they now recognize how low expectations for students and a grim outlook on opportunities for employment and higher education impact the youth of New Bedford.

UIA has proven itself as an effective organizing group on a number of different policy issues, and they are a respected political force in the city. Yet, UIA's experience working on the CRE curriculum speaks to the unique challenges of education organizing and the need to develop more effective strategies for collaborating with schools without forfeiting the valuable contributions that a CBO can make to the policymaking process as outside agitators.

In education reform, it is necessary to effectively communicate with various stakeholders. After all, "to the extent that people share a common language, this facilitates their ability to gain access to people and their information. To the extent that their language and codes are different, this keeps people apart and restricts this access" (Nahapiet & Ghoshal, 1998, p. 253). Thus, learning the language of power in the field of education is an essential part of creating viable policy solutions. Effective education activists are fluent in the technological, political, and cultural perspectives that shape policy, and this case study demonstrates how CBOs that do not develop this knowledge may struggle to fully participate in education policy debates.

UIA learned that it is imperative to have a strong understanding of the technical aspects of a reform, or an organization risks having the merits of their proposal delegitimized. They also came to understand the complex culture of education politics and how it differs from city politics on issues like health, crime, and poverty. Navigating education policy systems requires identification of the political and institutional insiders and knowledge of their roles within the system. And finally, they recognized the challenges that come in attempting to bridge cultures that have historically been disconnected. The decision to demonstrate their own commitment to the community by emphasizing the importance of volunteerism during the "Hope in Youth" rally was one way in which they sought to create trust with NBPS.

While adapting the language of education policy may help facilitate communication between stakeholders, this approach should not be interpreted as assimilation to the status quo. Rather, becoming adept in the language of education policy strengthens what Cornell West refers to as the prophetic voice (2004). By understanding the perspectives that guide education reform, CBOs can construct actions that resonate with educators, while simultaneously including the much-needed perspective of the community. When working in collaboration with educators, this approach creates the possibility for the development of more tailored and effective policies.

If education organizing is going to continue to flourish as an effective educational change strategy, CBOs will need to deepen their understanding of schools and reform challenges. One way that this might be accomplished is through partnerships with universities or by networking with education advocacy groups. Examples of partnerships at institutions like NYU, Harvard, and UCLA or with organizations like Annenberg demonstrate how mutually beneficial and empowering relationships can be established.

Creating effective education policy is a complicated process. Community organizations must be willing to learn about the culture of schools and reflect on the effectiveness of their organizing strategies in this environment. Traditional organizing practices may prove ineffective and require adaptation. Thus, as education organizing continues to grow, it will be important for CBOs to share not only the stories of their victories, but also the specific challenges that they had to overcome so that other communities will be better prepared to engage with education reform.

REFERENCES

Alinsky, S. D. (1969). *Reveille for radicals.* New York: Vintage Books.

Alinsky, S. D. (1971). *Rules for radicals: A pragmatic primer for realistic radicals.* New York: Vintage.

Baum, H. S. (2003). *Community action for school reform* Albany, NY: State University of New York Press.

Binder, A. J. (2002). *Contentious curricula: Afrocentrism and creationism in American public schools.* Princeton, NJ: Princeton University Press.

Bottery, M. (2003). The management and mismanagement of trust. *Educational Management & Administration, 31*(3), 245–261.

Bryk, A. S., & Schneider, B. (2002). *Trust in schools: A core resource for improvement.* New York: Russell Sage Foundation.

Chrispeels, J. H., & Rivero, E. (2001). Engaging Latino families for student success: How parent education can reshape parents' sense of place in the education of their children. *Peabody Journal of Education, 76,* 119–169.

City of New Bedford. (2000). Population, Retrieved on January 4, 2010 from http://www.newbedford-ma.gov/cd/pdfs/Demographics%20page%202-%20population.pdf

Crowson, R. L., & Boyd, W. L. (2001). The new role of community development in education reform. *Peabody Journal of Education, 76*(20), 9–29.

Evans, M. P. (2009). Inside education organizing: Learning to work for educational change. *Dissertation Abstracts International,* AAT 3349521.

Fraga, B. (2007). New Bedford has highest unemployment rate in Mass. Retrieved from http://archive.southcoasttoday.com/daily/03-07/03-07-07/01business.htm

Fullan, M. (2001a). *Leading in a culture of change.* San Francisco, CA: Jossey-Bass.

Fullan, M. (2001b). *The new meaning of educational change.* New York: Teachers' College Press.

Gitlin, A., & Margonis, G. (1995). The political aspect of reform: Teacher resistance as good sense. *American Journal of Education, 103*(August), 377–405.

Gold, E., Simon, E. & Brown, C. (2002). *Strong neighborhoods, strong schools: Successful community organizing for school reform.* Chicago: Cross City Campaign for Urban School Reform.

Hands, C. (2005). Its who you know "and" what you know: The process of creating partnerships between schools and communities. *School Community Journal, 15*(2), 63–84.

Hargreaves, A. (2001a). Beyond anxiety and nostalgia: Building a social movement for educational change. *Phi Delta Kappan, 82*(5), 373–377.

Hargreaves, A. (2001b). Emotional geographies of teaching. *Teachers' College Record, 103*(6), 1056–1080.

Hargreaves, A. (2003). *Teaching in the knowledge society: Education in the age of insecurity.* New York: Teachers College Press.

Hoover-Dempsey, K. V., & Sandler, H. M. (1997). Why do parents become involved in their children's education? *Review of Educational Research, 67*(1), 3–42.

Horwitt, S. D., (1989). *Let them call me rebel: Saul Alinsky his life and legacy.* New York: Vintage Books.

House, E. R. (1981). Three perspectives on innovation: Technological, political, and cultural. In R. Lehming & M. Kane (Eds.), *Improving schools: Using what we know* (pp. 17–41). Beverly Hills, CA: Sage Publications

House, E. R., & McQuillan, P. J. (1998). Three perspectives on reform In A. Hargreaves (Ed.), *International handbook of educational change* (pp. 198–213). Great Britain: Kluwer Academic Publishers.

Hubbard, L., Mehan, H., & Stein, M. K. (2006). *Reform as learning: School reform, organizational culture, and community politics in San Diego.* New York: Routledge.

Huberman, M. (1989). The professional life cycle of teachers. *Teachers College Record, 91*(1), 31–57.

Lareau, A. (2000). *Home advantage: Social class and parental involvement in elementary education.* Boulder, CO: Rowman & Littlefield.

Lawrence-Lightfoot, S. (2003). *The essential conversation: What parents and teachers can learn from each other.* New York: Random House.

Lima, J. (2000). Forgetting about friendship: Using conflict in teacher communities as a catalyst for school change. *Journal of Educational Change, 1*(2), 1–26.

Lortie, D. C. (1975). *Schoolteacher: A sociological study* (2nd ed.). Chicago: The University of Chicago Press.

Massachusetts Department of Education. (2008). New Bedford–Enrollment/Indicators. Retrieved March 1st, 2008, from http://profiles.doe.mass.edu/state_report/gradrates.aspxhttp://profiles.doe.mass.edu/home.asp?mode=o&so=-&ot=5&o=1156view=enr

Mathison, S. (1988). Why triangulation? *Educational Researcher, 17*, 13–17.

Mawhinney, H. (2004). Deliberative democracy in imagined communities: How the power geometry of globalization shapes local leadership practice. *Educational Administration Quarterly, 40*(2), 192–221.

Mediratta, K., Shah, S., & McAlister, S. (2008). *Organized communities, stronger schools: A preview of research findings.* Providence, RI: Annenberg Institute for School Reform at Brown University.

Mediratta, K., Shah, S., & McAlister, S. (2009). *Community organizing for stronger schools: Strategies and successes.* Cambridge, MA: Harvard Education Press.

Merriam, S. B. (1998). *Qualitative research and case study applications in education.* San Francisco: Jossey-Bass.

Miles, M. B. & Huberman, A. M. (1994). *Qualitative data analysis: an expanded sourcebook.* Thousand Oaks, CA: Sage Publications.

Nahapiet, J., & Ghoshal, S. (1998). Social capital, intellectual capital, and the organizational advantage. *Academy of Management Review, 23*(2).

Oakes, J. (1992). Can tracking research inform practice? Technical, normative, and political considerations. *Educational Researcher, 12*–21.

Oakes, J., & Rogers, J. (2006). *Learning power: Organizing for education and justice.* New York: Teachers College Press.

Olivos, E. M., (2006). *The power of parents: A critical perspective of bicultural parent involvement in public schools.* New York: Peter Lang.

Payne, C. M. (2008). *So much reform, so little change.* Cambridge, MA: Harvard University Press.

Rogers, J. (2006). Forces of accountability? The power of poor parents in NCLB. *Harvard Educational Review, 76*(4), 611–641.

Rooney, J. (1994). *Organizing the South Bronx.* Albany, NY: SUNY Press.

Rossman, G. B. & Rallis, S. F., (2003). *Learning in the field* (2nd ed.) Thousand Oaks, CA: Sage.

Sarason, S. B. (1990). *The predictable failure of educational reform: Can we change course before it's too late?* San Francisco: Jossey-Bass Publishers.

Schutz, A. (2006). Home is a prison in the global city: The tragic failure of school-based community engagement strategies. *Review of Educational Research*, 76(4), 691–743.

Sergiovanni, T. J. (2000). *The lifeworld of leadership: Creating culture, community, and personal meaning in our schools*. San Francisco: Jossey-Bass.

Shannon CSI. (2008). Senator Charles E. Shannon, Jr. Community Safety Initiative, Retrieved from http://www.shannoncsi.neu.edu/community_partners/new_bedford/

Shirley, D. (1997). *Community organizing for urban school reform*. Austin, TX: University of Texas Press.

Shirley, D. (2002). *Valley interfaith and school reform: Organizing for power in south Texas* (1st ed.). Austin, TX: University of Texas Press.

Shirley, D., & Evans, M. P. (2007). Community organizing and no child left behind. In M. Orr (Ed.), *Transforming the city: Community organizing and the challenge of political change* (pp. 109–133). Lawrence, KS: University of Kansas Press.

Smalley, S., & Ellement, J. R. (2006, May 27th). A mother's slaying stuns New Bedford: Police say shooting may be retaliation for earlier killing. *The Boston Globe*.

South Coast Facts Brief. (2007). Center for Policy Analysis, University of Massachusetts, Dartmouth, Retrieved December 28th, 2009 from http://www.umassd.edu/seppce/policyanalysis/scfacts.html

Stake, R. E. (2002). Case studies. In N. K. Denzin & Y. S. Lincoln (Eds.), *Handbook of qualitative research* (pp. 435–454). Thousand Oaks, CA: Sage.

Stinchcombe, A. L. (1989). An outsider's view of network analyses of power. In R. Perrucci & H. R. Potter (Eds.), *Networks of Power: Organizational Actors at the National, Corporate, and Community Levels*. New York: Aldine de Gruyter.

Tyack, D. & Cuban, L. (1995). *Tinkering toward utopia: A century of public school reform*. Cambridge, MA: Harvard University Press.

Urbon, S. (2008, January 12th). Tension builds in wake of incident at New Bedford High School. *Standard-Times*, retrieved from http://www.southcoasttoday.com/apps/pbcs.dll/article?AID=200801120324

Waller, W. (1932). *The sociology of teaching*. New York: John Wiley & Sons, Inc.

West, C. (2004). *Democracy matters: Winning the fight against imperialism*. New York: Penguin Books.

Winfield, L. F., & Hawkins, R. (1993). *Longitudinal effects of chapter 1 schoolwide projects on the achievement of disadvantaged students*. Washington, DC: Office of Educational Research and Improvement (ED).

Zachary, E., & olatoye, s. (2001). *A case study: Community organizing for school improvement in the South Bronx*. New York: Institute for Education & Social Policy, New York University.

CHAPTER 8

PIONEER PARENTS AND CREATING PATHWAYS FOR INVOLVEMENT

A Historical Case Study of School Change and Collective Parental Involvement

Erin McNamara Horvat

ABSTRACT

Ample evidence points to the important role of parent and family involvement in the school success of students. Yet, developing meaningful and effective home and school partnerships is often difficult, especially in low income urban communities. Erin McNamara Horvat presents data from a historical case study of one urban public K–8 school over a 30-year period. The author examines the nature of this home and school partnership over time, paying special attention to: 1) the collective nature of the parental involvement, 2) the important role of ideology in the development of the partnership, and 3) the ways in which the school created pathways for authentic parental involvement in the school.

Including Families and Communities in Urban Education, pages 161–185
Copyright © 2011 by Information Age Publishing

The role of parental involvement in schools has a long and varied history (Cutler, 2000). Some have touted increased parental involvement as a "fix all" for the problems facing schools in recent years (Epstein & Sheldon, 2002). Others have explored the differential abilities of parents to affect their children's experiences in school, based on social class and race differences (Lareau, 2000, 2003; Lareau & Horvat, 1999; Lewis & Forman, 2002; Stanton-Salazar, 2001). Many of these studies have focused on individual efforts of parents to affect their own child's school experience. There is far less research that has examined the effects of collective parental action in schools (but see Cucchiara & Horvat, 2009). In other words, we know less about how parents work together to change school communities than we do about how parents use networks to affect their own child's educational experiences. The current research also lacks attention to the interactive nature of parental involvement, focusing instead on one actor—the parents or the school—rather than the relationship between the two (Bryk & Schneider, 2002). It is also clear from examinations of current practice in large urban school districts such as the one in this study that we have had limited success in developing effective strategies to foster, promote and effectively harness parental involvement in schools.

This study contributes to our understanding of how collective parental involvement can play a critical role to positive school change. By investigating how parents worked collectively to create change in a school community, this study examines an under-researched area and also contributes to our understanding of how collective parental involvement can be a powerful tool in the engine of school reform. The single school case study presented here provides insight into how collective parental involvement contributed to the transformation of a school community over an extended period of time. This study focuses on two critical questions: 1) How and why did parent networks form and function in this school and community? And 2) What conditions at the school precipitated and supported this parent activism?

While leadership, neighborhood context, extraordinary teachers and programs were critical to the success of the school, I focus here on the motivation behind the early efforts of white, middle class "pioneer parents" to become involved in the school and the way that the school created an environment that welcomed individual and collective parental involvement. Specifically, I find that while the relationship between the parents and the teachers and administration was not always easy, these "pioneer parents" came with a particular sensibility that made the relationship work. My data also show that the school personnel were open to and created pathways for this involvement. I argue that the efforts of the pioneer parents, combined with a school that created pathways for involvement, were critical factors in the transformation of this school and may yield insights into the elements necessary to create strong school communities.

FAMILIES AND SCHOOLS

Decades of research have clearly established the critical importance of family involvement in schooling (Epstein, 2001; Hiatt-Michael, 2008; Weiss, Bouffard, Bridglall & Gordon, 2009). Strong connections between home and school have been shown to improve students' academic achievement and progress through the educational pipeline (Henderson & Mapp, 2002; Jeynes, 2007; Leithwood & Jantzi, 2006). Despite the clarity in the literature on the great importance of family involvement with, and connection to school, there remain two critical puzzles that have occupied researchers. The first is unpacking how parental and family involvement differs across race and social class. While it is clear that family involvement matters for all students, researchers have also found that some parents and families are able to have a greater positive influence on the school careers of students than others (Abrams & Gibbs, 2002; Crozier, 2001; Crozier & Davies, 2007; Diamond & Gomez, 2004; Lewis & Forman, 2002). Mapping the terrain of these differences is a critical endeavor as researchers and practitioners address the second puzzle: how to create strong and useful linkages between home and school for all children. Below, I review what we know about the differential impact of parents and family on students in school, highlighting the ways in which race and social class affect the quantity and quality of these connections and their importance. Then I turn to the research on how strong and useful connections that draw on the resources of all parents can be fostered in school communities.

Social class has always played a role in what kind of education parents provided for their children. Historically, parents were constrained by what they could spend on their child's education, while in the present day with universal free public education, parents' influence is most keenly exercised by the choices they make as to where to enroll their children in school and their capacity to interact effectively with school agents and influence the educational career and trajectories of their children (Crozier 1999; Diamond & Gomez, 2004; Hiatt-Michael, 2008; Weiss, Bouffard, Bridglall & Gordon 2009). The relationship between parental background and the efficacy of parental involvement in school has been increasingly examined. While many scholars argue that parental involvement of any type is positive, other scholars have focused on the differential ability of parents and families to support their children in school and have also focused on race and cultural barriers (Delgado-Gaitan, 1991; Diamond & Gomez, 2004; Lareau & Horvat, 1999).

Racial, ethnic and cultural differences between parents and families and school agents have often proven to be barriers to effective partnerships between the home and school. Researchers have identified race-patterned differences in expectations for interaction as one barrier (Crozier, 2001;

Lareau & Horvat, 1999; Lewis & Forman, 2002). Cultural differences between home and school have presented another barrier (Crozier & Davies, 2007; Delgado-Gaitan, 1991; Lopez, Scribner & Mahitivanichcha, 2001). These barriers between the home and school, be they based on class, cultural or race differences, share one critical feature: a lack of familiarity with or social distance from the norms, patterns of interaction and expectations of school environments, which are largely guided by white, middle class norms and expectations (Crozier & Davies, 2007; Lareau & Horvat, 1999). Recent models for effective home-school relationships have acknowledged the importance of this disconnect and have begun to examine the ways in which schools have been complicit in the exclusion of parents (Abrams & Gibbs, 2002; Crozier & Davies, 2007; Weiss, Bouffard, Bridglall & Gordon, 2009) and have sought to develop the capacity of schools and their agents to connect with parents from a variety of different racial, cultural and class backgrounds. The study presented here provides a historical perspective from one school community that grappled with these race and class issues, and illustrates the way in which both the school and its agents as well as the parents reached across barriers to create pathways for involvement.

While it has been well established that strong home and school connections have multiple positive effects, recent work has attempted to identify the critical features of successful partnerships. Like Weiss and her colleagues (Weiss, Bouffard, Bridglall & Gordon, 2009) as well as many other researchers (for example Epstein, 2001; Hiatt-Michael, 2006), this study points to the importance of a two-way relationship aimed at supporting the growth, development and maintenance of strong home-school and community connections. Epstein and her colleagues talk about overlapping spheres of influence, and Weiss and colleagues talk about "co-constructed shared responsibility." Further, home and school connections and partnerships prosper when school agents hold themselves accountable for effectively reaching parents and assisting them with their needs on an ongoing basis, as others have found (Lopez, Scribner & Mahitivanichcha, 2001). Like Sanders and Harvey (2002), I argue that reciprocity among parents, teachers and school leaders was critical to the development of an effective partnership, as were authentic opportunities for involvement (Auerbach, 2010), and the respectful and inclusive approach taken by parents. This approach is in contrast to other recent reform efforts mounted by largely white, middle class or professional parents who take an individualistic approach, emphasizing the benefit of the reform or change for their children, while ignoring the needs and desires of other families or teachers in the school (Cucchiara & Horvat, 2009; Edelberg & Kurland, 2009). The data presented here that document sustained school improvement over a 30-year period highlight the importance of a reciprocal approach that treats all parents as partners in the effort, and recognizes the importance of teachers, parents and administrators working in cooperation towards a shared goal.

METHODS

The Monroe School (a pseudonym) was selected for study due to the remarkable strength of the school community and its unique history of parental involvement. This single school site was selected in order to provide a deep and nuanced understanding of the change that had occurred over time at this particular school site, and the way in which the change took place. While the utility of single site case studies may be limited in terms of the generalizability of the findings, and historical or retrospective data can be affected by concerns related to "euphoric recall" (Walker, 1996, p. 223) where respondents overly romanticize the past, this design is well-suited to understanding a phenomenon in depth. Understanding change over an extended period of time necessitates the adoption of a historical perspective. This historical case study examining one school over a 30-year period represents a unique opportunity to understand how parents, situated in the context of the wider community, worked with the school and its agents to create change at the school over time.

Monroe is a K–8 neighborhood school of 417 children located in the city center of a large northeastern U.S. city I call Brickton. Like many other large northeastern cities, Brickton experienced a significant period of decline as industry closed up or moved out during the 1960s and 1970s (Sugrue, 2005; Wilson, 1987). The schools became increasingly populated by poor and minority families left in the wake of the white, middle class exodus. In the early 1980s, however, young, professional civic-minded families began to slowly repopulate the city. It is against this backdrop that the Monroe school community underwent a period of transformation that took place over a 30-year period. In the late 1970s, the school was one of the worst in a largely failing district and, with dwindling enrollment, was slated for closure. The student population was largely black and poor. Currently, Monroe enrolls a racially diverse population. Further, the school's results on the state standardized assessment are significantly above that of the district average, and have risen steadily over the last decade.[1] In addition, the school is one of three or four public K–8 schools located in the city's core that draws a large number of applicants from outside of its catchment area. Moreover, some families now deliberately purchase homes inside the school's catchment area boundaries so that their children can attend Monroe.

The primary data collection strategy for this study was a mix of participant observation and interviews. Interviews were conducted with key parents, teachers, administrators and former students. Between October, 2005 and June, 2006 I interviewed 32 individuals associated with the school: 21 parents, 5 teachers, 3 principals, 2 former students, and 1 former staff member. Of those interviewed, 26 self-identified as white, five as black or African American, and one as other. The participants also came from a range of time periods at the school. I interviewed nine people who were associated with the school during the early years (1974–1984), 13 from the middle years (1982–1994) and 16 from the recent past (1993–2006).[2] Of the parents that I interviewed, eleven held Bachelor's degrees while nine did not. Six of the parents had been or were currently a Home and School President or Co-President.[3]

Each interview lasted between 60 and 90 minutes. The interviews were semi-structured. After gathering background information on each participant, the interviews focused on each participant's involvement with the school, their perceptions of the changes that had taken place at the school, and the process by which these changes were initiated and carried out. Most often, the interview was conducted in the participant's home or a mutually agreeable neutral location such as a local library or coffee shop. All interviews were audio recorded and later transcribed and coded.

I spent 25 hours observing at the school. I chose to observe in settings where I would be likely to see the school community as a whole and where I would see and meet parents. I did not collect observational data from classrooms. I observed at the Harvest Day Celebration, Winter Concert, Spring Musical, Play Day, Home and School meetings, school dismissal time, prospective parent tours and other such events. I would also make casual observations when I would stop by the school briefly. While limited, these observations gave me a sense of the school community as it is today and provided a window onto the types of involvement parents have at the school, and the way the school feels to the students who attend there.

MONROE'S SCHOOL AND COMMUNITY

This neighborhood, like most in Brickton, the historic city in which the study took place, is densely packed with homes and businesses. The school's neighborhood has long been home to artists as well as public housing projects. The neighborhood is located not far from the central business district of the city and within an area commonly identified as part of the central core of this large and sprawling city. The streets here are narrow and tree-lined. While many of the homes in the area date to the early 1800s, there are also many newer homes built by developers in the 1980s. Immediately surrounding the school is a block of neat row homes, some with garages. A few blocks from the school, there is a commercial strip of stores, restaurants and other businesses. Around the corner sits a well-maintained playground and tennis court. Also located in this neighborhood are two major arts organizations, one for visual arts and the other for music. While in the mid 1970s and early 1980s, homes could easily be bought here for between $50,000 and $100,000 and far less at times, many homes in this neighborhood now sell for between $600,000 and $800,000.

Today, the school has an unusually high level of parental involvement. Its character is more like that of a private or charter school, where parents are involved in almost every aspect of school life, from special events like the Harvest Festival and Play Day that provide fun for the children and a sense of community to all members of the school, to substantial fundraising efforts like the Candy Sale, which raised $8,000, and an auction that raised $10,000. Moreover, parents appear to work in concert with the principal to battle cuts from the district and to enhance the school by working on projects such as getting the school air conditioned and wired for computers.

In addition, the school appears to revel in and celebrate the racial and ethnic backgrounds of all of its students. In the 2005–2006 year, the racial make-up of the school was 39.8% African American, 49.6% white, 5.0% Asian, 4.1% Latino and 1.4% other.[4] For the 2004–2005 year the racial and ethnic breakdown was similar with 46.6% African American, 44.6% white, 4.8% Asian and 4.0% Latino. These proportions are relatively consistent over the last four years. The portion of the population receiving free and reduced price lunch in 2005–2006 was 46.6%, while the average for the District was 72.8%. The racial make-up of the District overall for the 2005–2006 school year was 64% African American, 13% white, 6% Asian and 16% Latino. So while this school is more white and less economically challenged than the District overall, it still has a very mixed population both racially and socioeconomically.

Pioneer Parents and Pathways for Involvement

From the outside, Monroe does not look special. It is constructed in the same light brown brick used to build most schools in Brickton. It is not especially large or well landscaped. Like most of the other schools in the city, its doors are locked during school hours for security. Visitors to the school press a buzzer and the door is unlocked from inside to allow entrance. Once inside the building, however, the differences between this and other schools emerge. The school is spotless, bright and cheery. The brown concrete floors are polished to a high shine. The walls are decorated with children's artwork, colorful banners hang from the ceiling, and on the warm September day when I first visited the school, I heard the hum of air conditioning; unlike almost all other schools in the city, Monroe is air-conditioned.

In 1974, a group of largely white, college-educated parents, who had previously formed a babysitting cooperative and lived in the neighborhood, created a preschool program for their children in the school with the support of the principal. These "pioneer families" began the racial and social class integration at the school. It was from this initial group of parents that the foundation for parent activism began. Below, I describe the motivations of these pioneering parents, followed by a focus on two critical aspects of the school that facilitated and supported the sustained and meaningful involvement of parents in the school: 1) the openness to parental involvement on the part of all teachers and the critical role of one teacher in particular, and 2) the role of the arts program in providing a pathway for parental involvement at the school. Lastly, I explore how parents worked across race and class lines in partnership with the school over time.

Pioneer Parents and a Legacy of Involvement

Why did these pioneer parents want to invest in their neighborhood school and risk sending their children to a poorly performing racially segregated school? And how did they work in a collective and reciprocal way with the current black parents? Many cited the fact that they were "children of the 60s." For these parents, this meant they had a sense that they could create social change and do it across race lines. They came of age as young adults during a time (the late 1960s and early 1970s) when people did take political stances that affected their personal lives. They believed that they could create change, could make a difference in the world and, moreover, ought to try to make a difference. They felt that they could make a difference in a social and political sense. As one of these pioneering parents said, "I do remember how influential we were as parents. It was like, when we went to talk to the School Board, we were empowered." Another stated the parent motivation in the following way: "[We wanted to] make that school into a desirable, academically-happening school. Because that was our school, and here we were in the neighborhood, and we could make it into a good school."

These parents were also motivated by the desire to create a school community that would benefit their children. In addition to desiring to create larger social change through integrating the school, they felt that this integrated environment was good for their children. These early pioneer parents believed that their children would benefit from attending school with a rich mix of students. One white, middle class parent who was one of the first to send her white children into the all black school in 1974 talked about the kind of environment that she found at the school and the way in which it just made sense to commit to their neighborhood school:

That's one thing I would just say that was very obvious, that the teachers really loved the kids...You know, it was like that was perhaps what attracted us, and the feel you got, the vibe you got when you walked in the school. And so we picked that up. And we thought it was the right thing at the right time. We *knew* it was the right thing at the right time. And how could it not work? That was our feeling. How could this not work? So we just went in with this sense of, this all makes sense, doesn't it? You don't want to have a segregated school, you don't want to have a school that's 90% black. It's just not, I mean, how could you in this neighborhood that's not 90% black? And so what's to stop this school from being like the neighborhood that surrounds it?

Other parents shared this sentiment. Below, a parent whose children attended Monroe from 1985–1998 shared his perspective on parents who decide to leave the city and move to the suburbs when their children become school age. Comparing his children's experience to that of children raised in the suburbs he said, "The children in the suburbs might be a little more isolated because the suburban areas tend to be socioeconomic isolation for children and they end up having a strange view of the world because it's a narrow world." This sentiment was also expressed by a current parent who had had children in the school since 2000. I asked him why it was important for him to send his children to Monroe, and he responded by talking about the importance of placing his children in diverse environments early in life. He said,

I've met plenty of people who said that they didn't meet a black person or a Jewish person or a gay person until they were in college—it's always something foreign to them. It's almost too late at that point. You really need to have that respect early on in your formative years.

Another parent talked about how integration and working together across lines of race and gender was part of her consciousness. She said, "I mean, it's your philosophy of life. I mean, and that's really where we all grew up during the Civil Rights movement....And it affected us. I think that's where it stems from, absolutely." The parents sought out this school not only because they wanted to use their neighborhood school, but for the diversity that their children would experience by attending there. This is something that is valued by present day parents at the school. The Co-President of the Home and School Association at the time of data collection—who was black—commented on why parents continued to be involved with the school:

They [parents] want to affect their kids and make sure their kids get a good education. So they're going to be involved in it to help out whatever they can do that will help their child. I mean, they all look at, I guess they all, more or less looking at the same things I'm looking at, the diversity and making [sure] my child knows that even though the world is not just single race, it's multiracial. And to be multiracial you need to have that interaction. And I think all parents want to be able to show that "We can be involved with other parents to set that example for our children."

As another parent noted, what the children learn about the world and how to interact with different kinds of people stays with them.

It's Monroe. It's, it's the community, it's the school, it's the teachers, it's the parents, it's the students. It's, they're all working for one cause and a lot of the children, they go to other schools [after Monroe]. But, you know, what they learn in Monroe takes them to all those other places. They're successful where they go.

This idea that an integrated environment is one that will benefit their children was a shared sentiment among the parents with whom I spoke from all three chronological eras at the school. It was also a bedrock idea that guided the actions of the parents in their work in the school. Previous research has identified the need for effective partnerships to have common goals and a shared sense of mission (Bauch & Goldring, 1995; Bryk, Lee & Holland, 1993; Bryk & Schneider, 2002). The shared sense of purpose around diversity and the collective good was a theme that ran through data from all eras in the school.

These pioneer parents were people who felt that they could create change in their own environment and that this change would be good for society more generally. They also wanted to create a school environment that would benefit their children. They felt that their children would benefit from going to school with a racially and socioeconomically heterogeneous population. Lastly, they believed that parental involvement was critical to the success of the school. As one parent who lived in another region of the country wrote in an e-mail, "all of us knew that the success of the program depended on our participation and support. We worked hard, but we all had a common goal: to make the school the best it could be." Another parent said of their involvement at the school, "You have to work at it. You have to go, and go into that school, and make sure that it's happening. So in the pre-K we always had a parent there. There was one parent who was there." This finding echoes previous literature reinforcing the critical importance of parent involvement in creating positive school outcomes (Epstein, 2001; Henderson & Mapp, 2002; Hiatt-Michael, 2008; Weiss, Bouffard, Bridglall & Gordon, 2009). Moreover, these parents understood that their involvement was critical in many areas of school life, from raising money to volunteering in the classroom. This parent activism would have not created change, however, if it were not matched by welcoming principals and teachers who provided outlets for parental involvement.

Welcoming Teachers and the Key Kindergarten Teacher

While the motivations and commitment of the pioneer parents at Monroe were critical to the change that took place in this school community, these parents would not have been able to influence the school community had other conditions not been present at the school. Many people with whom I spoke referred to the early years at Monroe as "magical". As the following parent noted below, many people attributed some of that "magic" to the community and the parents; however, she and almost every interviewee acknowledged that the school had a core of capable and committed teachers.

> Perhaps part of the magic of that time was that we were all young, willing to experiment, and what had been a declining, rundown area was becoming quite a pleasant and chic place to live. The early years of the change were not always easy, but we were all committed to making sure the experience was a positive one for us and for our children.... I believe that having a nucleus of parents who cared made all the difference in the world in creating a positive learning environment for all our children ... I believe we were also very fortunate to have an amazing group of teachers who were willing to work with us to achieve success.

The school was blessed with a core of strong teachers. One teacher, however, stands out for the particular role she played in creating an expectation for parental involvement. Joanne Albright taught kindergarten at Monroe from 1980 to 1997. Through her efforts, more parents came to understand that they were key players in creating a school environment that benefited their children and that they were expected to support their children at home but also in school by working in the classroom on a regular basis, by going on the twice monthly class trips and assisting at school-wide events.

Despite the fact that the principal at that time did not understand the philosophy guiding her teaching or provide many of the resources that she needed to create her program, he did not stand in her way either, and parents were welcomed and needed in her classroom at all times.[5] This provided the opportunity for the teacher to interact with the parents and for parents to become committed to the school and their involvement there from the beginning of their children's academic careers. The kindergarten teacher effectively shaped parents' understanding of involvement that would stay with them throughout their children's attendance at Monroe.

The influence of this kindergarten teacher in creating the expectation for high levels of parental involvement and promoting parental involvement in her classroom was critical to the changes that occurred at Monroe. She created this expectation for involvement and promoted involvement by inviting and strongly requesting parental involvement in every aspect of her teaching. In fact, one of her colleagues went so far as to say that she required parents to spend time in her classroom. The standard practice in the district was and still currently is for the kindergarten teacher to meet individually with each student and parent during the first week of school. There is no group meeting. However, contrary to this district practice, Joanne held a meeting for parents at the start of the school year where she set out her expectations for them as a group and explained her philosophy. She told me,

> I said, "I want you to be to part of this. If you're a working parent, if you work in the area, you can come in at any time, you can help us out." I also explained in the beginning that if you are a parent that couldn't come in, I would love to have grandparents. That worked out really well. I had grandparents. I still meet them all over. Grandfathers, I had a lot of grandfathers. I would take anybody. I had a couple old maid aunts that were raising these little kids as the mother was working, that kind of thing. And I also let them know in the very beginning that even though I was prepared to set up the activities and I understood that I had full responsibility for the program, that they could help me and enhance me by giving me any ideas that they had, any good ideas. And they did that constantly.

Joanne created a culture of appreciation and involvement in part because she actually needed the parental involvement to carry out her program. Like others, (Auerbach, 2010; Epstein, 2001; Hiatt-Michael 2006; Sanders & Harvey 2002; Weiss, Bouffard, Bridglall, & Gordon 2009) I found that the reciprocal nature of her approach was critical to its success. Joanne's colleague, the art teacher, explains, "Joanne insisted the parents spend half a day in that room." As another teacher, who was at Monroe in the very early years before Joanne came said, "When Joanne came, parental involvement exploded." She could not take the children on the trips without parents. Parents provided real material resources that she needed in her classroom and she actively appreciated all that the parents could bring to her classroom and the children. She genuinely saw the parents as a part of her team. She explained,

> I want to explain my program to them, and explain to them what I expect of them. And so I started that. It [the meeting] was in the morning, from about 9 to 11. And I had the whole team there. The school nurse, who I worked very, very closely with. The principal came in and said hi. The speech teacher, Laura Jones, who was a very good friend of mine. This team.

She also explained her philosophy of education during this meeting.

> I think it's a two-way process. I explained to them my language arts program, that I teach sort of a thematic kind of teaching. And I gave them an example. I said "One of the themes that we probably will be doing are apples." And I

showed them how math and, you know, I showed them some of the things that we would be doing. I talked about trips and telling them that I thought that the community and the city was our classroom as well, and that we would be having a trip a month. I explained to them I sent home a monthly calendar in which I tell them all the trips for that month. I tripped about twice a month.

Joanne began collecting materials from parents and the school custodian such as old boxes and unused equipment. Her classroom was full of materials that other teachers realized they could use. She also got a large coffee pot for her classroom. Teachers and parents would come by her room to get coffee and borrow her materials. I asked her if she planned to create this sort of resource room where people could borrow things and where she intended to create a culture of involvement. She responded,

> No, it just happened accidentally. You know, just little things. But a coffee pot sometimes, and other teachers began to feel relaxed in my room. I had all kinds of stuff like the staplers, staple guns, glue guns, and the teachers would begin to say, "Ah, in Albright's room we're doing this and this." And so I would get notes all the time. "Could we borrow an extension cord?" "Can we borrow . . . ?" And I even got extra paper, because the parents were sending it in. By the end of the first year, you know, I had tons of stuff.

Not only did she have a wide assortment of materials, but after a few years, she had created an expectation among parents for involvement at the school. Joanne said,

> when they [parents] began to see what was happening and the parents were coming in every day to the kindergarten, they began to say, "Why isn't this happening in my other kids' class?" . . . And before I knew it, the next year they were asking the teachers, "Would you like some parent volunteers?" "What is it you would like?"

This culture of involvement was sustained through the creation of several avenues for continued parental involvement across the grades in the school, most notably through the arts program which I describe in the section that follows.

While Joanne Albright was able to make inroads in connecting with parents without the active support of the first principal, it is clearly important to have leader support. Subsequent principals built on the partnership foundation laid by the kindergarten teacher and her colleagues during the early years by actively supporting efforts to connect with parents and the community (see Horvat, Curci & Partlow, 2010) in creating lasting change and parental involvement. Similarly, others (Auerbach, 2010; Sanders &

Harvey, 2002) have found the support of the principal critical to establishing and sustaining authentic partnerships.

The other critical factor in the landscape of this school that supported the emerging partnership between parents and the school was the welcoming culture of the school clearly evidenced by these teachers (Bryk & Schneider, 2002). Over time, a culture of involvement was established and fostered at the school. This culture of involvement was critical for the ongoing growth and development of the partnership, as others have found elsewhere (Auerbach, 2010; Bryk & Schneider, 2002). Had the school not had other teachers promoting this type of involvement, home-school partnerships and the attendant changes occurring at the school might have ended with Joanne Albright. Another critical change took place at the school at the same time, however, that sustained and supported the foundation laid in kindergarten.

Providing a Pathway for Involvement: The Arts

In the 1975–1976 school year, Monroe applied for and received a grant to fund an arts program at the school. This arts program provided funds for four extra teachers, one each in Dance, Music, Art and Drama. While the addition of teachers and the accompanying reduced class size was important, equally important was the opportunity the arts program provided for parental and student involvement in the school. The outlet of the arts provided a way for the school to draw parents in to the school and provided a pathway for parents to be involved.

The arts program at Monroe was the best advertisement the school could ask for among the parent and broader civic communities. The teachers took students around to various venues in the community such as other schools, community centers and arts organizations for performances. They also invited the community in for performances and sought volunteers. This was a successful strategy, as the following teacher noted: "The word spread that Monroe has this, art, drama, music and dance. And parents love that, especially in [this neighborhood], because they respect that." One parent acknowledged,

> The arts and cultural opportunities offered at Monroe made it easy to want to be a part of their education, and I knew that supporting the teachers in this endeavor by raising money and by trying to help them with events would go a long way to making sure the program was a success. Having a group of similarly minded friends with children the same age as mine made it easy to be involved.

While the arts program was useful in drawing students and parents to the school, it also provided a way for parents to stay involved. For example, the school mounted a major musical production every spring that involved all aspects of the arts, including handmade costumes and sets. The entire school community galvanized around the annual spring production, for it could not take place without the substantial involvement of parents and teachers working together. When I asked one of the early pioneer parents which parents got involved, and whether just white parents or just middle class parents participated, she explicitly responded that all the parents supported the shows, found a way to be involved, and enjoyed it. She said,

> Everybody enjoyed doing the productions tremendously. And that brought all the kids, and all the parents liked it. Anybody could get involved, and everybody did get involved. The plays were good. And music and costume and make up and dancing. And everybody liked that. And that pulled them together real good. Everybody could work on the set, make costumes, help with the make up.

While often some parents come to schools with skills, talents or a sensibility that creates access at a school, all parents could find a way to be involved with the plays and the school found ways to reach out to all parents and students.

Moreover, the parents were actually needed, as the following quote from a parent indicates:

> the people, the principal and the teachers, actually wanted parental involvement and elicited their support. Part of this arts program required parental support because it took a lot of people. And some of the other activities took people, parents, to be involved. So it became self-fulfilling. I mean in growth, as it were, by promoting this type of activity.

Therefore, the growth took place because the school saw the need for the parents and the parents wanted to be involved. It was not inconsequential that a great deal of fun and learning happened in the bargain. After the foundation had been laid by Joanne Albright that set the expectation for parental involvement in the classroom, the arts program and the spring production in particular, provided an appealing pathway for parents to continue this level of involvement and support of the school.

Students also felt invested in the school and had fun with the program. As one parent said, "I think many of the children somehow understood and appreciated that their school was different, and given the wide array of arts in which they could participate, there really was something for everyone." This sentiment was echoed by the many teachers with whom I spoke, even those who were not part of the arts faculty. As one said, "I think the arts program was key to the success. It made kids happy. The kids wanted to come to school. When you're happy you want to come to school." The arts program was critical to creating a fun and engaging environment for the children and their parents. The productions and performances drew parents into the school and gave them something real and tangible to do once they were there.

Cultivating a Culture of Collaboration in Monroe

In the end, it was clear to all that the teachers knew they needed the parents, the parents wanted to be needed at school, and the two groups developed a longstanding relationship that both deemed essential to the development of the school. As one parent noted, the teachers and parents needed one another.

> You only need a few parents to either make a significant contribution of time or a relatively small but still very significant contribution of money that will really change the dynamic. And will suddenly make the teachers feel like, "Oh, somebody appreciates what I'm doing." And that helps them in their relationship with the children in general that they're getting a lot more community support. And community support often isn't a very large number of people. It's just a small number of people that really changes the dynamics. You need this sort of a small critical mass of parents raising funds to get involved.

For the most part, Monroe teachers shared this view that a strong relationship with parents was mutually beneficial. One of the arts teachers said,

> You have to nurture the relationship with parents. That bringing people into the school, they don't know that environment. Parents are not familiar with the school [except] for their child's room and they don't know that. So you have to create a relationship with them so that they feel safe coming in. And I did that intentionally. I purposely did that.

The parents who wanted to create change were met with a school environment that was willing to allow them into the school, providing ample opportunities for authentic and valuable service at the school. One of the parents said it best,

> Well, the administration first of all, has to be open to change. You have to have dedicated teachers. You have to have a very active parental force, because the changes come through them. But like I said, the administration and the teachers have to be open for all that. But the involvement has to be there. Because that involvement works both ways. If the teachers see that the parents are concerned, they're better teachers. If the administration sees

that they can rely on the parents to help them through something, they can be a little bolder. And then if the parents see that the school is really trying to educate their children the best, they're more willing to help. So it's, you know, back and forth.

While it was symbiotic in nature, this relationship was not without its bumps in the road. There were times when parents would infringe on teachers' authority. They might try to talk to a teacher without making an appointment, or come to visit in a classroom unannounced, or make unrealistic demands on behalf of their child. Regardless, the teachers understood that these types of problems came with the territory and that there was a substantial benefit to creating and maintaining a strong working relationship with parents. The teacher below was discussing some of these problems when I asked her if the benefit of having involved parents was worth the price teachers had to pay in aggravation at times. She responded,

> Absolutely. Absolutely. And there were times when people said, "Oh, no, there are too many parents. They're trying to run the school." And I said, "Yeah, but we need these parents. It's because of them that we have the things that we have in this school. They're willing to work hard." So this is the price that we have to pay. We cannot separate ourselves. Because if we do, we're not going to get that even balance that we need. And every once in a while you do have issues. You do have problems. But they work out.

The parents and teachers worked out the problems associated with parental involvement, and the children of this school were the direct beneficiaries of this effort.

While others have found that some formal mechanism to manage these partnerships is important to their success (Epstein, 1995, 2001; Goldring, 1993; Sanders, 1999), there was no formal action team or steering committee other than the standard Home and School organization that was deliberately focused on parent-teacher relationships. In spite of this, teachers and parents found ways to work together. One reason that parents and teachers were able to work together effectively may have been due to the remarkable stability of the leadership and teachers at this school (Davis, 2005). As noted earlier, the school was fortunate to have a core of strong teachers. These teachers and the leadership were very stable with only three principals in 30 years and over ten teachers who worked at the school for fifteen years or more. While the importance of stability and longevity of school staff was not an issue that was actively investigated in this study, it is reasonable to suspect that this longevity and stability contributed to the strength of the partnership and the ability of the parents and teachers to work out differences (VanVoorhis & Sheldon, 2005).

White and Black/Middle Class and Working Class Working Together

As noted earlier, many reform or school change efforts have been spear-headed by white middle class families and have excluded working class or poor parents of color (Cucchiara & Horvat, 2009; Edelberg & Kurland, 2009). While I was not able to interview as many poor or working class parents (4) or black parents (5) as I would have liked for this study, my data do indicate that the different groups of parents at the school found ways to work together over time. The Home and School partnership described above eventually involved not just the white middle class "pioneer" parents who provided the initial impetus. Over time, all parents—including black parents and parents of low socioeconomic status—got involved. As one of the "pioneer parents" said: "I mean, we eventually worked well with each other and it was a very integrated Home and School and school and it wasn't perfect but it worked."

Despite limited data from low income or working class parents or black parents, there were indications that parents worked across race and class lines. Parents from all eras pointed to the power of the arts to bring people together at the school over the years. A parent from the early years de-scribed how the background of a parent did not matter when they were working on one of the shows.

> Whatever their background was, it didn't matter. And it began not to matter to the parents, either, because you had everybody sitting up in [the art teach-er's] room sewing costumes. You had everybody painting scenery. It didn't matter after a while.

Not surprisingly, these efforts to work together often required parents to cross cultural barriers as well. An example of this can be found in the different fundraising efforts mounted by the Home and School. In the early years, the school developed a tradition of using spaghetti dinners that were held at the school to build community and raise money. In this tradi-tionally white ethnic Italian neighborhood, many families participated in these efforts. The Home and School would prepare the dinner, and fami-lies and community members would come and make a donation and eat dinner. As the "pioneer parents" made connections with the black families at the school, they began to have soul food dinners. One of the white par-ents described how she began to make inroads both with school staff and black parents:

> as I was in school and people got to know me a little bit, we became friends with some of the black women that were there, and the school people and the lunch ladies and all that. And all of a sudden there was this bridge hap-

pening [between the black and white parents] and we got more black people involved in the Home and School. And the soul food dinners happened and then we got all these black women to come in and cook. I never cooked greens. I never tasted them, let alone cook them. But, hey, they were in there, and I learned how to clean them and cut them and chop them and do all that. And we fried the chicken and we did that and it was a great success. And they did that for a number of years after that.

Another white Home and School President from the middle years described how important it was to provide opportunities for all parents to become involved. When asked how she involved all different kinds of parents at the school, she said:

> We would just say, 'Oh, can you help us?' And sometimes you can tell when a parent wants to help but they're kind of shy about it. "Oh, come on, we could use some more help," even though you've got 50 people behind the table. "Come and help us."

I asked about tensions during the interviews and often got responses similar to the one below. Here I had asked a white parent from the middle years: "Were there ever any tensions or disagreements at Home and School meetings about anything where you could see differences among these different groups at school?" She replied:

> I don't recall much ever. I'm sure there were some misunderstandings sometimes that people maybe felt. I would go out of my way to make sure if there was a committee we would not just make it an all-white bunch of mothers. Many of us did. I think we tried to—that big happy family thing . . . So I recall we kind of all got along pretty well.

As this parent indicates, like many "big happy families" there were disagreements and conflicts among different factions of parents at times.

Regardless, my data indicate that while the partnership between the home and school at Monroe was initiated by white, middle class parents, participation in the Home and School organization and other avenues for involvement in the school and classrooms was eventually shared across race and class lines. In addition, the leadership of the Home and School organization was shared by both black parents and white parents over time. For instance, the co-presidents of the Home and School were both black during the year of data collection. This collective, shared involvement across race and class is consistent with the values espoused by the pioneer parent who valued diversity and came to the work with a 1960s sensibility.

WHAT CAN WE LEARN ABOUT PARENTAL INVOLVEMENT FROM MONROE? IMPLICATIONS FOR POLICY AND PRACTICE

While the story of Monroe is far more complex than I am able to depict here, we are able to glean some insights into the critical elements of this home-school partnership. Below, I highlight three of these key elements relating to how the parent network formed and functioned at Monroe, including the conditions at the school that supported family involvement in education. The key elements included: 1) the importance of authentic opportunities for involvement, 2) the central role of ideology in creating a reciprocal partnership that involved families across race and class lines, and 3) critical organizational features of this partnership.

Authentic Opportunities for Involvement

It has been noted elsewhere that there is a certain tension between parents and school agents (Cutler, 2000; Horvat, Curci & Partlow, 2010; Waller, 1932). This tension for control at times limits the possibility for real and meaningful parental involvement (Crozier, 1999; Lareau & Munoz, 2010). As teachers and administrators are held accountable for the "results" of the school day, they may be less willing to spend valuable time and energy welcoming parents into the classroom and school and providing real opportunities for involvement. The data presented here indicate that real, meaningful and authentic opportunities for involvement were critical to the sustained success of the partnership at Monroe. As noted earlier, Joanne Albright needed parents to carry out her academic program and the arts program could not have mounted the impressive shows without the hundreds of hours invested by parents. Parents helped because they wanted to be of service, but also because they were truly needed. It is clear that one of the key features of this longstanding partnership in a successful urban school is the authenticity of the partnership itself. Elsewhere (Horvat, Curci & Partlow, 2010), I detail the relationships among the principals and the parents, noting the ways in which power and control at the school were negotiated over time. Like Auerbach (2010), I suggest that school leaders interested in forging stronger ties with parents need to locate avenues for authentic participation, and such participation by definition entails sharing a degree of power and control with parents and the community.

The Power of Ideology

I have outlined elsewhere the important role that ideology played in the participation of parents at Monroe (Cucchiara & Horvat, 2009). However it is important here to note the connection between the ideology of the pioneer parents and the structure of the resultant partnership. The parents who began the partnership at Monroe, and those who continued it in subsequent years held dear the civic values of diversity, inclusiveness and participation. The partnership that resulted from their efforts is not surprisingly a reciprocal two-way partnership that makes a real and meaningful difference in the lives of everyone in the school community. These parent and teacher partners envisioned a school that would benefit all of the children who attended it and would meet the demonstrated needs these students and families expressed. These values have been critically important to the partnership over time, providing a compass that has guided efforts over the years. These findings indicate that ideology does matter and the meaningful long-lasting reform is not simply a technical or organizational task separate from the ideals and values of those involved. Thus, as noted elsewhere (Cucchiara & Horvat, 2009), the longevity of partnerships and reforms are shaped not only by the ideologies underlying the effort. The continued existence and long term success of partnerships and reforms are also affected by the underlying beliefs and motivations of the participants.

Stability and an Early Start: Key Organizational Features

There are also key organizational features of the partnership that proved critical. The first is stability and longevity. As noted earlier, this school was fortunate to have had only three principals in 30 years and many high quality, senior, long-employed teachers. This stability was critical to the success of the partnership and the school. Success was not measured in months but in years, and this core of outstanding leaders and staff stuck with the school over time. For the most part, they stayed because they loved the work, they loved the children, and they loved the school. Creating exciting and meaningful professional homes for teachers and leaders that will attract and retain high quality educators is a key challenge for the profession and any serious reform effort. At Monroe, teachers were afforded the freedom to try new strategies. They also worked with parents who made the implementation of many of these strategies possible. Allowing able professionals to innovate and run their own programs was part of the Monroe culture (Hands, 2009). While current efforts aimed at improving accountability for teachers are not necessarily in direct opposition to such a philosophy, we have yet to determine how to attract high quality teachers and how to marry this spirit of innovation with current reforms aimed at "holding teachers accountable."

Lastly it is also critical to remember that the pioneer parents started when their children were young. They began as a babysitting co-op and approached the school when their children were ready for pre-school. It took years for the partnership to grow and develop. Starting early bought these parents critical time to work with the school and put in place a program that met their needs.

It is clear that successful schools are supported by parents and surrounding communities. However, research has also shown that it can be challenging for parents to find ways to connect at school, particularly economically disadvantaged and minority parents. This study shows how one school created opportunities for collective parental involvement and how both parents and school agents supported this activity. This study can provide other schools and parents with insight as to how to harness collective parental involvement to create strong school communities.

NOTES

1. In 2002, the District reported that 18.7% of students were at or above the proficient level in math while 20.8% were at that level in reading on the PSSA. Monroe's combined advanced and proficient level percentages for several consecutive years in reading are: 2002—39.1%, 2003—56.9%, 2004—70.2% and for math are: 2002—37%, 2003—45.1%, 2004—65%.
2. This accounting by era during which participants were associated with the school is meant to provide a rough idea of the type of data I have spanning the 30-year period. There is a degree of overlap among participants in terms of the eras they were associated with the school. Some individuals had been at the school for 30 years and were thus counted in two or more categories. The total, therefore, does not equal 32.
3. The website for Monroe describes the Home and School Association as "a group of parents and staff who assist the school in achieving its educational goals through advocacy, planning and fundraising." The Home and School Association can be compared to other commonly used terms such as Parent Teacher Organization or PTA that describe a parent advocacy and support group for the school. Officers for the organization are elected each fall and include a president (at times there are co-presidents), vice president, treasurer and secretary.
4. These statistics, as well as those below, were taken from the Brickton School District website.
5. While it was enough at this point for the principal to not get in the way of this teacher's efforts to build partnership, the support of subsequent principals was critical to the sustained development of school community partnership. This later involvement and support by the principal in the partnership and the principal's critical role in the success of partnerships is consistent with the dominant view in the literature (Hands 2009; Sanders and Harvey 2002).

REFERENCES

Abrams L. S., & Gibbs, J. T. (2002) Disrupting the logic of home-school relations: Parent involvement strategies and practices of inclusion and exclusion. *Urban Education, 37*(3) 384–407.

Auerbach, S. (2010). Beyond coffee with the principal: Toward leadership for authentic school-family partnerships. Paper presented at the 15th International Roundtable on School, Family and Community Partnerships, Denver, CO.

Bauch, P. A. & Goldring, E. B. (1995). Parent involvement and school readiness: Facilitating the home-school connection in schools of choice. *Educational Evaluation and Policy Analysis, 17*(1), 1–21.

Bryk, A. S., Lee, V. E., & Holland P. B. (1993). *Catholic schools and the common good.* Cambridge, MA: Harvard University Press.

Bryk, A. S., & Schneider, B. (2002). *Trust in schools: A core resource for improvement.* New York: Russell Sage Foundation.

Crozier, G. (1999). Is it a case of 'We know when we're not wanted'? The parents' perspective on parent-teacher roles and relationships. *Educational Research, 41*(3) 315–328.

Crozier, G. (2001). Excluded parents: The deracialization of parental involvement. *Race, Ethnicity and Education, 4*(4) 329–341.

Crozier, G., & Davies, J. (2007). Hard to reach parents or hard to reach schools? A discussion of home-school relations, with particular reference to Bangladeshi and Pakistani parents. *British Educational Journal, 33*(3) 295–313.

Cucchiara, M., & Horvat, E. M. (2009). Perils and promises: Middle-class parental involvement in urban schools. *American Educational Research Journal, 46,* 974–1004.

Cutler, W. W. (2000). *Parents and schools: The 150 year struggle for control in American education.* Chicago: University of Chicago Press.

Davis, D. (2005). Elementary teachers' perception of the sustainability of selected school reform: Ten years of school reform. Unpublished doctoral dissertation. Pepperdine University, Malibu, CA.

Delgado-Gaitan, C. (1991). Involving parents in the schools: A process of empowerment. *American Journal of Education* (November), 20–46.

Diamond, J. B., & Gomez, K. (2004). African American parents' educational orientations. *Education and Urban Society, 36*(4), 383–427.

Edelberg, J., & Kurland, S. (2009). *How to walk to school: Blueprint for a neighborhood renaissance.* New York: Rowman and Littlefield.

Epstein, J. (1995). Caring for the children we share. *Phi Delta Kappan, 76*(9), 701–712.

Epstein, J. (2001). Building bridges of home, school and community: The importance of design. *Journal of Education for Students Placed at Risk, 6*(1&2), 161–168.

Epstein, J. L., & Sheldon, S. B. (2002). Improving student behavior and school discipline with family and community involvement. *Education and Urban Society, 35*(1), 4–26.

Goldring, E. (1993). Principals, parents and administrative superiors. *Educational Administration Quarterly, 29*(1), 93–117.

Hands, C. M. (2009). Architect, advocate, coach and conciliator: The multiple roles of school leaders in the establishment of school–community partnerships and the impact of social context. In K. Anderson (Ed.), *The leadership compendium: Emerging scholars in Canadian educational leadership* (pp. 193–213). Fredericton, NB: Atlantic Centre for Educational Administration and Leadership.

Henderson, A. T., & Mapp, K. L. (2002) A new wave of evidence; The impact of school, family, and community connections on student achievement. Southwest Educational Development Laboratory. Austin TX: National Center for Family & Community Connections with Schools.

Hiatt-Michael, D. (2006). Reflections and directions on research related to family-community involvement in schooling. *The School Community Journal, 16*(1), 7–30.

Hiatt-Michael, D. B. (2008). Families, their children's education and the public school: An historical review. *Marriage and Family Review, 43*(1), 39–66.

Horvat, E.M., Curci, J.D., & Partlow, M.C. (2010). Parents, principals and power: A historical case study of "managing" parental involvement. *Journal of School Leadership, 20*(6), 702–727.

Jeynes, W. (2007). The relationship between parent involvement and urban secondary school achievement: A meta analysis. *Urban Education, 42*(1) 82–110.

Lareau, A. (2000). *Home advantage: Social class and parental intervention in elementary education.* Lanham, MD: Rowman & Littlefield Publishers.

Lareau A. (2003). *Unequal childhoods: Class, race and family life.* Berkeley, CA: University of California Press.

Lareau, A., & Horvat, E. M. (1999). Moments of social inclusion and exclusion: Race, class, and cultural capital in family–school relationships. *Sociology of Education, 72*(1), 37–53.

Lareau, A. & Munoz, V. (2010). Parents are not going to call the shots: Class and parent involvement in schooling. Paper presented at the Annual Meeting of the American Sociological Association, Atlanta, GA.

Leithwood, K., & Jantzi, D. (2006, January). A critical review of the parent engagement literature. Final report. Toronto, Ontario, Canada: Ontario Ministry of Education.

Lewis, A. E., & Forman, T. A. (2002). Contestation or collaboration? A comparative study of home-school relations. *Anthropology and Education Quarterly, 33*(1), 60–89.

Lopez, G. R., Scriber, J. D., & Mahitivanichcha, K. (2001). Redefining parental involvement: Lessons from high-performing migrant-impacted schools. *American Educational Research Journal, 38*(2), 253–288.

Sanders, M. G. (1999). Schools' programs and progress in the national network of partnership schools. *The Journal of Educational Research, 92*(4), 220–229.

Sanders, M. G., & Harvey, A. (2002). Beyond the school walls: A case study of principal leadership for school–community collaboration. *Teachers College Record, 104*(7), 1345–1368.

Stanton-Salazar, R. (2001) *Manufacturing hope and despair: The school and kin support networks of U.S.-Mexican youth.* New York: Teacher's College Press.

Sugrue, T. J. (2005). *The origins of the urban crisis: Race and inequality in postwar Detroit.* Princeton: Princeton University Press.

VanVoorhis, F. & Sheldon S. (2005) Principals roles in the development of US programs of school, family and community partnerships. *International Journal of Educational Research, 41*(1), 55–70.

Walker, V. S. (1996). *Their highest potential: An African American school community in the segregated South.* Chapel Hill, NC: University of North Carolina Press.

Waller, W.W. (1932). *The sociology of teaching.* New York: J. Wiley & sons.

Weiss, H., B. Bouffard, S. M., Bridglall, B. L., & Gordon, E. W. (2009). Reframing family involvement in education: Supporting families to support educational equity. Equity Matters: Research Review No. 5. New York: Teachers College Columbia.

Wilson, W. J. (1987). *The truly disadvantaged: The inner city, the underclass and public policy.* Chicago: University of Chicago Press.

PART III

AGENCY

CHAPTER 9

THE MATH/SCIENCE EQUITY PROJECT

Working With Educators to Increase African American Parental Involvement in Secondary Math and Science Course Placements

Roslyn A. Mickelson and Linwood H. Cousins

ABSTRACT

In this chapter, Roslyn Mickelson and Linwood Cousins examine the Math/Science Equity Project (MSEP), and its impact on educators, school cultures, and parental involvement as it intersects with the social organization of schooling. MSEP was designed to address tracking and how tracking affects the race gap in math and science achievement, by enhancing the participation of African American parents in their children's secondary school math and science course selections and placements. The authors describe MSEP and examine both the accomplishments and the struggles of the program in the communities of three high schools and their feeder middle schools in Charlotte, North Carolina. They found that the parents who participated resoundingly embraced the program's main intervention—the series of parental enrichment workshops. Post-workshop interviews indicated MSEP's enrichment

Including Families and Communities in Urban Education, pages 189–211
Copyright © 2011 by Information Age Publishing

workshops began to level a very uneven playing field because the workshops provided African American parents with the information, networks, and negotiation skills they typically did not possess but that many white, middle class parents already had and often used to their children's advantage. The authors report important lessons learned from this case study and outline strategic implications for future work in the intersection among African American parents, communities, and public educators.

The pervasive practice of curricular differentiation (tracking and ability grouping) sorts students into educational trajectories soon after they enter school (Kornhaber, 1997; Lucas, 1999; Oakes, 2005). As early as elementary school, most children are placed into ability groups for instruction in reading and mathematics. The process of identifying students for placement in gifted and special educational programs also begins at this time (Eitle, 2002; Kornhaber, 1997). Ideally, tracks or ability groups are designed to match students' abilities with a differentiated curriculum and instruction (Hallinan, 1992; Kulik & Kulik, 1987; Loveless, 1999). Within a given track, however, there is a wide range of student abilities. Often, a teacher's recommendation to place a student in a given ability group is based on the teacher's perception about that student's potential ability, a perception that may be influenced by stereotypes, teacher beliefs about different racial and class groups, or—in some instances—racist ideologies (Mickelson, 2001, 2003b; Oakes, Muir, & Joseph, 2000; Welner, 2001). Consequently, students with similar abilities are often assigned to different tracks.

The Math/Science Equity Project (MSEP) was a program designed to narrow the black-white gap in mathematics and science achievement in the Charlotte-Mecklenburg Schools (CMS) and to serve as a model for other urban minority communities struggling with racial gaps in academic outcomes. MSEP's point of entry into addressing the achievement gap was racially correlated tracking in math and science courses where black youth disproportionately learn in lower level tracks. MSEP was built around community workshops designed to enhance the involvement of black parents in their adolescent children's mathematics and science course placement process. The underlying logic of the intervention linked greater agency and empowerment through enhanced knowledge of the operations of the school system, parents' educational rights, mathematics and science concepts, and the course selection process to greater parental involvement. The logic of the program, extrapolated from findings reported in the literature (c.f., Epstein, 2002; Lareau, 2003; Lareau & Horvat, 1999), further assumed that informed, assertive, black parents would be more likely to push their children to enroll in more rigorous science and mathematics classes (Lareau, 2003; Lareau & Horvat, 1999; Williams, 2003). Greater black student enrollment in higher-level courses would, in turn, contribute to closing the achievement gap.

From 2002 through 2005, MSEP offered parents, educators, and community activists a concrete intervention that enabled them to eliminate racially correlated access to opportunities to learn in CMS. MSEP focused upon parental involvement as it intersects with the social organization of schooling, specifically tracking. Racially correlated tracking is a substantial contributing factor to the race gap in math and science achievement (Blau, Stearns & Lippman, 2003; Mickelson, 2001; Southworth & Mickelson, 2007). Black students are much less likely than their otherwise comparable white or Asian peers to be placed in college prep math and science courses during high school. One aspect of the placement gap is parents' role in managing their adolescents' educational careers, especially the academic course selection and placement process. MSEP was designed to enhance the participation of black students in college prep courses by empowering their parents' greater participation in the secondary school math and science course selections and placements.

MSEP was offered to families in the communities of three high schools and their feeder middle schools. The parental enrichment workshops provided participants with information about secondary school mathematics and science course sequences and their relationship to postsecondary education and professional careers. Parents also learned about their educational rights under the North Carolina constitution, they engaged in hands-on mathematics and science activities, and participated in role playing activities designed to enhance their sense of agency by equipping them to manage their children's educational careers. MSEP offered critical informational support about secondary course tracking practices, strategies for effectively engaging school officials, and informal network supports to black CMS parents who likely would not otherwise have had access to these.

Interviews with graduates of the program indicated that parents who participated in MSEP resoundingly embraced the program's parental enrichment workshops. Parent graduates of MSEP reported that the program directly contributed to their sense of what they were entitled to do as parents and motivated them to become more involved in their children's education. In these ways, MSEP was successful. MSEP encountered mixed success in recruiting parents to participate in the workshops, in retaining families throughout the process, and in obtaining follow-up interviews with parents who completed the program. Nevertheless, the findings from the follow-up interviews we collected indicate MSEP's enrichment workshops began to level a very uneven playing field. The workshops provided black parents with the information, networks, and negotiation skills they typically did not possess but that many white, middle class parents already had and often used to their children's advantage.

This chapter describes MSEP's operations, chronicles the benefits and challenges of collaborating with educators, and assesses the program's accomplishments and struggles. This case study offers strategic implications for future collaborative work among black parents, communities, and public educators. After a brief review of the literature that informed the Math/Science Equity Program's development, we present the background of MSEP and a detailed description. We present the program's organizational structure, the research design of the study, and findings. We conclude by drawing implications for future research, policy, and practice.

THE RELATIONSHIP OF TRACKING AND PARENTAL INVOLVEMENT TO RACIAL INEQUALITY IN EDUCATIONAL PROCESSES AND OUTCOMES

Once students are identified and placed into any program, ability group or level—whether gifted, regular, or special education— the instruction, curricula, and content to which they are exposed begin to differ from the experiences of students in other tracks. Compared to students in lower tracks, students in higher tracks tend to cover more of the formal curriculum each semester, are exposed to more challenging curricula and are taught in ways that encourage higher order thinking than students in lower tracks (Oakes, 2005). As students proceed along a given educational trajectory, the effects of the previous years' differentiated curriculum influence students' transitions to subsequent courses and schools.

The consequences of tracking manifest in both academic and social domains. Educational advantages accumulate for those in the top tracks relative to those in the bottom tracks because of the differences in opportunities to learn. Tracking tends to reinforce the learning problems of educationally disadvantaged students; these students are provided with less effective instructors, who teach the least rigorous curricula using the methods least likely to challenge children to learn (Finley, 1984; Ingersoll, 1999; Loveless, 1999; Lucas, 1999; Mickelson, 2001; Oakes, 2005). The cumulative effects of these differences over the course of students' educational careers contribute to their differential access to the opportunity structure upon completion of their schooling (Kornhaber, 1997; Lucas, 1999; Oakes, 2005).

A growing body of research suggests that tracking practices result in unjustifiable and disproportionate assignment of minority students to lower tracks. Racially stratified tracking and grouping are highly consequential because lower tracks offer far fewer opportunities to learn compared to higher ones. In these ways, racially stratified tracks create a discriminatory cycle of restricted educational opportunities for minorities irrespective of their academic abilities (Lucas, 1999; Lucas & Berends, 2002; Mickelson, 2001; Oakes, 1990; Oakes et al., 2000; Welner, 2001).

A number of scholars and educators recommend detracking as solution to this problem (Burris & Welner 2005; Mehan, Villanueva & Hubbard, 1996; Oakes, 2005; Rubin, 2006). Within the practical and political realities of the Charlotte-Mecklenburg School district, however, wholesale detracking was not a viable political option at the time that MSEP sought to address the racial gaps in mathematics and science course placements. Greater parental involvement in the course selection process emerged as a potential strategy to challenge the racially stratified aspects of tracking. By parental involvement, we are referring to active participation in educational decision-making, course selection, assisting and monitoring homework, or volunteering in the school (Epstein, 2002).

A host of studies show that parental involvement in the course selection and placement process is one key avenue through which differences in family background (socioeconomic status and culture) influence educational processes and outcomes (Epstein, 2002; Ho & Willms, 1996; Lareau 1987, 2003). Race, ethnicity, and social class shape the likelihood and nature of parents' involvement in course selection. White middle class parents are more likely to be involved in their children's education both at home and in school than parents from disadvantaged minority and lower class backgrounds (Chazen, 2000; Epstein, 2002; Moses & Cobb, 2001; Yonezawa, 1997).

To be sure, tracking is rarely done today in an overtly racist manner. In theory, adolescents, their parents, and educators jointly select secondary school courses and their track levels. Ideally, school personnel take into account students' prior performance, test scores and interests when they recommend courses and track levels. Adolescents choose courses, often basing their decisions on their own interests and goals, perceptions of their own abilities, course difficulty, and peer influences (Oakes, 2005; Schmidt, Shumow & Kacker, 2007; Shumow & Lomax, 2002). Parents are the third party in the process, but, in practice, parents' participation is related to their racial and social class backgrounds (Lareau 1987, 2003; Lareau & Horvat 1999). Parents of color and working class parents are less likely than white and middle class parents to have access to the necessary official information, informal social networks, cultural capital, or lived experiences that are increasingly necessary for parents to have in order to guide their children's educational choices (Malen & Cochran, 2008).

School reform efforts to address issues such as these are fraught with social, cultural and political challenges. In as much as universities can partner with schools, parents and communities, real and potential challenges complicate the potential role university representatives can play in addressing issues such as enhancing black parents' knowledge, networks, skills, and sense of empowerment. In the following section, we recount the experiences of one such program, which was a university-school district collaborative partnership created to build parents' and school personnel's agency for student achievement.

BACKGROUND OF THE
MATH/SCIENCE EQUITY PROGRAM (MSEP)

The Math/Science Equity Project (MSEP) was a program designed to narrow the black-white gap in mathematics and science achievement in the Charlotte-Mecklenburg Schools (CMS). MSEP was built around community workshops designed to enhance the involvement of black parents in their adolescent children's mathematics and science course placement and academic track. Charlotte is an interesting community in which to investigate race gaps in math and science outcomes. The community is known for its landmark *Swann v. Charlotte-Mecklenburg Schools* (1971) decision, in which the Supreme Court upheld the use of within-district mandatory busing as a remedy for segregated schooling. For almost 30 years, CMS was regarded as a model of how a school system could provide seemingly equitable, quality, desegregated public education through busing and other means.

While CMS was successfully desegregating schools at the building level, systematic tracking of academic classes resegregated students within schools. Previous survey research on CMS (Mickelson, 2001; 2003a) indicated that while CMS was desegregating its schools from 1975–1992, students were placed in racially correlated tracks throughout all secondary core academic classes within the schools, irrespective of the school's overall racial composition. For example, race differences existed in the probabilities of English course enrollment among CMS students in the four tracks (Regular, Advanced, Academically Gifted, and Advanced Placement/International Baccalaureate), even after controlling for prior achievement. Comparably able blacks and whites were in very different tracks, with whites more than twice as likely as blacks to be assigned to top tracks. This was especially marked in science and mathematics courses (Mickelson, 2001).

Unfortunately, many working-class and non-college-educated parents (who are disproportionately people of color) are less likely to know how to support or encourage their children's interest in science, technology, engineering, or mathematics (Mickelson, Cousins, Williams & Velasco, 2010). The authors reasoned that if black parents enhanced their existing knowledge about math and science coursework, social networks, and the kinds of informal information and official knowledge that middle class white families often share, they could more effectively manage their children's educational careers. Greater proportions of black adolescents would then enroll in higher-level mathematics and science courses. The authors readily acknowledge that institutional and cultural barriers to greater equality of educational opportunity most likely will persist despite this project. Lareau and Horvat (1999) describe moments of inclusion, when parents' efforts to participate in their children's education are favorably received by school officials, and moments of exclusion, when such efforts are thwarted. Keeping these challenges in mind, the MSEP's leadership team designed community-based parent enrichment workshops to enhance and strengthen black parents' social, cultural, and human capital regarding their adolescent children's academic course selection and placements.

MSEP'S HOME WORKSHOPS AND TEEN SUMMITS

MSEP presented its parental enrichment curriculum in three versions over a two-year period. The first version, the HOME Workshop (Helping Ourselves Mold Education), consisted of two-hour meetings held for six consecutive weeks on six consecutive Monday, Wednesday, or Thursday evenings. This amounted to a total of 12 hours of enrichment per workshop series for each participant. The second version, named Teen Summit, delivered the parent enrichment curriculum in four-hour sessions held on two consecutive Saturdays for a total of eight hours of enrichment per workshop series per participant. Another version of Teen Summit was presented on a single Saturday. Post-tests indicated participants found the daylong format tiring. Parents were less enthusiastic and they retained less information than those who attended the other two MSEP formats. The HOME Workshops and Teen Summits were conducted in both community venues (e.g., churches, recreation centers, and libraries) and on the university campus. A Teen Summit once was held on a middle school campus.

The variations in format and sites were introduced in an effort to adapt to the needs of the parents expected to attend the workshops. Each variation represents MSEP's struggle to maintain the delicate balance between the time required for the workshops to be effective and the time parents could practically afford to sacrifice from their busy schedules. The descriptions that follow provide an overview of the MSEP organization and program content in these workshops.

Workshop Curriculum

The parent enrichment curriculum presented at both the six-week HOME Workshops and two-week Teen Summits consisted of:

- Information about Mathematics and Science courses and their value in a student's educational career.

- Hands-on mathematics and science experiences in four gateway courses (Algebra, Geometry, Physics, and Chemistry).
- Curricular tracking and parental involvement in the related decision making processes.
- Parental educational rights, including North Carolina's constitutional guarantee for a sound basic education for all children.
- Strategies for effective parent–educator communications, including the difference between assertive and aggressive communication.
- Strategies for effective parent–child communications.
- Networking skills, particularly, building on existing parental and community networks.

Both the HOME Workshops and Teen Summits were designed to be convenient and flexible for parents. Consequently, all participants and their children were provided with lunch or dinner as well as transportation to and from the workshop. A set of youth workshops (one for students in grades K–6 and another for students in grades 7–12) were also designed to run concurrently with each parent workshop. The youth workshops focused on the development of valuable life skills (i.e., goal-setting and college planning), introduced students to topics in mathematics and science through engaging and culturally relevant experiences, and provided students with opportunities to discuss subjects pertinent to their lives (i.e., hip hop music's influence on youth). No data were collected on student participants other than noting their attendance.

In addition to the actual workshops, MSEP employed a number of other strategies to remain connected to parents and to provide them with additional resources that reinforced initial workshop dynamics. A program newsletter, *Letters from HOME*, was mailed to parents, schools, and community members every two months. The newsletter included articles of specific interest to parents of children in Charlotte-Mecklenburg schools, accessible articles about mathematics and science topics, educational resources in the Charlotte-Mecklenburg community, updates on mathematics and science related events geared to families in the Charlotte area, and information about MSEP. We also established a website at www.msep.uncc.edu (the website remains as an archive of the project), where the newsletters were posted along with extensive information about MSEP and links to other mathematics and science educational sites.

The Groups of Individuals Who Contributed to MSEP

A number of scholars, school personnel, community members and parents contributed their time and expertise to the development of MSEP and the program content.

Leadership and Program Teams. The program team was highly diverse in terms of discipline (sociology, anthropology, social work, and education), gender, and ethnicity. The leadership team was comprised of the Principal Investigators (the authors of this chapter), the Program Director (a postdoctoral fellow), and the Program Manager, while the program team extended beyond that of the leadership team to include university students. Between 2003 and 2006, 17 graduate and undergraduate students were trained as researchers and supported by the program: five black males, five black females, two white males, four white females, and one Indian female served as student research assistants for the program. The diversity of the team was consciously generated in order to reflect the diversity of the community MSEP served.

Community Advisory Council (CAC). The CAC, composed of ten community activists, parents and educators from the neighborhoods feeding into the three treatment site high schools, gave feedback to the leadership team regarding the direction and content of the workshops.

Academic Advisory Board (AAB). Several scholars with specific expertise relevant to the program served on an Academic Advisory Board. The AAB met in January 2003 and in December 2004. The eight members were presented with updates on activities, successes and challenges of the program during each one-and-a-half-day meeting. The AAB offered guidance relative to overcoming the challenges and better meeting the goals and objectives of the program.

Workshop Staff. MSEP hired several CMS educators and community members as consultants when the program staff's own expertise was inadequate. For example, MSEP used the expertise of a high school counselor to develop and teach the course selection and placement curriculum. A CMS physics teacher instructed adolescents in the physics of music during the Teen Summits, and an attorney with expertise in North Carolina educational rights developed the parents' rights curriculum. In all, six consultants provided the additional support necessary for effective programming. With the MSEP program thus described, we now turn to the strategies we used to examine the participants' experiences as a result of the workshops.

RESEARCH DESIGN, METHODS, AND DATA

MSEP was a National Science Foundation-funded research project designed as a quasi-experiment involving three sets of matched CMS high schools. One of the schools in each set served as the treatment site, while the other school in the pair served as the control site (see Mickelson, Cousins, Williams & Velasco, 2010 for details). Treatment and control schools were selected from distinct geographic regions of 525 square miles of Mecklenburg County. Parents of academically able black students in the three treatment high schools were eligible to attend the enrichment program. MSEP staff recruited parents through a variety of means including outreach through churches, community organizations, and school personnel who identified appropriate families based on adolescents' current math and science track and their academic potential. Counselors identified students who could perform better but who did not take challenging classes, and then sent MSEP's invitation to their parents. The most fruitful method of recruiting parents for the workshops, however, was an invitational letter sent to them sent by school counselors. Irrespective of the strategies by which participants were recruited, the parent participants were a self-selected group.

Sample

From early 2004 through late 2005, 99 African American adults (80 females and 19 males) attended at least one MSEP workshop; however, most of this chapter focuses on the 75 adults (61 female and 14 male) who *graduated* from HOME or Teen Summit. Graduation is defined as completing at least four sessions of the six-week HOME program or both days of the Teen Summit. Approximately 65 children age 13 and over and 34 children age 12 and under participated in the youth programs offered by HOME and Teen Summit. Although not all parents provided demographic data, additional attributes of parents who did provide data include 1 homemaker, 1 unemployed parent, 5 self-employed, and an almost even split between parents who held working class jobs (home repair, postal clerk, cafeteria worker, cashier, for example) and middle class/professional jobs or higher (ultrasound technologist, physician, real estate broker, teacher, hotel manager, for example). Additionally, 23 parents reported education of four or more years of college, and 41 parents reported one to three years of college education, including community college.

Only 25 of the potential 75 parent graduates of either HOME or Teen Summit programs for whom the project team had contact information agreed to a follow-up interview. Only 14 of the 25 interviews are used for this chapter. Of the 14 interviewees, 12 were women and 2 were men; 8 were married; 6 were single parents who were divorced or never married; all the women and men (not including spouses) had at least some college. We hypothesized that so few graduates responded to the opportunity to be interviewed because of participant mobility and burnout. Firstly, MSEP's contact information had become outdated, and the staff of interviewers could not contact every participant. Of those who were contacted, parents who had been excited about the program immediately after the workshops seemed to lose interest by the time they were asked to participate in the follow-up interviews. Table 9.1 presents the number of participants in various MSEP activities.

TABLE 9.1   Sample Characteristics

Subsamples Participating in Various MSEP Activities	N
Adults participating in at least one MSEP parent workshop	99
Adults graduating from HOME or Teen Summit	75
Children participating in youth programs	99
Graduates agreeing to follow-up interviews	25
Graduates completing full interviews	14

Data

One of three interview protocols was used for each of the 14 follow-up interviews with parents who participated in the workshops during the 2005–2006 academic year. MSEP developed the protocols to capture varying degrees of details about post-MSEP parental involvement activities, perceptions of the program's utility, and parents' future plans to engage and monitor their children's education. We also draw upon extensive field notes taken during community meetings, CAC meetings, HOME workshops and the Teen Summits. Interviews were tape recorded and transcribed. Analysis of the interviews and field notes followed qualitative research protocols.

Our approach was inductive in that we closely analyzed the interview responses to identify and code emerging themes and categories. Drawing from grounded theory (Glasser & Strauss, 1967), we explored and interpreted themes and categories by: a) immersing ourselves in the interview responses; b) moving back and forth between the application of existing theories and explanatory models and the exploration of new theories and models based on what emerged from the data (Berg, 2009); and c) focusing on sociopolitical and sociocultural contexts and the manifest and latent meaning of events. We analyzed the interview responses by conducting a content analysis of them to identify the themes and categories (Bernard, 2002; Maxwell, 1996) that were related to our inquiry. In addition, we focused on the interpersonal histories of each participant and the ways in which the histories reflected racial, social class and gender identities and motivations regarding educational aspirations within the participant's family. For example, in asking an open-ended question about the "role a parent should play in their child's education," respondents often gave a response about what they believe and why they believe it, sometimes interspersed with how they arrived at their beliefs.

Our analysis rested theoretically on the parent involvement literature as it intersects with educational research on race and social class (Barbarin, McCandies, Coleman & Hill, 2005; Brandon, 2007; Lareau, 2003; Lareau & Horvat, 1999). For example, Lareau and Horvat (1999) describe how during parent-school interactions, parents' distinctive cultural capital inter-acts with certain organizational and cultural systems in schools in ways that create what they call "moments of inclusion" and "moments of exclusion." This framework guided us in developing MSEP's curriculum to empower parents to maximize moments of inclusion. It also helped to guide our anal-ysis of the follow-up interviews. We report our findings below.

FINDINGS

Our findings focus on responses to two aspects of a central question: What happened when MSEP personnel and parent graduates of HOME and Teen Summit workshops attempted to work with school counselors, teachers, prin-cipals and other school officials? One aspect entails the support parents and MSEP received in response to their involvement with schools. The second aspect addresses the barriers that thwarted parent and MSEP involvement. In this chapter, we focus more on the former than the latter half of this issue because we have addressed barriers and challenges elsewhere (see Cousins, Mickelson, Williams & Velasco, 2008). We organize our findings into sec-tions about educator responses to MSEP parents' greater involvement, edu-cator cooperation with MSEP, and educator tensions with MSEP.

MSEP Parents' Greater Involvement

The follow-up interviews with the parents who completed MSEP work-shops investigated if they had been in touch with school officials, teachers and or staff since completing the workshop, if they had used any of the workshop material (i.e., parent involvement strategies, curriculum con-tent), and, if so, what were the outcomes of their interactions with educa-tors? The responses of the parents suggest not only that many of them be-came highly involved, but also that they gained access to the school officials who had the most influence on matters of course selection and placement (see Table 9.2). Equally important, school officials were largely accessible, responsive, and cooperative. For example, when asked whether they talked to school officials about course selection and placement in general, all in-terviewees said they had used MSEP content related to course selection and placement. Nine parents said they used strategies learned in the workshop about effectively communicating with school officials to either get infor-mation about courses or request that their children be placed in different courses. In several cases, the parents contacted several school faculty or staff members. For example, one parent reported a contact with a teacher, a

TABLE 9.2 Number and Type of Educator Contacts Among MSEP Graduates

Educator	N of Contacts
Teachers	12
Guidance Counselors	12
Principals	6
Vice Principals	6
AVID Coordinators	3
Math Coordinator	1
Parent Advocate	1
School Social Worker	1

principal and the AVID coordinator. Thus, the number of parent-educator contacts (42) exceeds the number of parents interviewed (14).

Interviews indicated that parents generally received what they wanted in their interactions with schools, although sometimes only after they asserted their "parental rights" and used other strategies they learned in the workshops. The excerpts below illustrate the nature of the parents' and school personnel's interactions.[1]

- Ms. Battle telephoned her child's guidance counselor who communicated with her via email about moving her child to a different math course. Ms. Battle received suggestions from her child's teachers about what the student could work on over the summer and about different classes the student could take in the coming academic year.
- Ms. Carrier's contacts have primarily been with the guidance counselor who "really answers just about everything, and once I talk to her, I see results. Like as far as their schedule and placing children in French for the foreign language [requirement]."
- Ms. Nielson's contact with the band instructor and guidance counselor helped to resolve a discrepancy about her child being in concert band or marching band. Both educators communicated with the parent, listened to her concerns, and answered her questions.
- Ms. Henderson reported that she had a collective meeting with her child's teachers and had spoken the day before to the guidance counselor. She let the teachers know what she needed, and they developed a strategy to better communicate with her and her child. As a result, her child's grades improved.
- Ms. Dennis had contacts with a science teacher. "She's been real good. She sends out emails and is real good with communication."

- Ms. Jenson stayed in contact with her child's math teacher by email. She found that teachers respond more quickly to emails. She was motivated to meet with several teachers as a result of the workshop, especially after she found out her right to meet with them and make decisions about her child's education. She said the meeting was

    > positive. [My child] still needed a whole lot of work, but it was positive and everybody just jumped on it. They were willing to help. At first I think they were a little defensive because they didn't know what I was coming in with since I called everybody together. And when they saw that I came asking for help, it was very powerful and we got stuff accomplished.

- Ms. Benjamin contacted her child's guidance counselor. She recalled "going back and forth" to get her child in a "certain course." The guidance counselor said no to a particular class and Ms. Benjamin, as a result of workshop content on parent rights, invoked her rights as a parent, telling the counselor she knew that " yes, her child *could* enroll in the course in question." As a result of Ms. Benjamin's efforts, the student enrolled in the higher-level course that the parent requested based on her familiarity with the proper math sequence for prospective college students.

The above accounts highlight a number of our findings. First, we noted that parents acted on rights they learned they during MSEP workshops. Second, acting on their rights meant that parents had to become engaged in the school. Our findings are consistent with previous research that shows that becoming involved in their children's schools offered benefits to the school, parent, community, and the child (c.f., Epstein, 2002). Finally, in many instances, the parents were able to get desired results—a change of course placement, a sense of caring from the educators, and, perhaps, a sense of empowerment in experiencing themselves as capable of fostering change in their own lives.

Educator Cooperation with the MSEP Program

School officials cooperated with MSEP in three stages to deliver the project. First, they agreed to let MSEP recruit prospective parent participants at their schools. Doing this meant their counselors and office staff provided MSEP with strategic support. Second, the teachers, counselors and coordinators actively participated as MSEP staff, planning workshops and delivering some aspects of workshop curriculum. Third, after the completion of the workshops, teachers and other schools officials responded to the efforts of MSEP parents who attempted to become more involved in their children's education (as described in the previous section).

At the district level, MSEP received general support from the CMS superintendent of schools, school board members, and several associate superintendents. The authors met with the superintendent prior to beginning the project in order to inform him of the goals and design of the project. He approved of the project and directed us to key school personnel. He expressed interest in discussing our prospective findings and, if appropriate, incorporating them into then-forthcoming parent involvement and course selection and placement activities in CMS at large. Several members of the school board provided broad support to MSEP by describing the sociopolitical issues in the school system. They offered to state their support to the superintendent, to midlevel CMS bureaucrats, and to community members who might be critical stakeholders in MSEP's implementation (see Hands, 2005, 2009, 2010 for a discussion of the importance of educator cooperation with parental involvement overtures).

At the school level (particularly in the middle and high schools that were part of our research design), most middle and high school principals supported our work, gave us access to their schools (i.e., teachers, staff, and site), and assisted us by permitting their clerical staff to mail invitations to parents identified as prospective participants in MSEP workshops. A number of them were initially cautious about our work due to politically volatile issues related to school racial inequality in Charlotte. Teachers and coordinators were also supportive, but in more direct ways. Several teachers, coordinators and school social workers assisted MSEP in recruiting parents, developing and implementing workshop curricula on math and science, the course selection and placement process, and suggesting strategies for parents to effectively interact with school officials on behalf of their children.

Educator Tensions with the MSEP Program

MSEP's relationships with CMS educators were not without tensions. The vast majority of building-level and district-level administrators were supportive, but those who were not posed serious obstacles to MSEP's success. For example, a principal of a middle school was unwilling to support MSEP because he believed the team was led by a white person, and that African American personnel were "fronts" for the real program leader. In his view, white people's interests were, once again, being pursued at the expense of the interests of African Americans. For this individual, MSEP's affiliation with UNC-Charlotte, a "white university", only compounded his negative image of MSEP (for a complete discussion of thwarted parent involvement and the other challenges presented by community members and school officials, see Cousins et al., 2008). In fact, MSEP was co-led by one white and one African American professor, and the postdoctoral fellow who designed and taught the science and mathematics portions of the parent workshops was an African American male. The majority of the student research assistants, parent, school, and community staff members were people of color.

The associate superintendent responsible for research and accountability presented a more systematic obstacle to MSEP's implementation. The project initially received tepid support from her. Among the reasons for her equivocal support was her concern for potentially damaging findings from our project about race disparities and inequality in course selection and placement due to the pervasive tracking practices in CMS. She approved MSEP's collaboration on parent recruitment with target schools and their personnel as long as their principals supported the project. After one year of MSEP's operation, she changed her mind and required MSEP leaders to obtain her office's formal approval of the project before school personnel—even at schools where we had successfully worked during the prior 12 months—were permitted to continue collaborating with MSEP on further parental recruitment. We applied for formal CMS approval for our project. In 2004, CMS's research approval process typically took four weeks. In MSEP's case, approval inexplicably took over three months. The lengthy approval process delayed MSEP's collaborative recruitment efforts for several months, damaging the project's momentum.

DISCUSSION, IMPLICATIONS AND CONCLUSION

Whether by design or unintended consequence, academic tracking and ability grouping result in children of color and students from lower income families learning in lower tracks compared to their white and middle class peers. Greater parental involvement can potentially increase the numbers of academically able students from working-class backgrounds and students of color who are placed in higher tracks.

Yet all parents are not equally equipped—in terms of experience, knowledge, willingness, and sense of empowerment—for effective engagement with school personnel on either the course selection or placement process. Prior research has indicated that certain parents—typically middle class whites—are more likely to have negotiation skills, education, and network connections that mesh with school practices and policies (Lareau, 1987; 2003). These parents utilize their assets in ways that contribute to the disproportionate middle-class white student enrollment in top ability groups and tracks.

Our findings suggest that African American parents see a world in which being African American means one is unlikely to get the best information or best opportunities in schooling, that success in the schooling of African American children requires the persistence of parents, and parents have to make one's child the top priority to "make success" in schooling (Mickelson, Cousins, Williams & Velasco, 2010).

Minority parents are more likely than middle class white parents to defer to educators' decisions about their children's course placement (Lareau & Horvat, 1999; Oakes, 2005). Minority parents do so because they often assume that educators' professional expertise trumps their own knowledge and experiences, and that they should not—or could not—advocate for a higher track placement for their child. Working class parents of color—especially those with limited English language proficiency—are the least likely of all parents to feel they have the relevant knowledge, language skills, or sense of empowerment necessary to effectively become involved in school decisions or to question school personnel (Oakes, Wells, Jones & Datnow, 1997; Yonezawa, 1997). Powerful, well-educated school administrators and teachers intimidate parents whose own educational experiences may have been unsatisfactory.

MSEP leadership reasoned that if black parents could enhance their knowledge and networks with the valuable informal and formal knowledge of schooling, they would be prepared to challenge practices that hamper their children academically—particularly in areas related to mathematics and science tracking. As a result, more black adolescents would enroll in and complete advanced mathematics and science courses (see Hoover-Dempsey, Bassler & Burow, 1995; Hoover-Dempsey & Sandler, 1995; 1997; Walker, Wilkins, Dallaire, Sandler & Hoover-Dempsey, 2005 for a discussion of the underlying model upon which we based these expectations). In an effort to facilitate this behavior, MSEP designed and implemented a set of community-based parent workshops aimed at providing a space for black parents to better understand and develop the necessary social, cultural, and human capital as well as the formal knowledge related to the schooling of their children. MSEP's workshops attempted to empower parents to be assertive, knowledgeable advocates for their children's educational careers, specifically by advocating for their sons and daughters to enroll in college preparatory tracks and advanced courses in mathematics and science.

School officials and administrators varied in their support of parent involvement and MSEP's activities. The CMS superintendent, some of his associates, and just about all principals, teachers and school staff in our project's target schools were supportive of the project. They explicitly gave their assurance that they would work with African American parents to improve parent involvement in general and math and science course selection and placement for African American children in particular. Many school-level officials and staff actually worked with MSEP as workshop instructors and developers to assure parent success. School-level staff worked with MSEP to recruit parents, and principals offered their buildings as sites for the workshops.

At the same time, several strategically placed individuals' distrust of MSEP personnel and the project, or fears that an open discussion of the systematic racial inequality in CMS would trigger hostile racial dynamics in certain communities thwarted the project's momentum, and ultimately, its ability to fully reach its target population. Although MSEP operated in a collaborative and constructive a manner, we still met official resistance to our efforts from some sectors of the CMS educational bureaucracy. Our curricular materials explicitly challenged the school system's "business-as-usual" approach to math and science enrollments. We do not minimize the political aspects of our research, especially as it relates to our effort to address race disparities and inequality in education. But as a bona fide research project, we sought to address issues that are uncomfortable and politically sensitive. To do otherwise would have left a source of educational inequality untouched.

Moreover, the dynamic of resistance around racial inequality in opportunities to learn took a different spin in the actions of several principals and district-level administrators. Although these educators were African Americans, they resisted MSEP as well as the level of parent involvement MSEP advanced. The desire to control public impressions of their school, information, and resources—which MSEP sought to address in the sociopolitical and sociocultural context of race and class relations in Charlotte—was as important to African American school administrators and staff as it was to white administrators (Cousins et al., 2008).

Implications

As this chapter illustrates, MSEP-type partnerships face barriers because many inequitable school processes, like tracking, are powerful mechanisms for maintaining the social, cultural and economic status quo that privileges some sectors of the community (Burris & Welner, 2005; Welner, 1999). We believe that at a macro level, MSEP-type university partnerships with parents, schools and communities can challenge and weaken such barriers and can effectively blunt the unintended consequences of school processes, like tracking, which exclude and disenfranchise some students, parents, and communities from full and equal participation in the educational process.

Our experiences in MSEP and CMS exposed the status quo nature of tracking and how tracking seems to be taken for granted, as a sort of "yeah it's there but we can't do anything about it" kind of phenomenon. At the same time, many teachers and administrators were eager to help MSEP, even though they were not sure of the program's direction or outcomes;

they were aware that some aspects of the educational system's status quo needed to challenged. Similarly, while parents and community members with whom we worked in MSEP were aware of tracking at some level (in that they did not see many African American children in college preparatory math and science courses), they appeared to believe they had little recourse except to say "it's racism." This seems to be how the power and perseverance of mechanisms of inequality such as tracking wear people down and suppress their expectations and hopes. Initial MSEP workshops were filled with such conversations among parents. After completing HOME workshops or Teen Summits, parents expressed a sense of their own capacities to effect change for their own children.

MSEP's largest shortcoming was the project's inability to systematically eliminate tracking in CMS's math and science courses. It also fell short of its goal of widespread community involvement and universal acceptance across the district. Some CMS educators welcomed the program because they believed in it; others saw its potential to improve students' outcomes on factors for which they and their schools were to be held accountable. For a minority of administrators, fear of change, distrust of "the other," or an unwillingness to challenge the status quo made their cooperation with MSEP impossible. At the same time, there is a silver lining for MSEP-type partnerships that focus on re-educating parents and others to circumvent and penetrate resistance to their educational rights and needs. Indeed, the conversations with parents during the follow-up interviews that we reported earlier were filled with parents' optimism, hope and a sense of new possibilities in relationship to their children's educational trajectories. As the follow-up interviews illustrated, parents were able to discuss their life histories and their motivations and expectations regarding their children. And perhaps more important, they described what they believed about education and what they practiced with their children regarding schooling. They shared with us their views on "their rights," new-found opportunities, and their accomplishments in engaging the schools on behalf of their children.

So, while wholesale detracking is not an option in CMS at the moment, our work in MSEP offers realistic hope and optimism for change. In the space between tracking and detracking lies numerous interim outcomes. MSEP demonstrated that parents, community members, and educators working together can expand some opportunities to learn math and science for a limited number of students previously marginalized from rigorous curricula because of racially correlated tracking. Participating parents gained confidence and skills, and as a consequence they were more likely to enroll their child in higher-level secondary math and science courses.

Despite the strengths and initial accomplishments of MSEP, it remains unclear as to what short- or long-term institutional effects MSEP has had on the core dilemma that prompted the program in the first place: racially correlated enrollments in college-prep mathematics and science courses. Some critics might say that making tracking work better for minority students misses the point: tracking hurts all students while it fosters white, middle-class educational privilege by excluding many working class and most students of color from rigorous college-prep classes (Welner, 2001). Therefore, tracking and ability grouping need to be eliminated, not made to operate more fairly. Such arguments have a great deal of merit.

While tracking remains virtually a universal feature of the structure of schooling, MSEP's parent enhancement workshops held the potential to be one component of a larger effort to reform public education in a more equitable direction while improving outcomes for the students whose parents participated in the program. MSEP appears to have altered the balance of power in the school-home-community sphere for the 99 adults who were involved in the program. Empowered black parents directly challenged racially disparate educational outcomes rooted in the race gaps in higher-level track enrollments. Although much more remains to be done before the race gaps in science and mathematics course enrollment and achievement are closed, MSEP's contribution was far from trivial for the families in Charlotte, North Carolina who participated in it.

NOTES

1. The names are pseudonyms to protect the participants' confidentiality.

REFERENCES

Barbarin, O., McCandies, T., Coleman, C., & Hill, N. (2005). Family practices and school performance of African American children. In V. McLoyd, & K. Dodge (Eds.), *African American family life: Ecological and cultural diversity* (pp. 227–244). New York: The Guilford Press.

Berg, B. L. (2009). *Qualitative research methods for the social sciences.* Boston: Allyn Bacon.

Bernard, H. R. (2002). *Research methods in anthropology: Qualitative and quantitative approaches.* New York: Altamira Press.

Blau, J. R., Stearns, E., & Lippman, S. (2003). Tracking the curricula. In J. Blau (Ed.), *Race in the schools: Perpetuating white dominance?* (pp. 133–158). New York: Lynne Rienner.

Brandon, R. (2007). African American parents: Improving connections with their child's educational environment. *Intervention in School and Clinic, 43*(2), 116–120.

Burris, C., & Welner, K. (2005). Closing the achievement gap by detracking. *Phi Delta Kappan, 86*(8), 594–598.

Chazen, D. (2000). *Beyond formulas in mathematics and teaching: Dynamics of the high school algebra classroom.* New York: Teachers College Press.

Cousins, L., Mickelson, R., Williams, B., & Velasco, A. (2008). Class and race challenges to community collaboration for educational change. *School Community Journal, 18*(2), 29–52.

Eitle, T. M. (2002). Special education or racial segregation: Understanding variation in the representation of Black students in educable mentally handicapped programs. *The Sociological Quarterly, 43,* 575–605.

Epstein, J. L. (2002). *School, Family, and community partnerships: Your handbook for action* (2nd ed.). Thousand Oaks, CA: Corwin.

Finley, M. (1984). Teachers and tracking in a comprehensive high school. *Sociology of Education, 57,* 233–243.

Glasser, B., & Strauss, A. (1967). *The Discovery of grounded theory.* New York: Sociology Press.

Hallinan, M. T. (1992). The organization of students for instruction in the middle school. *Sociology of Education, 65,* 114–127.

Hands, C. (2005). It's who you know and what you know: The process of creating partnerships between schools and communities. *The School Community Journal, 15*(2), 63–84.

Hands, C. M. (2009). Architect, advocate, coach and conciliator: The multiple roles of school leaders in the establishment of school–community partnerships and the impact of social context. In K. Anderson (Ed.), *The leadership compendium: Emerging scholars in Canadian educational leadership* (pp. 193–213). Fredericton, NB: Atlantic Centre for Educational Administration and Leadership.

Hands, C. M. (2010). Why collaborate? The differing reasons for secondary school educators' establishment of school–community partnerships. *School Effectiveness and School Improvement,* 12 February, 1–19.

Ho, S. E., & Willms, J. D. (1996). Effects of parental involvement on eighth-grade achievement. *Sociology of Education, 69,* 126–141.

Hoover-Dempsey, K. V., Bassler, O. C., & Burow, R. (1995). Parents' reported involvement in students' homework: Strategies and practices. *Elementary School Journal, 95,* 435–450.

Hoover-Dempsey, K. V., & Sandler, H. M. (1995). Parental involvement in children's education: Why does it make a difference? *Teachers College Record, 97,* 310–331.

Hoover-Dempsey, K. V., & Sandler, H. M. (1997). Why do parents become involved in their children's education? *Review of Educational Research, 67,* 3–42.

Ingersoll, R. (1999). The problem of underqualified teachers in American secondary schools. *Educational Researcher, 28,* 26–37.

Kornhaber, M. L. (1997). *Seeking strengths: Equitable identification for gifted education and the theory of multiple intelligences.* Unpublished doctoral dissertation, Department of Sociology, Harvard University, Cambridge, MA.

Kulik, C. L., & Kulik, J. (1987). Effects of ability grouping on student achievement. *Equity and Excellence, 23,* 22–30.

Lareau, A. (1987). *Home advantage.* New York: Falmer.

Lareau, A. (2003). *Unequal childhoods.* Berkeley: University of California Press.

Lareau, A., & Horvat, E. M. (1999). Moments of social inclusion and exclusion: Race, class, and cultural capital in family–school relationships. *Sociology of Education, 72,* 37–53.

Loveless, T. (1999). *The tracking wars.* Washington, DC: Brookings Institution.

Lucas, S. R. (1999). *Tracking inequality*. New York: Teachers College Press.

Lucas, S. R., & Berends, M. (2002). Sociodemographic diversity, correlated achievement, and de facto tracking. *Sociology of Education, 75*, 34–55.

Malen, B., & Cochran, M. (2008). Beyond pluralistic patterns of power: Research on the micropolitics of schools. In B. Cooper, J. Cibulka, & M. Fusarelli (Eds.), *Handbook of Education Politics and Policy* (pp. 148–161). New York: Routledge.

Maxwell, J. A. (1996). *Qualitative Research Design: An interactive approach.* Thousand Oaks: Sage Publications.

Mehan, H., Villanueva, I., & Hubbard, L. (1996). *Constructing School Success: The Consequences of Untracking Low Achieving Students.* New York: Cambridge University Press.

Mickelson, R. A. (2001). Subverting Swann: First and second generation segregation in the Charlotte-Mecklenburg Schools. *American Educational Research Journal, 38*, 215–252.

Mickelson, R.A. (2003a). Achieving the educational opportunity in the wake of the judicial retreat from race sensitive remedies: Lessons from North Carolina. *American University Law Review, 52*(6), 152–184.

Mickelson, R.A. (2003b) When are racial disparities in education the result of discrimination? A social science perspective. *Teachers College Record, 105*(6),1052–1086.

Mickelson, R. A., Cousins, L., Williams, B., & Velasco, A. (2010). Taking math & science to Black parents: Promises and challenges of a community-based intervention for educational change. In Carol C. Yeakey & William Tate, (Eds.), *Schools, neighborhoods, and social inequality.* Washington, DC: American Educational Research Association.

Moses, R. & Cobb, E.C. (2001). *Radical equations: Math literacy and civil rights.* Boston: Beacon Press.

Oakes, J. (1990). *Multiplying inequalities: The effects of race, social class, and tracking on opportunities to learn mathematics and science.* Santa Monica, CA: RAND.

Oakes, J. (2005). *Keeping track* (2nd ed.). New Haven, CT: Yale University.

Oakes, J., Muir, K., & Joseph, R. (2000, May). *Course taking and achievement in math and science: Inequalities that endure and change.* Paper presented at the National Institute for Science Education Conference, Detroit, MI.

Oakes, J., Wells, A., Jones, M., & Datnow, A. (1997). Detracking: The social construction of ability, cultural politics, and resistance to reform. *Teachers College Record, 98*, 34–59.

Rubin, B. C. (2006). Tracking and detracking: Debates, evidence, and best practices. *Theory into Practice 45*(1), 4–14.

Schmidt, J., Shumow, L., & Kackar, H. (2007). Adolescents' participation in service activities and its impact on academic, behavioral, and civic outcomes. *Journal of Youth and Adolescence, 36*, 127–140.

Shumow, L., & Lomax, R. (2002). Parental efficacy: Predictor of parenting behavior and adolescent outcomes. *Parenting: Science and Practice, 2*, 127–150.

Southworth, S., & Mickelson, R. A. (2007). The interactive effects of race, gender, and high school racial composition on college track placement. *Social Forces, 82*(2), 497–523.

Swann v. Charlotte-Mecklenburg. 402 U.S. 1,15 (1971).

Walker, J., Wilkins, A., Dallaire, J., Sandler, H., Hoover-Dempsey, K. (2005). Parental involvement: Model revision through scale development. *The Elementary School Journal, 106,* 85–105.

Welner, K. G. (2001). *Legal rights, local wrongs: When community control collides with educational equity.* Albany, NY: SUNY Press.

Williams, B. (2003). *Charting the pipeline: Exploring the critical factors in the development of successful African American scientists, engineers, and mathematics.* Unpublished doctoral dissertation, Emory University, Atlanta, GA.

Yonezawa, S. (1997). *Making decisions about students' lives: An interactive study of secondary students' academic program selection.* Unpublished doctoral dissertation, Department of Education, University of California, Los Angeles.

CHAPTER 10

SHAPING YOUTH'S IDENTITY THROUGH STUDENT-DRIVEN RESEARCH

Susan Yonezawa and Makeba Jones

ABSTRACT

In this chapter, Susan Yonezawa and Makeba Jones describe the ways in which their student co-researcher project, serving low-income, minority youth in several high schools, illustrates the importance of setting and identity to actively engage youth. The authors discuss the activities of the SCR project, specifically focusing on how teams of students engaged in action-oriented, student-driven research on their school communities to inform adults within their schools about needed changes to improve student achievement. While discussing the case of one SCR team, Yonezawa and Jones explain how the SCR activities encouraged students to expand their identities from high school students to researchers. They also describe the precarious nature of developing new and, therefore, tenuous identities in the contested terrain of interactions with school adults. The authors note, in particular, how students came to see themselves differently as they collaborated with university researchers and their peers.

Including Families and Communities in Urban Education, pages 213–232
Copyright © 2011 by Information Age Publishing

We propose that adults working with youth in school and community contexts consider the ways in which youth's identities are impacted by the settings we create in classrooms, extra-curricular academic programs and social clubs, community programs, and various youth development projects, for example. Opportunities and activities important to improving youth's future prospects in the adult world must engage youth in meaningful content connected to how youth see themselves (Nasir & Hand, 2008; Yonezawa, Jones & Joselowsky, 2009). Settings organized purposefully to elevate and expand how youth see their life prospects and future possibilities set the stage for engaged learning and social development (Newmann, 1992).

Research on educational settings in school and out of school tries to ascertain the social features of settings that impact youth. Features such as the structured or unstructured nature of activities in settings, the interactional relationships among actors in settings, and the cognitive requirements of tasks undertaken by actors during activities within various settings have become of increasing interest among scholars (Newmann, 1992; Tseng & Seidman, 2007; Yonezawa, Jones & Joselowsky, 2009). This work on educational settings emphasizes the social processes inherent in a given setting, and the ways in which various resources (physical, material, temporal, economic, human, etc.) are organized and utilized to shape the social processes of settings (Tseng & Seidmen, 2007). The purposeful organization of resources to construct a particular social process in which youth and adults participate in a given setting increases the likelihood that youth will be substantively or actively engaged in their own learning and development (Nystrand & Gamoran, 1991; Yonezawa, Jones & Joselowsky, 2009).

Youth identity is interwoven with their learning, development and engagement (Lave & Wenger, 1991; Newmann, 1992; Wenger, 1998). We draw from social and cultural traditions of sociology and psychology to understand identity as one's sense of self which is constructed by the multiple social worlds in which individuals participate, such as peer groups, family, work, school, church, clubs, sports, professional organizations, and so on (Collins, 1997; Davidson, 1996; Jones, 2000; Wenger, 1998). Youth identity, for instance, how self-confident youth are as students, their expectations for their futures, or their overall self-esteem level is shaped by the multiple social worlds and various settings that make up their lives (Davidson, 1996; Flores-Gonzalez, 2002; Nasir & Hand, 2008; Yonezawa, Jones & Joselowsky, 2009).

Identity as socially constructed through lived experiences across a variety of social domains means individual agency interacts with institutionalized cultural beliefs that typically marginalize racial minorities and women (Banks, 1993; Collins, 1997). In the social domain of school, youth's perceptions of their capability as learners or their expectations for their future prospects are influenced by the overall school culture and the culture in classrooms. Teachers, for example, who view their students' capabilities through lenses of race, class and gender, create a classroom culture where students are held to differential expectations for learning and academic success. How minority students activate their agency in response to classroom cultures of low expectations depends partly on self-perceptions of their social ranking in the world (Flores-Gonzalez, 2002). The values youth attach to social categories based on race, class, gender, language, or immigration status shape the extent to which classroom settings with disengaging cultures impact their identities negatively (Carter, 2005; Flores-Gonzalez, 2002).

The configuration of resources (i.e., human, material, temporal, physical, economic, etc.) in educational settings must be purposefully organized to offer youth an engaging cultural experience of respect, competency and expectations of academic success (Newmann, 1992; Yonezawa, Jones & Joselowsky, 2009). In these educational settings, the identities of youth can be supported and encouraged to grow as confident, productive learners. Understanding the relationship between setting and youth identity better equips us to learn how to elevate and expand the identities of youth with which we work, particularly youth of color from socio-economically disadvantaged backgrounds.

Our contribution to understanding the relationship between settings and youth identity is to promote a focus on improving youth engagement in education contexts by purposefully organizing settings around critical youth voice. By critical youth voice, we mean that young people actively and critically participate in the creation and re-creation of educational institutions they attend by helping to analyze these institutions from students' perspective and, in doing so, inform adults with power on how to improve educational policies and practices. We have spent ten years advocating for the active participation of students in their high school's reform efforts (Jones & Yonezawa, 2002, 2008b; Yonezawa & Jones, 2007). In our work, and in that of many of our colleagues who write about youth voice and youth empowerment, is the idea that adults working with youth can create settings that deliberately promote youth identities as agents of institutional change through foregrounding student's critical insights about their experiences in those institutions (Cook-Sather, 2007; Hopkins, 2008; Rogers, Morrell and Enyedy, 2007).

Our belief is that settings aimed at developing youth are enhanced by organizing activities around critical youth voice. In doing so, we can provide opportunities for youth to empower themselves in ways that increase their engagement in their learning and development, and their engagement in creating bright futures for themselves. In this chapter, we illustrate the ways in which setting and identity interact to provide a space in which low-income youth of color can test an unfamiliar identity, that of researcher, through the Student Co-Researcher Project (SCR). The project provides youth in low-income high schools an internship-like experience as educational researchers. We draw from data we collected from one student co-researcher team we worked closely with over a semester, during the 2008–2009 school year. More specifically, we describe how the settings we created encouraged and supported students to take on identities as researchers, albeit novice researchers.

History of Student Co-Research

Student co-research work has a long history beginning in the student power movement in the 1960s and 1970s (Levin, 2000). Decades later, Jean Rudduck and her colleagues described early meetings with groups of students trained to conduct research on issues in their schools and communities (Rudduck, Chaplain, & Wallace, 1996; Rudduck, 2007)

Since then, many researchers have engaged students in studying various contexts in which they live and learn. Alison Cook-Sather, for example, has involved students for over a decade in teacher training through her work at Bryn Mawr (Cook-Sather, 2007). She has argued that including students in such work benefits novice teachers as they develop their sense of how involved students could be in the evolution of their classrooms. Fine, Rubin, and Silva have worked with students in New York City and New Jersey to study classrooms and communities around civic engagement and political reform (Fine, Roberts, Torre & Bloom, 2004; Rubin & Silva, 2003). Rogers, Morrell and Enyedy (2007) have helped youth in Los Angeles examine cultural and linguistic differentiation (and the political ramifications of such differentiation) in low-income urban black and Latino communities.

Student co-researcher studies across this body of work have used various quantitative and qualitative research methodologies. As qualitative, social science researchers, our backgrounds determined the qualitative methodologies used by all student co-researcher teams.

THE STUDENT CO-RESEARCHER PROJECT IN THE SAN DIEGO UNIFIED SCHOOL DISTRICT

During the 2008–2009 school year, we worked with student co-researcher (SCR) teams at four high schools in the San Diego Unified School District (SDUSD). These four high schools all served low-income, minority African American, Latino and Asian students. For this chapter, we primarily focus on the SCR team at one high school as a case in point, to illustrate data trends. The SCR project is run by us through the research center for which we work, the Center for Research on Educational Equity, Assessment and Teaching Excellence (CREATE) at the University of California, San Diego (UCSD). CREATE is an education research center dedicated to improving learning, achievement and post-secondary opportunities for students in San Diego's most low-income and racially diverse neighborhoods and communities. We have created other student-driven projects in the past; however, the SCR project is our most recent attempt at creating an extra-curricular setting for high school students in which their schooling experiences drive the project. The SCR project invites a diverse group of high school students to engage in an internship-like experience as education researchers. We train students in social science research and guide them as they conduct an education study at their high school.

The project takes place in a range of settings from our university research center to various locations at the high school, such as the library, a teacher's classroom, school site computer lab and the staff lounge. We meet with a team of student co-researchers several times over the course of two to four months, depending on the frequency with which we can schedule meetings that coordinate with students' course schedules and other non-school responsibilities. In general, there are three phases to the student co-researcher project: 1) project launch, 2) data collection, and 3) presentation of research results. The project launch involves a full day at CREATE on the UC San Diego campus in which we introduce a SCR team to the research process and facilitate the team's decision-making about a research topic for their education study. Data collection usually takes place during one day at the school-site (a few teams have occasionally needed two days to complete all data collection). Students are released from class in order to conduct, for example, teacher and student interviews, classroom observations, and to administer surveys to students and staff. Lastly, teams present their research results to their school's faculty and administrators with a PowerPoint presentation explaining the SCR project, the team's study, and the important analytical points uncovered by the research.

In 2008–2009, we collected: 1) student-produced documents such as data collection instruments and personal reflections, 2) video and audio-tapes of team working meetings, 3) individual student co-researcher interviews about their experiences on the project, 4) principal interviews about the student co-researcher project, and 5) photos of student co-researchers collecting their data. Our research design took on an "applied" form as we constructed the SCR project to learn about the ways in which student co-research teams form, develop, and impact school-communities and the ways in which student participants are affected (Noblit, 1999).

In this way, we acted more like participant-observers than neutral, detached observers. We did so with a practical purpose: to guide students in their research and to learn how to improve the SCR project overall. Our focus was on the process we used to work with the SCR teams while keeping students' critical voices and identities at the forefront of our work as facilitators and coaches for the student research teams. We engaged in design-based research wherein we attempted, over several years, to create a model of youth engagement in an academic setting that would contribute to the school environments of the participating students and, in time, the communities the school served (The Design-Based Research Collective, 2003). In effect, the SCR project is designed to highlight critical youth voice as a lever of school–community change.

In the sections that follow, we describe the school–community context surrounding Lincoln High School and its SCR team. We then describe the settings we attempted to create for the students during each of the three phases of the student co-researcher project and the ways in which student's engagement in the project impacted their identities.

Lincoln High School

Lincoln High School, named after Abraham Lincoln, is located in southeastern San Diego. The area is largely residential with commercial businesses interspersed throughout but suffers from conditions of urban density, generational poverty, low wage employment, and increasing unemployment. In 2003, Lincoln closed due to a bond measure passed in 1999 by the voters within the attendance boundaries for the school. The measure authorized the creation of a new facility on the same property as the original school, which meant demolishing the original and much dilapidated buildings to make way for a state-of-the-art education facility. While the new facility was under construction, planning around how to create a college preparatory focus at Lincoln was underway. The "new" Lincoln was supposed to shed its historical reputation for poorly educating its largely African American and Latino student population. Through a multi-million dollar grant from the Bill and Melinda Gates Foundation, Lincoln High School re-opened in September, 2007 as a campus that housed four smaller learning communities in the form of autonomous small schools—the 9th grade Center for Social Justice, Center for Public Safety, Center for the Arts, and Center for Science and Engineering. All incoming freshmen were enrolled in the 9th grade Center for Social Justice. Students in grades 10–12 chose to attend one of the three remaining centers.

Upon opening in 2007, the campus received students from 77 different schools both in and out of California. The Lincoln campus served about 50% Latino students and about 40% African American. The remaining 10% of the student body included whites, Asian Americans, Filipinos and Pacific Islanders. The enrollment across the entire campus was approximately 2,300. Approximately 80% of students qualified for Free and/or Reduced Priced Lunches, which meant Lincoln received federal money under Title I. According to last year's data, about one third of students were classified as English Language Learners.

The 2009 Lincoln Student Co-Researcher group was housed within one center and drew 21 students from diverse academic, racial and ethnic backgrounds. All 21 students were juniors from one teacher's advisory period led by teacher Ms. Hays. The principal approached Ms. Hays about allowing students from her class to volunteer for the project, in lieu of the traditional advisory. Advisory classes were typically, though not always, non-core and non-elective courses designed to personalize school for students by offering regular opportunities to receive academic help from teachers, learn about academic support programs and post-secondary information about college, for example, and to strengthen relationships among school adults and students.

The Launch Day: Initiation into Novice Researcher

The student co-researcher project at the high school launched during a full day in the university center's conference room. The room consisted of rectangular tables formed in a semi-circle to facilitate interaction during research meetings, and bookshelves lined the walls with various education research journals, books, and community service awards given to CREATE.

The formal purpose of the launch day is always to introduce the SCR teams to social science research and help them begin designing a study of their choosing. But the informal purpose is also to bring the students to the university to immerse them in the "world" of researchers and academics from the start of their research project. We want to break youth from their routine as high school students and introduce to them the notion of a less controlling, more self-governing and hopefully, more self-fulfilling educational experience (Jones & Yonezawa, 2008a). We want the students to be active in the research training throughout the day. But we also hope they begin to see themselves differently, as novice researchers. To this end, we are sure to tell the students from the beginning that this is not a "high school" activity per se. They are responsible from start to finish for their own learning and engagement. As a concrete example, we expect them to *not* raise their hand and ask to go to the bathroom, stretch their legs, and so on. They are in a university setting where students are treated as adults able to take care of their own needs and keep up with the responsibilities of the academic tasks asked of them.

While in the conference room, each group of students participates in a social process in which they are treated as college students at a one-day workshop learning how to design and conduct legitimate education research. During the workshop students are given UCSD folders and "blue books," for note-taking and brainstorming. Through individual writing activities and discussion-based whole group and small group activities, the SCRs try on new and, for many, tentative identities as education researchers. (See Figure 10.1 for the Launch Day agenda.) Below we describe particular activities in the university setting, as well as their significance to students' engagement as emerging novice researchers.

An important part of the launch day is creating and discussing what we call group norms. We give the students guidelines on how to behave on a research team so that all students are comfortable actively participating. We craft a short list of obvious but important norms, including openness to learn from team members and suspension of judgment about possible research results. These norms encourage the students to think in ethical, professional ways before embarking on their project. The list also includes respect and kindness toward team members, a norm to help students develop positive and comfortable relationships. We invite the youth to discuss and critique the norms, as well as modify and add to the team "principles." Establishing group norms early on in the Lincoln student co-researcher project gave the students social guidelines for the whole-and small-group activities (Jones & Yonezawa, 2008a). Moreover, fostering positive social

---

CREATE-UCSD LAUNCH DAY AGENDA

1. Introductions
2. Introduce CREATE's work as an education research center
3. Goals for Today: Develop research question, study design, & data collection Instruments
4. Distribute UCSD folders and bluebooks for notetaking.
5. Whole group discussion—"What is research?"
   a. Ask students for examples from their experiences in schools/classrooms.
   b. Frame research as "inquiry into a problem in order to better understand it and develop solutions;" research/inquiry as everyday part of life, give examples.
   c. Ask students what are important characteristics of being on a research team?
   d. Pass out "Principles of Being on a Research Team" and discuss each principle. Ask students if they would like to add to the list.
6. Research Process:
   a. Framing the problem using: personal experiences, current and/or past events, books, journals, newspapers, internet, and other data already available.

Figure 10.1 Launch Day Agenda.

    b. Developing a research question (open-ended to allow for all possible answers/responses)

    c. Designing the study: The What, Who, Where, When and How

    d. Collecting data

    e. Analyzing the data

    f. Disseminating research findings

7. Determining "the problem" that needs to be investigated—Suggested activities:

    a. Ask students to write to a prompt that asks about their overall experiences in their school and in classrooms (see handout). Students share out. Chart students' responses and post on wall.

    b. Focus group activity, where facilitators ask the group to respond to/discuss a set of questions on their learning experiences in their school/classrooms. Chart discussion and post on wall.

    c. Show students prior data about their school, e.g., test scores, attendance, student surveys, demographic data, etc. Ask students to brainstorm hypotheses on why the data looks the way it does.

8. Developing a research question.

    a. Discuss criteria for "good" questions such as open-ended wording (not leading or biased), clarity of focus, not too narrow or too broad.

    b. List "starters" on the board, such as "In what ways . . . ," "How does . . . ," "What does . . . ," "To what extent do . . . "

    c. Students work in small groups to brainstorm possible research questions based on the problem or problems students identified. Groups share their questions. Do the questions match the problems students identified?

    d. Students vote on the top 1 or 2 research questions.

9. Study Design and Data Collection Instruments:

    a. Discuss/Review The What, Who, Where, When and How:

       – What is the focus of the study? What is the research question?

       – What kinds of information are necessary to collect to answer the question?

       – How will you collect the information?

       – Who do you need to talk to? When might you talk with them? How many people should you interview?

    b. Discuss "Principles of Good Interview Questions"

    c. Discuss tips for creating surveys

    d. Discuss tips for creating observation forms

    e. Students work in small groups to create data collection instructions

10. Next steps: Discuss future meeting logistics and next steps in conducting the study.

Figure 10.1 (continued)   Launch Day Agenda.

relationships among team members helped the group cohere as a novice research team.

As Penny Eckert (1989) showed in *Jocks and Burnouts,* high school can be a tough place filled with students positioned in various, hierarchical social categories in structures similar to adult society. Because the students in the teams were often from diverse academic and grade levels, as well as different social status backgrounds, we knew that for students to work together productively as a research team, each one needed solid standing among the other team members. We want every student to feel like an expert about the educational issues the group will investigate. Tensions certainly sprouted periodically among students, but these were instances where students' teasing turned to hotly contested irritations expressed through biting verbal jabs. Separating the students for a cooling off period diffused these isolated situations.

As facilitators for the student research team, we made sure to ground many of the launch day activities in students' first-hand school and classroom experiences and personal knowledge about Lincoln High School. Eliciting students' prior knowledge helped them view research as partly informed by researchers' personal experiences about real educational problems that constrain students' daily experiences in schools. As social scientists, we knew that studying what you love and being truly interested in your work would very likely help the novice researchers see the project through to completion (Becker & Richards, 2007). Grounding the framing of the research problem in students' prior knowledge and experiences encouraged them to think of themselves as researchers doing the work of university researchers. By the end of the launch day, the Lincoln team constructed a powerful research question—*How does support from staff and teachers affect student behavior and student motivation?*

Our knowledge and experience as professional educational researchers certainly helped guide the student researchers' study design. But we were careful that our research expertise did not overshadow the fundamentally student-driven nature of the SCR project. We were mindful to draw on students' prior knowledge and experiences to help them construct a sound research design. We tried to work alongside students as research team members. In the SCR project settings, we were not teachers, but facilitators. Students appreciated this approach. Jackie, one of the Lincoln researchers, said that we were not like their high school teachers in that "[Makeba and Susan] don't sit there and lecture and tell you exactly what you need to do. They let us think for ourselves. If they told us what we had to do it wouldn't be our own project." A student-centered approach to the launch day contributed to the substantive engagement we witnessed in the team. In students' end-of-day written reflections to us about their impressions of the launch day, many students wrote that they were surprised how much "fun" they had learning about research and that they were excited about their research topic. As we moved back into the school setting of Lincoln High School for subsequent meetings, we hoped we could sustain the momentum of students' exploration of an emerging novice researcher identity.

Doing Research: School Interactions that Promote and Detract

Although we do not have the space to detail the Lincoln SCR team's extensive data collection and analyses, suffice it to say that the team met several more times at Lincoln High to create and edit their data collection instruments and to practice data collection techniques.

The setting for these meetings was decidedly different from the CREATE conference room, but still unique for students at most high schools. With permission from the supportive principal, the meetings usually occurred in one of the small school's "penthouses"—the in-house name for a second floor faculty lounge. Given that the school was newly built, the faculty lounge consisted of a set of shiny, mahogany colored tables, maroon padded chairs that swiveled and rolled, and the regular refrigerator, tables, copy machine, and so on found in many staff lounges. The students also enjoyed the lovely set of French doors that opened and overlooked the school's main quad.

The "faculty penthouse" setting at Lincoln helped us maintain some of the atmospheric features of the launch day in the university setting. We always set the tone for each meeting by reminding students that they were education researchers, not high school students, and that their focus was on the research team and not on themselves. We continued with the students' training in researcher ethics, building rapport, gaining informed consent, and recording the data with notes and digital audio equipment. This work was markedly different than that regularly asked of them in their classroom settings; students were engaged in youth-driven, university-level education research. The physical space and almost luxury of the penthouse contributed contrast to the Lincoln students' usual classroom spaces for academic work. The contrast between the penthouse and classroom settings reinforced students' emergent researcher identities while students participated on the project.

A pivotal phase during the project is always the data collection day. On this day, the SCR teams are pulled out of class for the entire day to collect the interviews, conduct observations, and do other types of data collection they had designed for their study. What is unique about data collection day is that although the students are still within the school setting, their role within the setting is largely different on this particular day; they are novice researchers.

Data collection day begins with a 45-minute training review where students are reminded about rapport-building techniques for interviews, review the protocols and audio-equipment, and are given lanyard-style badges that identify them as "Student Co-Researchers" working with the university. We remind the students that when wearing the lanyards they represent more than themselves. Rather, they represent the SCR team and need to comport themselves as professional researchers. The students have much more freedom and responsibility on this day than is typical for high school students. They are given a set schedule at the beginning of the day of interviews and observations to conduct, which the team helps craft. But, as true researchers, if they are unable to conduct an interview or an observation for whatever reason, they are expected to occupy their time productively by accompanying another researcher on his/her data collection tasks, spending more time on their field notes, or lining up other interviews or observations in the moment.

The Lincoln student co-researcher team conducted interviews with 124 students, eight teachers, and two administrators. They also surveyed 269 students in the two months that followed the launch day at UCSD. By the end of the data collection day, the students were exhausted and exhilarated from their on-the-ground, first-hand encounters as researchers. In written reflections about their data collection experiences, several students wrote that they felt proud at their researcher skills, such as coming up with on-the-spot "follow-up questions [that] kept the students talking," as one student reported.

The data collection experience is key to the students' identity shift because although it happens on the school grounds, the ways in which the students interact with the "research subjects" in the setting (i.e., interviews with the teachers, administrators, and other students) are completely different. Using their emergent researcher lenses to frame their more formal interactions with interviewees, the SCR team members begin to see their peers and teachers in a completely different light, and, in doing so, they see themselves in a different light as well. We will discuss the latter in more detail in the last section. For instance, students shared that they would never initiate conversation with a student or a teacher they did not already know in their every day roles as Lincoln High students. Yet as novice researchers, they saw this task as part of their responsibility in carrying out the research project and they were able to set aside their ambivalence and nervousness to break this barrier to interacting with high school peers. We also heard typical exclamations such as Angela's that data collection was "intriguing—getting different opinions and perspectives of various people." Angela continued that "the teacher interviews were not only helpful, but they gave me a more secure and confident feeling towards our school environment." As Angela, other team members were struck by how different the teachers' perspectives were, compared to their own perceptions of Lincoln. Several student researchers' experienced the most surprise by some of the students' answers to interview questions. These team members did not expect that students' responses would paint a picture of Lincoln High that team members did not necessarily share. One student who interviewed one of the small schools' vice principals was particularly frustrated by her failed attempts to persuade the administrator to see her side of how to spend the school budget (clearly the interview dynamic broke from neutrality).

After data collection was completed, the Lincoln students met with us three to four times a month in the "penthouse" during their advisory class and completed activities to help them analyze their data, draw reasonable conclusions, and prepare a professional PowerPoint presentation for their teachers and administrators. We took this time to remind the students to think back to the launch day for their project on the UCSD campus and remember some of the ground rules we talked about for being a researcher working on a team: be open to hearing different opinions and separate yourself from the research. The analysis and presentation-building work proceeded well; students were able to distance their personal opinions about the data from the systematic analysis of recurring themes and patterns. The team worked well together in various small groupings to comb through the data and synthesize research results. We were at the end of a four month process, and the Lincoln students continued to cohere as a research team committed to uncovering new information that might inform positive changes to student achievement at Lincoln. But, as we would be reminded later, what researchers believe is important information is not always what their audience sees as important.

The social setting for all actors during data collection created a new and, initially, unfamiliar structure for how youth would interact with teachers and their peers. In the moment of interviewing a student or principal, team members' emerging novice researcher identities brushed up against their identities as Lincoln students. Students' personal experiences in classrooms and on the campus were sometimes contested by the stories they heard their peers tell during interviews about the quality of education at Lincoln. We did our best to prepare the students for these conflicting moments as researchers with personal knowledge of the research site. The students' firsthand experiences proved more memorable than our verbal cautions, however. The final phase of the student co-researcher project would also test students' emerging novice researcher identities.

Testing New Identities: When Students Challenge Teachers and Get "Push Back"

The culminating task of the Lincoln SCR team, as with all SCR teams, was to present their findings to their small school's faculty and administrators. The 45-minute presentation was scheduled during the faculty's regular meeting time after school. The students swayed nervously in the front of the "penthouse," while the teachers sat at conference tables, side couches and swivel chairs. The teachers listened quietly to the presentation, flipping handouts and examining the multi-colored and multiple graphs of interview and study data.

The SCR team had many important overall findings from their study, such as the following points.

- A majority of students who were interviewed said they feel supported by teachers.
- Students say that extra help after school both helps them/and would help them feel more supported
- A large percentage (over 90% of students interviewed) say they have at least one teacher they respect on campus.
- A significant percentage of students (approximately 33% of those interviewed) do not feel well supported at school for a variety of reasons.
- Peers remain a largely negative influence on students.
- Peers are disruptive in class, which negatively affects learning & teachers' attitudes.
- Females appear slightly better supported (or at least feel that way) than males by teachers and staff.
- Seniors feel significantly better supported by counseling than 10th and 11th graders.
- Very few 11th graders (35%) in particular report that they get information about scholarships, SATs, college, etc.

After presenting this information to the entire faculty, the SCR team opened the floor to questions. Quite a few teachers raised their hands and respectfully waited for the students to call on them. After three or four questions, we and the SCR team were reminded, suddenly, that the penthouse setting, the place where we had held so many SCR sessions, was no longer the same place when occupied by the entire school's faculty. The space, now teacher-dominated, was more contested, as the teachers brought with them opinions about research, the team's findings, and the Lincoln students as researchers.

One incident illustrates how students' emergent novice researcher identities can be contested through interactions with school adults. In this case, a key finding in the study was that many students at the school were ill-informed about the kinds of academic supports—tutoring, counseling, and so on—available. One student, Stephanie, who was in student government (ASB), remarked to the audience that ASB tries to communicate information via a bulletin board, but that student government members find it difficult to maintain timely information. She suggested to the audience that perhaps more communication could be done within teachers' classrooms via classroom bulletin boards, announcements, and so on. In particular, Stephanie argued that there was critical academic information that often failed to make it into the weekly announcements. It was notable how she took great pains in her comments to be respectful of teachers' workload and time constraints, as well as bending over backwards to clarify that she and the group do not blame the teachers for the weak overall communication at the school.

Yet, despite Stephanie's efforts to recognize teachers' constraints, one teacher in particular engaged in an abrasive questioning of the SCR team. In an exchange among the teacher, Stephanie and a third team member, the tone of the exchange pitted the student co-researchers' tentative researcher identities against that of a veteran teacher with over 25 years experience in education. During the interaction, the teacher asserted her power over the students by questioning the students' research conclusion that teachers needed to be more active in communicating important academic information to students. The students pressed on and, despite the teacher's sometimes demeaning tone, challenged the teacher's notions of student apathy with their own ideas of what it took to engage and connect with students at their high school so that they were properly informed.

In the end, the SCR team's advisory teacher Ms. Hays intervened by pointing out that she did not want the SCR team members to feel like they were getting "thrown under a bus." She underscored the importance of their research and the issues they raised by stating the findings made her "think about what goes on" in her classroom. The principal also responded at that time to address the teachers and to simultaneously support the students' critical voices by reinforcing that communication is a major issue school wide.

The Lincoln student co-researchers were caught off-guard by the tense exchange. Ultimately, the Lincoln students were beholden to their teachers and not to us; we certainly had little to no authority over the students' schooling at Lincoln. The change in the penthouse setting from student-dominated (as SCRs) to teacher-dominated shifted the power dynamics to the teachers. We worried students' novice researcher identities were too fragile under their teachers' authority, but unnecessarily, as we learned soon after the project ended. The student co-researcher project made a positive impression on the Lincoln students' self-confidence, as we discuss below.

Project Impact on Lincoln Students' Identities

By the end of the project at Lincoln, we learned that several student co-researchers had expanded their sense of themselves and of their possible futures. We asked a post-doc student working for our research center to interview the Lincoln student co-researchers independently about their experiences on the project. We share a few examples from students' interview transcripts to illustrate the impact their project participation had on their identities.

Jackie said in the post-project interview that she "can see" herself doing research. "Although the process was hard but it was fun because of the interaction with people you don't know." Jackie also learned new things about herself as a result of participating on the project. She reflected that she noticed that she is "more determined" than she had believed. Jackie explained, "Because doing something like this, me I procrastinate and I'm lazy, so I thought I would have gave up soon as we started doing real work. Surprisingly I stuck to it." When asked if the project influenced her motivation to go to college after high school, she firmly stated, "Oh most definitely, more motivated to go to college. High school the whole atmosphere is different. Seeing that we worked with college people and we actually do college work I would enjoy college more than high school. I'm ready to go to college."

So too did other students feel more informed about the college experience after participating on the project. Ana stated that she "realized that there's more fields" she could enter in college. She explained, "It's not like 'oh you can [only] go into science, math or literature.'" Picking up on Ana's comment, Stephanie, who joined Ana in the interview with the post-doc, continued that because they will be applying to colleges next year, the project helped her learn about "different types of fields and different types of degrees." She said, "Makeba and Susan were sharing with us their majors [when they went to college]. So it really kind of expanded our mind in knowing that we didn't have to choose one, it can branch off into your interests so you get to focus on things you're interested in."

The improvement of communication skills surfaced from students as important to their growth in the project. Ana said she now sees herself differently because she became "more comfortable talking to people face to face" than she was before her participation on the project. Similarly, Bobby said he learned about "communication and hard work." Talking to students he had never seen before on campus increased Bobby's confidence about communicating with people he did not know. He spoke with pride about how his teachers saw him differently as a result of his participation on the project. "Some of the teachers," Bobby told us, "see me as a shy student and during the presentation they were shocked."

We can be sure that the student co-researcher project was successful in creating a setting in which students' voices were a driving force in their education and in which students' identities were expanded. We can only hope that the confidence the Lincoln students gained from their fragile novice researcher identity remains as they finish their high school careers and make their way into the adult world.

CONCLUSION

Any effort aimed at helping youth in their social and academic development, be it a program inside of school or a project sponsored by a community organization, needs to carefully consider the role that setting and youth identity play in shaping engagement in the program or project. All youth, regardless of background and circumstances, need to see themselves in the work adults ask them to do. How we organize and arrange the resources and activities in settings is crucial to strengthening youth engagement in their own learning and development.

It is no accident that students Ana, Stephanie, Jackie and Bobby, connected the student co-researcher project to a "real" college experience. The SCR project is an academically oriented youth engagement activity aimed at students in urban, low-income schools. We organized the project by creating a social process in which students could safely share their knowledge, learn from others, and contribute to executing a "real" research project. In doing so, students shifted and expanded their identity to include an emerging novice researcher identity that was partly shaped by their personal experiences. The conviction in the voices of Jackie, Stephanie, Bobby and Ana could positively affect their future choices and actions in their school–community.

However, even the most thoughtfully organized settings cannot control the response and reaction of adults who also participate in the settings youth occupy. Making an impact on the school–community through critical youth voice takes time and patience. It is not a quick fix for school improvement. We know that the structures, cultures and politics of schooling are intertwined with conceptions of race, class, and gender, to name a few social categories, in complicated ways, including teachers' perceptions of ability and learning (Oakes, 1985, 1992; Oakes, Wells, Datnow, & Jones, 1997). In retrospect, we should have better prepared the Lincoln students for the range of reactions by their teachers. We could have role-played with students the kinds of hard-hitting questions and concerns teachers might bring up after hearing the presentation. In the real world of research, researchers need to anticipate counter-explanations for research results and discuss why their particular interpretation merits consideration. Moreover, we realized after the fact that one activity in which youth and adults interact around the research results was grossly insufficient to accomplish our goal of elevating critical youth voice in the improvement work of schools. The power dynamic between youth and school adults is strong and can easily eclipse students' voices and insights. Youth and adults need consistent and multiple opportunities over time to dialogue about issues both believe are important to improving the school community. The settings in which such critical dialogue takes place needs to position young people and adults as equal experts who are open to listening to and thinking about each other's perspective. Enlisting school leaders to act as facilitators for such critical conversations might help level the power distribution and push the impact of the student co-researcher project beyond the participating student researchers and into the relationships between students and school adults. More importantly, critical youth voice can be a lever of institutional, social and cultural improvements in the broader school community, and a model for actively engaging young people in civic participation in their local communities.

REFERENCES

Banks, J.A. (1993). The canon debate, knowledge construction, and multicultural education. *Educational Researcher, 22*(4), 4–14.

Becker, H. S., & Richards, P. (2007) *Writing for social scientists.* Chicago: University of Chicago Press.

Carter, P. (2005). *Keepin' it real: School success beyond black and white.* New York: Oxford University Press.

Collins, P. H. (1997). Comments to Hekman's "Truth and method: Feminist standpoint theory revisited." *Signs, 22*(2), 725–78.

Cook-Sather, A. (2007). Translating researchers: Re-imagining the work of investigating students' experiences in school. In A. Cook-Sather & D. Thiessen (Eds.), *International handbook of student experience in elementary and secondary school* (pp. 829–872). Dordrecht, The Netherlands: Springer.

Davidson, A.L. (1996). *Making and molding identity in schools: Student narratives on race, gender, and academic engagement.* Albany: State University of New York Press.

The Design-Based Research Collective. (2003). The design-based research: An emerging paradigm for educational inquiry. *Educational Researcher, 32*(1), 5–8.

Eckert, P. (1989). *Jocks & burnouts: Social categories and identity in the high school.* New York: Teachers College Press.

Fine, M., Roberts, R., Torre, E., & Bloom, J. (2004). *Echoes of brown: Youth documenting and performing the legacy of Brown v. Board of Education.* New York: Teachers College Press.

Flores-Gonzalez, N. (2002). *School kids/Street kids: Identity development in Latino students.* New York: Teachers College Press.

Hopkins, E. A. (2008). Work-related learning: Hearing students' voices. *Educational Action Research, 16,* 209–219.

Jones, M. (2000). *Navigating high school: A study of Black students' schooling and social agency.* Unpublished dissertation. Los Angeles: University of California, Los Angeles.

Jones, M., & Yonezawa, S. (2002). Student voice, cultural change: Using inquiry in school reform. *Equity and Excellence in Education, 35*(3), 245–254.

Jones, M., & Yonezawa, S. (2008a). Use student inquiry to investigate the learning experience in racially mixed classrooms. In M. Pollock, (Ed.) *Everyday antiracism: Concrete ways to successfully navigate the relevance of race in school* (pp. 212–216). New York: The New Press.

Jones, M., & Yonezawa, S. (2008b). Student-driven research: When students gather and analyze data about their school everyone learns something. *Educational Leadership, 66*(4), 65–69.

Lave, J., & Wenger, E. (1991) *Situated Learning. Legitimate peripheral participation.* Cambridge: University of Cambridge Press.

Levin, B. (2000). Putting students at the centre of education reform. *Journal of Educational Change, 1*(2), 155–172.

Nasir, N. S., & Hand, V. (2008). From the court to the classroom: Opportunities for engagement, learning and identity in basketball and classroom mathematics. *Journal of the Learning Sciences, 17*(2), 143–180.

Newmann, F. (1992). *Student engagement and achievement in American secondary schools.* New York: Teachers College Press.

Noblit, G.W. (1999). The prospects of an applied ethnography for education: A sociology of knowledge interpretation. *Particularities: Collected essays on ethnography and education.* New York: Peter Lang.

Nystrand, M., & Gamoran, A. (1991). Instructional discourse, student engagement, and literature achievement. *Research in the Teaching of English, 25*(3), 261–290.

Oakes, J. (1985). *Keeping track: How schools structure inequality.* New Haven: Yale University Press.

Oakes, J. (May 1992). Can tracking research inform practice? Technical, normative, and political considerations. *Educational Researcher,* 12–21.

Oakes, J., Wells, A.S., Datnow, A., Jones, M. (Spring 1997). Detracking: The social construction of ability, cultural politics, and resistance to reform. *Teachers College Record, 98*(3), 482–510.

Rogers, J., Morrell, E., & Enyedy, N. (2007). Studying the struggle: Contexts for learning and identity development for urban youth. *American Behavioral Scientist, 51*(3), 419–443.

Rubin, B. C. & Silva, E. M. (2003). *Critical voices in school reform: Students living through change.* New York: RoutledgeFalmer.

Rudduck, J. (2007). Student voice, engagement and school reform. In A. Cook-Sather & D. Thiessen (Eds.), *International handbook of student experience in elementary and secondary school* (pp. 587–610). Dordrecht, The Netherlands: Springer.

Rudduck, J., Chaplain, R., & Wallace, G. (Eds.). (1996). *School improvement: What can pupils tell us?* London: David Fulton.

Tseng, V. & Seidman, E. (2007). A systems framework for understanding social settings. *American Journal of Community Psychology, 39,* 217–228.

Wenger, E. (1998). *Communities of practice: Learning, meaning, and identity.* Cambridge: Cambridge University Press.

Yonezawa, S. and Jones, M. (2007). Using students' experiences in the classroom to evaluate and inform secondary school reform. In A. Cook-Sather & D. Thiessen (Eds.), *International handbook of student experience in elementary and secondary school.* Dordrecht, The Netherlands: Springer.

Yonezawa, S., Jones, M. & Joselowsky, F. (April 2009). Youth engagement in high schools: Developing a multidimensional, critical approach to improving engagement for all students. *Journal for Educational Change, 10,* 191–209.

PART IV

STRATEGIES FOR INCLUSION
AND PROGRAM ASSESSMENT

CHAPTER 11

FROM MISTRUST TO COLLABORATION

Using Transformational Social Therapy to Support Participation in School–Community Educational Reform in a French *Banlieue*

Novella Keith

ABSTRACT

Collaborative relationships are held as all important in school reform, but the research and practice literature provides little guidance on how to create them across social divides marked by mistrust and even violence. Using a qualitative case study methodology, Novella Keith provides a detailed analysis in this chapter of a successful practice, Transformational Social Therapy (TST), as it was applied in a school–community planning project in the French equivalent of an inner city. TST combines a variant of action research, consensus-based community organizing, and techniques from group therapy to facilitate dialogue, information sharing, and the development of action plans. The author examines the TST theory of action, grounding it in the research on intergroup conflict and collaboration, organizational change, and trust and

Including Families and Communities in Urban Education, pages 235–266

mistrust. TST helps reweave social relationships and the development of trust by providing supports for the emotional understanding of self and other. The case study analysis selects four moments that appeared central to moving the initially mistrusting and reluctant would-be partners toward collaboration. The first moment shows that agency was exercised through dynamics including victimization, blame, rebellion, exclusion and violence. Encouraging participants to give free expression to their grievances and related emotions was a key to the second moment, gaining their participation and beginning to build trust leading to collaboration. The third and fourth moments illustrate how these very expressions created spaces in which participants could show their vulnerability and how this process, perhaps strangely and counter intuitively, provides an important key to human connection.

INTRODUCTION: THE PROJECT AND THE CONTEXT

This chapter examines a process, Transformational Social Therapy (TST), which is designed to foster collaborative action to address problems in organizations and communities where fractured relationships and mistrust create blocks to collaboration.[1] The case details collaborative planning in a school–community network, the Maville–TST School Success Project, which took place between April 2005 and October 2006 in one of the *banlieues*[2] on the outskirts of Paris, France. Maville (a fictitious name) is an economically depressed town that is home to a large multi-ethnic population, both French-born and immigrant, with roots in North and West Africa and other European and non-European countries. The area is considered volatile and, in fact, riots that were widely reported internationally exploded there and in other banlieues in October 2005, while this project was taking place (Coleman, 2006). At the time project activities began, tensions in the community were high and many of the local schools—among the lowest performing in France—were in disarray and closed off from each other and the neighborhood. Mandates from a recently revived national education reform policy that called for school–community collaborative planning provided an opportunity and some resources, and the principal of the lead school in the network, Collège Picasso (a fictitious name) invited the Charles Rojzman Institute, the hub for TST activities, to facilitate the planning process.

Between April and October 2005, TST facilitators worked first with a group of students over two weekends (in April and May) and subsequently with a group of educators, parents, and community members, also for two weekends (in May and October). The process continued into 2006 and 2007. The intervention with students and adults used a process that is the trademark of TST: it combines a variant of action research (Toulmin, 1996), consensus-based community organizing (Eichler, 2006) and techniques from group therapy (Yalom & Leszcz, 2005) to facilitate dialogue, information sharing (or "collective intelligence"; see Rojzman, 2009; Senge, Scharmer, Jaworski, & Flowers, 2004), and the development of action plans. The intervention succeeded in creating the groundwork for collaboration in an environment where the starting point had been mistrust and violence, and by October 2005 a group of students, teachers, parents and community members were able to have an open dialogue that subsequently informed the action plans. The meetings also helped initiate collaborations between educators, parents, and community-based social workers and organizers (Héraud, 2007). The project continued into 2006 and the French Ministry of Education provided funding for more intensive follow-up in 2007–2008.

I became interested in studying this intervention because it seemed to provide an answer to a pressing question: how to create school–community partnerships in circumstances where the starting point is mistrust, avoidance, and fear. The problems in Maville were in some ways similar—though in some ways much worse—to those that face school–community partnerships in U.S. cities, which are my main area of interest for research and practice; in addition, the TST process has been heralded in France and elsewhere as part of new interventions that contribute to humanizing education "for the 21st century" (Tarpinian, 2010). What was the theory of action and what aspects of the process might account for the results?

This chapter explores these questions using a qualitative case study methodology. I focus on the first four sessions, two with the students and two with the adults, so as to understand how trust and relationships are built initially in contexts such as Maville. The chapter begins with a brief description of the setting, which is followed by a discussion of TST, its main tenets, and related theory and research. The literature review provides evidence of the need for understanding the process through which TST engenders collaboration and support for the TST approach. This discussion is followed by an account of the research methods and the presentation and analysis of the data. The conclusion summarizes the main findings.

THE CONTEXT

The Maville-TST project was responsive to and supported by the third wave of a French national educational reform initiative dating to 1981, which had created Priority Education Areas (*zones d'éducation prioritaires* or ZEPs) targeted for compensatory funding to address inequalities in economic and educational attainment. In 1999, the second wave of the policy created Networks of Priority Education (*réseaux d'éducation prioritaire*, or REPs), designed to promote collaboration and mutual learning among feeder schools (pre-primary, primary, and middle) in the ZEPs; however, many of these networks did not remain active, including the one in the REP Picasso (named for the lead middle school, Collège Picasso), where this project took place (Héraud, 2007). The policy was revived in 2004–2005, in the wake of scathing reports, the threat of riots and a new government (Hargreaves, 2009; Pugin, 2007). Especially targeted were schools in the most volatile high poverty areas with the lowest educational achievement, which were now named Striving for Success Networks (*réseaux ambition réussite*). Maville has 20 preprimary schools, 21 elementary schools, eight collèges (middle schools), five lycées (high schools) and four tertiary institutions. All the pre-tertiary institutions in Maville fall within ZEPs. The REP Picasso included five elementary schools, three preschools, and the middle school.[3]

A historic shift in the French national government's practice of allocating the same level of funding for all schools, the new policy was part of a larger agenda providing compensatory funding to address "the challenges associated with minority ethnic cultures and social disadvantage" (Hargreaves, 2004, p. 227). France has the highest Muslim population of Western Europe (5 to 6 million, or approximately 9% of its population). Severe discrimination directed especially against youth and families of Muslim origins made the *banlieues* areas of seething resentment that periodically exploded in urban rioting. A 2004 study of "sensitive neighborhoods" with a high Muslim population, conducted by a police agency, reported that half of these neighborhoods "showed worrisome signs of community isolation...from social and political life" (Lawrence & Vaisse, 2006). According to 2006 reports, youth unemployment in the département (administrative region) of Seine-Saint-Denis, which includes Maville, stood at 50 percent—the highest in Europe (Chrisafis, 2006). The poverty rate stood at 18 percent, or 5.5 percentage points higher than that of the greater Paris region, and the income of some 60 percent of households in Maville and nearby towns (compared to 35 percent in the Greater Paris region) was low enough to be exempt from income taxes (Lawrence & Vaisse, 2006). Academic attainment is similarly inequitably distributed. What was always a differentiated educational system has become more strikingly so. Trica Keaton, who conducted a multi-year ethnographic study of Muslim girls in Seine-Saint-Denis, reports that

> schools in these outer cities are plagued by material inequalities, intensive tracking toward dead-end vocational studies, and high failure and dropout rates magnified by under-resourced conditions. In the late 1990s, concerns over inferior facilities, inadequate funding, crushing course loads, high teacher turnover, low salaries, and the elimination of critical teaching positions in a system in which classroom sizes have doubled and tripled over the years ignited massive teacher and student protests. (Keaton, 2005, p. 407)

The renewed emphasis on educational reform came partly in the hope that improvements in education could pacify young people and ease ever present threats to the public order (Chrisafis, 2006; Hargreaves, 2004).

Calling for local-level planning and action to improve educational achievement, the policy constituted a measure of decentralization in a system that is otherwise tightly administered at the national level and includes a national curriculum. Planning would bring together teachers and administrators from network schools, families, and civic and municipal organizations, under the joint leadership of an administrator from the National Ministry of Education (Inspecteur de l'éducation nationale) whose position was roughly equivalent to a district superintendent, and the principal of Collège Picasso, the middle school that the children in the network would attend.

The social environment would make collaboration exceedingly difficult, however, given seemingly intractable problems in both school and community. The percentage of young, inexperienced, and white teachers in the schools was high, as was teacher turnover (Pugin, 2007). Many schools, including those in the REP Picasso, had a garrison mentality; they did not welcome parents and neighbors, and the latter, in turn, perceived them as foreign enclaves. Collège Picasso, the middle school in the network that is the site of this study, was considered one of the most difficult schools in France (Héraud, 2007). This is the context in which the principal of Collège Picasso suggested a TST intervention by the Charles Rojzman Institute.

FROM MISTRUST TO COLLABORATIVE ACTION THROUGH TRANSFORMATIONAL SOCIAL THERAPY

TST interventions are based on a process developed by French social psychologist Charles Rojzman.[4] Rather than healing individuals, as its name might suggest, TST focuses on reweaving the fabric of social relationships that are torn apart by various expressions of violence. TST works through small groups of ten to fifteen people who are personally affected by a local problem and reflects the social divisions and divergent perspectives on the problem (the "primary group"). The group is taken through a developmental process that enables participants to move from violence and mistrust to collaboration. Violence here is defined broadly to include not only physical aggression but also emotional harm to self and others, such as abuse, shaming, and rejection. As in the field of peace studies, violence is understood to have intrapersonal, interpersonal, institutional, and structural dimensions and to include phenomena such as discrimination, marginalization and social isolation (Galtung, 1969). The TST process is based on the understanding that violence is an unhealthy adaptation to meeting one's basic human needs. Violence is thus the symptom of a more deeply underlying problem generated by social contexts that do not provide healthy pathways for meeting one's need for respect, affiliation, safety, agency and the like (i.e., see Staub, 2003b). The TST process is geared to creating a group in which participants can meet their needs in healthier ways. As the process creates self-awareness and heals relationships among participants, they become motivated to collaborate.

A particular kind of trust comes into play here: trust that grows from emotional understanding and emotional supports and can thus withstand and even grow through constructive conflict. Through this process, group members are able to get beyond communication that conforms with cordial relations (Keith, 2010), and engage in open, democratic dialogue that potentially yields creative and workable approaches to organizational or community problems (Yankelovich, 1999). Here the TST primary group is connected to decision makers who are invested in working with the group to implement action proposals.

What follows is a brief discussion of TST theory and practice in light of its supports from the literature. I also look at the literature on trust and mistrust as it relates to promoting collaboration in settings such as Maville. Whereas much of this literature focuses on behaviors or cognitive processes, TST is in line with a relatively new emphasis in research and practice that looks at both emotions and cognition (Eisenberg, 2006). This section establishes the theoretical framework for the subsequent analysis of data from the Maville-TST School Success Project.

Transformational Social Therapy: Theory and Practice

TST is informed by a comprehensive theory of change that takes into account the interconnectedness of the person, social institutions, and society at large, or what social scientists refer to respectively as the micro, meso, and macro-levels. As Emirbayer and Mische (1998) assert, our identity and our agency incorporate all these levels as well as temporal dimensions: our past, both historical and personal, our present experiences, and our goals and plans for the future. How we act in particular circumstances is not determined by these factors—there is fluidity and possibility—but we are not entirely free to make and remake ourselves (Booth, 2008; Bourdieu & Wacquant, 1992; Lasky, 2005).

TST's theory of change centers on understanding oneself and others in the context of social institutions, with a particular focus on the emotions that underlie violence and on their transformation (see Greenberg, 2008; Scheper-Hughes & Bourgois, 2004). Accordingly, the essence of violence resides in a denial of the humanity of the other, as when the other is thought to be so different from oneself and so devoid of the emotions that make us human as to make relationships and communication impossible (Anzaldúa, 1987; Said, 1978). Violence is thus different from conflict, which entails engagement with the other, expressing, as needed, our disagreement, anger, hurt, and other emotions. Conflict can thus rebuild relationships that violence severs (e.g., see Melchin & Picard, 2008).

Expressing emotions, including negative ones, is an important part of TST: a supportive environment helps participants let down their masks (Craig, 1994; Goffman, 1959) and speak openly about their fears, frustrations, failures, pain, prejudices, and violence. In the process, participants share information which, coming from multiple perspectives, typically enables the group to develop new understandings of the problem. Solutions thus emerge that are generally more viable than is the case when planning and decision making are either expert-driven or not informed by multiple perspectives. The literature refers to this sharing of information as collective intelligence, a fast-growing practice that is based on the evolving model of the learning organization and on complexity theory (Atlee, 2003; Boud, Cressey, & Docherty, 2006; Hamilton et al., 2004; Page, 2007; Senge, Scharmer, Jaworski, & Flowers, 2004; Taylor, 2003). The central idea is that expert approaches to problems are not viable in fast-paced environments marked by complexity; in these contexts, dealing with complex problems requires pulling together information from multiple sources, and especially from diverse perspectives. In particular, those who are on the ground, experiencing a problem first-hand, constitute a vital new source of information. Page's (2007) own cutting-edge research demonstrates the superior outcomes produced by diverse groups. A key question then centers on how diverse groups can come to share information and generate a genuine collective intelligence from the exchange. Pierre Levy (1995) makes the important distinction between the exchange of information and the co-construction of knowledge, suggesting that the latter is less frequent and much more difficult to achieve. A collective is not necessarily intelligent and might be overly conformist. Collective intelligence, according to Levy, requires bringing together groups that include as much diversity as possible—of opinion, capacities, knowledge base—so participants can engage in collective reflection and dialogue that valorizes diversity and leads to a creative and productive synergy (Zara, 2004). Given that diverse groups are often separated by prejudices and violence, Rojzman adds the important insight that before truthful information can be shared, one must foster sufficient trust to allow members of diverse groups to get beyond in-group conformity, mutual suspicions, stereotypes, and prejudices.

Rojzman's account of the emotions involved in inter-group enmity and violence conforms with studies of prejudice and inter-group bias (Hewstone, Rubin, & Willis, 2002; Pettigrew, 2008) and genocide (Staub, 2003b). As Ervin Staub's voluminous research demonstrates, at the intra-personal level, we experience negative feelings toward a stranger when the stranger brings out our fears, which may be evoked by real or imagined dangers, and are different for different people; while some may fear being judged or rejected, others may anticipate aggression, whether physical or emotional, and still others may be fearful because they do not understand what is going on and what is expected—a fear of too much uncertainty and of the unknown, in the context of confident expectations of harm—one of the definitions of mistrust. These negative emotions and their accompanying attitudes and behaviors are complicated by the severing of social bonds across different social groups and by vicious cycles of prejudice and stereotypes. The social capital literature refers to this problem, though the focus is not on the emotional subtext (Dika & Singh, 2002). Social dominance theory makes the final linkage from this intergroup level to the macro level: power plays, social hierarchies, ideologies, and cultural and political factors interact to produce group-level and structural oppression, directing these expressions toward outgroups (Sidanius, Pratto, van Laar, & Levin, 2004). As these authors assert, it is important to consider and study interactions across these levels.

TST takes this caution to heart: its starting point are basic human needs and the ways individuals, groups, institutions, and sociopolitical structures interact and, in the process, create more or less healthy environments for meeting such needs (Eckersley, 2006). As Eckersley and others suggest, social environments can be pathological when extreme social selfishness and acquisitiveness lead some to disregard others' well-being. According to Staub (2003a, 2003b), although specifics may vary, researchers generally agree that human needs include affiliation and belonging, meaning, recognition, certainty, safety, and power (defined as "the capacity to act"). An important insight is that tensions around meeting these needs are never fully resolved: they begin early in life and become an important and mostly unconscious influence on how we respond to our environment (Daniele & Gordon, 1996). Enacting good or evil, in Ervin Staub's (2003a) purposefully moral language, is related to experiences in our childhood as well as to processes of social dominance, including histories of colonial dominance and out-group oppression. The connection to the emotional realm is through pain and fear experienced when our emotional and existential needs are not met. In this sense, as Eckersley and many other social commentators have argued, modern Western culture is itself promoting pathologies.

Changes in the social environment, including societal crises, can make people regress toward pathologies such as paranoia and its potential for hatred and violence; they can also, however, turn the tables and promote altruism and positive connections to others (Staub, 2005). For instance, unresolved needs for safety or love in early life, in contexts characterized by social selfishness and the lack of proverbial safety nets may contribute to excessive fears of being attacked, rejected, and abandoned and, in a move to projection, generate tendencies to interpret the actions of feared or unknown others as attacks against which we must protect ourselves. This is the main import of the well-known research into the authoritarian personality (Adorno, Frenkel-Brunswik, Levinson, & Sanford, 1950; Fromm, 1941/1969; Fromm, 1955) and the political psychology of Nazism and genocide (Staub, 2003b) that saw the light in the aftermath of the rise of the Nazi and Fascist regimes. According to these authors, relations to authority such as blind obedience, compliance, and participation in mass actions led by autocratic and dictatorial leaders are a pathological way of satisfying psychic needs for certainty, affiliation, and power.

Contributing to this well-known literature, TST group practice applies these insights to interrupt pathological intergroup behaviors and support the kind of personal development that favors collaboration and democratic action (Rojzman & Rojzman, 2007). When a facilitator intervenes by changing the group's social environment in ways that reduce fears, it creates a space for the emergence of healthy relationships. Indeed, one of the very few interventions that manage to create school–community collaboration in urban settings, starting from mistrust, is James Comer's School Development Program, which is based on promoting healthy adult development and adult relationships (Comer, 2004). Comer's premise is that circumstances experienced as threatening—so often present in impoverished and isolated neighborhoods and their schools—can bring forth survival and aggressive energies that exist in all of us. The disruptive and even violent child is acting out the aggression and violence expressed by the meaningful adults in his or her life. The task of the reformer, then, is to develop supports for adults and organizations that care for and educate children so that they can "channel their energy into improving conditions and outcomes for students rather than expressing it in harmful adult conflicts" (Comer, 2004, p. 164).

Building Trust from Mistrust

Since the 1990s, many studies of collaborative or participatory school reform have established the importance of trust, provided guidance on how to foster it, and documented positive learning outcomes resulting from relationships of trust, which foster collaboration and engagement inside schools and between school and community (see Bryk, Bender Sebring, Allensworth, Luppescu, & Easton, 2010; Bryk & Schneider, 2002; Cook-Sather, 2009; Gordon & Seashore Louis, 2009; Jeynes, 2003; Kensler, 2008; Tschannen-Moran, 2001). However, with the exception of Comer's SDP, few practices are available to help school leaders, educators, and change agents engage in collaborative reforms in communities wracked by deep social divisions, poverty and its accompanying ills, and power asymmetries—sites where school–community interactions are likely to include a surfeit of conflict, fear, mistrust, aggression, and incivility. As one telling example, Bryk and Schneider's (2002) study of the Chicago school reform found that in the initial stages of reform, fully two-thirds of the schools most in need of improvements were either left behind or struggling, with the former generally located in racially isolated high poverty neighborhoods.

The paucity of supportive practices for intervening in these environments is matched by the state of research on trust. In an extensive and growing research literature on trust and trust building there are few studies on mistrust and on how to move from mistrust to collaboration (Kramer, 1999; Lewicki & Wiethoff, 2000). Lewicki and Wiethoff propose that mistrust is not merely the absence or the opposite of trust. Whereas trust involves confidently positive expectations and beliefs about the other person or group, distrust involves confidently *negative* expectations and beliefs about the other, which means *fear* of the other. Following this line of thought, Saunders and Thornhill (2004) consider trust and mistrust in relation to a desire to reduce complexity and uncertainty with regard to one's expectations about others: "mistrust reduces complexity and uncertainty by removing favourable expectations and allowing unfavourable expectations to be seen as certain" (2004, p. 495). Kramer interestingly connects several threads in the literature: as Grovier asserts, distrust has been defined as a "lack of confidence in the other, a concern that the other may act so as to harm one, that he does not care about one's welfare or intends to act harmfully, or is hostile" (in Kramer, 1999, p. 587). Suspicion has been viewed as one of the central cognitive components of distrust (Lewicki & Wiethoff, 2000) and has been characterized as a psychological state in which perceivers "actively entertain multiple, possibly rival, hypotheses about the motives or genuineness of a person's behavior" (Kramer, 1999, p. 587).

Further, the literature on categorization alerts us to the presence of category-based distrust and suspicion (i.e., directed to different identity groups), where outgroup members are evaluated as less honest, open, and trustworthy than members of one's own group (Kramer, 1999) and even as less prone to experiencing distinctly human emotions (Leyens et al., 2003). Furthermore, the anxiety and other negative emotions that characterize interactions across social divisions may strengthen stereotyping and prejudice, hamper communication, and increase distrust (Dovidio, Gaertner, & Kawakami, 2003). Some studies suggest that trust building and reduction of mistrust operate differently in dominant and subordinated groups (Dessel & Rogge, 2008).

Shared goals, respect, reflective inquiry, and feelings of interdependence are commonly regarded as central to collaboration (on professional learning communities, see Stoll, Bolam, McMahon, Wallace & Thomas, 2006). However, these are not likely to come easily when relationships start from suspicion and unfavorable expectations. Let me quote Bryk & Schneider (2002) at some length:

> Embedded in the daily social routines of schools is an interrelated set of mutual dependencies among all key actors: students, teachers, principals and administrators, and parents. These structural dependencies create feelings of vulnerability for the individuals involved; this vulnerability is especially salient in the context of asymmetric power relations, such as those between parents and local school professionals. A recognition of this vulnerability by the superordinate party (in this instance, the local school professionals) and a conscious commitment on their part to relieve the uncertainty and unease of the other (that is, poor parents) can create a very intense, meaningful social bond among the parties. (2002, p. 20)

Bryk and Schneider's comments remind us of the importance of context. Rather than looking for generally valid definitions of trust and mistrust and ways of enabling collaboration where mistrust reigns, we need to start by considering that the process involves relationships between a trusting agent and a trusted one (or vice versa, mistrusting and mistrusted agents), interacting in their particular context (Kramer, 1999, p. 574). Here, micro, meso, and macro come together: what are the personal, organizational, and even national histories, narratives, and memories that provide the interpretive lenses for one determining that another's intentions are harmful and their actions are suspicious? Considering the earlier discussion, we also need to take into account how individuals' basic human needs are being met, and the pain, fear, and violence that emerge from pathological adaptations to meeting one's needs; the realm of the emotions must be included in the picture.

Table 11.1 brings together the main points in the above discussion. Based on the TST theory of change and supportive research, it highlights the actions the TST facilitator undertakes in order to enable a group to move from mistrust to collaboration and the underlying rationale for those actions: changing the group environment so as to create healthy ways for members to meet their basic needs. The table provides the framework in light of which the data are analyzed. The grand tour research question pertains to the correspondence between the theory of change and observable moves from mistrust to collaboration in the TST groups. In other words, what I am testing here is the explanatory power of the theory.

Masks, emotions, needs and interventions do not break down neatly into categories and should be seen as fluid and interactive rather than fixed. The table constitutes a heuristic that guides the facilitator's interventions in the group. In the first column are some expressions and behaviors relating to mis-

TABLE 11.1 TST Approach to Moving from Mistrust to Trust and Collaboration

	Sources and Manifestations of Mistrust		Building Trust and Collaboration
1. Masks & Pathological Expressions	2. Fears, Violence & Related Emotional Reactions	3. Unmet Needs	4. TST Facilitator's Actions
Delinquency & rebellion from authority figures. Peer and in-groups as alternative sources of respect.	Humiliation & contempt. Victimization	Respect Recognition Valorization	Treat fairly & without bias. Recognize talents, capacities, knowledge, contributions.
Pathological cooperation (submit to authority).	Rejection & isolation: Feeling victimized; loneliness, being misunderstood, devalued, despised.	Affiliation Love Connection Community	Model acceptance and non-judgment; create bonds between people who would not interact; support free self-expression, including negative emotions & expectations; confidentiality in the group.
Racist/jingoistic discourse and rejection of racial mixing, immigrants, *others*. Being a victim and not responsible for one's actions, since they are reactions to the actions of powerful others.	Aggression (physical, emotional & symbolic): sense of powerlessness and helplessness.	Power Safety Security	Give power/authority to make decisions. Ability to make a difference in one's environment. Address denial of responsibility, sense of victimization, and Manichean worldview of victim/oppressor. Participants' roles shift from dependency to autonomy
Fanaticism; Manichean worldviews (either good or bad). Seek absolute truths, expert knowledge; insist on rigid structures, discipline, & controls.	The unknown: anxiety, doubt	Meaning Certainty Information Order	Reduce anxiety, reassure and maintain clear sense of direction. Ensure open flow of information. Help group appreciate complexity. Each member has partial truths that together lead to collective intelligence.

trust that may be present in the group, while the second column names emotions and expressions of violence connected to these behaviors. Here, it is important not to assume the posture of the expert who knows and analyzes participants, but to use the heuristic to interrogate the situation, considering the question: what might be going on here? (Charles Rojzman, personal communication). The third column names the needs that underlie the behaviors and emotions in the first two columns, which become a guide for the facilitator's interventions in the group (fourth column). These interventions are directed at creating enough safety and trust so participants will be motivated to take some risks in removing their masks, becoming vulnerable, engaging in authentic communication, and collaborating. The facilitator looks for central dynamics that revolve around the process of (a) reflecting and developing self-awareness; (b) moving from binary thinking, such as victim-oppressor, self-other, and in-group/out-group toward complex understandings of the situation; and (c) moving from a sense of victimization and powerlessness toward the assumption of responsibility and empowerment.

RESEARCH METHODS

The TST project began with a stakeholders' meeting that included principals and teachers from network schools, a member of the local Community Governing Council, the two lead administrators for REP Picasso, and Charles, the TST facilitator. The leadership team clarified and affirmed the goal of the project (to plan for specific local actions that would foster students' academic achievement) and the design of the intervention, which involved creating two groups that would go through the TST process: a student group comprised of nine 14- to 17-year-olds from 3rd and 4th forms (8th and 9th grades) at Collège Picasso; and a group of ten to fifteen adult participants that included educators and school professionals (social workers) from the different levels of schooling in the network, as well as parents and members of local community organizations. Both groups would approach their work as action research, learning to collaborate in order to become a vehicle for understanding the problem and proposing ways to address it. The student group would meet separately from the adults, since experience suggested the students would not speak freely in the presence of the adults. The facilitator would find an appropriate time to introduce the students' input and ideas into the adult conversation, in ways as yet to be determined. The leadership team then proceeded with recruitment of participants. The criterion for selection was maximum diversity: it was important that groups include vociferous critics and failing students and not only willing volunteers (Planning meeting transcript, March 14, 2005).

Participants for the student group were recruited through a flyer drafted by the TST assistant facilitator, Théa Rojzman, based on several days of observation at the school. The flyer is reproduced here to show the approach to gaining a population of discontented and failing students who would not normally trust or participate in any initiatives by the school.

SCHOOL ISN'T PERFECT?

In this school, there are students who are hurting, not doing well, afraid of failing; students who feel like they are alone, attacked, and victims of injustice. To all those who are having difficulties and are angry, who feel deceived, outraged, dissatisfied, or even happy (why not?), we propose four days of exchange and interactive research. We invite students in 8th and 9th grade to participate in a group of "young researchers"...The mission of this group will be to find solutions to deal students' problems, your own problems...Do you have anything to say, any ideas or criticisms? Come, you can change the school! (Rojzman, T., 2005a, p. 1)

Based on the TST theory of change, the flyer also named the emotions students might be experiencing, including negative ones. It did so without judgment and without naming a problem or the students as the problem. Instead, disengaged and disaffected students were asked to contribute their ideas so that the school might change. The flyer was posted on school walls and nine students responded, all known as troublemakers by school personnel and all ethnic French of North African and African origins. The recruitment method had produced the intended results.

Leadership team members recruited adult participants from schools, the neighborhood and local organizations. Given a few changes in membership, the adult group consisted of 14 to 16 participants and included parents (3 to 4), educators (9 to 11 teachers, school directors, assistant principal), community social workers (1 to 2) and representatives of community/civic organizations (1 to 3). Some overlap in participants' roles accounts for numeric discrepancies. The parents were all mothers who were of non-European ethnic origins and the community representatives and social workers included both white French and French "of color." All the educators were white French.

The student group met for two weekend sessions held prior to the adult group meetings (April 25–26 and May 2–3, 2005). Student representatives also participated in two meetings with the principal and vice-principal of Collège Picasso (April 26 and June 22, 2005), and six of the students also met subsequently with the adult group in October 2005, on the latter's invitation. The adult group met for a total of four weekends (May 23–24, 2005; October 17–18, 2005; March 2006; October 2006) of which only the first two are of interest here. Each day lasted around five hours. Group members also engaged in various related actions in between sessions.

Théa Rojzman collected and transcribed verbatim data for most of the group sessions and wrote thematic analytical summaries that included observable non-verbal behaviors. Charles Rojzman provided clarifications and further analytical commentary relating the project to TST theory and practice. Novella Keith translated data from the French, analyzed the data, searched for and reviewed related literature, and wrote the chapter. Data sources used in this chapter are verbatim notes of the planning meeting, all meetings with students and the first weekend meeting with adults, and thematic summaries of the two meetings with students and the second meeting with adults. Verbatim field notes, including direct quotations, are referred to as "field notes," followed by the date of the meeting and the page number(s) where the account appears in the transcript. Data, including direct quotations, from thematic summaries are referenced as Rojzman, T., 2005a (student data) and Rojzman, T., 2005b (adult data), followed by the page number(s) where the data appear in the document.

Data were interrogated in light of TST's theory of change and the reviewed literature on trust and mistrust. In an iterative process between the grand tour research question and the data, I selected four moments in the students' and adults' groups that seemed to provide rich details relating to the research question. The first moment is the initial encounter between the students and the TST facilitator (April 25, 2005). The main focus here is on the process of moving from mistrust to sufficient trust to enable collaboration. The second moment centers on the students' role-plays featured in a film (May 3–4, 2005) that was later shown to the adult group. The focus here is on the TST approach to developing trustworthy information with the students about the problem of school success. The third moment occurs when the adults watch the students' film (May 23, 2005) and illustrates the process through which adults establish the students as a source of trustworthy information that can be incorporated into collective intelligence for school reform. The fourth moment features a meeting between students and adults (October 18, 2005), which takes the form of a dialogue in which all participants consider one another trustworthy partners.

Data analysis followed the standard qualitative approach consisting of a search for themes that related to the theoretical framework and research question. As I interrogated the fit between the theory and the data, I paid particular attention to the ways the group process appeared to build trust and support collaboration. This approach is in line with "critical realist" research, which establishes the study of processes, contextualized through qualitative research (here, a case study), as a valid and powerful alternative to experimental research (Maxwell, 2005). The aim is not to establish a generalizable connection between context-free causes and effects, but to understand and interpret how events and actions in the particular and the local are connected, taking into full account the context-rich environments that constitute the site of social science research (Flyvbjerg, 2001). In so doing, we are provided with an internally rich way of linking causes and effects than sheds light on the intricacies of social life.

FROM MISTRUST TO DIALOGUE: FOUR KEY MOMENTS

Moment Four: "Should we meet again in three months?"
"No, no, in two weeks!"

I start with the last moment, at the end of the second session with adults, because this point marks the beginning of collaboration between the adult and student groups. Moments One to Three, presented subsequently, will look for the path that led to this moment. The adult group had viewed the students' film during their first session, in May 2005, and decided on the first day of their October session to invite the students to meet. Six students agreed to come. It is now the morning of October 18. The students arrive on time and participate fully in an intense three-hour dialogue on the theme of "what is a good day at school," during which no one asks for a break. At the end, when the facilitator suggests another meeting in three months, one of the students objects: "no, no, in two weeks!" (Field notes, October 18, 2005, pp. 10–15).

The meeting starts with the director of a primary school explaining the objectives of the meeting to the students—the group of adults has been trying to come to grips with the issue of school success but is having problems: they want things to work out, but they don't seem to be getting there. The adults would like to know from the students: "How do you see the problem of school success? What do you think can make a difference?" (Field notes, October 18, 2005, p. 1). As agreed by the adults the day before, the director proposes that teachers and students talk together about "a good day at school." The students agree. The adults start.

Before continuing the narrative, let me briefly comment on this introduction, which may have struck readers as somewhat unusual. What stands out is the way the students are being addressed: the adult admits to not knowing what to do and needing the students' knowledge. As the research on youth adult partnerships documents, adults generally find it difficult to enact their side of the partnership because they tend to relate to young people in ways that are either infantilizing and overly directive or too laissez-faire: the point instead is to act as guides, mentors, coaches—to provide young adult roles and trust young people to fulfill them, but not trust them blindly. They need appropriate adult guidance (Camino, 2005; Cook-Sather, 2002). In fact, earlier interactions among the adults revealed the same problematic relationship between teachers and parents, with the latter feeling either infantilized or marginalized by teachers (Field notes, May 24, 2005, p. 4). If the educators in this meeting are treating the students as partners, it makes sense to ask whether the process has changed their taken-for-granted attitudes and demeanors. Analysis of the process will address this point.

For the teachers, a good day at school comes down to two main issues. The first involves good relationships, good feelings, having a sense of work well done and students who are satisfied. "Everyone leaves happy" and the next day "we are motivated," and "we feel like coming back." There is an almost primordial sense about the importance of good relationships in school. The second issue pertains to meaningful work: not feeling useless, having the sense of teaching something important and of one's presence making a difference. For instance, one teacher remembers teachers who made him want to learn by giving him a larger perspective on the world. That is what he wants here, to produce "magical moments in the classroom." Thus, indirectly, this issue also has to do with relationships, not for their own sake, but for a proper role for adults in guiding, mentoring, and coaching the young (Field notes, October 18, 2005, p. 10).

The students start by saying they want an orderly environment without any fights and problems, teachers who understand them, but most importantly, they want to understand the materials the teacher is presenting and be able to get good grades: understanding the teachers should not require an enormous effort and teachers should slow down if needed, encourage the students and help them. The lively exchange includes the students' criticisms of the school and of teachers but also a sense of camaraderie with the adults. At one point, a student asks what school was like "before," for the adults who are present. He and his peers seem astounded that the adults, as students, were afraid, kept quiet, tried to avoid getting into problems, went to school mainly to see their friends and not especially because they liked school, and the adults "were always right." "Same as for us—the students exclaim—nothing has changed!" (Field notes, October 18, 2005, pp. 10–11). However, as it later transpires, unlike the adults, students now are not afraid of teachers but only of their older brothers, who will get physical and hit them, and of their parents' emotional reactions when things are not going well at school.

The conversation is wide-ranging, going from issues of scheduling and class size, to teachers who don't want to explain and just throw them out of class, the problem of labels that stick, from the beginning of the year ("troublemaker," "no good"), without the opportunity for change. As time goes on, participants take risks and speak frankly about their emotions and fears. For a student, a teacher's unjust punishment means lack of care and lack of love. A teacher admits to an increasingly lower tolerance threshold in the classroom, due to fearing loss of control. The adults do not simply agree with the students or make polite comments. They engage them, disagree, and throw back their own hard questions. When an adult asks the students about their own responsibility for the problems in school ("what if the students just aren't working hard enough, or aren't motivated?") the dialogue turns to the very meaning of the school that the students are asked to "be motivated" to attend, and a problematic match between the school's lack of clear focus and relevant curriculum, and the students' lack of a clear sense about their future. The adults also want to explore peer pressure and internal groups divisions among the students, and the students explain that, for them, the issue is not peer pressure but some students being weak; it is about life in the neighborhood and does not necessarily relate to life in school (Field notes, October 18, 2005, pp. 11–13).

Daniel Yankelovitch (1999) says "in dialogue, we penetrate behind the polite superficialities and defenses in which we habitually armor ourselves. We listen and respond to one another with an authenticity that forces a bond between us." He calls on Martin Buber's I and Thou to propose that "life itself is a form of meeting and dialogue is the 'ridge' on which we meet." (Yankelovitch, 1999, p. 15). Recalling Saunders and Thornhill (2004), showing our vulnerabilities is also a way of connecting and building trust. It seems evident that this sort of existential meeting is taking place here. Students and adults are partners in a conversation that interrogates the ridges where their lives meet and that seems to fit the definition of collective intelligence. Here, the understandings and constructions of problems that emerge from the different ways participants experience classroom and community yield a collective understanding of what it will take to change the school. In comparing this exchange with interpretations of the problem that both students and adults voiced earlier during the project, one is struck by the richness of this dialogue in producing insights, awareness, and information that could lead to appropriate local actions to address the problem. Information was not the only outcome, as there was motivation and energy that comes when people discover that they are not alone and they can in fact act as a team and with its support.

I cannot provide full supports for this statement given the space limitations of this chapter. Putting side by side the proposals for action the adults identified at the beginning of the process and at the end of the second weekend does provide suggestive evidence. Day 4 proposals seem to reflect new perspectives (e.g., the recognition of the oppressive nature of education), attention to the multiple dimensions of the issue (e.g., the importance of the affective domain in academic achievement), and appreciation of the ongoing creation of collective intelligence through "spaces for conversation." Beyond this brief comment, I must let readers reach their own conclusions.

Action Proposals Day 1 (May 23, 2005, 10)	Keys to School Success Day 4 (October 18, 2005, 16)
■ "Get parents to come to school for one or two weeks so as to reduce the discrepancies in the messages students receive from home and from school, as well as inform parents about how school works; ■ Bring all the stakeholders to the table, including parents, to learn about reciprocal expectations and put in place 'something in common'; ■ Help students develop by taking them on outings out of the neighborhood and motivate them to do well by showing them that their success is valued."	**THE SCHOOL:** ■ Consider the school schedule ■ Match school work to the rhythm of family life ■ Take into account different levels of student performance ■ Institute group work and peer supports ■ Further develop and stabilize teams, inside school and in the network ■ Create spaces for conversations ■ Find ways to make acceptable the legitimate violence of the educational system **AFFECTIVE DOMAIN** **[issues to be considered]:** ■ Motivation and effort ■ Being valued ■ Trust ■ Respect and consideration

Figure 11.1

My sense is that the difference between the two lists is not simply a matter of three more days the group spent together, but of the collective intelligence that resulted from collaboration. How did project participants become partners, each with trustworthy information to contribute to the project? It is time to return to the first moment and trace the steps to this conclusion.

Moment One: Give this project a grade

I begin with a somewhat detailed description of the initial meeting with students, because the analysis of transcripts shows that it exemplifies a process that was followed with each group and is part of the TST strategy for getting a group of mistrusting agents to move toward developing sufficient trust to participate (Charles Rojzman, personal communication).

It is the morning of April 25, 2005, later than the expected starting time. After some calls and reminders, nine students (seven boys and two girls, aged 14 to 17), the facilitator (Charles) and his assistant (Théa) are ready to start. Charles begins by explaining the overall project: a number of different groups are being brought together that include all the stakeholders in the educational system—parents, teachers, other educators, social workers, students and neighborhood representatives—in order to develop proposals on the topic of school success in this neighborhood. The demeanor of the students suggests a wait-and-see attitude: some are slumped in their chairs, others look indifferent, no one is smiling. Charles asks them to introduce themselves and also to say how they feel about the prospects of this project: "Do you believe that this work will bear results and help students succeed? Give it a grade, from 0 to 20." (April 25, 2005, pp. 1–2) The students' grades range from 7 to 12, as they talk about their hopes (good idea, it's good to think about this, it would be good if it could work), and about the obstacles they anticipate. Several themes emerge, captured by the following quotes: "teachers always want to be right;" "it might work for a while but then they will let it fall by the wayside;" "some teachers won't want to do it," they "won't listen," they "pay no attention;" "a week won't change much;" "there has to be give-and-take, and teachers always have the last word." One remarks that it's not only the teachers—some of the students don't want to change, either. At the end, Charles proposes an exercise addressing the question: who's responsible for the students' failure? He adds: "Complete the sentence: if we don't succeed it's because the students [blank]; or, because the teachers [blank]. Explain why." (April 25, 2005, p. 2)

This beginning is similar to that of the adults, who were asked to introduce themselves and also speak to the question of who was mainly responsible for problems pertaining to school success. Following these long introductions, the adults were then asked to pair up with someone whose views had perhaps shocked them, or with whom they had some significant disagreements. Referring to Table 11.1, the facilitator is intervening to change the group's social environment through the following: signaling that negative emotions, expressions and expectations are welcome, and not only positive or polite ones; creating opportunities for participants who are unlike one another to interact in a personalized and intimate (small group, pairs) setting and begin to develop personal connections that also help break up in-groups; engaging the group in reflection about responsibility for the problem, so as to encourage self-awareness and complex thinking; and addressing powerlessness and victimization by signaling that group members are collaborators whose experiential knowledge is a valued asset for institutional change.

Returning to the students (in a pattern that is also observed in the adult group), the exercise does not result in much perspective taking. Their narrative continues to construct teachers as the problem, providing examples of unfairness, preferences and biases that constitute a fundamental injustice. Students also name lack of consideration or attention to family problems that affect them, lack of care, teachers not seeing them except as categories of students, no one showing concern for them, and failure to provide academic support when needed. Charles does not point out to the students that they have failed to follow directions and have not done the exercise correctly, nor does he assert that they must also, necessarily, bear some responsibility for the problem. He listens and introduces probing questions: are all teachers like that (answer: no, not all); how are students responsible (answer: students create problems, as well, they're not all obedient; "we're not all saints, either!"). He also reminds them that one of the goals toward which they are working is to determine how to share their knowledge about the problem with the adult group. Here, he is behaving according to well-established group therapy practice: as Yalom and Leszcz assert, "the basic posture of the therapist must be one of concern, acceptance, genuineness, empathy. *Nothing, no technical consideration, takes precedence over this attitude*" (2005, p. 117).

Returning to Table 11.1 (column 1), the facilitator understands these expressions as masks. Listening for unmet needs (column 3), he may consider the conversation as indicating possible needs for recognition and affiliation. The facilitator responds by modeling openness and acceptance and asking reflective questions that may lead students to consider their binary constructions of reality. In this environment that appears to be non-judgmental and caring and is becoming relatively safe, students begin to exercise their agency in ways that act on the school environment rather than against it. Having seemingly understood the importance of reflection and awareness, one of them suggests making posters "to make teachers and students reflect." Another student proposes making a film, with scenes that show adults the students' view of how they get thrown out of class and eventually suspended from school. They begin by brainstorming words for teachers and for students. Théa comments: "a list of around one hundred words is quickly generated, many of which are quite violent toward the teachers. [The students] laugh and throw out the words without thinking" (TS students, 5). The brainstorming exercise also produces negative words for students. After small groups work on creating slogans from the words, the group decides on five slogans for students and 13 for teachers. The slogans for teachers include: "I treat you with respect, you treat me with respect," "Moussa, Kadhidja, Kader = Maxime, Bertrand, Géraldine" (meaning that students with Arab first names are not different from students with French first names), "Tell me when I'm doing well, too," "I exist, why don't you see me?" "We all want the same things." "Why don't you give me support?" "We need it to make progress." "Don't get physical." "If you're wrong, accept it." Slogans for students: "Put yourself in the teachers' place; their job's not easy," "School is not the hood," "Bastard, prick, fuck-up, these aren't words for school," "Pride, for both students and teachers, that's what gets us stuck in power games," "Problems between students and teachers are often created by misunderstandings. Do you agree?" (April 25, 2005, pp. 5–6).

Referring to Table 11.1, two issues seem to emerge. First, the students' slogans for the teachers can be heard through the filter of their own needs, which include not only recognition and affiliation, but also safety and information. Second, the slogans for their peers signal a beginning of owning some responsibility for the problem, which may create a path out of the sense of powerlessness induced by victimization and rebellion. On the second day, the students make up the posters and explore their ideas for the film. There is also a meeting with the principal to discuss the posters.

Moment Two: Of Clowns and Rabble

The following weekend is devoted to preparing and making the film. Two additional adults have been brought in by the Rojzman Institute to participate in small group work with the students. The first day serves to deepen understanding of the problems aired during the first session and help the students express themselves on the difficulties they experience as well as on their ideas about how to promote school success. Students are invited to create two stories in their small groups: one of a student who succeeds in school and another one of a failing student. They are asked to talk personally about their own lives in the context of their families, community, and school. The role of the adults is explained: they are not there to help the students, but to talk about their experiences in school, from their own perspective (May 2, 2005, pp. 1–2).

The emphasis on self-awareness through reflection and on speaking from one's personal experience is in evidence in both the student and the adult group and is part of well-established therapeutic practices that connect emotional experience with cognitive understanding and experience inside the group with what exists outside the group and in one's past. Yalom and Leszcz comment that "the self-reflective loop is crucial if an emotional experience is to be transformed into a therapeutic one" (2005, p. 30). They also explain how personal history and current life situations fit into the group's orientation to the "here and now":

> It is not that the group doesn't deal with the past; *it is what is done with the past:* the crucial task is not to uncover, to piece together, to fully understand the past, *but to use the past for the help it offers in understanding (and changing) the individual's mode of relating to the others in the present.* (Yalom & Leszcz, 2005, p. 155. Italics in the original)

Here, students are learning to relate to adults in a different way from usual—and thus experiencing healthy bonds with the adult world—by sharing their past and present experiences in school, home, and the neighborhood with those in the adults' past. The result is a nuanced discussion of the problem, which examines interactions among students and students and teachers. As the students reflect on their experiences, they begin to break down the binary categories that were part of their original masks, in which they inhabit a student world composed of clowns (*bouffons*) and rabble (*cailleras*). The clowns do well in school, don't question authority, never leave home, and are boring; the rabble don't succeed, don't see the point of school and thus rebel and have fun; they often have family problems and are always singled out as troublemakers in school. The students explain: "there are always some students who do well and others who don't." As they develop the scenes, however, one hears comments such as, "it's not always like that," "there are lots of different circumstances," and "there are different kinds of clowns; it's not necessarily bad to be a clown" (Rojzman, T., 2005a, p. 8). As binaries begin to give way to multiplicity and complexity, some of the students carefully define other categories. It transpires that their group is not comprised of unified rabble: there are conflicts brewing behind the masks of group unity, which point to in-group differences. In this context, the students develop and role-play nine scenes (May 3, 2005, pp. 7–9).

The following day brings more nuanced explorations of interactions between students, teachers, and parents and eventually eleven scenes are filmed: three scenes in a classroom, six scenes of meetings between teachers and parents, one scene of parents and a child, at home, and one of a meeting between students and teachers (May 4, 2005). Dialogues surrounding role-plays of good and bad teachers provide mounds of insight and information. A scene between parents and children at home shows the adults as more understanding of the children than a scene of parents meeting with a teacher. Nonetheless, the parents seem powerless, asking plaintively at times: "Why do you behave like that? What's going to happen to you—do you want to become a chamber maid?" Ashamed of their children's behavior, the parents don't seem to know what to do other than agree with the teacher. (PS students, 11)

How does a "good" adult behave? The initial picture of the good teacher depicts one who pays attention to the students' needs and maintains order by establishing an alliance with the students that at times creates an in-group against the administration. When students talk and do not pay attention, he asks for "some respect;" he is attentive to students and goes by their desks, asking how things are going and if there is a problem. When one student doesn't reply, the teacher asks another student to come sit by him and help him; he always speaks nicely and smiles; he lends his book to a student who does not have one. When a student is being disruptive in spite of these efforts, the teacher goes by him and says, "stop, otherwise the principal will say that I don't do my work well." These efforts result in less chaos, but the students are not engaged in the lesson. When asked why, students explain that the teacher is too permissive and does not have enough authority (Rojzman, T., 2005a, pp. 10–11). However, the student who plays the very strict (bad) teacher has trouble controlling the class. Asked if he's responsible for the chaos, he says no, "the students have just come back in from their break, sometimes they're just like that." Another student comments: "he is strict, but he's alone;" "on the one hand, I understand him, on the other, he's not necessarily right."

We see again a severing of binaries and more complexity. The students recognize that they need adults who are both responsive and responsible, who can guide them, and they do not know how to make that happen. In this context, the facilitator plays that adult: referencing Table 11.1, he is acting in ways that meet their needs in healthier ways: he follows their lead but not blindly so, treating them as responsible and knowing agents, while also providing gentle guidance. He is somewhat like a mentor, except that he does not have all the answers: they must make the road together. Similarly, working with adults in small groups to prepare the scenes creates an additional experience and demonstration for the students that collaboration between youth and adults is possible. In this room, an environment has been created that makes openness, trust and thus collaboration possible. I suggest that having met the students' needs in healthy ways provides a reasonable explanation for the transformation.

Moment Three: "I had no idea that they see us so well"

The session begins with Charles giving the adult group an account of the students' work, including the film they have prepared for the adults' viewing. Reactions are mixed, as participants voice expectations that the students' portrayals are likely to be stereotypes and caricatures, also noting that the expected—and excessive—criticism would only represent the views of problem students. Some of the participants remain shocked at hearing about the violence in some students' remarks about teachers. One even expresses disgust.

Charles agrees that the students' views are subjective and do not represent the views of all students. He also confesses that he is not sure how to proceed toward the goal of the groups being able to work together: "yesterday, the conversation was interesting, but whose fault is it? We are steeped in a sense of powerlessness. We can't change others. So we need to talk about how we can change, what can change in ourselves, here and now." The group, he adds, needs to find ways to work together, while incorporating the diverse motivations of students. He suggests reflecting on what each person in the group does that contributes to the problems. The idea is to have an exchange that is close to the lived reality of each one and goes beyond the structure of usual meetings: speaking not in the name of their group but personally about their own difficulties and responsibilities will enable the group to work on real problems, leading to solutions that can be adopted locally, and thus overcome feelings of powerlessness. A conversation ensues in which participants explore the risks and vulnerabilities involved in such an approach. Some are guarded, claiming their right not to make themselves vulnerable, but in the end all agree to work in this way. Against this backdrop, the group agrees to view the students' film. Following the film, an exploration of the adults' own schooling experiences, including their successes and failures, will enable them to reflect on the students' experiences in light of their own.

Based on TST theory (see Table 11.1), this exchange appears to be primarily about the participants' need for safety, power, and information. The facilitator names these themes, making them the subject of reflection about how to move out of powerlessness and toward joint action. The process is clearly guided by the facilitator, but the group is given the time it needs to express fears and other emotions before agreeing to move forward. Different kinds of power are in evidence: the power of self-awareness (as in naming and understanding one's emotional reactions); the power to maintain a sense of control over the process; and the power of becoming agents of institutional change which, as they agree, requires gathering the collective knowledge of the students as well as adults. A new light is thrown on collective intelligence in this particular context: co-constructing knowledge with diverse groups is much more than the technical matter of pooling together information from different and diverse sources. Rather, it requires delving into realms that participants may passionately want to ignore. In this context, gathering collective intelligence requires building trust by addressing the realm of emotions (fears and motivation for change) and valorizing the potential contribution of mistrusted others (here, the students). Having their emotions and power acknowledged appears to create enough safety and trust for participants to hear potentially painful information without falling into defensive postures.

As the film ends, the adults come to see that their fears were not entirely justified; the film reveals that the students are trustworthy partners with valuable knowledge to contribute to the project. Their keen observation of adults comes as a surprise, as one teacher comments, "I didn't realize they see us so well." After the film, trust is not fully established and fears have not disappeared. Indeed, the objective is only to create enough trust to be able to share knowledge and work together, and in some contexts it may be realistic to be afraid. One participant names a feeling others share: "sometimes I think, poor kids; then, other times, I wouldn't want to meet a group of them in the dark." At the same time, what happened in the group of students is also transpiring here: binary constructions are being replaced by more complex understandings. Gone is the sense that the portrayals of a few troublemakers should be dismissed because they are necessarily grossly biased. The students' violent expressions notwithstanding, their knowledge is now considered valid. What accounts for this change? Some comment on how well the students have captured the teachers' actions and feelings. Relations with parents and interactions among students also match the adults' impressions and knowledge and so seem realistic. Beyond this, what appears to move the teachers toward trust is the students' feelings: there is surprise about their concern and need for their parents to be involved in their schooling, as well as a sense of connection with the students' struggles. Research on categorization shows that we tend to attribute inherently human or "secondary" emotions (such as love, admiration, fondness, compassion) to our own groups, and not to others (Leyens, et al., 2003). Uniquely human emotions are internally caused and long lasting, rather than sudden and involve morality, cognition, and sensitivity (for instance, love, admiration, compassion, contempt, sorrow). One gets the sense that the film has humanized students in the eyes of the teachers: the students have complex feelings and needs, and in that sense they can be trusted. As the knowledge from the film begins to be integrated with the adults' knowledge, there is a sense that the wealth of diverse experiences is beginning to suggest some possible paths for action.

The process is not linear, however, and the ambiance at the end of this first session with adults contrasts markedly with their next meeting in October, in which the group was floundering. The day before the dialogue that introduced this section of the chapter, there is a great sense of urgency accompanied by a feeling of near-drowning in an "ocean of difficulties": a crisis-ridden start of the school year contrasted markedly with a voluntary-attendance summer school session in which students were pleasant and acted responsibly. The facilitator had intervened: "can I make a suggestion? For me, the only way to move forward is for everyone to be able to work together." This was the context for the group's decision to invite the students to meet with them. In preparation for the meeting, they had identified areas for information gathering (i.e., issues around peer group pressure and violence in class; how to get students and adults to communicate better about what happened in class) and worked on an exercise that had them remember themselves as they were in middle school: "you are the same as you were then, but you are attending this school, in this neighborhood. What's going on? How do you react?"

Through the exercise, the group had come to insightful realizations concerning similarities and differences between themselves as students and the young people in school now. At first, it seemed that "it is two different worlds that have nothing to do one with the other": as students, they had showed respect to the teachers and even if they detested some, they would never dare say it. Then came the realization: "the system was founded on fear of the teachers [and that] was what kept us quiet." "It relied on fear and injustice, but it worked;" and "the more violence there was from teachers, the more quiet the students got" (October 17, 2005, p. 6). The exploration of these differences that followed seemed to energize all participants: gone was the doubt and sense of powerlessness, and insight brought a renewed sense of purpose that was taken into the dialogue the following day.

CONCLUSION

How can we build trust and engender collaboration across social divides marked by mistrust and violence? Starting from this vexing and pressing question led me to a process, Transformational Social Therapy, that is known for its capacity to accomplish this goal. This chapter examined the TST theory of change in light of its supports from research and with regard to its explanatory power: could the theory draw useful and insightful connections between the various aspects of a process that ended in a productive dialogue among students, educators, parents, and neighborhood representatives? Analysis of the case study featuring the initial stages of the Maville-TST School Success Project highlighted four moments that appeared central to moving the initially mistrusting and reluctant would-be partners toward collaboration. The first moment showed that in the context under study, agency was exercised through dynamics that included victimization, blame, rebellion, exclusion and violence. Combined insights from the second and third moments also showed that encouraging participants to give free expression to these dynamics was a key to gaining their participation and beginning to build trust leading to collaboration.

The literature on partnerships affirms the importance of including participants' interests in the process: in Russell Linden's (2010) apt phrase, the point is to ensure everyone can answer affirmatively the WIIFM question, "what's in it for me?" In the context of Maville and perhaps more generally in the context of mistrust, the answer to this question involved being able to express one's grievances as well as one's emotions, including one's fears and violence. The third and fourth moments illustrate how these very expressions created spaces in which participants could show their vulnerability and how this process, perhaps strangely and counter-intuitively, provided an important key to human connection.

Theories are never proven and readers could well add that I have not explored disconfirming evidence. There is always the possibility that the facts of this case could be explained through some other pattern joining causes and effects. Nonetheless, I hope I have provided sufficiently reasonable arguments and evidence that TST, as a well-supported theory of change, does indeed have strong explanatory power in illuminating the path from mistrust to collaboration in the Maville case study. In addition to transforming relationships and providing new collective understandings to inform local reform, the analysis also shows the vital importance of appropriate facilitation. While processes such as inter-group dialogues tend to establish safety and trust by creating rules for behavior (Dessel & Rogge, 2008), the therapeutic foundations that inform TST assert that the modicum of safety and trust required for a group to overcome obstacles to collaboration can be created by intervening in the social environment of the group in ways that reduce social pathologies and support free communication and a move toward healthy relationships (Staub, 2005).

Finally, readers might point out that community participants are not visibly featured in the analysis. The transcripts do show clear divergences and frank disagreements, not only between teachers and parents and their constructions of each other and of schooling, but also among parents and representatives of community organizations. A measure of unpacking "the adults" and showing how their group went through a similar process as the students would thus have been interesting. I chose not to emphasize these issues both because of space limitations and because they did not seem as central as the story that led to the dialogue in the fourth moment. While all participants were essential to the process, reconnecting students and the adult world emerged in this case as a main task to be accomplished. The students embodied in their very identities the possibility of joining school, family and community. Healing relationships among the adults was thus part of working to restore their relationships with youth. The case should thus provide useful insights for building sound partnerships that include youth as well as community members in the search for trustworthy knowledge and solutions to problems of schooling in "difficult" contexts.

NOTES

1. An early version of this chapter was presented at the meetings of the American Educational Research Association (Keith, Rojzman & Rojzman, 2007).
2. *Banlieue* is often translated into English as "suburb," as they are located on the outskirts of cities. However, banlieues were traditionally working class and are now mainly impoverished areas with high unemployment that house families of immigrant origins and ethnic French (North African and African). I use banlieue to refer to these settings. For analyses of the multiple manifestations and causes of violence in the banlieues, see Canet, Pech, & Stewart, 2006; Le Goaziou & Rojzman, 2006.
3. See http://www.educationprioritaire.education.fr/
4. Unless otherwise noted, references to TST theory and practice are drawn from Rojzman, 2008, Rojzman, 2009, Rojzman & Pillods, 1999, and Rojzman & Rojzman, 2006. Supporting references from other sources are noted in the text.

REFERENCES

Adorno, T. W., Frenkel-Brunswik, E., Levinson, D. J., & Sanford, R. N. (1950). *The authoritarian personality*. New York: Harper & Brothers.

Anzaldúa, G. (1987). *Borderlands/La frontera: The new mestiza*. San Francisco: Aunt Lute.

Atlee, T. (2003). *The tao of democracy: Using co-intelligence to create a world that works for all*. Writers Collective.

Booth, W. J. (2008). The work of memory: Time, identity, and justice. *Social Research, 75*(1), 237–262.

Boud, D., Cressey, P., & Docherty, P. (Eds.). (2006). *Productive reflection at work; Learning for changing organizations*. London: Routledge.

Bourdieu, P., & Wacquant, L. J. (1992). *An invitation to reflexive sociology*. Chicago: University of Chicago Press.

Bryk, A. S., Bender Sebring, P., Allensworth, E., Luppescu, S., & Easton, J. Q. (2010). *Organizing schools for improvement: Lessons from Chicago*. Chicago: University of Chicago Press.

Bryk, A., & Schneider, B. (2002). *Trust in schools: A core resource for improvement*. New York: Russell Sage Foundation.

Camino, L. (2005). Pitfalls and promising practices of youth-adult partnerships: an evaluator's reflections. *Journal of Community Psychology, 33*(1), 75–85.

Canet, R., Pech, L., & Stewart, M. (2008, November 18). *France's burning Issue: understanding the urban riots of November 2005*. Retrieved December 5, 2009, from Social Science Research Network : http://ssrn.com/abstract=1303514

Chrisafis, A. (2006, April). *We will not be thrown away! France's student uprising*. Retrieved January 4, 2007, from The Nation at http://www.thenation.com/doc/20060424/chrisafis

Coleman, Y. (2006, January/February). *The French riots; dancing with the wolves*. Retrieved January 4, 2007, from Solidarity: http://www.solidarity-us.org/node/33

Comer, J. P. (2004). *Leave no child behind: Preparing today's youth for tomorrow's world*. New Haven: Yale University Press.

Cook-Sather, A. (2002). Authorizing students' perspectives: Toward trust, dialogue, and change in education. *Educational Researcher, 31*(4), 3–14.

Cook-Sather, A. (2009). I am not afraid to listen: Prospective teachers learning from students. *Theory Into Practice, 48*(3), 176–183.

Craig, R. (1994). The face we put on: Carl Jung for teachers. *Clearinghouse, 67*(4), 189–191.

Daniele, R., & Gordon, R. M. (1996). Interpersonal conflict in group therapy: An object relations perspective. *Group, 20*(4), 303–311.

Dessel, A., & Rogge, M. E. (2008). Evaluation of intergroup dialogue: A review of the empirical literature. *Conflict Resolution Quarterly, 26*(2), 199–238.

Dika, S. L., & Singh, K. (2002). Applications of social capital in educational literature: A critical synthesis. *Review of Educational Research, 72*(1), 31–69.

Dovidio, J. F., Gaertner, S. L., & Kawakami, K. (2003). Intergroup contact: The past, present, and the future. *Group Processes and Intergroup Relations, 6*(1), 5–21.

Eckersley, R. (2006). Is modern Western culture a health hazard? *International Journal of Epidemiology, 35*, 252–258.

Eichler, M. (2006). *Consensus organizing, building communities of mutual self interest.* Thousand Oaks, CA: Sage.

Eisenberg, N. (Ed.). (2006). *Social, emotional, and personality development* (6th ed.). New York: John Wiley & Sons.

Emirbayer, M., & Mische, A. (1998). What is agency? *American Journal of Sociology, 103*(4), 962–1023.

Flyvbjerg, B. (2001). *Making social science matter: Why social inquiry fails and how it can succeed again.* Cambridge, UK: Cambridge University Press.

Fromm, E. S. (1941/1969). *Escape from freedom.* New York: Henry Holt.

Fromm, E. S. (1955). *The sane society.* New York: Henry Holt.

Galtung, J. (1969). Violence, peace, and peace research. *Journal of Peace Research, 6*(3), 167–191.

Goffman, E. (1959). *The presentation of self in everyday life.* New York: Anchor Books.

Gordon, M. F., & Seashore Louis, K. (2009). Linking parent and community involvement with student achievement: Comparing principal and teacher perceptions of stakeholder influence. *American Journal of Education, 116*(1), 1–31.

Greenberg, L. (2008). Emotion and cognition in psychotherapy: The transforming power of affect. *Canadian Psychology, 49*(1), 49–59.

Hamilton, C., with Brown, J., Atlee, T., Scharmer, C. O., Bache, C., Parish, C., et al. (2004, May). *Come together: The mystery of collective intelligence.* Retrieved February 18, 2010, from http://www.enlightennext.org/magazine/j25/collective.asp

Hargreaves, A. G. (2004). Half-measures: Anti-discrimination policy in France. In H. Chapman, & L. L. Frader, *Race in France: Interdisciplinary perspectives on the politics of difference* (pp. 227–245). New York: Berghahan Books.

Hargreaves, A. G. (2009, September 24). *"Race" and the Republic.* Retrieved January 12, 2010, from Indiana University Center for European Studies: http://vimeo.com/7599513

Héraud, J.-L. (July 2007). *De la reforme au changement: Une étude de cas–La mise en oeuvre de la reforme Ambition Réussite dans le réseau d'enseignement prioritaire Garcia Lorca.* Université de Marne la Vallée, Master's Thesis.

Hewstone, M., Rubin, M., & Willis, H. (2002). Intergroup bias. *Annual Review of Psychology, 53,* 575–604.

Jeynes, W. H. (2003). A meta-analysis: The effects of parental involvement on minority children's academic achievement. *Education and Urban Society, 35*(2), 202–218.

Keaton, T. (2005). Arrogant assimilationism: National identity politics and African-origin Muslim girls in the other France. *Anthropology and Education Quarterly, 36*(4), 405–423.

Keith, N. (2010). Getting beyond anaemic love: From the pedagogy of cordial relations to a pedagogy for difference. *Journal of Curriculum Studies,* 1–34. (First published on December 7, 2009)

Keith, N., Rojzman, C., & Rojzman, T. (2007, April). Leading for difference: The implications of Transformational Social Therapy for leadership: The case of the Merveille (France)–TST School Success Project. Paper presented at annual meetings of the American Educational Research Association, Chicago.

Kensler, L. A. (2008). The ecology of democratic learning communities. Unpublished Ed.D. dissertation. Lehigh University, Bethlehem, PA.

Kramer, R. M. (1999). Trust and distrust in organizations: Emerging perspectives, enduring questions. *Annual Review of Psychology, 50*, 569–598.

Lasky, S. (2005). A sociocultural approach to understanding teacher identity, agency and professional vulnerability in a context of secondary school reform. *Teaching and Teacher Education, 21*(8), 899–916.

Lawrence, J., & Vaisse, J. (2006). *Integrating Islam: Political and religious challenges in contemporary France* (accessed March 31, 2007 ed.). Washington D.C.: Brookings Institution.

Le Goaziou, V., & Rojzman, C. (2006). *Les banlieues*. Paris: Le Cavalier Bleu.

Levy, P. (1995, October). *Pour l'intelligence collective [For collective intelligence]*. Retrieved July 19, 2005, from Le Monde Diplomatique: www. monde-diplomatique. fr/ 1995/ 10/ LEVY/ 1857#nb1

Lewicki, R. J., & Wiethoff, C. (2000). Trust, trust development, and trust repair. In M. Deutsch, & P. T. Coleman (Eds.), *The handbook of conflict resolution: Theory and practice* (pp. 86–107). San Francisco, CA: Jossey-Bass.

Leyens, J.-P., Cortes, B., Demoulin, S., Dovidio, J. F., Fiske, S. T., Gaunt, R., et al. (2003). Emotional prejudice, essentialism, and nationalism. *European Journal of Social Psychology, 33*, 703–717.

Linden, R. M. (2010). *Leading across boundaries: Creating collaborative agencies in a networked world*. San Francisco: John Wiley & Sons.

Maxwell, J. A. (2005). Causal explanation, qualitative reseach, and scientific inquiry in education. *Educational Researcher, 33*(2), 3–11.

Melchin, K. R., & Picard, C. A. (2008). *Transforming conflict through insight*. Toronto: University of Toronto Press.

Page, S. E. (2007). *The difference: How the power of diversity creates better groups, firms, schools, and societies*. Princeton, NJ: Princeton University Press.

Pettigrew, T. (2008). Future directions for intergroup contact theory and research. *International Journal of Intercultural Relations, 32*(3), 187–199.

Pugin, V. (April 2007). *La politique d'éducation prioritaire : bilans et perspectives*. Lyon, France: Millénaire : Le Centre Ressources Prospectives du Grand Lyon.

Rojzman, C. (2008). *Sortir de la violence par le conflit (Overcoming violence through conflict)*. Paris: La Découverte.

Rojzman, C. (2009). *Bien vivre avec les autres. (Living in harmony with others)*. Paris: Editions Larousse.

Rojzman, C., & Pillod, S. (1999). *How to live together*. St. Kilda, AU: Acland.

Rojzman, C., & Rojzman, T. (2006). *C'est pas moi, c'est lui: Ne plus être victime des autres (Trans. It's not me, it's him: How to stop being a victim)*. Paris: JC Lattes.

Rojzman, C., & Rojzman, T. (2007). Pour une réussite de l'école : voies nouvelles (Toward school success: new pathways). In A. Tarpinian, L. Baranski, G. Hervé, & B. Mattéi, *Ecole: Changer de cap: contributions à une éducation humanisante (Schools: Changing the habit: Contributions to humanizing education)*. Paris: Chronique Sociale.

Rojzman, T. (2005a). Thematic summary, student group. Unpublished notes.

Rojzman, T. (2005b). Thematic summary, adult group. Unpublished notes.

Said, E. (1978). *Orientalism*. New York: Pantheon Books.

Saunders, M. N., & Thornhill, A. (2004). Trust and mistrust in organizations: An exploration using an organizational justice framework. *European Journal of Work and Organizational Psychology, 13*(4), 493–515.

Scheper-Hughes, N., & Bourgois, P. (2004). Introduction: Making sense of violence. In N. Scheper-Hughes, P. Bourgois, & P. Blackwell, *Violence in War and Peace* (pp. 1–32).

Senge, P. M., Scharmer, O. C., Jaworski, J., & Flowers, B. S. (2004). *Presence: Human purpose and the field of the future.* Cambridge, MA: Society for Organizational Learning.

Sidanius, J., Pratto, F., van Laar, C., & Levin, S. (2004). Social dominance theory: Its agenda and method. *Political Psychology, 25*(6), 845–880.

Staub, E. (2003a). Notes on cultures of violence, cultures of caring and peace, and the fulfillment of basic human needs. *Political Psychology, 24*(1), 1–21.

Staub, E. (2003b). *The psychology of good and evil: Why children, adults, and groups help and harm others.* New York: Cambridge University Press.

Staub, E. (2005). The roots of goodness: The fulfillment of basic human needs and the development of caring, helping and non-aggression, inclusive caring, moral courage, active bystandership and altruism born of suffering. In G. Carlo, & C. Edwards (Eds.), *Moral motivation through the lifespan* (pp. 34–72). Lincoln, NE: University of Nebraska Press.

Stoll, L., Bolam, R., McMahon, A., Wallace, M., & Thomas, S. (2006). Professional learning communities: A review of the literature. *Journal of Educational Change, 7,* 221–258.

Tarpinian, A. (2010, January 6). *Politique et école. La dimension anthropologique (Politics and schools: Anthropological perspectives.* Retrieved February 1, 2010, from Psychologie de la Motivation: //www.le-cercle-psy.fr/politique-et-ecole-la-dimension-anthropologique_sh_24792

Taylor, M. C. (2003). *The moment of complexity: Emerging network culture.* Chicago: University of Chicago Press.

Toulmin, S. (1996). Concluding Methodological Reflections: Élitism and Democracy Among the Sciences. In S. Toulmin, & B. Gustavsen, *Beyond Theory: Changing Organizations Through Participation* (pp. 203–225). Amsterdam and Philadelphia: John Benjamins Publishing.

Tschannen-Moran, M. (2003). Fostering organizational citizenship in schools: Transformational leadership and trust. In W. Hoy, & C. G. Miskel (Eds.), *Studies in organizing and leading schools* (pp. 157–180). Charlotte, NC: Information Age Publishing.

Yalom, I. D., & Leszcz, M. (2005). *The theory and practice of group psychotherapy* (5th ed.). New York: Basic Books.

Yankelovich, D. (1999). *The magic of dialogue: Transforming conflict into cooperation.* New York: Simon & Schuster.

Zara, O. (2004, November 17). *Pour le management de l'intelligence collective (Managing collective intelligence).* Retrieved July 2, 2005, from Le Journal du Net: http://www.journaldunet.com/management/0411/041158zara.shtml

CHAPTER 12

MAPPING FAMILY–SCHOOL PARTNERSHIP PROGRAMS THROUGH THEORIES OF ACTION AND LOGIC MODELS[1]

Janet Chrispeels and Margarita González

ABSTRACT

In this chapter, Janet Chrispeels and Margarita González explore the theory of action and logic models of two parent education programs to reveal the unique aspects of each and the opportunities for learning that they afford their participants. Both programs aimed to help Latino families gain an understanding of the American educational system and how they could be active participants. One program was designed to reach the largest number of parents possible, whereas the other program targeted a smaller group to develop parent leaders. Understanding the theory of action and logic models was essential for designing appropriate evaluation strategies and instruments. The findings show that both programs implemented many of the components of their espoused theory of action and model and thus demonstrated a match between their espoused theory and theory-in-use. The authors' evaluations

Including Families and Communities in Urban Education, pages 267–299
Copyright © 2011 by Information Age Publishing
267

showed that the two programs had different outcomes consistent with their logic models and could be judged equally successful based on their goals.

Increasing attention is being given to parent education programs offered by intermediary organizations (Annenberg Institute on Public Engagement for Public Education, 1998; Gonzalez & Chrispeels, 2005; Henderson, Jacob, Kernan-Schloss & Raimondo, 2004; Lopez, Kreider & Coffman, 2005; Mediratta et al., 2008). As Henderson et al. (2004) pointed out, the work of these groups ranges from education to advocacy to organizing. These organizations usually offer their programs in collaboration with schools. The organizations provide the curriculum and instructor, and the school informs the parents about the workshops and supplies childcare and meeting space. Some of these intermediary organizations have broadened their curriculum beyond basic parent education and parent involvement practices to encompass leadership development. Themes addressed can include parent organizing, strategic planning, action research, public dialogue and debate, and shared decision-making (Annenberg, 1998; Mediratta et al., 2008).

Lopez et al. (2005) investigated four non-profit organizations offering parent education programs that promoted parent involvement in decision-making, democratic participation and leadership. Using a capacity-building framework, she described how these organizations successfully built capacity at the individual level by providing parents with the knowledge and skills necessary to understand and effectively work with the school system. At the relational level, the organizations supported parents as leaders and catalysts for change; and at the organizational level, they developed support systems for school-family relations.

Delgado-Gaitan (1991) tested a university-sponsored community-based model of parent empowerment and involvement. She formed a committee of Latino parents and community members, Comité de Padres Latinos (COPLA), which collaborated with school officials but operated independently. Through COPLA, parents as a collective set educational agendas, invited school officials to participate, and brought issues and solutions to the table. Delgado-Gaitan contrasted COPLA with the more traditional models in which the school invites the parents, sets the agenda, controls the setting, and determines the parameters for involvement. Over time, COPLA came to be an integral part of the school district and continues to create a context where fair and effective negotiations with the school system are possible.

Another collaboration of this kind has been reported by Bechely (1998) between Center X at the UCLA School of Education and Information Studies and the parent communities at two Los Angeles high schools. Center X's goals were to provide parents with the necessary knowledge about changes in curriculum and instruction and skills allowing them to lead for social justice by redefining their role as important stakeholders and decision makers.

Their Advanced Curriculum Leadership Project guided parents to assume roles as "policy partners" through a mini-research project with a social justice agenda.

Although these studies represent important steps in understanding the role of intermediary organizations, little work has been done to explore how an organization's theory of action shapes parents' opportunities for learning and influences program design, processes and outcomes. In addition, identifying an intermediary organization's approach may be essential in conducting a fair evaluation of its outcomes. In this chapter we use the concepts of theory of action and logic models to compare and contrast two parent education programs offered by two intermediary organizations: the Parent Institute for Quality Education (PIQE) Parent Education program and the Mexican-American Legal Defense and Educational Fund (MALDEF) National Parent-School Partnership Program. We also highlight findings from evaluations of these programs using their respective logic models to illustrate how program inputs, outputs and outcomes were influenced by their theories of action. Finally, we discuss the importance to community organizers, educators, and researchers in understanding a program's theory of action and logic model and conclude outlining the challenges of evaluating parent education programs.

THEORY OF ACTION, LOGIC MODELS, AND EVALUATION DESIGN

Social scientists have struggled to understand how to approach the relationship between individuals and micro-level processes and the macro-level structures of organizations and the context in which individuals live and interact (Coleman, 1986). How are the intentions and purposeful actions of individuals to be connected to the macro-social environment? A theory of action helps to explain this relationship and serves as a framework for exploring the work of organizations' collective and individual members' actions. It is grounded in the concept of activity theory, which recognizes that ideas are historically developed and actively constructed by humans in the moment (Engeström, 2000; Jonassen & Rohrer-Murphy, 1999). In this chapter we explore the ways in which two different parent education programs represent activity systems. An activity system involves the production of an object, in this case, a parent education program. The production of the activity involves a subject (the individual or a collective of parents who attend the classes), and tools (curriculum and activities of the class), and the actions and operations that affect the outcome (parents' participation) (Engeström, 2004; Jonassen & Rohrer-Murphy, 1999; Nardi, 1996). The parent education classes (system of activity) are situated in the larger context of the organization offering the classes, the community in which they are held, and the norms and rules of the community that shape and influence how the activity can be carried out. We argue that to understand and evaluate how and in what ways parent education programs serve families, we should begin with the theory of action espoused by the program developers. The theory of action helps to surface underlying assumptions that guide the program strategy (e.g., focusing on recruiting a small group of parents for leadership training versus recruiting 100–200 for parent education). By exploring the programs as activity systems, it is possible to discover the opportunities for learning and actions that the classes create for individual parents and for the collective.

Logic Models

Related to activity theory is the concept of logic models, which have primarily been formulated by program managers and evaluators to capture an organization or program's activities (McCawley, n.d.). A typical logic model includes a description of the situation and assumptions that prompt an action. In the case of both parent education programs that are the focus of this chapter, the situation that drives their work is the inequitable educational outcomes for Latino students, especially students of immigrant parents. A key assumption is that if immigrant parents are given information about how the American educational system works, they will be able to play an active role in their child's education and address some of the inequities. Thus educators welcoming the programs to their schools and evaluators would first want to ensure that the program serves the intended audiences.

Inputs (time, money, resources, partners, facilities and equipment) are often identified next, as these are essential for carrying out a program. In other words, how will the activity be accomplished, who must be involved and for how long? The outputs or flow of work of the activity/program must also to be determined. What will the process entail and who is the program intended to serve? A logic model also includes the organization's short and long-term outcomes. What will constitute success for program developers and participants? Program designers and evaluators can use logic models to identify environmental factors or unique community situations that need to be taken into account in both development and evaluation. Logic models, in a linear fashion, help to provide details of the activity system from the organization's standpoint and show potential or intended causal relationships between actions and outcomes. The logic model can be used to frame and guide an empirical study or evaluation of an activity system (in this case parent education programs).

Overview of Evaluation Designs, Questions, and Studies Conducted

The authors were asked by both organizations to evaluate their respective parent education programs. For evaluations of both programs, we used a mixed-methods approach collecting quantitative survey data and qualitative data from participants and program staff. We provide a brief overview here and in the relevant sections describing each program provide the details.

The first evaluation of the Parent Institute for Quality Education (PIQE) involved a matched pre-post survey design as well as an in-depth, year-long ethnographic study of the program being enacted in two elementary schools serving high percentages of Latino children (Chrispeels & Rivero, 2001; Rivero, 2006). The in-depth qualitative nature of this study enabled us to identify the program's theory of action and surface its logic model. The second evaluation of PIQE involved greater number of participants in a quasi-experimental design of matched pre-post assessment of parent participants in 20 schools in Los Angeles Unified School District (Chrispeels & Gonzalez, 2002, 2004). The third study was conducted at one large middle school in Los Angeles and used a random assignment experimental design (Chrispeels, Gonzalez & Arellano, 2004). A fourth small-scale study in one high school in the Central Valley of California tracked student achievement and college preparatory readiness for one year. Students whose parents attended PIQE were matched with students whose parents did not attend (Chrispeels & Bolivar, 2007). Student records of these students were reviewed at the start of the PIQE program (fall semester) and re-reviewed at the end of the school year. In the findings section, we will also discuss the results of a review of PIQE's pre-post surveys of its teacher workshop in 13 schools.

We have conducted only one evaluation of the Mexican American Legal Defense and Education Fund Parent School Partnership (PSP) program (Bolivar & Chrispeels, 2010; Chrispeels, Gonzalez, Bolivar, & Rodarte, 2007). To fully understand the PSP program, the evaluation involved several phases: document collection and review, interviews with program staff, pre-post surveys of attendees in fall of 2005 in four cities, in-depth study of the PSP program in two schools in Los Angeles Unified School District, and finally a half-day focus group with graduates of the PSP program in the Los Angeles Region. Table 12.1 provides a comparison of the evaluations conducted of the two parent education programs, and Table 12.2 presents the evaluation questions for each. As can be seen in Table 12.2, the questions reflect both similarities and differences. Question 2 in particular was developed to capture in what ways the PIQE program might be fostering individual parent actions to support their child's learning. In contrast, in Question 2 of the PSP program evaluation, we wanted to know in what ways the program might be fostering individual and collective community

TABLE 12.1 Comparison of Evaluation Design Shaped by Theory of Action and Logic Models

PIQE Evaluation Design	MALDEF PSP Evaluation Design
1. Ethnographic study of the PIQE program involving observation of classes in two schools, review of program documents, pre-post survey of parents in the two schools, interviews of founder, and instructors and follow-up interviews of parents six to nine months after the program concluded. Data used to develop theory of action and logic model (1999–2000).	1. Interviews of PSP directors and regional facilitators and review of program documents to identify program's theory of action and logic model (Summer 2005).
2. Quasi-experimental study using pre-post parent survey with a larger sample of parent participants (n = 2500) in 20 schools in Los Angeles (Winter/Spring 2002).	2. Quasi-experimental study using pre-post parent survey with participants (n = 130) in four states (CA n = 51, GA n = 13, IL n = 11, TX n = 53).
3. Randomized experimental study (treatment and control groups) with a large sample of parents (T = 150, C = 100) in one middle school in Los Angeles. Parent surveys & teacher surveys regarding growth of PIQE and non-PIQE students (Spring 2003).	3. Qualitative study conducted of two PSP classes in Los Angeles using observations of classes, review of class materials, video-taping of graduation ceremony, focus interviews of parents (30 in groups of five parents). Teachers asked to follow students completing a pre-post survey of PSP students.
4. Study to explore impact of PIQE on high school students. Comparison of students whose parents attended PIQE with matched comparison group (Fall 2006–Spring 2007).	4. Strengths-Based Inquiry with 28 past graduates in Los Angeles to explore ways program has sustaining impact (Spring 2006).

TABLE 12.2 Comparison of Evaluation Questions Shaped by Theory of Action and Logic Models

PIQE Evaluation Questions	MALDEF PSP Evaluation Questions
1. Has the PIQE program influenced parents' knowledge of the education system and parenting practices in support of their children's learning? Has the program influenced parents' decision to encourage children to attend college?	1. Has the PSP program influenced parents' knowledge of the education system and enhanced leadership skills? Has the program influenced parents' decision to encourage children to attend college?
2. What actions have parents taken *individually* to support their child's learning?	2. What actions have parents taken *individually and collectively* to address school and community issues?
3. Do teachers perceive changes in students whose parents attend PIQE?	3. Do teachers perceive changes in students whose parents attend PSP?

action. As will be shown, the evaluation questions and instruments reflect each program's theory of action and logical model.

THE PARENT INSTITUTE FOR QUALITY EDUCATION (PIQE)

The Parent Institute for Quality Education (PIQE) is a non-profit organization founded in San Diego in 1987. PIQE conducts three distinct programs in twelve regions in California. Recently offices have been established in Texas, Virginia, and Minnesota. This chapter focuses primarily on evaluations of the basic nine-week parent education program conducted in California elementary, middle and high schools. At the conclusion of the basic program in some schools, community aides make coaching calls to parent graduates to remind them of what they learned in the PIQE classes and encourage them to remain active. A teacher workshop is also available in an all-day Saturday format or in three to four after-school sessions. The teacher component is designed to prepare the school staff to successfully work with PIQE families, but relatively few schools have offered this workshop compared to the number offering the basic program. The basic education program constitutes the core of PIQE's work, has reached over 500,000 families in California, and has been the focus of our evaluation studies.

The purpose of the nine-week parenting program is to assist families in becoming actively involved in the education of their children. Three main goals are addressed in the nine-week parent program: (a) increase parents' knowledge and skills about the school system and how to support their children's education, (b) encourage home and school involvement, and (c) promote expectations for their children to attend college. The program particularly stresses the importance of parents in promoting their children's school success. The underlying principle guiding PIQE's work is that parents, especially Latino immigrants, care deeply about their children's future but need access to important mainstream, middle class school information and strategies to facilitate the home and school involvement expected by teachers. It is assumed that parents will respond when presented with opportunities to gain culturally valued knowledge and form networks with other families. PIQE mainly focuses on Latino families, though it also offers classes to several other immigrant groups and has teaching materials translated into English, Russian, Cambodian, Korean, Chinese, and Armenian.

Program Contents and Approach

PIQE offers three versions of its basic program for parents, one at each level of schooling: elementary, middle and high school. The program consists of nine weekly sessions of 90 minutes each. The first session is an orientation introducing parents to the contents and purpose of the program, while seeking parent input about their needs. At this session, a five-point star with the paths to success is given to each participant. Each point of the star outlines a step parents must take to assist their children in succeeding in the U.S. school system. These steps are reviewed at each subsequent session. After the orientation, the following six sessions cover the content: home–school collaboration, motivation and self-esteem, academic standards, understanding the school system, and promoting college attendance. The middle school and high school programs place more emphasis on understanding the courses needed for college admission, the role of the counselor in placing students in a college-prep program, the perils of drugs and gangs, and financial aid for college. The secondary programs often schedule a visit to a college campus. Although each session has a unique theme, the importance of reading, meeting with teachers, and college attendance are continually highlighted (Rivero, 2006). The eighth session is a parent forum with the school principal, teachers and counselors. The last session is a graduation ceremony with district and school officials and PIQE staff attending to celebrate the parents. To become a PIQE graduate, parents must attend a majority of the content sessions. Parents are strongly encouraged to attend the graduation ceremony with their children, relatives and friends. They are asked to offer testimonials about the program's significance to them and some receive special awards for perfect attendance.

The number of parent graduates since the program's inception in 1987—over 500,000 in the 12 regions throughout the state, impacting the lives of more than one million students—indicates the reach and sustainability of the program. For example, in the Los Angeles Unified School District, the program is conducted every quarter in 20 to 25 schools (elementary, middle and high) with approximately 3,000 participants. In 2005, PIQE launched a partnership with California State University (CSU) to provide the program in areas near to the 23 university campuses. This CSU partnership program is specifically designed to increase the likelihood of college attendance (PIQE, 2008). Since the inception of the partnership, approximately 200 parents have graduated in each of the 23 regions every year. PIQE's theory of action and logic model help to illustrate how the design and logic of the program leads to these outcomes.

PIQE Theory of Action

Based on a review of PIQE documents (PIQE, n.d.), observations of the classes, and interviews with the founders and instructors (Chrispeels & Rivero,

2001; Rivero, 2006), we identified five underlying principles that seem to reflect PIQE's theory of action.

1. Train a critical mass of parents (100–200) at each school who will become *individual advocates* for their children.
2. Recruit parents through telephone calls made by community aides (many of whom are parents who have or had children in the school) who are paid per call if parents attend the orientation session. To ensure continued attendance of parents, link part of the instructors' stipends to the number of graduates.
3. Hire instructors who are committed to meeting the needs of Latino families, have similar backgrounds of poverty and struggle, speak the parents' language, and have successfully navigated the American educational system so that they can serve as *cultural brokers* (Delgado-Gaitan, 1991).
4. Provide parents with an opportunity to learn about the American educational system, parenting skills, tips for homework support, college requirements and financial aid, and they will then be able to be advocates for their children, become actively involved in their education, and increase the likelihood they will graduate from high school and enroll in college.
5. Schools will respond if sufficient numbers of individual parents make well-informed requests.

PIQE Logic Model

Based on the analysis of the PIQE theory of action and the program contents and methodology, we constructed a logic model to reflect the resources (inputs), goals and activities (outputs), and the short and long-term intended outcomes of the program. This logic model guided the evaluation questions and design of the evaluation studies. Figure 12.1 displays PIQE's Logic Model.

PIQE Evaluation Studies: Designs and Data Collection

The authors conducted four research and evaluation studies of PIQE programs in southern California, between 1999 and 2007. As previously mentioned, Chrispeels and Rivero (2001) and Rivero (2006) conducted the initial study using a matched pre-post parent assessment of program attendees as well as a year-long ethnographic study in the two elementary schools. We reviewed program documents to determine goals, program

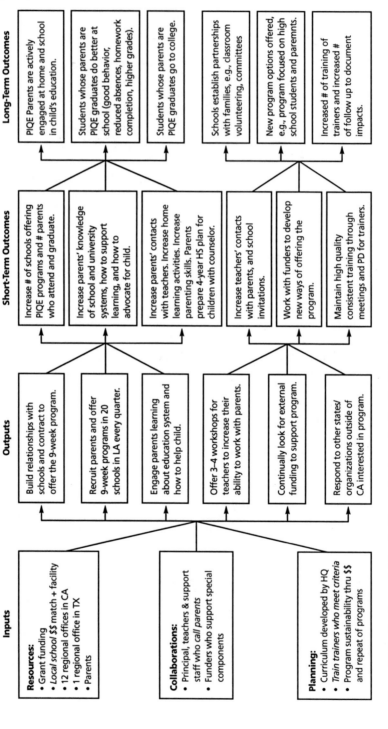

Figure 12.1 Logic model for the Parent Institute for Quality Education program.

content and processes; observed all classes in two schools for the duration of the program; and interviewed the founder, three facilitators, and 12 parents, six to nine months after the conclusion of the classes (Chrispeels & Rivero, 2001; Rivero, 2006).

The ethnographic study provided extensive data on the founder's motivation and the environmental situation that led to the program design, parent recruitment strategies, organization and conduct of the classes, the expected requirements and role of program facilitators, and anticipated short- and long-term outcomes. This initial study provided the basis for the authors to identify PIQE's theory of action and logic model. The founder revealed that the major goal of PIQE was to help parents understand how vital they were in their child's education and provide sufficient knowledge about the American education system so they could become actors at home and in the school. Thus the evaluation needed to focus on the level of knowledge gains in regard to the school system, college requirements, and how parents might help at home, and the actual actions of parents as a result of attending the PIQE classes.

Also as previously mentioned, we conducted two additional studies of PIQE in 2002 and 2003 in schools in one region/district of Los Angeles Unified School District. The study in 2002 involved a quasi-experimental pre-post design to assess program processes and short-term outcomes in 20 schools: five elementary, 13 middle, and two high schools. With more than 2,500 parents involved, it was possible to use more sophisticated statistical tools such as Structural Equation Modeling for theory-building about the pathway of factors that contribute to parents being able to assist at home and at school (Gonzalez & Chrispeels, 2005).

In the 2003 study, a randomized experimental design was used to evaluate the program in one middle school to determine the short-term effects on parents' knowledge and engagement with their children's education. In this study, as parents came to the orientation (approximately 200), half of the parents were assigned to one room and the other half to a second room. We asked all parents attending the orientation to complete a survey. Then all of the parents in one of the rooms were asked to delay taking the program for nine weeks. They were given ten dollars as a thank you gift for completing the survey. Approximately eight weeks later, PIQE staff re-contacted these parents and invited them to return for the class. The delayed-treatment parents became the control group and the survey was readministered to them when they returned. In this study, teachers were also given a pre-post survey to determine if they noted changes in students' behavior, attendance, or homework return. Teachers did not know which students were in the control and which were in the experimental (PIQE) program. These data from teachers provided some insights into potential long-term effects of PIQE on students when their parents attend PIQE class-es (Chrispeels, Gonzalez & Arellano, 2004).

Summary of Findings from PIQE Studies

Using the PIQE Logic Model, Figure 12.1, as an organizing framework, we present important findings from these studies of the PIQE program.

Inputs. Through a review of records, we found that PIQE is able to secure both external funding support and school support to offer its programs throughout California. Based on observation of classes across multiple sites, PIQE is delivering the program as intended and outlined in its printed ma-terials (Rivero, 2006). PIQE instructors seem to effectively retain the inter-est of parents, typically graduating between 75 and150 parents, depending on school size (Chrispeels & Rivero, 2001, Chrispeels & González, 2002). Table 12.3 presents the number of participants, graduates and number of pre-post matched surveys[2] collected from the elementary, middle and high schools in the Los Angeles study. Table 12.4 summarizes the demographics of participants from these 20 schools. Over 97% of the participants identi-fied themselves Hispanic; 85% received free or reduced-price lunch. Thirty-eight percent reported they had no English reading fluency, and 29% indi-cated their fluency was limited. Only 17% of the parents indicated they had graduated from high school and 5% had some college.

Outputs. An important output of the PIQE program is securing school participation and expanding the program to new regions. Data from a range of sources indicate PIQE staff is successful in securing schools to offer the full nine-week program as indicated by the operation of 12 regional centers and the number of participating schools in California. The establishment

TABLE 12.3 Data Summary of Participants Who Attended the PIQE Program in 20 Schools in Los Angeles Unified School District

School Level	Number of Participant Schools	Number of Students Enrolled at School	Number of Parents Enrolled at PIQE	Number of Parents who Graduated from PIQE[a]	Number of Parents Pre- and Post-Tested	Percent of Parents Pre- and Post-Tested[b]
Elementary	5	6,879	803	634	388	61
Middle	13	23,566	1,800	1,451	697	48
High	2	4,243	191	160	71	44
Total	20	34,688	2,794	2,245	1,156	51

[a] Participants who attended at least 4 out of 8 sessions
[b] Percentage estimated from the number of Participants who Graduated from PIQE

TABLE 12.4 Description of PIQE Parent Participants in 20 Elementary, Middle and High Schools in Los Angeles Unified School District

A) Participant–Child Relationship

| | Percentage of Participants per School Level | | | Total |
Relationship	Elementary	Middle	High School	Percentage
Mother	78.1	69.0	69.0	72.1
Father	16.7	27.8	23.9	23.9
Guardian	0.8	0.7	1.4	0.8
Other	2.6	1.3	2.8	1.8
No data	1.8	1.1	2.8	1.5
Total	100.0	100.0	100.0	100.0

B) Participant Ethnicity

African	0.0	0.4	0.0	0.3
Asian	0.0	0.1	0.0	0.1
Caucasian	0.0	0.4	1.4	0.3
Hispanic	98.2	96.8	95.8	97.3
Other	0.3	0.6	0.0	0.4
No data	1.5	1.6	2.8	1.6
Total	100.0	100.0	100.0	100.0

of the partnership with the California State University system and centers in Minnesota, Virginia, and Texas suggest that PIQE is forming new partnerships and extending its reach to new geographic areas. To maintain this level of outreach, key PIQE staff devotes considerable energy to contacting potential funders and grant writing. In the past two years over a million dollars in funding has been secured each year from a wide-range of foundations and funding agencies (PIQE financial reports, 2008 and 2009).

Another important output in the logic model is assisting parents to gain knowledge of the American educational system and the role they can play. Based on observations of the classes, PIQE instructors make explicit the implicit norms and expectations of the dominant middle-class culture of American schools (e.g., reading at home, attending school meetings, helping with homework) (Chrispeels & Rivero, 2001; Rivero, 2006). The instructors were observed to act as cultural brokers (Delgado-Gaitan, 1991) by comparing the U.S. system to education in Mexico and pointing out similarities and differences to parents. Opening up this information channel to parents represents one component of socio-cultural capital, which Coleman (1988) identified as enabling parents to support children's learning.

A third output indicated in the logic model is a teacher workshop, which represents a much smaller dimension of the overall PIQE programs. Most schools participating in the basic nine-week parent program do not offer the teacher workshop. In 2007 a small-scale evaluation was completed of the teacher component offered to 300 teachers in 16 schools in Los Angeles and El Monte. A pre-post assessment of teachers in 13 of the 16 schools indicated there was a positive short-term effect. Teachers reported they valued the strategies they learned, especially about how to reach out to parents. In follow-up interviews, one teacher said she was now making home visits and another said that she makes an explicit effort to greet parents every day. Teachers also indicated they were now more aware of their responsibility in making parents welcome. As one teacher commented, "We as educators could make the difference in students and families' lives." They also indicated a better understanding of parents' perspectives as well as the need for more positive communications with parents (Chrispeels, 2007). Future studies need to explore if there are schoolwide changes or implementation of new practices (long-term outcomes) when the teacher component is offered.

Short-term outcomes. The fourth column of the logic model addresses short-term outcomes, which are critical to sustainability, long-term outcomes and organizational survival. For purposes of this chapter, we focus primarily on the parent outcomes documented in our studies of PIQE (Chrispeels & Gonzalez, 2002; Chrispeels, Gonzales, & Arellano, 2004; Chrispeels & Rivero, 2001; Rivero, 2006). The findings suggest PIQE parents gained new knowledge through deliberate and intentional participation in a parent education program. This knowledge became the primary predictor influencing the parents' individual actions to support their children's education at home and at school. As shown in Table 12.5, the PIQE program specifically impacted five outcomes related to parental involvement: home learning activities, parenting, college expectations, improved perceptions of parent self-efficacy, and parent-school connection. Table 12.5 displays the pre-post mean score gains and the effect sizes for each variable for the elementary schools participating in the 20-school Los Angeles study (Chrispeels & Gonzalez, 2002). As shown, the effect sizes varied from low (Home–School Connection, 0.11) to high (Knowledge, 1.06), with most outcomes falling in the moderate range. One mother of three reported how she acted on the knowledge gained: "I never knew it was important to read at home to my children. I wish I had known with my boys; now we read all the time to my three-year-old daughter." Her comment is typical of most graduates and supports the quantitative findings about the important knowledge gains.

With this significant gain in knowledge, it is not surprising there was a statistically significant growth in the other variables such as Parent-Child Interaction (praising the child and spending time talking to my child, ES = 0.25); and Home Learning Activities (reading or reviewing homework, ES = 0.32) although effect sizes are still in the low range. As parents

TABLE 12.5 Comparison of Pretest and Posttest Results Showing Significance and Effect Sizes of PIQE Program

Category	Scale Range	Pretest		Posttest		Significance (2-tailed)	Overall Effect Size
		Mean	SD	Mean	SD		
Home Learning Activities	1–5	3.82	1.407	4.22	1.089	.000	0.32
Academic Knowledge	1–3	1.66	0.703	2.36	0.635	.000	1.06
Parent–Child Interaction	1–5	3.93	1.347	4.17	1.081	.004	0.25
Home–School Connection	1–5	2.55	0.965	2.67	0.907	.300	0.11
Parent Self-Efficacy	1–4	3.11	0.747	3.28	0.605	.000	0.42
Parental Role	1–4	3.61	0.628	3.78	0.496	.000	0.31
College Expectations	1–4	3.56	0.528	3.74	0.398	.000	0.32

Note: SD = Standard Deviation
PIQE Elementary School Parents (5 schools, 388 parents)

gained knowledge, there was also significant growth and a low to moderate gain in effect size in parents' Self-Efficacy (ES = 0.42), in College Expectations for their children (ES = 0.32), and an understanding of their Parent Role (ES = 0.31).

There are at least two possible explanations for the low effect size in the variable Home–School Connection (ES = 0.11). First, the pre-post time frame may be insufficient for parents to actually take action. Follow-up interviews in the first study (Chrispeels & Rivero, 2001; Rivero, 2006) indicated that by the end of the year all parents interviewed had been to see their child's teacher, suggesting that the post-assessment in the ninth week may be too short to measure a change in home–school connections. This need for more time is confirmed in the experimental study conducted in one Los Angeles middle school. Data from this study also indicated that by the end of the year, teachers reported that PIQE parents had made more positive contacts with them than had the control group. A second explanation may be that the focus of the PIQE parent program is on the parents. The program does not address the school invitations to attend school activities or parents' perceptions of these invitations, which Epstein (1991) and Hoover-Dempsey and Sandler (1997) found to be important for increasing home–school connections.

Long-term outcomes. The fourth component of the logic model is the long-term outcomes, several of which were identified in Figure 12.1. Two long-term outcomes are particularly important for the program and for funders: changes in parent behavior and student outcomes. Long-term parent outcomes are difficult to assess because of the challenges of following a group of parents, many who are highly mobile, over time. In Rivero's (2006) study, she interviewed parents six to nine months after the classes ended, which begins to provide a longer-term perspective than the post-survey at nine-weeks. Parents recounted their current behaviors in supporting their children such as reading regularly, using more positive praise, controlling TV viewing and setting up college funds. These findings suggest that parents were persisting in practices that they learned in the PIQE classes.

A second critical long-term outcome is the impact of PIQE on students' school success and college going rates. It is too early to assess the impact of the PIQE partnership with the California State Universities on college attendance rates. However, a longitudinal study conducted by Vidano and Sahafi (2004) compared 351 San Diego County high school graduates whose parents had attended PIQE with the general results for Latino students in the region. They found promising outcomes that suggest the need for more rigorous matched comparison group studies. For example, (a) the dropout rate was 7% versus 41% for Latinos in the county; (b) the college attendance was 79% versus 52% for the county; (c) from this 79% of the 351 PIQE students, 51.4% enrolled in a Community College and 27.8% were admitted to a four year University; and finally, (d) study participants admitted to four year college equaled 19% versus 7% in San Diego County.

In the experimental study of one middle school in Los Angeles, in the end-of-year teacher assessment, teachers reported that students whose parents attended PIQE in January had higher attendance, greater completion of homework, and more positive contact from PIQE parents in comparison to the control group (Chrispeels, Gonzalez & Arellano, 2004). In a one-year follow-up of the basic PIQE high school program's effects on students, Chrispeels and Bolivar (2007) found that students whose parents attended the PIQE program completed more college preparatory courses with a C or better and had higher attendance than a matched comparison group. These findings suggest the need to follow students from high school into college to more rigorously document the ways PIQE may be increasing college attendance of Latino students.

THE MEXICAN-AMERICAN LEGAL DEFENSE AND EDUCATIONAL FUND (MALDEF)

The Mexican American Legal Defense Fund (MALDEF) was founded in 1968 in San Antonio, Texas as a national non-profit organization born out of the Civil Rights movement. Its mission is to protect and promote the civil rights of the Latino population in the United States and to empower the Latino community to fully participate in American society (MALDEF, 2007). Although the organization is known for its litigation, it emphasizes leadership development, educational outreach and collaboration to achieve its goals while using litigation as a last resort.

In its effort to promote the civil rights of Latinos in the United States and to provide opportunities for their active participation in society, MALDEF implemented a Parent School Partnership (PSP) Program in 1989. The goal of PSP is to provide information and develop the skills of parents to be effectively involved in ensuring an equitable and college-preparatory education for their children. Parent School Partnership programs at the time of the study offered programs in Los Angeles, Chicago, Houston and Atlanta, but currently Houston is no longer participating. Since 1989, about 5,000 parents have graduated from PSP programs. To expand the reach of its PSP program, MALDEF also provides a national "training of trainers" program for representatives of other community-based organizations. These other agencies have used the MALDEF curriculum to offer the program in diverse communities throughout the U.S., but at the time of the evaluation MALDEF did not have information regarding the level of implementation by these other agencies. Currently MALDEF enters into a formal agreement with those requesting to be certified to teach the PSP curriculum and requires reports from these agencies on the number of classes conducted at each site per year and the number of participants who graduate.

Program Contents

The Parent–School Partnership program is a leadership development program that consists of 12 content sessions and two to four field visits conducted in 12 to 16 weeks. The sessions are led by a MALDEF instructor and address topics such as Parents' Rights and Responsibilities, Structure and Function of the School System, College Requirements and Financial Aid, and Leadership and Group Process Skills. The last topic, Leadership and Group Process Skills, is woven throughout the program. Parents have the opportunity to practice them as they engage in role-playing, analyze scenarios, and undertake group action research projects. Similar to the PIQE curriculum, the school principal and counselors present to the parents. Unique to PSP, school board members and city officials are also invited as guest speakers to share information and answer parents' questions. To prepare for these meetings, parents work in small groups to write questions in advance to ask of the presenters.

A requirement for graduation is conducting a group action research project. In an early session, parents brainstorm a list of concerns, and then, based on interest, form a small action team with others to address one of the identified issues. At the graduation ceremony, each team from across multiple schools where the program was offered presents its project design and results. Based on observations and review of documents, the MALDEF facilitator develops parents' leadership skills by providing them with planning protocols, tips on how to approach public officials, strategies for teamwork, and guidance in their action projects.

MALDEF's Theory of Action

Drawing on interviews with MALDEF national and regional directors and review of program documents, we identified five principles that seemed to capture MALDEF's Theory of Action.

1. Changes in the educational system require both legal challenges and the development of parent leaders.
2. To bring about change, a small, dedicated cadre of 15 to 20 parents should be developed to be leaders and advocates for their children and other children in the school and community.
3. Instructors who speak the language of parents and know how the political system works can serve as cultural brokers.
4. Parents need to know how to access political and educational systems to exercise their rights. Learning how to access one system facilitates access to other systems (judicial, economic, social, political).
5. Change will come through collective action of parents if they know the norms and expectations of the American educational system, develop leadership skills, and engage in individual and collective action during and after the PSP Program.

MALDEF Logic Model

Based on the analysis of the PSP Theory of Action and the program contents and processes, a logic model was constructed to reflect the resources (inputs), goals and activities (outputs), and the intended short-term and long-term outcomes of the program (see Figure 12.2). This logic model guided the evaluation questions and design of the study.

Evaluation Study Design of the Parent School Partnership Program

To evaluate its implementation, assess its effectiveness in developing Latino parent leadership in education and map future steps for improvement, a study of the Parent School Partnership program was conducted by

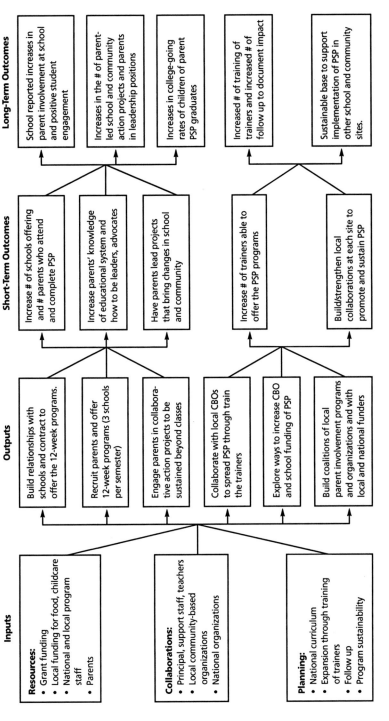

Figure 12.2 Logic model of the MALDEF Parent School Partnership program.

the authors and a team of graduate/undergraduate researchers from the University of California, San Diego and the University of California, Santa Barbara between 2006 and 2007. To provide a comprehensive evaluation of the MALDEF PSP program, a three-phase design process was used. The first phase involved meeting with national and regional PSP directors and staff either in person or via a telephone conference with the other sites to learn about the program and co-plan the evaluation. In addition, six individual interviews were conducted with the director of the PSP program, the national director of the program, a trainer of trainers, and the local facilitator in Los Angeles and by telephone with the facilitators in Houston, Atlanta and Chicago. Information gathered from these meetings and interviews and a review of program documents allowed us to identify the theory of action and the components of the logic model.

The second stage consisted of a quasi-experimental pre-post parent survey of parents attending PSP classes in fall of 2006 in Los Angeles, Houston, Chicago and Atlanta. The pre-post instrument was similar to the one used in the evaluation of the PIQE program but included three new variables (leadership, actions toward college attendance, and school invitations) and new items added to other variables aligned to assess the theory of action of the PSP program. For example, the *parent expectations* variable explored beliefs about the importance of higher education and the child's ability to attend college (similar to the PIQE survey) and asked about enrollment in advanced classes or taking the SAT. Table 12.6 compares the variables assessed in the PSP study with those of PIQE.

TABLE 12.6 Comparison of Program Variables Assessed in the PSP Program with PIQE Program

Pre-Post Variables Used to Assess PSP	Pre-Post Variables Used to Assess PIQE
Parent knowledge of education system and child's progress	Parent knowledge of education system and child's progress
Parent sense of self-efficacy	Parent sense of self-efficacy
Parental role and responsibilities	Parental role and responsibilities
Parent-child interactions	Parent–child interactions
Home learning activities	Home learning activities
Parent expectations	College expectations
Parent action to support future college attendance	
Participation at school and community	Home–school connections
Parent perceptions of school invitations and openness	
Parent Leadership	

Because of the proximity of the researchers to Los Angeles, the third phase of the evaluation involved an in-depth study of the PSP program at the two Los Angeles schools. We observed most of the classes of the 12-week program at one school and three classes at the second school. The same facilitator led the classes at both schools; and there were more observed similarities than differences between the two schools. Each elementary school served similar populations (98% Hispanic students and 89% receiving free or reduced-price lunch). At the conclusion of the program at each school, three bilingual research assistants conducted three focus groups with the parents (five parents to a group for a total of 15 parents at each school). One researcher also attended and video-taped the graduation ceremony. Teachers in these schools were also asked to complete a pre-post survey of the students whose parents had attended PSP to track progress across the year.

From these interviews and discussions with the facilitator and the national PSP director, we learned that some graduates of the program had actually established their own parent organizations. With the help of MALDEF's PSP staff in Los Angeles, 65 parents who had graduated in the past five years were contacted and invited to a half-day focus group session at MALDEF headquarters. MALDEF provided childcare and breakfast. We grouped by region the twenty-eight parents who attended into four focus groups of seven parents each. A native Spanish-speaking research assistant as well as a MALDEF staff member led each group. The purpose was to learn about their collective actions since graduation. These sessions were audio- and video-recorded and later transcribed for analysis.

Summary of Findings

We summarize key findings from this comprehensive study of the Parent School Partnership (PSP) program using the logic model categories as a framework. The framework helps to highlight similarities and differences in terms of inputs, outputs and short- and long-term outcomes of PSP compared to PIQE.

Inputs. As highlighted in their theory of action, the aim of the PSP program is to develop a small cadre of leaders. PSP staff work with two to four schools each semester and focus on reaching and developing a cadre of 15 to 20 parent leaders in each class. We found this pattern of number of schools involved and number of participants consistent across the four national sites based on interview data from the facilitator as well as attendance records. Table 12.7 presents the parent demographic data from classes that occurred in the four cities in the fall of 2006. As can be seen from this table, the ethnicity, primary language, English fluency and educational level of

TABLE 12.7 Demographic Data of Parents Attending PSP Classes Fall 2005 in Four Cities

Demographics	Los Angeles	Houston	Atlanta	Chicago
Child Grade Level (Oldest Child enrolled at school site)				
Elementary (K–5)	84%	61%	47%	78%
Middle/High School (6–9)	26%	39%	53%	22%
Free/Reduced-Price Lunch	81%	85%	78%	58%
Relationship				
Father	5%	1%	15%	33%
Mother	72%	93%	68%	46%
Other	23%	6%	17%	21%
Ethnicity				
African-American	1%			
Asian			2%	
Latino	75%	96%	86%	82%
White	1%			
Other/Missing data	1%	4%	12%	18%
Country of Origin				
USA	1%	4%	2%	3%
Mexico	54%	80%	83%	79%
Other/Missing data	45%	16%	15%	18%
Years in USA				
1–5 years	3%	12%	25%	6%
6–10 years	21%	40%	32%	30%
11–15 years	27%	28%	9%	21%
16–20 years	18%	11%	7%	12%
21+ years	11%	4%	5%	6%
Primary Language				
English	2%	1%	3%	
Spanish	78%	95%	85%	82%
Other/Missing data	20%	4%	12%	18%
English Fluency				
None	24%	13%	36%	18%
Beginning	32%	60%	27%	39%
Intermediate	17%	20%	15%	21%
Advanced	7%	1%	5%	3%
Educational Level				
Elementary school (K–5)	11%	13%	12%	6%
Middle school (6–8)	30%	33%	32%	24%
High school (9–12)	33%	32%	22%	30%
Some post-secondary	2%	11%	5%	15%
BA/BS	2%	3%	7%	6%
MA/MS	1%	1%	2%	
Other/Missing data	21%	7%	20%	19%
Occupation				
Homemaker	59%	67%	36%	27%
Worker	40%	27%	54%	67%
Manager/Business	1%	6%	10%	6%

the parents were relatively similar across the sites and were not substantially different from the parents served by the PIQE program.

Similar to PIQE, schools are asked to provide space for the class to meet and for childcare, but unlike PIQE, there is no charge to the school for the class. Observations at the two Los Angeles schools indicated that the PSP program enjoyed the support of the principals, and both principals made presentations to the parent classes. Funding for the PSP program is primarily provided through grants from foundations and corporations made to MALDEF. MALDEF does not apply for or accept government funding for its programs or operations, and as a result it usually has a smaller budget for parent work when compared to other well-established parent education programs, including PIQE. As indicated in the logic model, a unique aspect of the PSP program is collaboration with other agencies as a strategy for spreading the PSP program. The director of the PSP program and the director of the Training of Trainers component indicated that it is primarily through the trainers program that the PSP program extends its reach to other communities and agencies working with Latino families.

Outputs. The second component of the logic model is outputs. All four cities in the study were able to find schools that wanted to offer the program; and they had a waiting list of other schools wanting to offer the program. At the time of the study, the Chicago office had just been opened and the program was being offered for the first time, which indicates that the PSP program was able to expand its reach to a new area. However, the directors in Houston and Atlanta indicated they worked alone in offering the program and were struggling to keep up with the demands of program implementation. Lack of funding for the PSP program prevented them from hiring an assistant, indicating the program may struggle at times in its output goal of securing additional funding.

Similar to the PIQE program, another important output was to increase parents' understanding of the American educational system and the roles they can play. Observations of the two classes in Los Angeles, as well as survey and interview data from the focus groups, indicated that parents were provided information about the educational system by the instructor and guest speakers such as a school board member, the principal, and city officials. During the observations, parents engaged in role-play on how to interact with officials and worked in small groups to develop questions to pose to their guests. Program documents and observations of the classes also indicated that the instructors informed parents about norms of participation such as not raising one's voice or putting things in writing and, similar to PIQE, the facilitator also discussed typical teacher expectations of parents. The knowledge gains of the parents will be explored in more depth in the section on short-term gains.

A critical and unique component of the PSP program's theory of action and an essential output is to engage parents in collaborative action research projects. The observations of the classes offered in Los Angeles, the parent focus groups, and the interviews of the national and regional directors indicated that these action projects represented the heart of the PSP program. The results of these action projects documented in the in-depth study in Los Angeles will be discussed in the next section

Short-term outcomes. A variety of short-term outcomes is indicated in the logic model based on the theory of action. Two important outcomes that were documented through the survey data and the focus group interviews with class participants and PSP graduates are (a) knowledge gains and increased individual leadership actions by participants, and (b) collaboratively developed and implemented action projects designed to solve community and school problems.

Similar to the PIQE study, parents were asked to complete a pre/post assessment. For purposes of this chapter we focus on pre/post survey results from Los Angeles and Houston, where the matched sample sizes were sufficient for trustworthy analysis, 51 and 53 respectively. As can been seen in Table 12.8, there were gains in knowledge with large effect sizes similar to PIQE (1.34 in Los Angeles and 1.53 in Houston).

The interview data support these quantitative findings about knowledge gains about how the American educational system works, and what roles parents can play. One mother commented:

> First of all, I learned how to speak with people to ask for things. Having good background knowledge to say what it is we want to say and to know whom to speak with more than anything. [We have learned] where to go and how to address them.

Another mother added:

> Before, I used to almost have to fight with the school and the teacher, because of not knowing the appropriate steps. The school didn't pay me any attention... Today I address them in writing and they have been paying attention to me, also... I know what there is above, that if my concerns are not heeded or resolved, I could go [higher up].

A third mother indicated she is now able to "ask more specific questions that before I couldn't ask." She attributed this to "having more information and more capacity to ask those deeper questions." As Lareau (1989, 2003), and Horvat, Weininger, and Lareau (2003) have shown, these responsibilities and ways of interacting are implicitly understood in middle class parent culture, but often go unrecognized by parents from lower socio-economic status or working class culture.

Latino parents often risk dangerous border crossings and illegal status in search of a better life for their children. Both PIQE and PSP provide

TABLE 12.8 Pre-Post Survey Results from Parents Participating in the PSP Program in Los Angeles and Houston Fall 2005

Category	Los Angeles (N = 51)						Houston (N = 53)					
	Pre-Survey	SD	Post-Survey	SD	Change	Effect Size	Pre-Survey	SD	Post-Survey	SD	Change	Effect Size
Mean Parent Knowledge	3.47	1.153	4.86	0.922	1.39***	1.34	2.92	1.170	4.32	0.657	1.40***	1.53
Mean Parent Expectations	5.36	0.743	5.74	0.325	0.38***	0.71	4.88	0.731	5.22	0.552	0.34**	0.53
Mean Parental Role	5.18	0.781	5.42	0.533	0.25*	0.37	4.69	0.844	4.95	0.503	0.26*	0.39
Mean Parent Self-Efficacy	4.98	0.743	5.39	0.506	0.42***	0.66	4.29	0.898	4.81	0.505	0.52***	0.74
Mean School Invitations	5.10	0.755	5.38	0.401	0.28**	0.48	4.64	0.864	4.84	0.551	0.20	0.28
Mean Parent–Child Interactions	5.31	0.966	5.61	0.558	0.30**	0.39	5.39	0.776	5.55	0.405	0.16	0.27
Mean Participation at School	3.89	1.033	4.68	0.900	0.79***	0.82	3.01	1.338	3.80	0.829	0.79***	0.73
Mean Home Learning	4.93	0.937	5.42	0.521	0.49***	0.67	4.22	1.221	4.84	0.645	0.62***	0.66
Mean Parent Leadership	2.81	1.445	3.99	1.263	1.18***	0.87	2.08	1.076	3.52	0.923	1.44***	1.44
Mean Actions Toward College	3.42	1.104	4.43	1.067	1.01***	0.93	2.92	1.178	3.98	0.833	1.06***	1.05

$* p < .05;$ $** p < .01;$ $*** p < .001$

information about U.S. colleges and universities, requirements for admission, and financial aid. As shown in the PSP survey data, there were significant gains from the pre-post test in terms of "visit colleges or universities" (>.01), "talk with counselors to ensure child is enrolled in classes that qualify for university"(>.05), and "talk to child about courses required for university" (>.01). The overall effects sizes were also large (.93 in LA and 1.05 in Houston). In the interviews, parents confirmed these findings and stressed how valuable it was learning about financial aid. One mother stated, "For me the most important and useful class was the one about college, what roads [the children] need to take, the requirements and the tools they need to get there." Another one echoed the comments of several when she reported, "The most important thing I learned was about the possibility of asking for loans or other financial aid for my son to go to college."

A key short-term outcome was to have parents lead projects that brought changes to their school and community. The pre-post survey data for both Los Angeles and Houston showed large effect sizes in terms of parent leadership (.87 and 1.44 respectively). Through observations of the classes, video taping of the graduation ceremony and focus group interviews, details regarding the leadership outcome in the Los Angeles PSP program emerged. As a result of their small group projects, cars were stopped from using the school yard and nearby street as a drag-strip; parents persuaded the principal to offer an intersession for their children during one of their long winter breaks (the school operates year-round and one group of children is always on break); parents organized an evening session with teachers to foster greater communication and collaboration; and parents secured a portable classroom for a computer center that the principal had not been able to do on his own. A surprising finding was that parents formed small groups of their own initiative and continued to pursue new action projects beyond the ones the facilitator had guided them to undertake. This finding suggests that the PSP program may be achieving one of its important long-term outcomes, which is to increase the number of parents in leadership roles.

Long-term outcomes. During the interviews with the directors, we learned that several areas in the Los Angeles region (Pasadena, Whittier and San Fernando Valley), PSP graduates have created and are leading three parent organizations. Through a half-day focus group session with these with graduates, parents shared that the organizations they founded operate at both the district and school level. In one school PSP graduates created a school-based parent center. In other cases they had founded district or region-wide organizations that offered parenting classes, participated in policy setting meetings, traveled to the state capital to lobby for Latino rights, and organized cultural and community service events. These findings suggest that the parents not only learned how to take action under the guidance of the PSP facilitator, but also how to identify problems on their own and organize for action. From the experience of undertaking an action research project, they realized as one mother said, "[We need to work together] because together we are strong. A group of people filing a petition can get something done because if it's just one or two people they don't pay attention to us."

LESSONS LEARNED FROM UNDERSTANDING THEORIES OF ACTION AND LOGIC MODELS

From indentifying the theory of action and creating logic models of these two programs, we were able to surface important themes that needed to be addressed in the evaluation designs, such as understanding the leadership component of the Parent School Partnership Program, and investigating how the Parent Institute for Quality Education is able to recruit and retain so many parents in its programs. Similar quantitative and qualitative data collection approaches were used in the evaluation designs (e.g., pre-post assessments, observations, review of program documents, and interviews of participants and directors). The qualitative data surfaced important insights about the programs' designs and how they met parents' needs. The larger number of participants and schools involved in the PIQE program made it possible to use an experimental design and more sophisticated statistical analyses.

The evaluations surfaced important similarities between the two programs. Both programs are offered by intermediary agencies that served as cultural brokers to help link Latino families and schools. Through these programs, parents gained valuable knowledge and insights into the American educational system and as a result were able to help their children. Particularly important for parents in both programs was the increased awareness of the requirements that must be met to attend university and the potential for financial support. In both programs parents and students seemed to benefit. Table 12.9 summarizes the findings from the PIQE and PSP studies.

Alignment of Theory of Action and Logic Models with Evaluation Results

A theory of action could be considered a program's espoused theory and the logic model as the activity system needed to enact the theory of action. The evaluations of these programs help to determine if the espoused theory is the theory in use (Argyris & Schön, 1974), and when

TABLE 12.9 Summary Comparison of Findings from PIQE and MALDEF Evaluation Studies

PIQE Findings	MALDEF Findings
1. Program had a large effect on parents' knowledge of school system, how to help child, and college requirements.	1. Program had a significant effect on parents' knowledge of the school system, college requirements, and *leadership skills*.
2. Parents increased expectations for college attendance and engaged in more home learning activities, had more self-confidence and engaged in more parent-child interactions (moderate effect sizes) but there were no significant differences in home–school connections.	2. Parents engaged in program-guided individual and collective actions to solve individual and school problems. Parents engaged in self-motivated individual and collective actions to meet own child and other children's needs. PSP graduates established their own sustaining parent organizations as a result of PSP participation.
3. Teachers perceived changes in students' homework return, attendance and parent contacts. High school students completed more of the college prep requirements.	3. Teachers reported slight improvements in homework return, academic engagement and grades in class and significant changes in parents actions such as attending parent-teacher conferences, volunteering in class and help to ensure homework is returned.

enacted what are the outcomes. The evaluations of these two programs indicate that both are implementing many key components of their logic model. In other words, there is a reasonable alignment between their theory of action, theory in use and expected outcomes. PIQE's theory of action focuses on the goal of reaching as many Latino families as possible and its logic model reflects the necessary inputs and outputs to achieve this goal. The organization's ability to secure funding and recruit districts and schools to offer its programs is impressive. In addition, the significant knowledge gains of the parents and the indication that these gains led to changes in behavior and increased support for their children's educational achievement also attest to alignment between program actions and goal accomplishments.

PSP's theory of action with its goal of enhancing parent leadership skills has designed a program that enabled parents to bring about change when they were guided by the program. Also noteworthy was the finding that, once equipped with these skills, parents in some areas continued on their own to collaborate to solve other school and community problems and in some cases to establish formal parent organizations that continued to play a role five years after the parents had graduated from PSP (Bolivar & Chrispeels, 2010).

Benefits of Identifying a Parent Program's Theory of Action and Logic Model

After interviewing the program directors and reviewing documents, we were able to identify the theory of action of each of the parent education programs and develop a logic model. When presenting their programs, the directors implicitly described a theory of action; however, when seeking funding or recruiting schools to offer the program, they may find it beneficial to explicitly present their theory of action and a logic model that shows how inputs lead to specific outputs and outcomes. In this age of accountability, being able to show the link between inputs and outcomes is essential.

Educators or community agencies wishing to offer parent education programs should ask program directors to explain the theory of action (assumptions and processes) clearly, and explore the relationship between what the program offers and its expected outcomes (logic model). As can be seen from the evaluations of these two parent education programs, both had positive outcomes. They both increased parents' knowledge considerably about the educational system and their role in that system. They had different results or outcomes in terms of number of parents served and actions parents would take during and subsequent to the program based on their theory of action.

For us as evaluators, identifying the theory of action of the respective parent programs was essential in designing the initial parent surveys and questions we would ask in interviews so that they reflected the program goals and potential outcomes. The logic model facilitated our investigation of the multiple dimensions of the program that might be contributing to its outcomes, even though these dimensions (e.g., fundraising or trainer of trainers model) may not be the primary focus of the evaluation.

Program Evaluation Challenges

Based on the evaluations of these two programs, we identified a number of challenges. Administering surveys to non-English speaking parents, many of whom are not fully literate even in their spoken language, required considerable skills and assistance. Reading the surveys proved the best means of data collection, so that no parents felt disenfranchised in providing their opinions. Obtaining the assistance of the instructors was essential; however, they were reluctant to give up class time to administer the survey.

Designing and conducting an experimental, random assignment evaluation proved difficult and ethically challenging. Parents came to school wanting the program. Once at the school, some parents were asked to delay treatment. Given the difficulty for many of these low-income parents to organize time to participate in such a program, we knew that, even with follow-up calls, some parents would not return to take the class later. We found randomization did not yield different results compared to a pre-post evaluation design. Since both the pre-post design and the experimental study yielded similar results across multiple studies, we suggest a pre-post design is adequate to evaluate parent education programs, especially those involving parents who are voluntarily attending.

These studies showed the importance of collecting both qualitative and quantitative data to understand the full effects of parent education programs. The quantitative studies illustrated that these programs do have an effect and showed the areas of greatest effect. Through the qualitative studies, details about the actions parents took to support their children became visible in ways the survey data did not reveal. Missing in the literature, however, are longitudinal studies of parent education programs that would more adequately document the long-term outcomes desired by the programs and shown in the logic models. Both educators and intermediary agencies offering parent involvement programs in their schools could benefit by collaborating to track students over several years to determine if there are long-term effects on learning outcomes. Interviews with parents over time would increase understanding of which knowledge gains seem to most influence parent actions. The opportunity to meet with parents who had previously graduated from the Parent School Partnership program four to five years earlier showed the importance of keeping records of graduates. This retrospective look through graduates' eyes enabled us to identify the long-term outcomes of helping parents to develop leadership skills. These impacts and long-term outcomes had not been fully surfaced or appreciated. Since both of these programs have an outcome of encouraging college attendance, designing a longitudinal study that tracks students whose parents attended the programs when their children were in middle or high school would make an important contribution to the literature. From the evaluation of both of these programs, however, we would caution expecting short-term gains in student learning from a nine to 12 week parent education program. The results of these studies suggest there are some short-term positive gains for students in terms of attendance and homework return. Raising student test scores is an unrealistic outcome expectation for both of these programs. The long-term goal of college attendance is a factor that parents can influence and is worth exploring as an outcome.

NOTES

1. An earlier version of this paper was presented by the authors at the Annual Meeting of the American Educational Research Association, New York, April 25, 2008.

2. The number of matched surveys is considerably lower because the pre-survey was only given once, many parents join the classes after the first session, and those in the first session may not have attended the last session to take the post-survey.

ACKNOWLEDGMENT

The authors would like to thank their colleagues Elvia Rivero, Jose Bolivar, and Marisol Rodarte and the undergraduate students who assisted us in transcribing all the interviews for their contributions to the studies reported on in this chapter. We would also like to thank the anonymous reviewers and the editors, Cathy Hands and Lea Hubbard, for their excellent suggestions that greatly strengthen this chapter.

REFERENCES

Annenberg Institute on Public Engagement for Public Education. (1998). *Reasons for hope, voices for change.* Providence, RI: Brown University, Author. Retrieved October 2009 from http://www.annenberginstitute.org/pdf/Reason1.pdf

Argyris, C., & Schön, D. (1974). *Theory in practice: Increasing professional effectiveness.* San Francisco, CA: Jossey-Bass.

Bechely, L. N. (1998). *Building parent leadership in curriculum reform through school/university collaboration.* Paper presented at the annual meeting of the American Educational Research Association. San Diego, CA.

Bolivar, J., & Chrispeels, J. H. (May, 2010). Enhancing parent leadership through building social and intellectual capital. *American Journal of Educational Research, 47*(2).

Chrispeels, J. H. (2007). *Evaluation of the Parent Institute for Quality Education Teacher Workshop.* Report prepared for the Margaret E. Casey Foundation and Parent Institute for Quality Education, University of California, San Diego.

Chrispeels, J. H., & Bolivar, J. (July, 2007). *Parent Institute for Quality Education: Destined for university high school study.* Report prepared for the Walter S. Johnson Foundation and the Parent Institute for Quality Education, University of California, San Diego..

Chrispeels, J. H., & González, M. (2002). *The Impact of the Parent Institute for Quality Education on Families in Los Angles Schools.* Evaluation Report prepared for the Los Angeles Unified School District Evaluation Department and Parent Institute for Quality Education, University of California, Santa Barbara.

Chrispeels, J. H., & González, M. (2004). *Effects of education programs on Latino parents' knowledge, beliefs and practices in middle schools.* FINE Research Digest, School of Education, Harvard University.

Chrispeels, J. H., González, M., & Arellano, B. (2004). *Evaluation of the Effectiveness of the Parent Institute for Quality Education in Los Angeles Unified School District.*

Evaluation Report. Retrieved January 31, 2008 from http://www.piqe.org/Assets/Home/ChrispeelEvaluation.htm

Chrispeels, J. H., González, M., Bolivar, J., & Rodarte, M. (2007). *MALDEF Parent School Partnership Program. Final Evaluation Report.* San Diego, CA: University of California, San Diego.

Chrispeels, J. H., & Rivero, E. (2001). Engaging Latino Families for Student Success: Understanding the Process and Impact of Providing Training to Parents. *Peabody Journal of Education, 76*(2), 119–169.

Coleman, J. S. (1986). Social theory, social research and a theory of action. *The American Journal of Sociology, 91*(6), 1309–1335.

Coleman, J. S. (1988). Social capital in the creation of human capital. *American Journal of Sociology, 94,* 95–120.

Delgado-Gaitan, C. (1991). Involving parents in the schools: A process of empowerment. *American Journal of Education, 100*(1), 20–46.

Engeström, Y. (2000). Activity theory as a framework for analyzing and redesigning work. *Ergonomics, 43*(7), 960–974.

Engeström, Y. (2004). "New forms of learning in co-configuration work", Journal of Workplace Learning, *16*(1), 11–21.

Epstein, J. (1991). *School, Family, and Community Partnerships.* Boulder, CO: Westview Press.

González, M., & Chrispeels, J. H. (2005). *Effects of parent education programs: Knowledge, beliefs and practices of Latino families in middle schools.* Paper presented in the American Educational Research Association (AERA) annual meeting in Montreal, Canada, April 11–15, 2005.

Henderson, A. T., Jacob, B. Kernan-Schloss, A., & Raimondo, B.(2004). *The case for parent leadership.* Lexington, KY: Pritchard Committee for Academic Excellence.

Hoover-Dempsey, K., & Sandler, H. (1997). Why Do Parents Become Involved in Their Children's Education? *Review of Educational Research—Spring 2007, 67,* 3–42.

Horvat, E. M., Weininger, E. B., & Lareau, A. (2003). From social ties to social capital: Class differences in the relations between schools and parent networks. *American Educational Research Journal, 40,* 319–351.

Jonassen, D. H., & Roher-Murphy, L. (1999). Activity theory as a framework for designing constructivist learning environments. *Educational Technology Research and Development, 47*(1), 61–79.

Lareau, A. (1989). *Home Advantage: Social class and parental involvement in elementary education.* London: Falmer.

Lareau, A. (2003). *Unequal childhoods: Class, Race, and Family Life.* Berkeley, CA: University of California Press.

Lopez, M.E., Kreider, H., & Coffman, J. (2005). Intermediary organizations as capacity builders in family education involvement. *Urban Education, 40,* 1, 78–105.

McCawley, P. F. (n.d.). *The logic model of program planning and evaluation.* Boise ID: University of Idaho Extension. Retrieved January 12, 2010 from www.uiweb.uidaho.edu/extension/LogicModel.pdf

Mediratta, K., Shah, S., McAlister, S., Fruchter, N., Mokhtar, C., Lockwood, D. (2008). *Organized communities, stronger schools: A preview of research findings.* Providence, RI: Annenberg Institute for School Reform.

Mexican American Legal Defense and Educational Fund (MALDEF). Retrieved May 10, 2007 from http://www.maldef.org/about/mission.htm

Nardi, B. (1996). *Context and Consciousness: Activity Theory and Human-Computer Inter-action.* Cambridge: MIT Press.

Parent Institute for Quality Education (PIQE) (n.d.). Retrieved March 18, 2008 from http://www.piqe.org/

Rivero, E. (2006). *A study with an ethnographic perspective: A new perspective on Latino families and children's schooling.* Unpublished doctoral dissertation. University of California, Santa Barbara.

Vidano, G. & Sahafi, M. (2004). *Executive Summary: Longitudinal PIQE performance evaluation.* San Diego, CA: San Diego State University, College of Business Administration and Marketing Department.

PART V

CONCLUSION:
THEMES FROM INITIATIVES INCLUDING FAMILIES
AND COMMUNITY MEMBERS IN EDUCATION

CULMINATING REMARKS ON FAMILY AND COMMUNITY INCLUSION IN URBAN EDUCATION

Catherine M. Hands and Lea Hubbard

In the first volume of this book series, the editors, Denise Armstrong and Brenda McMahon, raised some queries that are fundamental to the planning and development of inclusionary practices and programs. Among others, they posed the questions,

> What practices need to be instituted to ensure high academic and social expectations for all students? What programs can be adopted to guarantee equity of access and outcome? What procedures can be implemented to ensure that students and their parents are involved decision-makers? (McMahon & Armstrong, 2006, p. 316)

When we began this book, we were looking to address these questions and the fundamental issues that arise with them through an examination of what it takes to establish effective partnership programs among families, schools and communities in urban settings. We noted the pressing need to meet the varied requirements and desires of equally diverse groups of people in urban settings with regard to education issues. We also recognized the similarly urgent need to promote public education as a means for meeting those requirements. Schools of choice, such as independent, charter and magnet schools may not be available or accessible for all students. Vulnerable groups, such as newcomers to the country, families identified as low-income and members of ethnic minority groups may not have the means to access schools to meet their specific requirements. Hence, the need is great for public education and neighborhood schools in particular to foster inclusive practices.

Like the authors who have contributed to this book, we too were committed to the idea that family–school–community partnerships were one way to approach the issue of meeting those needs in urban education. We have been reading about the importance of family and community engagement for decades, and we have been impressed by the compelling research evidence that suggests students and their families in particular benefit from a cadre of collaborative activities with school and district personnel.[1] In that case, why are parent and community engagement not more prevalent, particularly in urban educational settings? And why are authentic, mutually beneficial partnerships so difficult to create and to maintain? In examining these central issues, we turned to school change, or reform, literature. As with any change—including the addition or modification of collaborative activities within an organizational community—there is level of dynamism resulting from the altered relationships among members. We saw the need to focus on the elements that shaped the relationships and the resulting actions that followed school change in order to deeply examine the inner workings of interactions that promote—or fail to promote—family and community engagement in education.

Structure, Culture and Agency Matter

We have learned much about the pitfalls and possibilities of engaging diverse groups in urban educational settings. In particular, we found the structure-culture-agency framework useful in assisting us to understand the issues. The partnership initiatives discussed in this book achieved varying degrees of inclusion. When we looked at the reasons behind this, they invariably involved structural, cultural or agentive elements that either supported or failed to support family and community engagement in education.

Lacking an awareness of, or ignoring structural issues such as the hierarchy and procedures within the education system and how they interact with political system, and similarly lacking an understanding of the culture of these organizations and the perspectives of the educators, presents problems for collaboration. It makes it difficult for citizens, either individually or as part of a collective, to engage productively with school and district personnel on educational issues and to affect change in education (Chapter 7), especially in circumstances where there may be some resistance to family and community engagement.

By the same token, it is equally if not more important that school personnel understand the cultures or more broadly, the contexts of the communities they are serving. We are mindful that the education delivered needs to be relevant. Schools and districts cannot operate as separate entities from the communities, for they are required to hone practices to meet the changing needs of communities they serve (Crowson & Boyd, 2001) or run the risk of cultivating a culture of family–school–community relations characterized by dissatisfaction at best and animosity at worst (Chapters 4, 5 and 6). These practices include developing opportunities and strategies—structures—for including families and community members in education issues that impact their children and the broader community, and that enhance their ability to participate.

We were struck by the degree of interconnectedness of structural, cultural and agentive issues. We noted that even with structures in place that supported inclusion, in the absence of a school or district culture that favored family and community engagement in education, individuals outside of the school remained there. With cultures and personnel who were supportive of family and community engagement, we saw that without structures consistent with this culture that enable participation, there were limited opportunities for engagement. Similarly, the agency of school and district personnel, families and community members all contribute in varying degrees to shaping the school culture and the structures that support inclusion and engagement.

Educational Hierarchies Continue to Influence Structures, Cultures and Individuals' Agency

Several themes were evident with regard to structural, cultural and agentive elements, and family and community inclusion in education. The continued existence of a hierarchy means that school and district personnel need to authentically welcome family and community engagement. It is not enough to institute policies to that effect, for the inclinations of those who are charged with the responsibility of interpreting and implementing those policies determine what those policies look like in practice (Clune, 1990). With a school culture that truly welcomes family and community engagement, we see the possibility for strong partnership programs in which families and community members are meaningfully involved in education, through the development of structures such as collaborative activities (Chapter 8). Without this type of culture, we see that teachers' and school and district leaders' positions of power and agency in school-related issues limit both the extent of the involvement and implementation of the suggested changes made by others, and the longevity of initiatives (Chapters 3, 9 and 10).

Instead of delving into an examination of the merits and drawbacks of hierarchies, and the question of whether they should still exist in the educational arena, we look at the current organizational structure of the education system as it is, when we ponder next steps for promoting family and community inclusion. Time, finances, organizations to steer partnership development such as action teams, and school-level agency in the form of leadership and guidance are required to establish partnerships that enhance family and community member participation in education (Sanders, 1999). Previous research highlights the importance of school and district support. If school personnel are the ones who need to initiate opportunities for families' and community members' engagement (Davies, 2002; Epstein, 1995, 2001), what does that support look like at the school, district, state or provincial levels? A contextualized examination of the structures in place to promote engagement would be helpful. We do not refute the usefulness of knowing the requisite components of partnership programs, or having examples of partnership practices.[2] These facilitate program development. It is our opinion, however, that there needs to be an intimate understanding on the parts of researchers and school personnel regarding how the components fit together in particular circumstances so that the components and the partnership practices that are established can be tailored to the specific contexts of individual schools. We have begun this type of study with this book, but we realize there is room for further case study investigation and reflection in this area.

School Personnel's Philosophies of Education Need to be Consistent with Inclusion in Order for Partnership Practices to be Developed

At the base of any change in partnering practices is the presence of a philosophy among individual educators that is conducive to inclusion. How is that best achieved? Again, when looking at the types of support needed for school personnel to establish partnerships with families and community members, there have been calls for university programs to supply learning opportunities in this area. Indeed, there are some promising pre-service teacher and principal programs for delivering strategies to engage families (see for example Dotger & Bennett, 2010). Professional networks for inservice school personnel are also a source for building a repertoire of partnering strategies (Hands, 2005a). Yet, knowing how to engage families and having some strategies and examples of collaborative activities for doing so do not necessarily mean that school personnel view parent and community engagement and inclusion in education as necessary in general or in their specific educational contexts.

If engagement in education is an avenue for families' and community members' democratic participation in their society (Harvard Family Research Project, 2002), and relationship-building, dialogue and power-sharing are central to socially just, democratic schools (Auerbach, in press), how is this message and underlying philosophy that education is everyone's responsibility (Hands, 2005a) transmitted and internalized among educators across the education system? What existing and potential roles can state and provincial policy makers, district personnel, and university faculty in pre-service programs play? What roles do social and professional networks and professional learning communities play in shaping school personnel's philosophy regarding the place of parents, grandparents, business owners, doctors, teachers, before- and after-school program coordinators, recreational center directors and the like, in education? Can or should family and community engagement in education be presented from an ethical perspective as essential, rather than viewed as optional, based on the preferences of the school personnel? For certain, there are no easy answers. What seems clear, however, is a need for school personnel to support partnerships as being necessary philosophically and practically for the academic and social wellbeing of their students, and consequently for their own benefit as educators and that of their schools.

The Power of Language

The language used to describe relations and interactions among school personnel, families and community members provides us with insight into the philosophical underpinnings and the types of structures in place to promote or challenge inclusion (Chapter 2) and the cultures that are evident. Further, language itself can be used to limit family and community involvement in educational issues at the school or district levels (Chapters 4, 7) with the use of "eduspeak": words and terminology that are familiar within educational settings but not part of the common lexicon. Conversely, language and capacities associated with its use, such as communication and negotiating skills, can promote greater levels of collaboration (Chapter 9).

Elsewhere, the importance of partners using a common language, of being "on the same page," and of communicating needs and negotiating partnership goals is discussed (see for example, Hands, 2005b; Hanson, 2003). This comes from interaction over time, opportunities to communicate and the development of trust (Chapter 11). These elements form the building blocks of collaborative work (Earl, Katz, Elgie, Ben Jaafar & Foster,

2006; Hands, 2009). Indeed, we see the capacity for distrust and the resulting communication among strategically placed personnel in the district's hierarchy and community members to limit the breadth of an initiative designed to promote inclusion and engagement (Chapter 9).

The Importance of Assessment

Once the requisite trust and communication is in place for the development of engagement initiatives, several levels of assessment are key elements of inclusionary practices such as family–school–community partnerships. In their useful ASPIRE model, McMahon and Armstrong (2006) outline the phases that are essential to change processes. The overlapping phases include the assessment, synthesis, planning, implementation, review and evaluation of programs, policies and activities as they relate to equity and social justice issues in a school environment. Of the six phases, four entail assessment practices, in which information about people, programs, policies and procedures are collected and reflected upon by a school community (McMahon & Armstrong, 2006). Similarly, scholars in the area of family and community engagement advocate conducting audits to determine the current state of partnership practices and evaluating the collaborative activities at the end of an interval of time (see Harvard Family Research Project, n.d.; National Network of Partnership Schools, n.d.).

Promoting Partnerships and Sustaining the Ones that are Developed, through Assessment

Assessment is crucial, as it forms the basis for critical reflective practice and research, which are precursors to the establishment of partnerships that meet the needs of the participants. Equally importantly, one needs to assess who is involved in the collaborative activities and to what extent, as well as how the activities are meeting or not meeting the needs of all of the participants once established. The importance of assessment here is three-fold. First, assessments allow collaborative activities to be tailored to participants' needs. The feedback provided once the activities are underway allows for the individuals involved to make modifications as necessary to the partnerships to ensure inclusion (Hands, 2005b). Second, sustainability is unlikely without some way to measure or determine the impact of the initiative on parent or community engagement. There needs to be a method of promoting accountability and explicitly demonstrating the impact of the family and community engagement initiatives (Harvard Family Research Project, n.d.). Related to this point, assessment can be used to persuade others, including educators and policy makers and community members, that partnerships are of value to students' academic and social well-being as well as to families, communities, schools and to school personnel themselves. Positive assessments in particular have the potential to influence potential partners to view family and community engagement and collaborative activities favorably and to become involved.

While assessment is touted as an important element in school reform literature, strategic leadership in education (see Davies & Davies, 2010) and partnership research (Harvard Family Research Project, 2005), difficulties sometimes arise when attempting to carry out assessments. Even with an understanding of how to assess student achievement, school or district leaders or teachers may not have the strategies or capacity to conduct the assessments that suit their program design and evaluation needs (Hands, 2008). Overviews of different types of assessment methodologies provide descriptions of the strategies and the circumstances under which they are best suited (see for example Harvard Family Research Project, 2005). Yet, it is necessary to know how they might work in practice. Logic models are one of the most popular tools for assessment, and we see their application to two community-based parent programs in the book (Chapter 12). What becomes clear is the importance of assessment strategies, such as a clear theory of action and logic model, for any engagement initiative. It is essential to understand the outcomes to be accomplished, how they are to be achieved and for which specific groups, not only to gain the interest and support and others, but for evaluative purposes while the initiatives are ongoing or at their conclusion. Without specified goals and this type of assessment, it is unlikely that family and community engagement initiatives will become more prevalent or less of a challenge to establish and sustain over time. Indeed, perhaps assessment is the key to addressing the main questions posed in the beginning section of these final remarks.

> Ultimately the goal is to provide equitable education for all students. This takes an act of courage that requires the faith and creative energy of all and is dependent on the multiple visions and talents of the communities. It requires a critical analysis of the urban landscape and the skill and will to work with others to reconfigure it on behalf of the students. (McMahon & Armstrong, 2006, p. 319)

Toward that goal, it is our hope that this book provides a picture of family and community engagement in urban education in its complexity. Through the structure-culture-agency lens, we can develop a comprehensive and realistic perspective of the challenges and possibilities for collaboration.

NOTES

1. There are a number of organizations that have compiled bodies of work on the impact of family and community engagement in education. See for example, the U.S.-based National Network of Partnership Schools, The Harvard Family Research Project, and SEDL (prior to 2007, the Southwest Educational Development Laboratory).

2. The National Network of Partnership Schools has a website (www.partnership-schools.org) with examples of actual strategies used by schools and submitted for inclusion in an annual compendium of promising partnership practices.

REFERENCES

Auerbach, S. (in press). Beyond coffee with the principal: Toward leadership for authentic school-family partnerships. *Journal of School Leadership.*

Clune, W. H. (1990). Three views of curriculum policy in the school context: The school as policy mediator, policy critic, and policy constructor. In M. W. McLaughlin, J. E. Talbert, & N. Bascia (Eds.), *The contexts of teaching in secondary schools: Teachers' realities* (pp. 256–269). New York: Teachers College Press.

Crowson, R. L., & Boyd, W. L. (2001). The new role of community development in educational reform. *Peabody Journal of Education, 76*(2), 9–29.

Davies, B., & Davies, B. J. (2010). The nature and dimensions of strategic leadership. *International Studies in Educational Administration, 38*(1), 5–21.

Davies, D. (2002). The 10th school revisited: Are school/family/community partnerships on the reform agenda now? *Phi Delta Kappan, 83*(5), 388–392.

Dotger, B. H., & Bennett, J. (2010). Educating teachers and school leaders for school–family partnerships. In D. B. Hiatt-Michael (Ed.), *Promising practices to support family involvement in schools* (pp. 129–149). Charlotte, NC: Information Age Publishing.

Earl, L., Katz, S., Elgie, S, Ben Jaafar, S., & Foster, L. (2006, May). How networked learning communities work: Volume 1 The Report. Report prepared for the National College of School Leadership Networked Learning Communities Programme.

Epstein, J. L. (1995). School/family/community partnerships: Caring for the children we share. *Phi Delta Kappan, 76*(9), 701–712.

Epstein, J. L. (2001). *School, family, and community partnerships: Preparing educators and improving schools.* Boulder, CO: Westview Press.

Hands, C. (2005a). *Patterns of interdependency: The development of partnerships between schools and communities.* Unpublished doctoral dissertation. University of Toronto, Ontario, Canada.

Hands, C. (2005b). It's who you know and what you know: The process of creating partnerships between schools and communities. *The School Community Journal, 15*(2), 63–84.

Hands, C. M. (2008, October). *Parent Engagement Office evaluation of district parent engagement initiatives: Final report.* Report submitted to the Parent Engagement Office of the Ontario Ministry of Education.

Hands, C. M. (2009). The evolution of trust relationships in school–community partnership development: From calculated risk-taking to unconditional faith. In L. Shumow (Ed.), *Promising practices for family and community involvement during high school* (pp. 53–69). Greenwich, CT: Information Age Publishing.

Hanson, K. (2003). Strong school–community partnerships: Opening the windows of public education. *Leading & Managing, 9*(2), 153–159.

Harvard Family Research Project. (2002). Concepts and models of family involvement. Retrieved on March 11, 2004 from http://www.gse.harvard.edu/hfrp/projects/fine/resources/case_study/intro.html#top

Harvard Family Research Project. (2005). Evaluation methodology. *The Evaluation Exchange, 11*(2). Retrieved from http://www.hfrp.org/var/hfrp/storage/original/application/d6517d4c8da2c9f1fb3dffe3e8b68ce4.pdf

Harvard Family Research Project. (n.d.). Evaluation. Retrieved from http://www.hfrp.org/evaluation

McMahon, B. J., & Armstrong, D. E. (2006). Framing equitable praxis: Systematic approaches to building social just and inclusionary educational communities. In D. E. Armstrong & B. J. McMahon (Eds.), *Inclusion in urban educational environments: Addressing issues of diversity, equity, and social justice* (pp. 301–322). Charlotte, NC: Information Age Publishing.

National Network of Partnership Schools (n.d.). Partnership planner retrieved from http://www.csos.jhu.edu/p2000/pdf/partnership-planner.pdf

Sanders, M. G. (1999). Schools' program and progress in the National Network of Partnership Schools. *The Journal of Educational Research, 92*(4), 220–232.

ABOUT THE CONTRIBUTORS

EDITORS

Catherine Hands obtained her Ph.D. in Educational Administration after a career as an elementary teacher. Since earning her doctorate, Catherine has been appointed to the School of Leadership and Education Sciences as an Assistant Professor in the University of San Diego's Leadership Studies department, where she taught in the principal preparation program as well as in the department's leadership programs. Catherine currently works as an educational researcher and consultant with school boards and educational organizations in Ontario, Canada in the areas of curriculum, policy, family engagement and professional learning communities. Catherine's research interests include educational leadership, school–community relations, schools as communities, parent involvement in schooling, values and ethics in education, social justice, professional learning communities, and educational reform. She maintains an active research agenda in these areas and has presented and published work regionally, nationally and internationally.

Lea Hubbard, Ph.D. is a Professor in the School of Leadership and Education Sciences at the University of San Diego. She has written and co-authored numerous books and articles on educational leadership and school reform, as well as the academic achievement of minority students. Dr. Hubbard's research focuses on educational inequities as they exist across race, class and gender. Her latest book, *Reform as learning: When school reform collided with school culture and community politics in San Diego* (2006), illustrates the social and political construction of district led educational reform. It offers a refined social theory that combines socio-cultural theories of learning with organizational life and policy adaptation. Working internationally, Dr. Hubbard has taken students to study education reform in South Africa, Costa Rica and next year she expects to conduct research in New Zealand.

Including Families and Communities in Urban Education, pages 313–317
Copyright © 2011 by Information Age Publishing
All rights of reproduction in any form reserved.

AUTHORS

Elvira G. Armas, Ed.D. is the Associate Director of the Center for Equity for English Learners (CEEL) at Loyola Marymount University. Concurrently, Dr. Armas works with the Los Angeles County of Education (LACOE), Multilingual Academic Support Unit as an English Learner Consultant providing professional development for school teams, school districts, and educational leaders. In her career as an educator she has served as a bilingual classroom teacher, mentor, trainer, district advisor, staff developer and curriculum materials developer. She has also taught reading, writing and second language learning methods as well as language foundation courses for schools of education at the university level. Her research interests include teaching and learning in biliteracy programs, professional development, and parental involvement and programs in biliteracy programs.

Julie H. Carter is an Assistant Professor of Foundations and Secondary Education in the Department of Curriculum & Instruction at St. John's University where she teaches courses in social foundations, educational research methods, and social studies methods. Her research interests include social foundations, urban school reform, and grassroots movements as these resonate with new urban teachers, parents, and students.

Janet Chrispeels is professor of Education Studies at the University of California, San Diego and director of the Joint Doctorate in Educational Leadership. Her research interests include school and district reform and change processes, leadership teams at all levels of the system and parent and community engagement.

Linwood H. Cousins is a social worker and cultural anthropologist who studies the cultural characteristics of race, ethnicity, and social class among African American families and communities, with an emphasis on how culture influences schooling and racial identity. He currently serves as Director of the School of Social Work at Western Michigan University.

Michael P. Evans is assistant professor of family, school, and community connections at Miami University's School of Education, Health, & Society. His research interests include interdisciplinary approaches to educational change, community organizing for school reform, and teacher preparation.

Susan C. Faircloth, Ph.D. is an Associate Professor of Education at the Pennsylvania State University. She is interested in the factors that account for the disproportionate referral and placement of American Indian and Alaska Native students in special education programs and services in the early grades, the role of Head Start programs and services in the education of young native children, and the moral and ethical dimensions of school leadership. In addition to teaching and research, Dr. Faircloth is the director of a personnel preparation grant, "Principals for Student Success." The purpose of this project is to prepare aspiring American Indian and Alaska Native school leaders. She is currently completing a research fellowship with the American Indian/Alaska Native Head Start Research Center at the University of Colorado Denver.

Mary Finn retired as Director of the Urban Education Institute at the University of Buffalo in 2002. As a founding member of the Education and Labor Collective (ELC), she has coordinated several national forums among teachers, university faculty, and union activists. Her course on Grassroots Organizing for Social Justice was co-taught (with Patrick Finn) in the department of teacher education at Antioch University, Los Angeles from 2007–2009.

Margarita Gonzalez is currently the Director of Consolidated Projects and Migrant Education at the Santa Maria-Bonita School District in California. She was Director of Research and Evaluation in the Center for Educational Leadership and Effective Schools at the University of California Santa Barbara and is a former school administrator and classroom teacher. Her work has focused on district and school leadership, systemic reform, English learners and family–school partnerships. E-mail: mgonzalez@smbsd.net

Erin McNamara Horvat is Associate Professor of Urban Education at Temple University in Philadelphia PA. Professor Horvat's research agenda has explored how race and class shape access throughout the educational pipeline focusing especially on the role of social and cultural capital in shaping families' interactions with schools, often drawing on Bourdieu's theoretical framework. Professor Horvat has been motivated by a desire to understand how interactions between individual and structural forces shape educational outcomes and life chances, including explorations of how race and class affect school and college experiences, college access and high school dropout and reentry.

Magaly Lavadenz, Ph.D. is currently a professor in the Language and Culture in Education Department and Director of Bilingual/Bicultural Education and TESL at Loyola Marymount University. She is also the Founding Director of LMU's Center for Equity English Learners (CEEL). Dr. Lavadenz has held leadership positions in numerous education related associations. She is a past president of the California Association for Bilingual Education (CABE), founding president of the California Association of Bilingual Teacher Educators (CABTE) and is currently president-elect for the California Council on Teacher Education. Her research interests include the education of Latino and bilingual teachers, the experiences of the Central American immigrant community, public policy affecting language use and education, and biliteracy development.

Lauri Johnson is an Associate Professor in the Department of Educational Administration and Higher Education at Boston College, where she teaches courses in educational research methods, diversity issues, and leadership for social justice. She is currently investigating the role of parent, community, and teacher activism on the historical development (1968–2008) of school district policies to promote educational equity in London, Toronto, and New York City.

Makeba Jones is an Associate Project Research Scientist at the Center for Research on Educational Equity, Assessment and Teaching Excellence at the University of California, San Diego. Her research interests include urban secondary school reform, student voice, educational engagement, and school policy.

Novella Keith is an associate professor of urban education in the Department of Educational Leadership and Policy Studies at Temple University. Her research centers on democratic practice and theory that enable connections across social divides. This chapter is drawn in part from a forthcoming book, *Engaging in Social Partnerships: A Professional Guide for Successful Collaboration in Higher Education* (Routledge, 2011).

Roslyn Arlin Mickelson is a Professor of Sociology, Public Policy, Information Technology, and Women's Studies at the University of North Carolina at Charlotte. Mickelson's research focuses upon the political economy of schooling and school reform, particularly the relationships among race, ethnicity, gender, class, and educational processes and outcomes. Currently, Mickelson is writing a book synthesizing social and behavioral science research on the effects of school and classroom composition on educational outcomes.

Bonnie Stelmach completed a doctorate in Educational Policy Studies at the University of Alberta in 2006. She has a Master of Arts in Educational Philosophy from Simon Fraser University. Bonnie's professional experiences include high school teaching in rural and northern Alberta, and at an international school in Chiang Mai, Thailand. Her work as a supervisor of the Alberta Initiative for School Improvement at a school division in Peace River, Alberta led her to an interest in policy focusing on engaging parents in schools. Bonnie began as an Assistant Professor in the Department of Educational Administration at the University of Saskatchewan in 2006. Her other research interests include rural education, Aboriginal educational issues, and the development of scholarly identity within corporatizing university contexts.

Susan Yonezawa is Associate Director of the Center for Research on Educational Equity, Assessment and Teaching Excellence (CREATE) at the University of California, San Diego. She has published numerous articles about youth voice, engagement and equity-minded educational reform in publications such as Theory Into Practice, the American Educational Research Journal, Educational Leadership, and the Journal of Educational Change.

LaVergne, TN USA
25 March 2011
221556LV00001B/42/P